Wave Theory for Alternative Investments

Riding the Wave with Hedge Funds, Commodities, and Venture Capital

STEPHEN TODD WALKER

New York   Chicago   San Francisco   Lisbon   London
Madrid   Mexico City   Milan   New Delhi   San Juan
Seoul   Singapore   Sydney   Toronto

1 2 3 4 5 6 7 8 9 0   DOC/DOC   1 5 4 3 2 1 0

ISBN   978-0-07-174286-3
MHID   0-07-174286-7

Library of Congress Cataloging-in-Publication Data

Walker, Stephen (Stephen Todd)
   Wave theory for alternative investments : riding the wave with hedge funds, commodities, and venture capital / by Stephen Walker.
      p. cm.
   Includes bibliographical references and index.
   ISBN 978-0-07-174286-3 (alk. paper)
      1. Investments—Mathematical models. 2. Elliott wave principle. 3. Technical analysis (Investment analysis) I. Title.

   HG4515.2.W35 2011
   332.64′5—dc22   2010029853

To my loving wife, Dorothy, and MTS

Contents

Acknowledgments

I would like to thank the following individuals, who influenced my work:

Amir Abolfathi, Nancy Abrams, Steve Adams, Tom P. H. Adams, Tony Adams, John Adler, Michael J. Ahearn, Theo Albrecht Jr., Jörn Aldag, Ken Allen, Daniel P. Amos, Stephen Anderson, Maxwell H. Anderson, David Anderson, Michael Andreottola, Armando Anido, Wallis Annenberg, Asif Ansari, Richard Archuleta, Micky Arison, Bernard Arnault, Mandeep Arora, Anil Arora, Charles Arsenault, Jud Askins, Mark Aslett, Jatin Atre, Bill Austin, Amir Avniel, Michael Axelrod, Ashar Aziz, Irving L. Azoff, Kevin Bacon, David Bagley, Safi R. Bahcall, H. C. Bailly, Frank and Sandra Baldino, Steve Ballmer, Chris Barbin, Sol Barer, Roger Barnett, Mark Barnett, John R. Barr, Craig Barratt, Carol A. Bartz, Curtis Bashaw, Bami Bastani, Whitney Basson, Chris Battaglia, William C. Bayless Jr., Murray Beach, Max Beach, David Bear, Steve Bearak, Kevin Becker, Daniel Beem, John Belizaire, Leonard Bell, Keith Belling, Moshe BenBassat, Richard Bendis, Amir Ben-Efraim, Marc Benioff, Gregory Bentley, Christiaan Antonius Van Den Berg, Todd Berg, Josh Berman, Dorrit J. Bern, Paul L. Berns, Ira Bernstein, Collins Betty, Jeffrey L. Bewkes, Jeffrey P. Bezos, Gina Bianchini, Martin A. Bieber, Brian Bischoff, Jamie Bischoff, Lars Bjork, Lawrence J. Blanford, Friedhelm Blobel, Timothy Block, Peter Boneparth, Peter J. Boni, Otho Boone, Doug Boothe, Greg Bosch, Al Boscov, Michael Boyce-Jacino, Richard J. Boyle Jr., Tucker Boyton, Richard M. Bracken, Angela F. Braly, David A. Brandon, Jonathan A. Brassington, Dale Bredesen, MD, Steven Brill, Glenn A. Britt, Greg Brogger, Pierre R. Brondeau, Edgar J. Bronfman Jr., Paul Brooks, Ellen L. Brothers, Donald Brown, Carl Buchholz, Jim Buckmaster, Lothar Budike Jr., Jonathan Bush, Neil Bush, Wolf Busse,

Chris Butler, Ray Butti, Roy Calcagne, Robert M. Calderoni, Robert J. Capetola, Dr. Robert and Mrs. Barbara Capizzi, William V. Carey, Todd Carmichael, Michael H. Carrel, Rachel Carson, William A. Carter, Rick J. Caruso, Chris Cashman, James Cassano, Peter Castaldi, S. Truett Cathy, Marc Cenedella, Olivier Chaine, John T. Chambers, S. Kumar Chandrasekaran, Fred Chang, Tom Chappell, Dov Charney, Michael Chasen, Amit Chatterjee, Timothy Childs, Y. C. Cho, Susan Choe, Blake and Julie Christoph, Chan and Eun Hee Chung, George Church, David St. Clair, Andrew S. Clark, Joe Clark, Richard T. Clark, Paul E. Clayton Jr., Peter Cocoziello, Arie Cohen, Jason W. Cohenour, Charles Collier, Doug Conant, John Condron, Warren D. Cooper, Peter Cooperstein, David M. Cordani, Jim Corl, Dick and Pat Corl, James M. Cornelius, James M. Cornelius, Donald L. Correll, Jon Costanza, Tom Costello, Philippe Courtot, Bruce G. Crain, Scott Crane, Rose Crane, David Crane, Neil Creighton, Pete Crnkovich, Gordon Crovitz, James Q. Crowe, Chris Crowell, John Crowley, Tom Curtin, C. David Cush, John P. Daane, Ashraf Dahod, Declan Daly, Mark Daniel, Robert Dann, Philippe P. Dauman, Derek Davis, Robert Davis, Jay Prakash Dayal, Ric and Maria DeBastos, Michael S. Dell, Donald A. DeLoach, Aynsley Deluce, Bill Demas, Felix Dennis, Paul J. Diaz, Lewis W. Dickey Jr., Colin Digiaro, Steve DiGiovine, Yossi Dina, John M. Dionisio, Bhat Dittakavi, John Dobak, James L. Dolan, John J. Donahoe, Scott Donahue, Jeffrey F. O' Donnell, Jack Dorsey, Michael R. Dougherty, J. Allen Dougherty, Sean Downs, Carl Dranoff, Francisco D'Souza, Richard J. Dugas Jr., Colin Dyer, Bernie Ecclestone, Amir Ben Efraim, Maigread Eichten, Michael Ellenbogen, Brian P. Elliott, John Elliot, Lawrence J. Ellison, Matthew Emmens, Richard P. Eno, Alan Epstein, Laura Eppler, Tom Erickson, Matt Espe, John R. Ettelson, Nim Evatt, Herb Evert, Thomas J. Falk, Liz Faville, John Fazio, Bruno Fedele, Russ Felker, George Fellows, Edward Fenster, Michael Fertik, Howard Fillit, Jeff and Linda Fine, Ed Finn, Tom First, David Fischell, Dan Fishback, Scott N. Flanders, Larry S. Flax, Larry Flick, Eli Florence, James P. Fogarty, Alan J. Fohrer, Lyle Fong, Steve Forbes, Neal F. Fowler, Rob Frankenberg, Matt Freeman, Kevin Frick, Tim Froehlich, John Frost, Jeff Frumin, Andy J. Funk, Edwin C. Gage, Joseph Galli, Elkan R. Gamzu, Dr. Jean-Pierre Garnier, Shawn Gee, Scott Geftman, Georges Gemayel, Paul D.

Geraghty, Steve Gerard, Seth Gerszberg, Eitan Gertel, Levy Gerzberg, Marco Giannini, Daniel Glassman, Richard Glikes, Ben Goldberg, Greg Goldman, Steve Goodman, Howdie Goodwin, Zorik Gordon, J. Warren Gorrell Jr., Alex Gorsky, Rich Gotham, Thomas E. Gottwald, Hugh Grant, Ron Graves, Paul Graziani, William D. Green, Gary G. Greenfield, Michael Gregoire, Chris Gronet, Dr. Chris Gronet, Erminia Guarneri, Sunny Gupta, Matt Gureghian, Vahan H. Gureghian, Brian de Haaff, David C. Habiger, Bob Hall, Seth Hallem, Lawrence Hallier, Richard Halloran, Edward Hannah, Joel A. Harden, Shawn Hardin, Kevin Hartz, Faheem Hasnain, Reed Hastings, Jeffrey S. Hatfield, Russell J. Hawkins, Frank W. Haydu III, Joshua Hebert, Marc Hedlund, Scott Heiferman, John Helm, Frederick Henderson, J. Richard Hendrick III, Gerri Henwood, Kelly Herrell, Dave Hersh, Rick Hess, Bill Higgins, Larry Highbloom, Leo Hindery Jr., Charles Hoeveler, Reid Hoffman, Pat Hoffman, Lucinda Holt, Ray Hood, Joseph Hopkins, Christine Horton, Ara K. Hovnanian, Tony Hsieh, Larry Hsu, Tom Hughes, Cameron Hughes, David T. Hung, Mark V. Hurd, Jeffrey R. Immelt, Chaim Indig, Jason and Sarah Ingle, Michael Jackson, Jess S. Jackson Jr., Paul Jacobs, Varun Jain, Dwight Jelle, Steven P. Jobs, William R. Johnson, Kevin R. Johnson, Rod Johnson, Jack Johnson, Kristopher B. Jones, Mel Karmazin, Andrew Kassner, Jeffrey Katzenberg, William Kay, Harry Kazazian, Scott Kelley, Dennis Kelly, David Kelly, James A. C. Kennedy, Kevin Kennedy, Danny Kennedy, John Kessock, George and Elizabeth Keszeli, Jack Kettler, Joe E. Kiani, Jason Kilar, Daniel J. Kim, Dr. Joseph Kim, Ranch C. Kimball, Jeffrey B. Kindler, Mark Kingdon, John Kish, Russel Klein, Kenneth R. Klein, Jeff Klinger, Eric Klinker, Ron Konezny, Alan Konn, Josh Kopelman, Steven Korman, Donald L. Kotula, Richard W. Kramp, Lee Kranefuss, David S Krause, Edward Krell, Ryan Kugler, C. Scott Kulicke, Ramesh Kumar, Girish Kumar, Gene Kunde, Margaret Kuo, Josh Kurtz, Taishi Kushiro, Scott Lang, George Langan, John Lauck, John C. Lechleiter, Stephen and Deb Lee, Stan Lee, Young Lee, John Chase Lee, Todd P. Leff, Chase Lenfest, Rick A. Lepley, Brad Leve, Domenic and Barbara Leve, Arnold and Esther Levine, Howard R. Levine, Art Levinson, Dr. Melvin Levinson, Zohar Levkovitz, Ben Lewis, Richard Tzar Kai Li, Yanhong Li, Carl Liebert III, David Lincoln, Edward H. Linde, Wilson Ling, Jay Litkey, Andrew N. Liveris, William and Veena

Loftus, Doug Lopenzina, Bob Lord, Jeffrey Lubell, Ira Lubert, Jeffrey Lurie, Maria L. Maccecchini, John Mack, Harry Macklowe, Harry D. Madonna, Gregory B. Maffei, Andrea Maggitti, Beth Maggitti, Mary Ellen Maggitti, Timothy J. Mahoney III, Victoria Maitland, Subhash Makhija, Rick Malcolm, Bradley L. Mallory, Narendra and Shaila Manocha, Art Mann Sr., John M. Maraganore, Mort Marcus, Robin Marino, Chris Marino, Paul A. Maritz, Brian A. Markison, Ron Marshall, John Martin, Tim Martin, John C. Martin, Bill Marvin, Steve Masapallo, Bob Mazzarella, Jim Mazzo, Mark McAllister, Shaun E. McAlmont, Daniel P. McCartney, William L. McComb, Robert A. McDonald, Jerry McEntee, Paul McGarty, Betsy and Joe McGill, Karl McGoldrick, Al McGowan, Kerry McGrath, Harold McGraw III, Scott A. McGregor, Patrick J. McHale, Chris McIntosh, Frank J. McKee, William S. McKiernan, Betsy McLaughlin, Bryan McLeod, Frances McMorris, Mark McNulpy, Tom and Kathy McPherson, Sandra McQuain, Mark Mednansky, Ed and Ursula Meese, Kenneth R. Melani, Adam S. Metz, Alan B. Miller, Craig Mitnick, Albert Momjian, Sal Monastero, Todd Montpetit, Leslie Moonves, Ned Moore, Keith Morgan, Ryan Morgan, Arlene M. Morris, William T. Morrow, Mick Mountz, Richard Muirhead, Peter Mullen, James C. Mullen, Geoff Murphy, Glenn K. Murphy, Jerry Murrell, Phaneesh Murthy, Elon Musk, Ronald Naples, Shantanu Narayen, Bob Nardelli, Zachary Nelson, Brian Nelson, Pat Nesbitt, Joe Neubauer, Sean and Kris Nevins, William J. Newell, James Newman, Steven Nichtberger, MD, Samuel Norvell, Daniel T. H. Nye, Glenn Oclassen, Patrick J. O'Dea, Michael R. Odell, Jason Olim, Carmine T. Oliva, William O'Neil, Brian O'Neill, Kathy P. Ordoñez, Jeffrey P. Orleans, Andrew Ory, Paul S. Otellini, Peter and Jean Ottmer, John Palermo, James Papada III, Arthur L. Papas, Doc Parghi, Bob Parsons, Jeff Pascoe, Arete Passas, Aaron Patzer, Jeff and Alicia Payne, George Paz, Roger S. Penske, Jerome A. Peribere, Steve Perlman, Isaac Perlmutter, David Perme, Mark Perry, Daniel L. Peters, Derek Pew, Olivia Pietrunti, Elisabet de los Pinos, David Pittinsky, Charles P. Pizzi, Paul Pluschkell, Lou Polisano, Frank Pompei, Mark Popp, Masahiro Popp, Fred Poses, Bernard J. Poussot, Christopher Pratt, Moshe Pritsker, Mary G. Puma, John K. Purcell, Paul Purcell, David E. I. Pyott, Michael Rapino, Ray Rastelli, Jerry S. Rawls, Eric Raymond, Gary T. Read, Dr. Andrew

Reaume, Joseph M. Redling, Stewart and Lynda Resnick, Stewart A. Resnick, Thomas Ressemann, John S. Riccitiello, Josef H. Von Rickenbach, Milton Riseman, Ronald A. Rittenmeyer, Lyndon Rive, Brian Roach, Brian L. Roberts, Seymour Robin, Bruce Robinson, Rick Rodriguez, Jim Rogers, John Roos, Martin F. Roper, Matt and Kiki Rosenberg, Harry Rosenberg, Howard Ross, Shira Rubinoff, Brian Ruby, Bill Rutter, Dick Sabot, Paul Sagan, Gerald L. Salzman, Alan Salzman, Marvin Samson, Robert S. Sands, Dr. Deepak Santram, Peter Sartorio, Bob Sasser, Paul C. Saville, Jitendra S. Saxena, George A. Scangos, John Scardapane, Mr. and Mrs. John Schade, Jack and Suzette Schade, Mike and Linda Schade, John C. Schafer, Ted E. Schlein, Eric E. Schmidt, John H. Schnatter, Howard Schultz, Roger Schwab, Severin Schwan, Jonathan I. Schwartz, Norman Schwartz, Luis Scoffone, Ivan G. Seidenberg, Glen T. Senk, Clint Severson, John Shackleton, Neil Shah, Jay Shah, Jeremy Shane, Kevin W. Sharer, Isadore Sharp, Alan Shaw, Ray Shaw, Pop Shenian, Joyce Shenian, Ken Sherman, Jonney Shih, Robert J. Shillman, Gary Shinner, Bruce J. Shook, Gerald B. Shreiber, Evan Shumacher, Charles Siegel, Myriam Siftar, Richard Silfen, Josh Silverman, Fred Simeone, Michael Simon, William Slattery, Frank Slootman, Steve Slovick, Larry J Smart, Sally J. Smith, Philip Smith, Alexander W. Smith, Halsey Smith, Tom and Ilene Smith, Del and Mary Margaret Smith, Ed Snider, David B. Snow Jr., E. Y. Snowden, Sheridan Snyder, Pascal Soriot, Paul Southworth, Carl Spana, Mark E. Speese, Judy Spires, Joel Spolsky, M. J. Sprinzen, Joanne and Woody Spruance, Willie Staats, Edward W. Stack, Eric Stang, Christopher Starr, Paul H. Stebbins, Dan Steere, David Steinberg, Leonard Stern, Barry S. Sternlicht, Julia A. Stewart, Charles W. Stiefel, Louis Stilp, Howard Stoeckel, Sir Howard Stringer, Scott Strochak, Brian Sugar, Taylor Swift, Robert Switz, Tom Szaky, Brian Tanigawa, Lew Tarlini, Mark Taylor, John M. Tedeschi, Natalie Tejero, Mark B. Templeton, Murli Thirumale, Kent Thiry, Randy H. Thurman, James Tisch, Annette M Tobia, Robert Toll, Alan Trefler, Joseph M. Tucci, Jill Tufano, Steve Tullman, Craig J. Tuttle, Tien Tzuo, Daniel L. Vasella, Gregory Veksler, Sridhar Vembu, Ron Vigdor, Al Vilamil, Arkady Volozh, Mike Volpi, Dennis Wahr, Stephen G. Waldis, Dr. and Mrs. Barry R. Walker, Alin Wall, Tim Wallace, Robert Walsh, William G. Walter, Alex Wang, Michael R. Ward, Peter Warwick,

Rob Weber, Steve Wedan, Wendell P. Weeks, Brian and Liz Weese, Daniel R. Wegman, Doug and Sharon Weiherer, Jeff Weiner, Liane Weintraub, Gregory S. Weishar, Alberto Weisser, Steve Weisz, Tom Werner, Thomas H. Werner, David J. West, Christoph H. Westphal, John A Westrum, Peter Wetherill, Terrie T. Wetle, Craig A. Wheeler, Mark Whelan, Miles D. White, James D. White, Russell J. Wilcox, Tom Wilde, Doug Wilder, Dan Willard, Evan Williams, Kevin Williams and Victoria Werth, Jack H. Wilson Sr., Jon Winer, Terry E. Winters, Ken Wisnefski, Andrew Witty, Alan Wolberg, Jonathan S. Wolfson, Ben Wolin, John M. Woolard, Mathew Work, Jeffrey Yabuki, Jerry Yang, Bhat Dittakavi, Harold III and Sharon Yoh, Karen Yoh, Jimmy Yoh, Mike and Gail Yoh, Jeff and Suzanne Yoh, Harold Jr. and Mary Yoh, William Yoh, Joe Yorio, David Yost, Payam Zamani, Jim Zierick, Robert Zipkin, Nehemia Zucker, Mark Zuckerberg, Ron Zwanziger.

Disclaimers and Disclosures

This book is designed to provide accurate and authoritative information in regard to the subject matter covered and the information, analysis and data contained herein are based on sources believed to be reliable. The author and Stratosphere, LLC do not, however, guarantee the timeliness, accuracy or completeness of the information provided. The author has been associated with a number of leading investment banking firms in his career but the opinions in this book are his alone. All information and opinions herein are subject to change without notice and are not intended to be the primary basis for any investment decision. The strategies described do not address individual financial objectives and may not be suitable in every situation. The appropriateness of a particular investment or strategy depends on an investor's particular circumstances and objectives. The author and Stratosphere, LLC do not intend to render individual financial, investment, tax, legal, accounting or other professional advice or services in this book. If personal advice or services are required, the reader should engage a competent professional. Nothing in this book should be construed as a recommendation about the advisability of purchasing or selling any particular security. The charts and graphs are for illustrative purposes only, and past performance of any security described in this book is not necessarily indicative of and does not guarantee comparable future results. All investments are made at the reader's own risk, and none of the publisher, the author or Stratosphere, LLC shall be liable or can be held responsible for any losses or damages, including without limitation special, incidental, consequential or other damages, incurred as a result of actions taken or not taken on the basis of the information, opinions or strategies set forth or described herein. The author, the author's clients and/or Stratosphere, LLC may invest in securities mentioned in this book.

Alternative investments are speculative and include a high degree of risk. They are typically highly illiquid, because, among other things, they often involve (i) securities that are not registered under the Securities Act of 1933 and/or (ii) securities that are subject to legal or contractual restrictions or requirements relating to their purchase, holding or sale, or the exercise of rights and performance of obligations with respect to them. Most alternative investments are also very volatile. Investors could lose all of, or in some cases more than the original amount of, their investment. For these reasons, they are suitable only for experienced and sophisticated investors who are capable of understanding and assuming the risks involved and who are willing to forego liquidity and put capital at risk for an indefinite period of time. Some of the other risks involved in and factors affecting the price of the types of alternative investments discussed in this book are set forth below:

Gold. Risks of investments in actual gold or securities backed by actual gold include but are not limited to forgery, fraud, theft and loss. Prices of all types of investments in gold can be affected by, among other things, (i) speculation; (ii) hedging; (iii) expectations regarding inflation; (iv) supply and demand; (v) currency exchange rates; (vi) interest rates; (vii) global or regional instability; or (viii) political, financial, economic and regulatory conditions or events.

Commodities. Risks include but are not limited to geopolitical risk, leverage, speculation and fraud. Prices can be affected by, among other things, (i) changes in supply and demand relationships; (ii) governmental programs and policies; (iii) national and international political and economic events, armed conflict and terrorist activity; (iv) changes in interest and exchange rates; (v) trading activities in commodities and related contracts; (vi) technological change, climate change and weather conditions; and (vii) the price volatility of a specific commodity.

Hedge funds. Risks include but are not limited to (i) little or no regulation; (ii) leveraging, short selling and other speculative investment practices; (iii) lack of transparency regarding underlying investments; (iv) unavailability of pricing or valuation information; (v) reduction of profits by high fees, some of which are not based on profitability; (vi) complex tax structures and delays in distributing important tax information; and (vii) the potential for regulatory changes.

Venture capital funds. Risks include but are not limited to (i) business risks involved in investing in smaller, less established companies; (ii) availability of future capital or other financing; (iii) lack of liquidity of underlying investments; and (iv) dilution of underlying investments.

* * * * *

Trademarks and service marks used in this book are the property of their respective owners.

Introduction

My finance career started at Alex. Brown in the early 1990s. Alex. Brown was founded in 1800 and considered the oldest investment firm in the United States. Known for its initial public offerings (IPOs), Alex. Brown attracted some of the wealthiest clients in the country. Virtually all great companies in the United States were taken public by Alex. Brown, including Microsoft, Amazon, eBay, and Starbucks. According to Susan Watters, "Alex. Brown is also the top-volume underwriter of corporate securities and the largest over-the-counter trader outside New York. And the partners here mean to keep things just that way."[1] In 1993, Alex. Brown had 28 IPOs, Morgan Stanley 17, DLJ 13, Lehman 13, Prudential 12, Bear Stearns 11, Smith Barney 11, and Goldman Sachs 10. In 1993, Alex. Brown raised $1,193.6 million for companies going public versus Goldman Sachs with $747.7 million. Alex. Brown had 14 lead managed IPOs, whereas Goldman only had 8 such offerings. In April 1994, Alex. Brown was ranked first for "Firms that served as managing or co-managing underwriters for 10 or more 1993 venture backed IPO's."[2] In addition to being assigned companies to work with, I also introduced many of Alex. Brown's successful IPOs to the firm. Over the years, I was able to work with some of the wealthiest individuals in the nation.

I was adept at asset allocation and diversification, but my skills flourished with a relatively new but rapidly growing area known as alternatives. What exactly are alternatives? Alternatives can be defined as any asset class other than equities, bonds, or cash. Alternatives offer a viable option to the bond and equity markets. According to *On Wall Street* magazine, "Generally speaking, alternative investments include just about anything outside the traditional asset classes of stocks, bonds and mutual funds."[3] Alternatives came to fruition mostly in the 1980s with real estate and venture capital. My ability to discover the best alternatives and know when to use them led me to be chosen as one of the youngest directors in Alex. Brown's history. The rate at which I attracted high-net-worth clients and brought in business was unheard of at the time. I recall my name being listed in the *Wall Street Journal.* The national manager of Alex. Brown, Tim Schweizer, pulled me aside and said, "You have a real talent for identifying exceptional opportunities. You will go far." But everyone at Alex. Brown worked hard and was talented; the competition was immense. Alex. Brown was considered by many to be the crown jewel of Wall Street. Determined to be more successful than my peers, I worked morning, noon, and night searching for terrific growth companies and compelling ideas. As a result, I discovered a number of the best companies for Alex. Brown to take public. An article titled "Alex. Brown Shows Wall St. How It's Done" in *Investor's Daily* stated: "Alex. Brown & Sons Inc. may be a regional broker, but it's a national powerhouse when it comes to taking young growth companies public. It can also take credit for bringing more small and medium-size growth companies public than most other firms."[4]

Before a company went public, it raised funds through private equity or venture capital. According to David F. Swensen, "More than 1,300 venture partnerships were active in the United States at the end of 2003."[5] Both institutions and high-net-worth clients invest in private placements, which enable investors to own part of a private company. Many investors like to own private companies—including Warren Buffett through his company, Berkshire Hathaway Inc. According to the *Wall Street Journal* in 2008, "Since the beginning of 2006, Berkshire has spent nearly $17 billion buying private companies lock, stock, and barrel, including an Israeli cutting-tool maker and a distributor of electronic components."[6] Buffett is arguably one of the most astute investors in the country, and he invests heavily in private companies. Over the years Buffett decreased his public equities and increased his investments in private companies. "As recently as 1995, 73.5% of Berkshire's total assets consisted of a portfolio of publicly traded stocks that (at least in theory) any knowledgeable investor could have replicated. As of June 30, 2008, though, Berkshire's stockholdings made up just 25% of its total assets."[7] His performance investing in both private and public securities has been quite good.

Alternatives and Waves

During my investment career, I observed that venture capital and the rest of the alternatives (just like equities and bonds), tend to move in waves (patterns, cycles, or trends). Large-cap growth equities were in favor from 1994 to 1999, and then out of favor from 2000 to 2008. Fixed income was in vogue from 2000 to 2002, and then out of favor from 2003 to 2006. Alternatives are not too dissimilar with waves or periods when they are in favor or out of favor. For example, real estate investment trusts (REITs, another alternative investment) were out of favor from 1989 to 1999. They were one of the worst-performing asset classes. However, REITs came back with a vengeance from 2000 to 2006. Not surprisingly, they were out of favor from 2007 when the real estate bubble burst until mid–2009.

Although asset allocation is important, dynamic asset allocation (as opposed to static allocation) is imperative:

> Risk premiums appear to be stable over very long periods of time, but that's mostly an illusion if we adjust for the real-world time horizons of clients. In fact, these premiums vary through time, as a large and growing body of academic research and real-world evidence tell us. The only question is how best to manage money in a world where the premiums fluctuate. The basic answer is that investors shouldn't rely totally on static asset allocation strategies.[8]

An investor should know when to catch a wave or let it go. Sometimes missing an opportunity is better than chasing one. There is a proper time and place to invest with any security. Alternatives require one to be extra alert. One must be cognizant not only of the particular alternative asset class they are contemplating investing in, but also the overall or general market. Is the market in an uptrend or downtrend? Is the market overheated or did it correct (a polite Wall Street term for crash)? Examining waves with alternatives can be fruitful and help investors make the right decisions.

Besides my observations with venture capital and the IPO market over time, I learned that wealthy investors wanted what others cannot have. For instance, in the late 1990s BT Alex. Brown had a fund of funds with buyout firms. At the time, U.S. private equity had been attracting more than

$10 billion annually since 1992, with a record $50.9 billion raised in 1997. Annualized over 10 years, the U.S. buyout universe returns through December 1997 exceeded 20%. There are a number of excellent leveraged buyout (LBO) firms, but Bain was the first one I got to know. At the time, Bain was a relatively small LBO firm in Massachusetts formerly run by Mitt Romney. Romney was so successful growing Bain into a powerhouse that he leveraged the profits of his success into his 2008 run for President of the United States by contributing $40 million of his own money toward his campaign. Romney remains a savvy businessman and legendary figure in the LBO world.

I noticed that Bain and the other LBO firms did well even in difficult market periods. During the time of the terrorist attacks on September 11th, Enron, WorldCom, Kmart, Global Crossing, Martha Stewart going to jail, and other unusual or calamitous events, the fund produced a +22.5% Net IRR (from 2001 to June 30, 2008). Bain did very well in a tough period and appeared to correlate very little with the market. Unlike equities, I noticed that many alternatives besides LBO firms performed well in adverse market conditions and helped diversify clients' portfolios.

The trends that I identified with alternatives were immensely useful in helping to diversify client portfolios, especially during difficult markets such as 2000–2002 or 2008–2009. In an ideal world, one can generate positive returns in both good and bad environments. Hedge funds are supposed to do well regardless of the direction of the market. The best hedge fund managers are those who discuss preservation of capital. Any hedge fund that promises or flaunts returns should be avoided. Hedge funds that have high returns might seem attractive but also might carry too much risk; they should receive extra due diligence to better understand the strategy or risk that the manager is incurring. No security is guaranteed. Rates of return will vary.

Although many hedge funds suffered in 2008 and 2009, the asset class performed far better than mutual funds and other equity vehicles such as indexes or exchange-traded funds (ETFs). Hedge funds will likely attract new assets:

> Hedge funds lost an average 19% in 2008. But the global downturn actually increased institutional investors' appetites for alternatives. According to a survey by Greenwich Associates in June 2009, about

a fifth of institutions polled said that despite losses, they plan to increase allocations to hedge funds and private equity.[9]

A number of hedge funds had exceptional performance despite the market woes. For example, Mulvaney Global Markets Fund Ltd. had a return of +85.47%, JWH Global Analytics +72.40%, and Dighton Aggressive SP +63.30% as of October 31, 2008. Hedge funds and private equity have outperformed the S&P 500 over the past decade:

> Institutional investors have long used private equity and hedge funds to achieve overall returns far higher than those eked out by individuals. In the 10 years ended Dec. 31, 2009, Hedge Fund Research's Fund Weighted Composite Index gained 7% per year, an average, while the Thomson Reuters U.S. Private Equity Performance Index returned an annual average of 17%. That compares with a 13% cumulative loss for the Standard & Poor's 500-stock index.[10]

Tumultuous periods offer the best test to see how a particular asset class might hold up or be decimated. Not surprisingly, gold performed the best out of all asset classes and continued to shine even when the equity market started to pick up again. Gold is an important asset that many investors overlook. In fact, gold is one of the few assets that can be used as an inflation hedge. Some even view gold as a currency.

One can deduce a lot about alternatives during the stock market crash of 2008–2009. Except for the Great Depression, there is no other time over the last century that adversely affected so many different types of asset classes all at once. Halloween (October 31) 2008 was not the typical merriment. "U.S. stocks have lost $7.5 trillion in market value since indexes hit a record on Oct. 9, 2007, one year ago. That exceeds the gross domestic products of China and Japan, and is in the same ballpark as the U.S. national debt."[11] Virtually every investor (individuals as well as institutional) was spooked; there existed an investment crisis with global proportions affecting every corner of the earth.

Developed as well as undeveloped nations were on the verge of collapse. Every day investors were bombarded with negative sentiment about Wall Street: "fears of an economic catastrophe," "global sell-off," "facing a meltdown," "stock market plunge," "global shakeout," "no more blood to bleed," "neck-snapping volatility." Fear was rampant. Trillions of dollars have been lost worldwide, leaving many investors mentally exhausted, fearful, and despondent. According to Bloomberg in 2008, "The slowing world economy wiped out $32 trillion in capitalization this year."[12] Financial storms are similar to hurricanes in that they move fast. As Daniel Defoe described a storm in *Robinson Crusoe*:

> While I sat thus, I found the air overcast and grow cloudy, as it would turn to rain; soon after that the wind rose by little and little, so that in less than half an hour it blew a most dreadful hurricane. The sea was all on a sudden covered over with foam and froth, the shore was covered with the breach of the water, the trees were torn up by the roots, and a terrible storm it was; and this held about three hours, and then began to abate, and in two hours more it was stark calm, and began to rain very hard.[13]

The month of September commenced with a tsunami of losses. James Picerno reported that "September was extraordinary for many reasons, including the hard truth that losses infected virtually everything, everywhere. In dollar terms, no asset class was spared, save cash. Even there, the classic safe harbor wasn't universally safe, depending on how you defined cash."[14] Frozen like deer in front of headlights, there appeared to be nowhere to turn for investors.

Although such negative news only exacerbates matters (fear is contagious), severe problems existed. With such gut-wrenching volatility, many investors were left puzzled about what to do or where to seek safety. Many withdrew from the equity markets at the bottom. "Investors reacted to September's stock market conflagration by stampeding out of the door. They pulled a net $63.54 billion out of stock, bond, and hybrid funds. In contrast, August's $12.14 billion exit was a calm grade-school fire drill."[15]

A History of Volatility

As investors are aware, many banks were lost in the Depression. During the Depression, more than 1,000 banks failed because there was no FDIC (Federal Deposit Insurance Corporation). However, the Fed acted quickly this time, having learned from past mistakes of slow reaction during the Depression.

The Great Depression was not far removed from the global market collapse in 2008–2009 in that the United States teetered on the edge of another abyss. In a sense, the acquisition of my old firm, Alex. Brown, signified the beginning of the end for investment firms on Wall Street because it involved the merger between a bank and an investment firm.

After the Depression, Congress enacted the Glass-Steagall Act, which separated investment firms and commercial banks. According to *Bloomberg Markets,* "Glass-Steagall, which was passed in 1933, was intended to prevent bank executives from lending to companies they owned and to keep investment banking and securities firms from tapping into funds held at commercial banks."[16] In 1999 Glass-Steagall was repealed with the passage of the Gramm-Leach Bliley Act, which allowed investment firms to merge with commercial banks.

According to Peter Temple in his book *Hedge Funds: Courtesans of Capitalism,* "Investment banks run the biggest risks. But a disturbing recent trend has been the quest for size among investment banks, and also the degree to which some commercial banks have, since the effective demise of Glass-Steagall, increased their exposure to investment banking and proprietary trading."[17] Citigroup promoted the idea of the "universal bank," which was an unmitigated disaster. In retrospect, repealing Glass-Steagall might have been a mistake. It created a monster:

> Cracks in Wall Street's façade appeared soon after the repeal of Glass-Steagall in 1999. Investment banks became commercial banks, lending money without credit insight or a deposit base. Commercial banks became brokers, selling securities without market insight. And with the rise of credit-default swaps, which are used to insure bond or loan holders against borrowers missing debt payments, they all became insurers without underwriting standards.[18]

The result of allowing banks to procure securities and investment firms to arrange mortgages soon became catastrophic:

> What worked for Wall Street during the housing boom of 2002–06, when normally illiquid assets such as subprime mortgages were made

liquid, didn't work when housing prices started to fall. The result: global bank write downs of $518 billion; the evaporation of $19.5 trillion of market valuation; a $29 billion government pledge to backstop the sale of Bear Sterns to JP Morgan Chase; a federal takeover of Fannie Mae and Freddie Mac, the largest mortgage lenders in the U.S.; the bankruptcy of Lehman Brothers; the shotgun wedding of Merrill Lynch and Bank of America; and the $85 billion Fed bailout of AIG.[19]

The 2008–2009 storm hastened the pace of mergers and acquisitions between banks and investment firms, but this was nothing new. In 1999, the Gramm-Leach Bliley repealed the 1933 Glass-Steagall Act, which permitted Bankers Trust (a commercial bank) to acquire Alex. Brown (an investment firm). I remember the acquisition well. At the time, I viewed it not only as the demise of a legendary institution but an ominous sign for the future. Less than a decade later, an unbridled storm began. Similar to a rogue wave out at sea, the Volatility Index (VIX) reached an all-time high of almost 80. For investors, there were few places left to hide during 2008. Figure I.1 shows exactly how volatile the world became in 2008.

To put things into perspective, volatility levels doubled that of the Asian Crisis, Long Term Capital Management, September 11th, and Enron. While the U.S. Government helped support many of the failed financial institutions, Henry Paulson made the strategic decision to let Lehman Brothers Holdings Inc. fail. At the time, this decision might have been prudent. However, the collapse of Lehman Brothers Holdings Inc. adversely affected the credit default swap market, not only with the credit default swap insurance Lehman sold but also the billions of dollars other firms wrote on Lehman's debt. Credit default swaps are essentially derivative contracts on bonds. The chain reaction of events that followed could be described as the perfect storm. Investors learned quite a bit about investing during this period with both good and bad experiences (mostly bad).

Few investors understood the magnitude of the credit default swap (CDS) market. The CDS market is only part of the overall derivatives market. The *Economist* reported that "The overall market for over-the counter derivatives shot up to $455 trillion at the end of 2007. Some $62 trillion of that were credit-default swaps (CDSs), whose supercharged growth continues in spite of the crunch."[20] Steve Forbes noted that "American households, until recently, had net assets of $56 trillion."[21] Comparatively, the world's assets were around $195 trillion as of the end of 2007. *Harvard Business Review* reported that "The value of the world's financial assets—including equities, private and public debt, and bank deposits—has soared from $12 trillion in 1980 to $195 trillion in 2007."[22] Essentially, contracts on options, swaps, and futures far exceeded their underlying assets.

Because of this widespread turmoil, numerous asset classes were adversely affected, such as municipal bonds, bank loans, corporate bonds, convertible bonds, high-yield global bonds, domestic equities, mutual funds, preferreds, foreign equities, emerging market stocks, large-cap equities, midcap equities, and small-cap equities. Even U.S. Treasuries were negatively affected. Basically, no asset class was safe:

U.S. stock-market declines during October were so deep and wide that even tame investments were pummeled. Losses from the steep

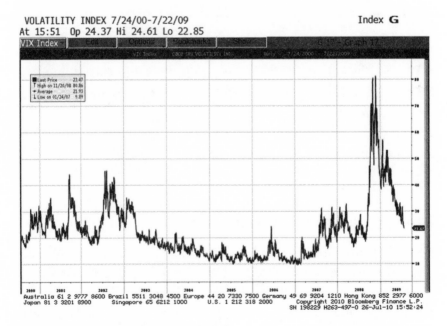

Figure I.1 Volatility Index 2000–2009

lunge that began just over a year ago now top those from 2000–2002. The average diversified mutual fund of U.S. stocks returned a negative 18.7% in October, according to preliminary figures from fund tracker Lipper Inc.; as of Thursday, that average fund was down 40% since the Dow Jones Industrial Average hit a record high on October 9, 2007. By comparison, during the previous bear market, between March 10, 2000, and the bottom on October 9, 2002, the average diversified stock fund lost a total of 34.9%. The past month has been a vivid reminder that sometimes, no matter how conservative an investor you think you are, you're going to get hit. Those who sought havens in what were once considered the safest of stocks saw their holdings battered as fears of a serious recession mounted. Even those who shunned stocks for once-boring bond funds saw their portfolios dragged down as the ripples of the credit crisis expanded outward. There were few places to hide. The average return for diversified U.S.-stock funds is a negative 34.7% for the first 10 months, which suggests 2008 is shaping up to be the worst year for mutual-fund investors in the nearly 50 years for which Lipper has such data.[23]

Traditional asset classes were destroyed, but even some of the alternatives were adversely affected, which typically is not the case. Hedge funds, for example, did well in 2000, 2001, and 2002, whereas the stock market performed poorly in each of these years. The S&P 500 was down –9.10% in 2000, –11.90% in 2001, and –22.10% in 2002. The Hedge Fund Research, Inc.'s (HFR) Funds of Funds Index returned +4.10% in 2000, +2.80% 2001, +1.00% in 2002.

Alternatives and Diversification

Quite a few institutions threw money into alternatives as a result of hedge fund performance from 2000 to 2002. By September 30, 2004, *Pensions & Investments* reported that the top-50 pension investors had added $4.6 billion to hedge funds or hedge fund-of-funds. Out of 50 of the largest pensions, 18 invested in hedge funds. Moreover, "U.S. institutional investors allocated nearly $500 billion to alternatives in the year ended June 30, 2004, according to data from Greenwich Associates Inc.'s annual survey. About $210 billion was invested in equity real estate, $185 billion invested or committed to private equity; and $90 billion in hedge fund of funds."[24]

Alternatives might sometimes fall with traditional asset classes like stocks and bonds, but for the most part, they hold their own. There are several reasons to utilize them for diversification: hedge funds outperformed equity mutual funds, there is a difference between short-term correlations and long-term ones, and diversification works when there are genuinely different sources of return. All three of these are valid reasons as to why alternatives are useful for diversification.

Many securities typically viewed as safe ones became illiquid or lost a lot of value during the 2007–2008 market collapse. The definition of risk was essentially rewritten in a few months. In *Against the Gods: The Remarkable Story of Risk*, Peter L. Bernstein states, "The prevalence of surprise in the world of business is evidence that uncertainty is more likely to prevail than mathematical probability."[25] In the *Risk Within*, James Picerno believes most risk rests with equities:

> Portfolio risk, for good or ill, is still almost fully reliant on stocks. The lesson: Don't focus exclusively on the whole at the expense of the pieces in risk management. Each component contributes to overall risk, which leads to two critical questions: 1) How much of the total volatility does each component contribute? And 2) How do those individual contributions change, if at all, after shifting the asset mix?[26]

Each component of a portfolio should be examined to determine the overall risk. Alternatives offer a wide variety of options for investors and can help build well-diversified, risk-adjusted portfolios:

> Given the gyrations in the financial markets, some investors are abandoning stocks and bonds and seeking refuge in unusual alternatives—parking spaces, for instance, and condos in Peru. Sales of exotic livestock are up. The U.S. Mint has seen a gold-coin rush. Investors have long turned to hard assets in market downturns, the idea being that if you invest in something real, it won't disappear, even if its value declines.[27]

Exploring Alternatives

Diversification can lead to alternative investments as obscure as coins, diamonds, art, or wine. Indexes of alternatives are evolving in many unlikely areas. Although the alternatives market is vast, there are three central alternatives one should initially explore: hedge funds, commodities, and venture capital. All three of these areas exhibit patterns, trends, or cycles that I call *waves*. I will focus on these three primary alternatives, offer examples of alternative vehicles for investors, and show how one might use them for diversification purposes. Understanding these alternatives and their waves can be useful in diversifying a portfolio.

Diversification is a means to lower risk or standard deviation. It is a common risk management tool. The objective is to have minimal covariance with the securities in a portfolio. Covariance is simply a measure of how much or how little two variables change together. By diversifying and owning different types of securities that do not move in lockstep together, risk will most likely be reduced. Alternatives can lower risk. Alternative investments can help diversify away beta. Beta is a measure of the volatility, or systematic risk, of a security or a portfolio in comparison to the market as a whole. Hypothetically, if one has two portfolios, one with alternatives and one without, the portfolio with alternatives from 2000 to 2009 exhibited less volatility, a lower beta, and higher returns. In Figure I.2, portfolio A had 60% U.S. Equity, and 40% U.S. Bonds with a total CAGR of 1.92%, total volatility of 12.69%, and total Beta of 0.589. Portfolio B had 20% U.S. Equity, 30% U.S. Bonds, 12.25% Hedge Funds, 12.25% Real Estate, 12.25% Commodities, and 12.25% Gold with a total CAGR of 6.61%, total volatility of 8.16%, and a total beta of 0.338.

Alternatives Investing

Depending on the individual investors' specific needs and objectives, certain alternatives might be more appropriate than others when making asset allocation decisions. Alternatives are not suitable for every investor. Some might not be appropriate at all depending on risk tolerance and net worth. According to David F. Swensen, "Asset allocation represents the most powerful implement in a rational investor's toolbox. By using the basic principles of diversification and equity orientation to build a foundation that

Asset Class	Index	Beta	Historical Volitility (2000-2009)	Compound Annual Growth Rates (2000-2009)	A	B
U.S. Equity	S&P 500	1	21.10%	−1.00%	60%	20%
U.S. Bonds	Barclays U.S. Capital Aggregate Bond Index	−0.029	2.90%	6.30%	40%	30%
Hedge Funds	HFRI Fund Weighted Composite Hedge Fund Index	0.317	11.10%	6.30%		12.25%
Real Estate	NAREIT (Real Estate Investment Trusts)	0.905	24.30%	10.60%		12.25%
Commodities	Barclays CTA Index	−0.084	23.50%	9.00%		12.25%
Gold	Handy & Harman Spot Gold Price	0.059	11.90%	14.30%		12.25%
Total Total CAGR Total Volitility Total Beta					100% 1.92% 12.69% 0.589	100% 6.61% 8.16% 0.338

Figure I.2   Adding Alternatives to Portfolio: Risk, Return, and Beta

Source: Author

accommodates individual characteristics and risk preferences, investors establish a framework that promises superior investment outcomes."[28] By preserving capital through the use of alternatives, one can take advantage of market corrections. *Wealth Manager* magazine reports: "Hedging with alternatives reduces volatility and loss during tough market conditions which, literally, allows advisors to buy when there's blood in the streets."[29]

Alternatives can be used in combination with equities and bond allocations. Rydex SGI notes that "These investments are typically characterized as having low correlation to traditional investments—that is, their movements are generally unrelated. This low correlation may service to 'hedge' or help protect traditional portfolios during sideways or down markets."[30] Just like stocks and bonds, one needs to be cognizant of waves.

Some of the worst percentage changes in the S&P 500 since 1929 were seen in the month of October 2008. Three of the biggest percentage drops in the index are as follows: October 1929 (−19.9%), October 1987 (−21.8%), and October 2008 (−16.9%). Throughout the history of stock and bond markets (about 200 years in the United States) and even longer in Europe, there have been moments of extreme volatility. Nassim Nicholas Taleb, in *The Black Swan*, examines how people react to explosive, unforeseen events, "A black swan can be defined as a highly improbable event with three principal characteristics: First, it is an *outlier*, as it lies outside the realm of regular expectations, because nothing in the past can convincingly point to its possibility. Second, it carries an extreme impact. Third, in spite of its outlier status, human nature makes us concoct explanations for its occurrence *after* the fact, making it explainable and predictable."[31]

Looking at past negative events is not alarming, but when you are in the middle of a storm or negative event, it can be quite traumatic and confusing. Investors tend to make poor decisions that can also be irrational at times. Bigger storms, such as rogue waves, sometimes affect securities that typically are safe. The market turmoil in 2008–2009 affected many investments that investors thought conservative, such as municipal bonds or money market funds. Storms in the past are no different. Take, for instance, the crash of 1973–1974, when the S&P 500 fell −43% from December 1972 to September 1974. As cited in Peter L. Bernstein's *Against the Gods*:

> This was a dark time, one marked by a series of ominous events: Watergate, skyrocketing oil prices, the emergence of persistent inflationary forces, the breakdown of the Bretton Woods Agreements, and an assault on the dollar so fierce that its foreign exchange value fell by 50%. The destruction of wealth in the bear markets of 1973–1974 was awesome, even for investors who had thought they had been investing conservatively.[32]

Alternatives frequently have high minimums ranging from $500,000 to $100 million. Historically, millionaires use a fair number of alternatives; *Wealth Manager* magazine notes that "households with total investable assets over $1 million have the highest exposure to alternatives of all asset ranges."[33] Additionally, the 26th U.S. Trust Survey of Affluent Americans revealed that, "40 percent of those with total assets of $25 million or more are invested in hedge funds, compared to only 17 percent of high net worth individuals with investable assets under $25 million."[34] According to *Private Wealth Management,* 76.4% of those with assets of more than $20 million have an interest in hedge funds as compared with 5.5% interest of investors with assets between $500,000 and $1 million.[35] Quite a few Forbes members invest in alternatives. For example, Dirk Ziff and family sold a business and allocated a large amount of the proceeds into alternatives:

> He and his two brothers founded Ziff Brothers Investments in the 1990s, after the $1.4 billion sale of their family's Ziff-Davis publishing empire. They invested in various public and private-equity ventures, including hedge funds. The family fortune was estimated by Forbes at more than $10 billion.[36]

Alternatives typically include higher costs and also might be illiquid. However, many mutual fund companies, banks, and other financial organizations realize the demand for both liquid and lower-priced alternatives. New vehicles for alternatives are entering the market at a rapid rate. ETFs now offer liquidity and minimums as low as $1,000. According to Rydex SGI, "Alternative strategies and asset classes are becoming available in the form of mutual funds and exchange traded funds (ETFs), thereby providing individual investors greater access."[37]

The real estate market collapse and credit crisis of 2008 provides investors with more data to help learn how alternatives can be used in building better and more diversified investment portfolios. One could draw a number of comparisons between the 1970s crisis and the subprime meltdown credit crises in 2007 and 2009:

> While we have been in a credit crisis for more than 14 months, there can be no mistaking the telltale signs of the panic phase of the crisis that first became evident in the week of September 15. We are in the midst of what the academic Charles Kindleberger called the "revulsion state" of a crisis—indiscriminate and contagious selling

of distressed assets that leads "banks to stop lending on the collateral of such assets." When such fear grips the markets, investors (and speculators) are quick to generalize—punishing many for the sins of few. That's the most dangerous phase of any crisis—when market implosions start to take on a self-reinforcing life of their own. The most important thing I can say about financial panics is that they are temporary—they either die of exhaustion or are overwhelmed by the heavy artillery of government policies.[38]

Yet the biggest difference was the availability of the alternatives market to reduce risk for investors. By adding more asset classes that have low correlation with one another, one can increase returns while similarly lowering risk. Diversification applies not only to difference asset classes (such as equities or fixed income), but within asset classes. For instance, one might diversify across different sectors or geographic areas. Investment styles such as small, mid, or large cap growth or value investing can be used to further diversify. The idea of proper diversification is also expressed in Peter L. Bernstein's "The Strange Case of the Anonymous Stockbroker":

> Investors diversify their investments, because diversification is their best weapon against variance of return. . . . As Poincaré had pointed out, the behavior of a system that consists of only a few parts that interact strongly will be unpredictable. With such a system you can make a fortune or lose your shirt with one big bet. In a diversified portfolio, by contrast, some assets will be rising in price even when other assets are falling in price; at the very least, the rates of return among the assets will differ. The use of diversification to reduce volatility appeals to everyone's natural risk-averse preference for certain rather than uncertain outcomes.[39]

Therefore, the fewer asset classes one uses in constructing a portfolio will increase risk and lower returns. There is no greater risk than a single-stock position. Having advised hundreds of corporate executives with single-stock positions, I have witnessed many who diversified and were protected as well as a number of individuals who refused to sell any shares.

Table I.2 Change in Net Worth on the Forbes 400 between August 29 and October 1, 2008

Name	Net Worth on August 29	Net Worth on October 1
Sheldon Adelson	$15.0 billion	$11.0 billion
Charles Ergen	$8.1	$5.9
Lawerence Ellison	$27.0	$25.4
Carl Icahn	$12.0	$10.4
Sergey Brin	$15.9	$14.4
Larry Page	$15.8	$14.3
Harold Hamm	$7.0	$5.5
Bill Gates	$57.0	$55.5
Michael Dell	$17.3	$15.9
Dan Duncan	$7.6	$6.3
Kirk Kerkorian	$11.2	$10.0
Jeffery Bezos	$8.7	$7.6

Source: Net Worth on the Forbes 400, *Forbes 400,* October 27, 2008. Used with permission.

Billionaires typically are well diversified, but many with large single-stock positions (that they were unable to sell because the shares were restricted) dropped precipitously. In Table I.2, a number of Forbes members lost a staggering amount of their net worth in the 2008 downturn.

If one examines closely the Forbes 400 list, the individuals and families who remain on the list over long periods tend to be the most diversified. Take for example, the Pritzker family, which holds companies with approximate revenues of more than $11 billion a year. The family that founded Hyatt not only manages 212 Hyatt hotels, but owns a diversified portfolio of real estate that includes apartment units, luxury retirement communities, industrial and office parks, and a commercial complex. They also own Marmon Group, an industrial company that holds 150 businesses that are mostly involved in manufacturing; have a large stake in heath-care companies; and are invested in a variety of other companies. On top of owning Conwood Co., the second-biggest snuff producer in the United States with $300 million in annual sales, they also have a large stake in Royal Caribbean and run several casinos.[40] The family is involved in many other alternative investments. John Pritzker "runs [a] private equity fund [and] invests in retailing, hospitality, entertainment and resorts. Tony and J. B. Pritzker run a venture capital fund and invest in technology manufacturing."[41]

Alternatives in a Postrecession Economy

One does not need to be a billionaire to invest in alternatives. The alternative space is mushrooming and open to any class of investor. Hedge funds frequently have high minimums which explains why they used to be accessible only to high-net-worth or institutional investors. Years ago, a million-dollar minimum was commonplace for hedge funds and other alternative investments. Robert F. Whitelaw and Sujeet Banerjee note that: "In 1982, the Securities and Exchange Commission (SEC) restricted access to these funds to accredited investors, defined as investors with at least $1 million in investment assets or a trailing income stream of over $200,000 per year."[42] Today, minimums have dropped to a hundred thousand (and in some cases even less), increasing both the interest and percentage of investment flowing into alternatives.

Whitelaw and Banerjee also note that "More and more investors are seeking out alternative investments. Industry research suggests that high-net-worth investors are allocating upwards of 20% of assets into alternative investment strategies-up from 3% in 2000."[43] (See Figure I.2.) The *Wall Street Journal* reported that "the institute for Private Investors in New York

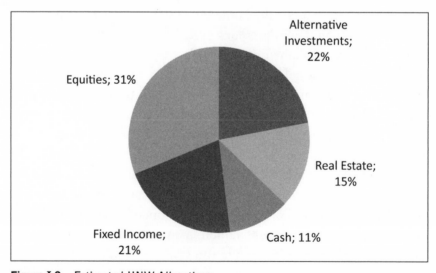

Figure I.2   Estimated HNW Allocations

Source: Robert F. Whitelaw and Sujeet Banerjee, "Hedge Funds for the Rest of Us," *Journal of the Indexes,* July/August 2007. Used with permission.

found that wealthy families allocated about 42% of their portfolios in 2004 to alternative investments such as hedge funds, private equity, venture capital and real estate."[44] Newer asset classes have evolved, such as mutual funds (with hedge fund–like characteristics), and have minimums now as low as $1,000; virtually all investors have access. Alternative investing will continue to expand.

As stated in the Rydex report, "Alternatives 2.0: What Is the Prudent Investor to Do?":

> We believe that the fundamental rationales for alternative investing remain sound—i.e., many alternatives are sound in their fundamental characteristics and seek to allow managers greater expression of their ideas; and they are still relevant in their application by investors, who seek to improve portfolio efficiency. The challenge for the future is to retain fidelity to the basic character and utility of alternatives (i.e., strategy flexibility freedom and higher portfolio efficiency), but adopt a new frame of reference regarding implementation within portfolios, particularly as a tool for reducing risk.[45]

Contrary to popular opinion, the world is not going to end. As I told my son when we were at a wedding in Chicago (where it rained for three days straight), "It does not rain forever." The sun surely did arrive, but it did so on Monday—we'd left on Sunday. Every asset class was affected in the epic downturn with the real estate meltdown and credit crisis of 2008–2009. Alternatives have been criticized recently in the downturn, but they are a viable asset class, and there is reason to believe they will have a strong rebound. Alternatives are beginning to show light, and institutional investors (the "smart money") are noticing.

Before problems occurred in 2008, a tremendous amount of money was flowing into alternatives. According to *Pensions & Investments*, "About 40% of manager hires by U.S. institutional investors in 2007 went into alternative investments."[46] The real estate market was overvalued. A deadly combination of arrogance, avarice, and naivete helped contribute to the real estate blowup. After reaching an all-time high with real estate in 2007, both individual and institutional investors plowed more money into real estate, ignoring the obvious impending correction. Alternatives are not immune and will correct on occasion. While real estate did poorly, other alternatives did well, such as gold. Some even had positive returns, depending on the type of alternative. As everyone knows, a recovery typically follows a recession. It is my belief that alternatives will not only prosper this time around but will most likely skyrocket. The LBO market appears to be thriving in 2009. *BusinessWeek* reported, "With the economy in tatters, corporate dealmaking remains anemic. But at least one group is feasting: vultures. Hostile takeovers and other unsolicited bids accounted for 11% of the acquisitions announced in the past 12 months."[47] Similarly, the venture capital area is bouncing back. According to the *San Francisco Business Times*, "A few weeks short of its second birthday, Hyperion Therapeutics landed a $60 million venture capital gift amid one of the biotech industry's worst funding droughts."[48]

There are early signs that the "smart money" or institutional money is seeking more alternatives. According to *Pensions & Investments*, first, "CalPERS' investment committee voted June 15 to increase the system's private equity allocation by four percentage points to 14% and raise fixed income by one percentage point to 20%, as well as create a 2% cash allocation."[49] Second, a survey conducted by the Oxford University Center for Employment, Work, and Finance, Oxford, England [and] co-sponsored by *Pensions & Investments*, "Analyzing SWFs through Proxy: The Oxford Survey of SWF Asset Managers," claims that sovereign wealth funds will be adding alternatives.[50] Third, "Worldwide institutional investor search and hiring activity [for hedge funds] remained positive so far this year [2009]."[51] Finally, the State of Wisconsin Investment Board decided to add hedge funds: "[A] first-time allocation to hedge funds is also possible, according to recommendations in an asset allocation study presented to the Madison-based board, which oversees a total of $78 billion."[52]

Hindsight is always 20/20. The time to make money, however, is to invest low and sell high. In my view, now is the time one should be adding alternatives to a well-diversified portfolio. It is time to get out the surfboard. I believe alternatives move in waves, and this next wave will be worth riding. Investors in equities and fixed income lost trillions in the downturn (most of which will be gone forever). Owning alternatives might be the solution. However, investors must do their homework and decide what may or may not be suitable for his or her portfolio. Hitting a wave at the right moment takes years of practice and patience. Both equities and bonds left investors shell-shocked with the 2008 stock market collapse. Alternatives, on the other hand, performed reasonably well. According to the *New York Times*, "When the global markets plummeted after Lehman Brothers declared bankruptcy in September last year, a handful of alternative investments remained stable or even made money for investors."[53]

Based on how alternatives have performed in good years as well as extremely difficult years with adverse market conditions, there will most likely be less interest in stocks and bonds going forward. Despite the recent market correction, investors will continue to seek nontraditional alpha. *On Wall Street* reported that "The expectation is that by 2010, demand for alternatives by U.S. institutional investors will grow to 10.8% or $3.3 trillion out of total assets of $30.3 trillion, according to a report publish by Freeman in 2004 based significantly on data from *Pension & Investment's* annual directory of the 200 largest U.S. pension funds."[54] Although trillions are presently invested in alternatives, the space is still relatively new and in its infancy. The financial landscape has changed forever. Banks and investment firms are one in the same now. Investors lost money not only with equities but asset classes that historically have been safe, such as bonds or money market funds. Those who own alternatives are adding to them and investors who have never contemplated owning alternatives are beginning to take notice and see how they might be added to a portfolio to be properly diversified. No matter if it is an individual or institution, investors are seeking alternatives. Investors should consider all asset classes, especially those they do not fully understand, because that is where an investor will likely find the best opportunity going forward.

Riding the Wave

Before exploring various alternatives, I review Wave Theory in Chapter 1 and how it can be applied. Chapter 2 is devoted to understanding waves with alternatives. Chapter 3 is about how waves work and how one might apply Wave Theory as an investor. Part 2 is about venture capital. Chapter 4 defines venture capital. Chapter 5 covers the history of venture capital. Chapter 6 concerns market dynamics with venture capital. Chapter 7 discusses venture capital advantages and disadvantages. Chapter 8 reviews venture capital performance. Chapter 9 summarizes the various investment vehicles with venture capital. Part 3 is about commodities. Chapter 10 involves an overview of commodities. Chapter 11 discusses investing with commodities. Part 4 is about the precious metal gold. Chapter 12 is an overview of gold. Chapter 13 discusses gold waves and investments. Part 5 is about hedge funds. Chapter 14 is an overview of hedge funds. Chapter 15 discusses the overall hedge fund market. Chapter 16 discusses the advantages and disadvantages of hedge funds. Chapter 17 reviews hedge fund performance. Chapter 18 summarizes a number of hedge fund vehicles.

I have trained many wealth managers over the years and part of this training entails a thorough knowledge or education regarding alternative investments. Similarly, I have given many talks to senior advisors interested in learning about alternatives. Further, I have educated many institutional as well as private clients about alternatives and how they might be used as part of a well-diversified, risk-adjusted portfolio.

When I discuss or introduce an alternative, I typically share my experience or background involving a particular alternative. One could study many different attributes of alternatives, but I believe it is prudent to know or be able to define each alternative. Likewise, I have found learning about an alternative's history is important. Besides the past, one should also consider the current market for each alternative as well as the overall market.

Anyone contemplating adding alternatives to their portfolio should explore both the advantages and disadvantages associated with each alternative. Although there is no guarantee of performance continuing into the future, one should examine the performance of every alternative, as well as the vehicle selected to gain access to the alternative. The manager, fund, index, or other means of investing will vary greatly and should be carefully selected for the investor.

All securities have risk, and alternatives are no different. Understanding risk is crucial in this regard. Over time, I compiled a list of recommended reading and Web sites to help further explore each alternative. Investment vehicles for alternatives are growing at a rapid rate and changing on a daily basis. There are nuances among every investment vehicle that one might consider to gain access to a particular alternative.

Finally, I make it a habit to constantly look toward the future. No one possesses a crystal ball, but it is not impossible to identify a certain trend or wave forming with alternatives. Understanding an alternative and events transpiring at the time is a good idea. For example, fighting or going against a trend such as market downturn is not wise and should be avoided.

Throughout Wave Theory with alternative investments, I attempt to follow this format so that a reader can easily compare and contrast each alternative in terms of my experience with alternatives: definitions, history, market, advantages/disadvantages, performance, risk, recommended reading and Web sites, and investment vehicles and outlook.

PART 1

WAVES

RIDING THE WAVE

Chapter 1

Wave Theory

Wave theory is simply the belief that all securities move in waves (patterns, cycles, or trends). History sometimes repeats itself, but with alternatives an investor can typically see similar waves repeating themselves. Equities move in waves. Fixed income moves in waves. Cash moves in waves. There is now enough data to support the notion that alternatives also move in waves. Besides these asset classes, there can even be styles such as "value" or "growth" investing that move in waves. Securities can also move in tandem, forming huge waves in epic downturns or sharp rallies. Realizing this, one can either make a lot of money or lose a lot of money while investing. After the Dow Jones dropped from 14,164 to 6,469, many investors sold securities at precisely the wrong time and lost trillions of dollars. Ironically, when the market started to recover and passed 10,000, many of these same investors attempted to jump back in and chase the market after they sold at the very bottom of the market. The individual who coined the expression "buy low, sell high" was not unintelligent. Yet investors (ones who are not paying attention to waves) frequently follow the news media and make the erroneous mistake of buying high and selling low.

Waves are found among all asset classes, including the fastest growing and compelling asset class: alternatives. In other words, there are distinct waves found within the alternatives asset class. Since more data became available in recent years, it is apparent that waves exist with alternatives. Those of the main alternative groups—hedge funds, commodities, and private equity (venture capital)—all have identifiable waves. One must be cognizant of waves found with alternatives to lower risk and maximize returns. Otherwise, the results can be lackluster if not devastating.

Mergers and Acquisition Waves

There is very little written about waves in finance, and although several individuals have touched on the subject, none have written about alternatives and waves. Alternatives are a relatively new asset class and can be difficult to understand. Those who have discussed waves in the past tend to review them with regard to various aspects of finance, not asset classes. For example, Allen, Brealey, and Myers's *Principles of Corporate Finance* explained that there are merger and acquisition waves:

> Mergers come in waves. The first episode of intense merger activity occurred at the start of the 20th century and the second occurred in the 1920s. There was a further boom from 1967 to 1969 and then again in the 1980s and 1990s (1999 and 2000 were record years). Each episode coincided with a period of buoyant stock prices, though there were substantial differences in the types of companies that merged and the ways they went about it.[1]

Robert F. Bruner also wrote about waves in *Applied Mergers and Acquisitions*, in which he describes "five periods of heightened merger activity; hereafter, I will call these 'waves'."[2] The fifth wave, or his Wave 4b (which I will call *Wave 5*), was caused by a few large scale mergers and acquisitions (M&A) deals. According to Bruner, "Following the 1990–91 recession, M&A activity increased briskly in all segments of the economy and all size categories. The announcement of a few large deals signaled to some observers a 'paradigm shift' in M&A where old rules about strategy, size, and deal design were being replaced with new rules."[3]

The graph in Figure 1.1 shows M&A activity in terms of deals and depicts one of the M&A waves described by Bruner. If one combines all of the M&A waves over the last century, Figure 1.2 depicts a long-term trend of M&A waves (patterns, cycles, or trends).

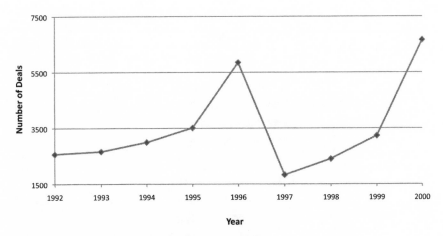

Figure 1.1   M&A Activity in Wave 5: 1992–2000

Source: Data from Robert F. Bruner, *Applied Mergers and Acquisitions* (New York: Wiley, 2004), 74–75. Used with permission.

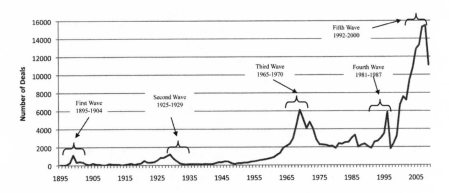

Figure 1.2   M&A Activity Since 1895

Source: Author.

Long before Bruner, Joseph Schumpeter noted "cycles" with M&A activity. Schumpeter originated the concept of creative destruction. His ideas have been widely applied to theories of evolutionary economics.[4] Understanding M&A waves with economics is helpful because of their effect on alternatives. Alternative asset classes (such as venture capital or leveraged buyout funds) depend on the M&A market because it is an exit strategy or a means to take a profit or cash out. The M&A market has shown distinct waves, especially over the past 30 years (Figure 1.3).

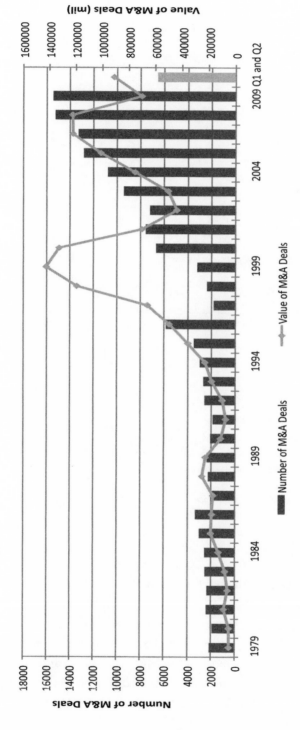

Figure 1.3 30 Years of Global Mergers and Acquisitions Activity

Source: Author.

Whether one measures the number of M&A deals or the dollar value of these deals, it is apparent that waves exist.

Initial Public Offering Waves

The discovery of waves with alternatives might be beneficial to a plethora of investors from retail and high net worth to institutional investors. Also, waves with alternatives might assist venture capital–backed private companies contemplating going public as well as investors in venture capital (pre-initial public offering [IPO]) or even buyers of IPOs. Wave Theory can help a lot of different people, including entrepreneurs who would like to take a company public. Chief executive officers (CEOs) of fast-growing emerging companies (e.g., health care, technology, consumer), should be aware of the point at which they are approaching a wave before going public. Depending on where a venture capital–backed company stands with regard to a wave, the CEO or venture firm might decide to wait or hold off for a more opportune time to go public—that is, be one of the first to go catch the wave. IPOs at the pinnacle of any market tend to have precipitous drops.

Similar to M&A, there are distinct waves with the IPO market. Whether one examines the number of IPOs or value in IPO deals, it is quite apparent that the IPO market (like the M&A market) travels in distinct waves as depicted in Figure 1.4. Hilary Kramer wrote the following about IPO waves in *Ahead of the Curve*: "IPOs are big waves that should be surfed only by investors who can stomach the big-wave risks associated with them.... IPO waves can be big, and the payoff can sure be big, too."[5]

Before 1999, there was a strong wave correlation between M&A and IPO markets. After this time, the M&A wave was robust, whereas the IPO market suffered. There were a number of variables that explained this phenomenon. The Sarbanes-Oxley Act was introduced to regulate new companies. However, it made it more expensive for young, fast-growing companies to arrange an IPO. Many went public in foreign markets (such as the London-based Alternative Investment Market) to save money. Others elected to become part of a larger conglomerate (M&A) to help them finance growth. Thus, M&A increased while IPOs decreased after 2002. Figure 1.5 portrays the number of M&A deals versus the number of IPO deals.

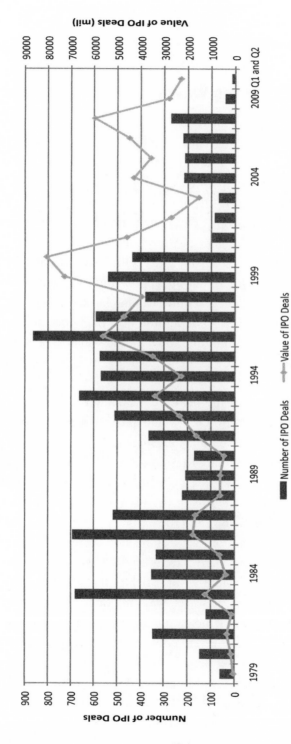

Figure 1.4 30 Years of U.S. Initial Public Offering Activity

Source: Author.

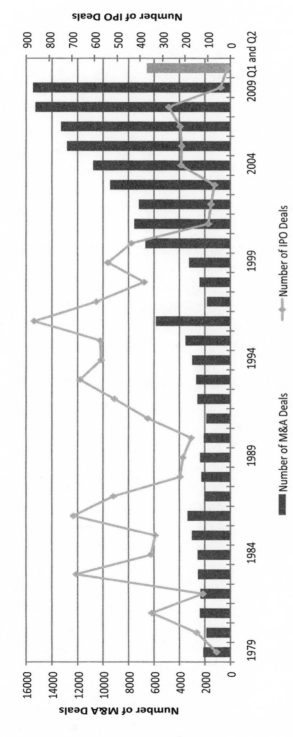

Figure 1.5 30 Years of Global M&A versus U.S. IPO Activity

Source: Author.

One can clearly see from this graph the huge growth in M&A deals since 2000. The IPOs during this period declined precipitously.

Waves and Economics

Investment waves were first depicted by the Russian economist Nikolai Kondratiev (1892–1938). Besides his wave ideas with investing, he is known for being a proponent of the New Economic Policy—a program during the Lenin years that allowed a small bit of capitalism. Kondratiev was imprisoned and later executed for his economic views. David Barker summarized Kondratiev's theories in *The K Wave*:

> The first matter to be covered when considering the Kondratieff long wave's effect on investments concerns timing. An economic cycle of 50 and 60 years duration is questionable as a precise investment-timing instrument. You cannot use the K Wave to say what will happen next month or even next year with precision in any market. However, the K Wave's long-term trend impact on financial markets is critical information. The K Wave's impact can make or break an investor's long term returns—and even determine a company's survival. Investors should incorporate the most important elements of K Wave Theory into their general decision-making process.[6]

Other economists wrote about reoccurring waves or cycles. Waves are inevitable, just like mortality. We cannot avoid waves just like we cannot escape death. As Herman Melville described in *Moby-Dick*, "...the waves should rise and fall, and ebb and flow unceasingly; for here, millions of mixed shades and shadows, drowned dreams, somnambulisms, reveries; all that we call lives and souls, lie dreaming, dreaming, still; tossing like slumberers in their beds; the ever-rolling waves but made so by their restlessness."[7] Life is filled with waves, both good and bad. Even if there is an occasional bad wave, it is not the end of the world because it is a "cleanup process," as referred to in Chevallier's *Greenspan's Taming of the Wave*:

> Greenspan emphatically proved in the 1990s that, even if down waves can't be escaped overall, depressions can be avoided. Thus, creative destruction can be made to work in your favour. In other words, the

clean-up process can be shortened by adequate monetary policies and depression need only be endured as worst-case scenarios. Hence, what the world needs in the future will be central bankers able to tame the wave, 'a la Greenspan.'[8]

Waves and Mathematics

Waves are not new to mathematics. In fact, Figure 1.6 shows that simple mathematical waves can be added together to create a graph that resembles one of an alternative wave.[9]

The exact formula used to create this wave is not important. The central importance is the general shape of the graph. Although these waves are hypothetical, similar waves in real life might represent a spike in prices from a war, hurricane, or other significant event.

A number of famous mathematicians wrote about waves. For instance, the Fibonacci number sequence was developed from the Italian mathematician Leonardo Fibonacci's book, *Liber Abaci*, which helped explain natural phenomenon. Mathematician Leonardo de Pisa (Fibonacci sequence of numbers) first wrote about patterns that were later used for analyzing alternatives.

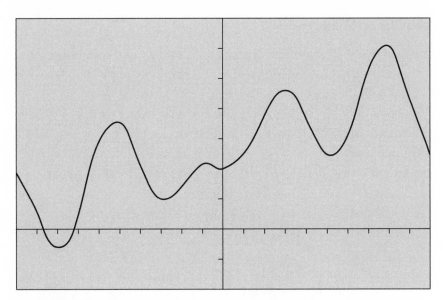

Figure 1.6 abs(sin(.3x)) +.2x + 2 + sin(x) +.2sin(.5x) + sin(30x)

Source: Author.

What may be surprising is just how pervasive the Fibonacci numbers are in Elliott's analysis of the stock market. Tracing most bear markets, he found that they move in a series of 2 impulsive waves and 1 corrective wave, for a total of 3 waves [like the beginning of the series]. On the other hand, his research showed that a bull market usually jumps upward in 3 impulsive waves and 2 corrective waves, for a total of 5 waves [following the Fibonacci sequence]. A complete cycle would be the total of these moves, or 8 waves.[10]

Albert Osborne, a wave mathematician from the University of Turin, wrote about rogue waves. Just like the securities market, normal waves can become unstable. It is believed that huge waves can leap up out of nowhere. "Quantum physics has at its heart a concept called the Schrodinger Equation, a way of expressing the probability of something happening that is far more complex than the simple linear model."[11] Schrodinger's theory, "An Undulatory Theory of the Mechanics of Atoms and Molecules," published in the *Physical Review* (December 1926), was based on the research of L. de Broglie in what he called *phase-waves* ("ondes de phase"). This view was essentially that material points are wave systems.

Waves and Securities

It is fairly well known that equities (both foreign and domestic), fixed income, and cash have identifiable waves. Ralph Nelson Elliott described "waves" with the stock market long ago. Elliott was born more than a century ago on July 28, 1871, and observed waves with the securities market. Elliott's observations of stock market behavior began coming together in 1939 into a general set of principles that applied to all degrees of wave movement in the stock price averages.[12] Elliott believed the stock market is affected by repetitive waves. Further, Edwards and McGee wrote *Technical Analysis of Stock Trends*, which was first published in 1948. Essentially, the book showed that stocks move in identifiable patterns, which repeat themselves as a result of supply and demand.[13] Finally, money management firm BlackRock depicted trends or patterns with equities, fixed income, and cash over the past 20 years in *Asset Class Returns: 20-Year Snapshot* (Table 1.1):

Table 1.1 Asset Class Returns: 20-Year Snapshot

BLACKROCK

Rank	1989	1990	1991	1992	1993	1994	1995	1996	1997	1998	1999	2000	2001	2002	2003	2004	2005	2006	2007	2008	2009
Best	Lg Cap Growth 35.90%	Fixed Income 9.00%	Sm Cap 46%	Sm Cap 18%	Int'l 32.60%	Int'l 7.80%	Lg Cap Value 38.40%	Lg Cap Growth 23.10%	Lg Cap Value 35.20%	Lg Cap Growth 38.70%	Lg Cap Growth 33.20%	Fixed Income 11.60%	Fixed Income 8.40%	Fixed Income 10.30%	Sm Cap 47%	Int'l 20.20%	Int'l 13.50%	Int'l 26.30%	Lg Cap Growth 11.80%	Fixed Income 5.20%	Lg Cap Growth 37.20%
	Lg Cap Core 31.60%	Cash 8.40%	Lg Cap Growth 41.20%	Lg Cap Value 13.80%	Sm Cap 19%	Cash 4.20%	Lg Cap Core 37.60%	Lg Cap Core 23.00%	Lg Cap Core 33.40%	Lg Cap Core 28.60%	Int'l 27.00%	Lg Cap Value 7.00%	Cash 4.40%	Cash 1.80%	Int'l 38.60%	Sm Cap 18%	Lg Cap Value 7.10%	Lg Cap Value 22.30%	Int'l 11.20%	Cash 2.10%	Int'l 31.80%
	Lg Cap Value 25.20%	Lg Cap Growth -0.30%	Lg Cap Core 30.40%	Lg Cap Core 7.60%	Lg Cap Value 18.10%	Lg Cap Growth 2.70%	Lg Cap Growth 37.20%	Lg Cap Value 21.60%	Lg Cap Growth 30.50%	Int'l 20.00%	Sm Cap 21%	Cash 6.20%	Sm Cap 3%	Div Portfolio -9.80%	Lg Cap Value 30.00%	Lg Cap Value 16.50%	Div Portfolio 5.40%	Sm Cap 18%	Fixed Income 7.00%	Div Portfolio -22.80%	Sm Cap 27.20%
	Div Portfolio 21.50%	Div Portfolio -3.00%	Div Portfolio 26.20%	Div Portfolio 7.50%	Div Portfolio 13.30%	Lg Cap Core 1.30%	Sm Cap 28%	Sm Cap 17%	Sm Cap 22%	Div Portfolio 17.00%	Lg Cap Core 21.00%	Div Portfolio -1.10%	Div Portfolio -4.80%	Lg Cap Value -15.50%	Lg Cap Growth 29.80%	Lg Cap Core 10.90%	Lg Cap Growth 5.30%	Lg Cap Core 15.80%	Div Portfolio 6.00%	Sm Cap -34%	Lg Cap Core 26.50%
	Sm Cap 16%	Lg Cap Core -3.10%	Lg Cap Value 24.60%	Fixed Income 7.40%	Lg Cap Core 10.10%	Div Portfolio -0.30%	Div Portfolio 27.40%	Div Portfolio 13.60%	Div Portfolio 20.60%	Lg Cap Value 15.60%	Div Portfolio 13.70%	Sm Cap -3%	Lg Cap Value -5.60%	Int'l -15.90%	Lg Cap Core 28.70%	Div Portfolio 10.50%	Lg Cap Core 4.90%	Div Portfolio 13.00%	Lg Cap Core 5.50%	Lg Cap Value -36.90%	Div Portfolio 20.80%
	Fixed Income 14.50%	Lg Cap Value -8.10%	Fixed Income 16.00%	Lg Cap Growth 5.00%	Fixed Income 9.80%	Sm Cap -2%	Fixed Income 18.50%	Int'l 6.10%	Fixed Income 9.70%	Fixed Income 8.70%	Lg Cap Value 7.40%	Lg Cap Core -9.10%	Lg Cap Core -11.90%	Sm Cap -21%	Div Portfolio 23.50%	Lg Cap Growth 6.30%	Sm Cap 5%	Lg Cap Growth 9.10%	Cash 5.00%	Lg Cap Core -37.00%	Lg Cap Value 19.70%
	Int'l 10.60%	Sm Cap -20%	Int'l 12.10%	Cash 3.90%	Cash 3.20%	Lg Cap Value -2.00%	Int'l 11.20%	Cash 5.30%	Cash 5.30%	Cash 5.20%	Cash 4.90%	Int'l -14.20%	Lg Cap Growth -20.40%	Lg Cap Core -22.10%	Fixed Income 4.10%	Fixed Income 4.30%	Cash 3.10%	Cash 4.90%	Lg Cap Value -0.20%	Lg Cap Growth -38.40%	Fixed Income 5.90%
Worst	Cash 9.90%	Int'l -23.40%	Cash 6.40%	Int'l -12.20%	Lg Cap Growth 2.90%	Fixed Income -2.90%	Cash 6.00%	Fixed Income 3.60%	Int'l 1.80%	Sm Cap -3%	Fixed Income -0.80%	Lg Cap Growth -22.40%	Int'l -21.40%	Lg Cap Growth -27.90%	Cash 1.20%	Cash 1.30%	Fixed Income 2.40%	Fixed Income 4.30%	Sm Cap -2%	Int'l -43.40%	Cash 0.20%

Source: BlackRock, Asset Class Returns: 20 Year Snapshot, www.colorado.metlife.com/files/23151/20Yr_Asset%20Class_Returns.pdf, accessed 2009. Used with permission.

Large Growth versus Value Waves

From the above BlackRock graph, one can see that large-cap growth investing was popular from 1989 to 1991. From 1992 to 1993, large-cap growth investing did not do as well but rallied from 1994 to 1999. However, large growth then remained out of favor from 2000 until 2006. In 2007, large-cap growth was the best-performing asset class. Growth moves in waves. When large-cap growth investing does well, value investing typically does not. The contrapositive is true; when value investing does well, growth does not. Figure 1.7 helps show waves with the Russell 1000 Growth versus Russell 1000 Value.[14]

Large- versus Small-Cap Waves

In 1999, before the bubble imploded, growth was in vogue while value did poorly. If one invested heavily in growth at this time (after a long growth wave), one would be investing at an all-time high, which Alan Greenspan described as "irrational exuberance."[15] The value wave then took over from 2000 until 2007—a really long wave to ride. Frequently, when there is a large-cap wave, small caps do not perform as well. The antithesis is true:

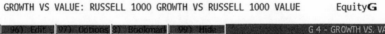

Figure 1.7 Growth versus Value: Russell 1000 Growth versus Russell 1000 Value

Source: Bloomberg. Used with permission.

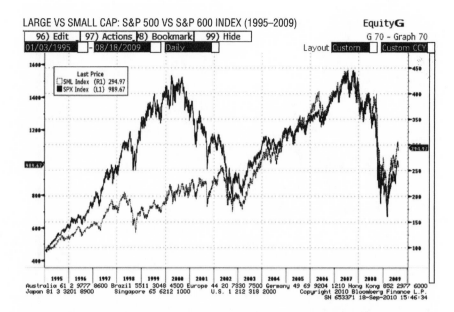

Figure 1.8 Large versus Small Cap: S&P 500 versus S&P 600 Index (1995-2009)
Source: Bloomberg. Used with permission.

when small caps are in favor, large caps usually do not do as well. Figure 1.8 exemplifies large-cap outperformance versus small-cap outperformance.

Fixed-Income versus Equity Waves

Fixed income was the best-performing asset class from 2000 to 2002 and then was one of the worst-performing asset classes from 2003 to 2006. Fixed income tends to do well when equities are underperforming. For instance, fixed income performed the best out of any asset class in 2008 (including cash). However, when equities have strong returns, bonds frequently are not performing well, as shown in Figure 1.9 with the S&P 500 versus Barclays Bond Index Fund from 1993 to 2009.

Foreign versus Domestic Equity Waves

Foreign equity moves in waves as much as domestic equity. Foreign equity investing performed poorly from 1989 to 1992. However, from 1993 to 1994, it was the best performing asset class. From 1995 to 1997, foreign equity moved out of favor but gained traction again from 1998 to 1999. Foreign investing moved out of favor again during 2000–2002. Foreign equity did

STOCKS VS BONDS: S&P500 VS BARCLAYS BOND INDEX FUND (1993-2009)   EquityG

Figure 1.9   Stocks versus Bonds: S&P 500 versus Barclays Bond Index Fund
(1993-2009)

Source: Bloomberg. Used with permission.

well from 2003 to 2007 but was one of the worst-performing asset classes in
2008. It is interesting to note that foreign-equity investing over time has
become more closely aligned with domestic-equity investing primarily
because the United States is part of a global economy. According to the 2009
"Top 100" in *Forbes*, only 7 out of the top-20 largest companies in the world
were based in the United States. Historically, the number of U.S. companies
on the list was far greater. In fact, the United States had 11 out of the top-20
global companies in 2005.[16] This new wave might help investors learn the
importance of foreign-equity investing and that the United States is an integral part of the global economy. One might be remiss to not own foreign equities in his or her portfolio. Figure 1.10 depicts the Dow Jones compared with
the MSCI (Ex USA) from 1989 to 2009.

Long-Run versus Short-Run Waves

Although one can clearly see waves with value versus growth investing, equities versus fixed-income investing, foreign versus domestic investing, small-
cap versus large-cap investing, there exist larger waves from the market in
general. For example, if one charts the Dow Jones from 1929 to 2009, a total
of 18 waves are identifiable (Figure 1.11).

Figure 1.10 Domestic versus Foreign: DJIA versus MSCI EX USA Index (1989-2009)
Source: Bloomberg. Used with permission.

Figure 1.11 Dow Jones Performance 1929-2009
Source: Bloomberg. Used with permission.

Smaller waves might appear insignificant when examining waves over long periods, but they become much more traumatic or even exaggerated up close. The longer the period, the more likely the tendency to smooth out volatility for various asset classes. In other words, one might not notice the asset class fluctuating as one might see in the short run. Equities, for instance, appear attractive and low risk in the long run. But in any given year, equities can drop precipitously, such as evidenced in 2008. Time dampens the wild swings in the market so that equities average 9% to 10%. One might be tempted to put all their money in equities after examining the S&P 500 because in the long run the market moves up. In the short run, there is volatility, and an investor can examine the rocky waves.

Hypothetically, if one examined the market for a shorter period (1995–2009), one could see two massive market declines in which trillions of dollars were lost by investors and the United States experienced unprecedented volatility (Figure 1.12).

If one peers closer as a scientist does while sharpening the focus of his or her microscope, one can see the waves even more vividly. For example, the uptrend or trough-to-peak exhibited from January 1997 to March 2000 is distinct. The bull market rally revolved around the Internet and technology sector. During this period, the market reached a historic high (Figure 1.13).

Figure 1.12 Bull versus Bear Waves

Source: Bloomberg. Used with permission.

Figure 1.13 Trough to Peak (January 1, 1997–March 23, 2000)

Source: Bloomberg. Used with permission.

Figure 1.14 Peak to Trough (March 24, 2000–October 10, 2002)

Source: Bloomberg. Used with permission.

Yet we know nothing exists that can actually grow to the sky; there will be a correction. The tide turned after March 2000, when growth investing turned to value investing (Figure 1.14). The nonstop barrage of negative news lasted several years, with many unforeseen events taking place one after another, such as 9/11, Enron, and Martha Stewart being hauled off to jail.

Cash Waves

Buying equities in this downturn would be tantamount to surfing in a parking lot—it will not happen. Catching a falling knife is a bad idea. When stocks start falling, run for cover. One might argue that you cannot time the market. However, it is quite clear from Figure 1.14 that investors were not limited to a few days from which they had to exit the market or go to the sidelines; they had three years of warning signals.

Cash moves in waves. Overall, cash was out of favor 14 out of 20 times during a two-decade horizon (1989–2008), according to BlackRock's *Asset Class Returns: 20 Year Snapshot.* Over 20 years, cash was never the number-one-performing asset class. However, it was the worst performer five times and the second worst performer eight times over those same 20 years. Cash was out of favor from 1995 to 1999 but rallied from 2000 to 2002. However, from 2003 to 2007, cash was not a top performer when the equity markets were up. During the horrible downturn in 2008, cash was only the second-best performer (after bonds). Fidelity did a study regarding money markets as a percentage of all mutual funds compared with the S&P 500 (Figure 1.15). The research revealed that investors tend to build cash positions at precisely the wrong time. In other words, investors frequently miss the wave. As Fidelity summarized, many investors "have been slow to reallocate to stocks in the early stages of a new bull market."[17]

Alternatives and Waves

Alternatives move in waves (patterns, cycles, or trends) just like other securities. "Technical and fundamental factors affect price. Forecasting price movement based on the fundamental approach requires the study of supply and demand factors affecting the price of a commodity or financial instrument. Technical analysis, on the other hand, requires the study of

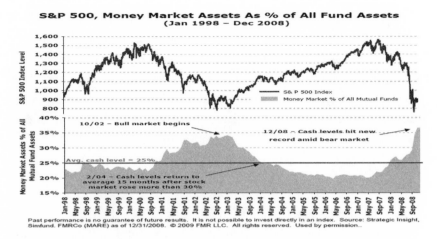

Figure 1.15 Money Market Wave

Source: Fidelity Investments, "The Perils of Herding to Cash," Fidelity Investor's Publications (March 13, 2009). Used with permission.

historical price movement and current market activity."[18] Similar to equities, a technical analysis can be used for making an investment decision:

> [A] technician is concerned with market action only. The basic issue here is not that fundamentals are what ultimately moves price—the technician concedes the point. The technician believes it is virtually impossible for most of us to know all the fundamentals that affect price at any given time. By the time the news reaches most of us, it has been disseminated so widely that it has been discounted in price. Because a trader makes or loses money via price movements, the technician believes this is what should be studied. In other words, the technician believes price is the ultimate fundamental.[19]

Hypothetically, one could use both technical and fundamental analysis for evaluating an investment in gold. Fundamentalists do not view charts. If it is an equity, fundamentalists explore economic, industry, and company analysis in order to obtain a stock's fair value as well as a future value. A company's market share, management, product, services, financials, competition, and other variables are examined. Unlike a technician, fundamentalists will also examine economic factors such as inflation, interest rates, or anything else regarding the economy. Lastly, a fundamentalist would examine the supply and demand for the products in a particular industry. Research reports are issued by banks and other independent third-party research. Due to their complexity, a prudent investor might consider both technical and fundamental analysis when considering alternatives. Certain Alternatives exhibit multiple waves over very short periods of time as evidenced by gold, where technical analysis might be extremely useful in addition to fundamentals. Fundamentally, gold is a volatile commodity that frequently has its price affected by a variety of factors.

Commodity Waves

Other alternatives, such as wheat, might not be as fast paced as oil. Yet technical and fundamental analysis might be helpful in making a wise investment decision. Regardless, all alternatives have waves. Alternatives are affected by many factors at any given time, just as they represent many waves at one time (Table 1.2).

Prudent investors must be cognizant of such waves and factors that could either adversely or positively affect their investment. Otherwise, one could lose a lot of money. Take, for example, the GSCI Commodity Index (Table 1.2). Part of this index includes oil. From July 29, 1999, to July 7, 2008, the GSCI Index grew to the sky. But as we are now aware, nothing grows to the sky (hindsight is 20/20). If one rode this index to astronomical highs, however, there is a time when one should take a profit. You cannot win forever; it is statistically impossible. Ask anyone betting only on red in roulette. Eventually, you will hit 00 or black. Figure 1.16 tracks the performance of the S&P 500 Goldman Sachs Commodity Index (GSCI) over this period.

If one were marked by avarice and held this index too long, the result would be devastating. Likewise, if one paid no attention to the commodity

Table 1.2 Goldman Sachs Commodity Index

# of Components	24
% Energy	70.50
% Grains	10.04
% Industrial Medals	7.70
% Livestock	4.43
% Precious Metals	3.00
% Softs	4.33
% Other	0.00

*Weighting current as of 8/3/09.

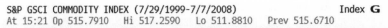

Figure 1.16 S&P GSCI Commodity Index (7/29/1999-7/7/2008)

Source: Bloomberg. Used with permission.

wave that transpired and bought at the high, they would be annihilated. Figure 1.17 depicts the worst time to invest as well as the best. One cannot always buy low and sell high. However, wave riders can develop good timing and/or be aware of the wave. Waves come and go.

Although this 10-year graph of the S&P GSCI Commodity Index shows a recent wave, it is nothing new. Hypothetically, if one used another index, such as the Reuters-CRB Index, and went back further in time, there were at least five occasions of commodity waves or rallies with commodities (Table 1.3).

Table 1.3 Commodity Waves Ranked by Percentage Gain of Reuters-CRB Index (CCI) (1971-2008)

	Low		High		Percent Rally
2001–08	Oct–01	182.83	Jul–08	615.04	236.40%
1971–74	Oct–71	96.40	Feb–74	237.80	146.70%
1977–80	Aug–77	184.70	Nov–80	337.60	82.80%
1986–88	Jul–86	196.16	Jun–88	272.19	38.80%
1992–96	Aug–92	198.17	Apr–96	263.79	33.10%

Source: Commodity Research Bureau (February 29, 2009).

Figure 1.17 S&P GSCI Commodity Index 10 Years (7/29/99-7/29/09)
Source: Bloomberg. Used with permission.

Similar to stocks, bonds, and cash, certain patterns or waves exist with commodities as a whole and also with individual commodities. For example, one can create a periodic table similar to BlackRock using individual commodities such as industrial metals, energy, precious metals, agriculture, or livestock (Table 1.4).

As one can plainly see, industrial metals did not perform well in 2002. Yet from 2003 to 2006, they are the best-performing commodities. From 2007 to 2008, however, they were one of the worst performers.

If one views a large body of water from a plane, no matter what the conditions are, it will appear as if there are no waves and that everything is calm. However, if you are swimming in the ocean, you will be much more cognizant of the waves, much like a surfer.

Venture-Capital Waves

Like commodities, venture capital has waves. Figure 1.18 shows a wave with venture capital for a short time (2003–2008).

Table 1.4 Periodic Table of Commodity Returns 1999–2009

1999	2000	2001	2002	2003	2004	2005	2006	2007	2008	2009*
Energy 92.39	Energy 87.54	Precious Metals 0.52	Energy 50.71	Industrial Metals 40.05	Industrial Metals 27.55	Industrial Metals 36.32	Industrial Metals 60.93	Energy 41.92	Precious Metals 0.48	Industrial Metals 29.91
GSCI Index 40.92	GSCI Index 49.74	Livestock -2.87	GSCI Index 32.07	Energy 24.57	Energy 26.09	Energy 31.19	Precious Metals 24.08	GSCI Index 32.67	Livestock -27.42	Energy 8.05
Industrial Metals 30.75	DJAIG Index 31.84	Industrial Metals -16.48	DJAIG Index 25.91	DJAIG Index 23.93	Livestock 25.49	GSCI Index 25.55	Agriculture 13.35	Agriculture 28.31	CCI-TR Index -28.6	DJAIG Index 7.79
DJAIG Index 24.35	CCI-TR Index 14.26	CCI-TR Index -17.18	Precious Metals 23.29	GSCI Index 20.72	GSCI Index 17.28	DJAIG Index 21.36	CCI-TR Index 10.75	Precious Metals 27.94	Agriculture -28.88	GSCI Index 6.55
Livestock 14.36	Livestock 8.57	DJAIG Index -19.51	CCI-TR Index 18.42	Precious Metals 19.55	CCI-TR Index 12.45	CCI-TR Index 19.75	DJAIG Index 2.07	CCI-TR Index 17.21	DJAIG Index -35.65	Precious Metals 5.7
Precious Metals 3.89	Agriculture -1.08	Agriculture -23.09	Agriculture 11.36	CCI-TR Index 11.32	DJAIG Index 9.15	Precious Metals 18.63	Livestock -6.74	DJAIG Index 16.23	GSCI Index -46.49	CCI-TR Index 2.47
CCI-TR Index 2.06	Precious Metals -1.24	Energy -40.44	Industrial Metals -0.61	Agriculture 6.59	Precious Metals 5.65	Livestock 3.46	GSCI Index -15.09	Industrial Metals -5.64	Industrial Metals -49.02	Agriculture -4.94
Agriculture -18.86	Industrial Metals -4.26	GSCI Index -31.93	Livestock -9.45	Livestock 0.03	Agriculture -20.15	Agriculture 2.35	Energy -26.79	Livestock -8.63	Energy -52.38	Livestock -11.49

*As of 6/30/09.
Source: Author.

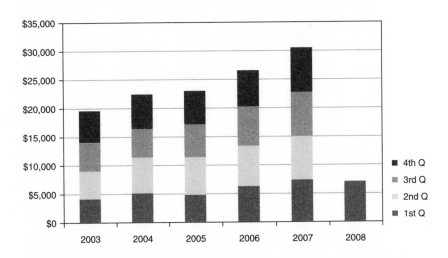

Figure 1.18 A Difficult Quarter: Transaction Volume by Quarters, in Millions.

Source: PricewaterhouseCoopers/National Venture Capital Association Money Tree Report; data: Thomson Reuters. Used with permission.

Yet venture-capital waves have existed for decades. Figure 1.19 shows the number of venture-capital deals along with the value of the venture-capital deals over the past 30 years.

Hedge-Fund Waves

Investors should step back and examine waves to see where they are at the moment. Whether it is real estate, commodities, or private equity, all alternatives have waves. Table 1.5 compares hedge funds with equities, fixed income, and cash over the last decade.

Thus, Wave Theory pertains not only to securities such as stocks, bonds, or cash but to alternatives as well. Alternatives are relatively new and evolving. They are becoming actual asset classes to compete with equities, fixed income, and cash. Because information is sometimes hard to locate and in some cases nonexistent, the alternatives world can be challenging for investors to navigate. One can clearly see waves with alternatives such as hedge funds, commodities and gold, and private equity (venture capital). No one can predict the future. However, history tends to repeat itself, and there are distinct waves (patterns, cycles, or trends) with alternatives. Surfing the alternative waves takes courage. As Sri Sathya Sai Baba said, "Have faith in yourself, when you have no faith in the wave, how can you get faith in the ocean?"[20]

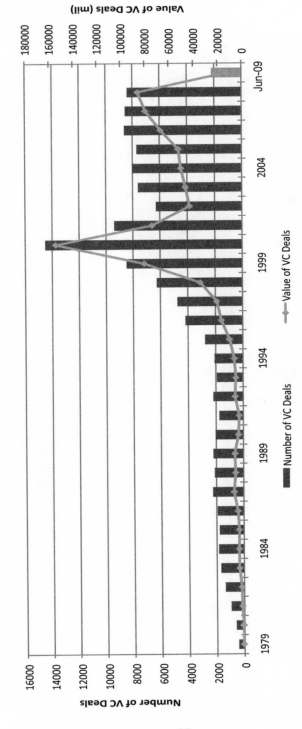

Figure 1.19 30 Years of Global Venture Capital Activity

Source: Author.

Table 1.5 The Wave Chart: 10-Year Ranking of Asset Class Returns

	1999	2000	2001	2002	2003	2004	2005	2006	2007	2008
Better Performing	EM Equity 66.40%	US REITs 26.40%	US REITs 13.90%	Real Assets 24.70%	EM Equity 56.30%	US REITs 31.50%	EM Equity 34.50%	US REITs 35.10%	EM Equity 39.80%	Managed Futures 14.10%
	Developed Asia Equity 57.60%	US TIPs 13.20%	US Fixed Income 8.40%	Managed Futures 12.40%	Europe Equity 38.50%	EM Equity 26.00%	Private Equity 28.30%	Europe Equity 33.70%	Real Assets 31.00%	Real Assets 5.80%
	Private Equity 34.80%	US Fixed Income 11.60%	US TIPs 11.80%	US TIPs 11.60%	Developed Asia Equity 38.50%	Private Equity 24.90%	Developed Asia Equity 22.60%	EM Equity 32.60%	Private Equity 20.50%	US Fixed Income 5.20%
	Hedge Funds 31.30%	Managed Futures 7.95%	High Yield Bonds 5.80%	US Fixed Income 10.30%	US REITs 37.10%	Europe Equity 20.90%	Real Assets 17.90%	Private Equity 27.00%	Europe Equity 13.90%	US TIPs 2.40%
	US Equity 21%	Hedge Funds 5.00%	Hedge Funds 4.60%	US REITs 3.60%	US Equity 29%	Developed Asia Equity 19.00%	US REITs 12.20%	Real Assets 23.20%	US TIPs 11.60%	Hedge Funds −9.00%
	Europe Equity 15.90%	Private Equity 3.10%	Real Assets 2.10%	High Yield Bonds 2.10%	High Yield Bonds 27.90%	High Yield Bonds 12.00%	Europe Equity 9.40%	US Equity 16%	Hedge Funds 10.00%	Private Equity −22.70%
	High Yield Bonds 3.90%	High Yield Bonds −4.20%	Managed Futures 0.80%	Hedge Funds −1.50%	Private Equity 23.40%	US Equity 11%	Hedge Funds 9.30%	Hedge Funds 12.90%	Managed Futures 7.60%	High Yield Bonds −26.20%
	US TIPs 2.40%	Real Assets −6.70%	EM Equity −2.40%	EM Equity −6.00%	Hedge Funds 19.60%	Hedge Funds 9.00%	US Equity 5%	Developed Asia Equity 12.20%	US Fixed Income 7.00%	Developed Asia Equity −36.40%
	Real Assets 0.50%	US Equity −8.40%	Private Equity −7.70%	Private Equity −7.70%	Real Assets 19.40%	US TIPs 8.50%	US TIPs 2.80%	High Yield Bonds 12.00%	US Equity 7%	US REITs −37.70%
	US Fixed Income −0.80%	US Equity −9%	US Equity −12%	Developed Asia Equity −11.90%	US TIPs 9.4$	Real Assets 5.50%	US Fixed Income 2.40%	US Fixed Income 4.30%	Developed Asia Equity 5.30%	US Equity −38%
	Managed Futures −1.20%	Developed Asia Equity −25.80%	Europe Equity −19.90%	Europe Equity −19.90%	Managed Futures 8.70%	US Fixed Income 4.30%	High Yield Bonds 2.30%	Managed Futures 3.50%	High Yield Bonds 2.70%	Europe Equity −46.40%
Worse Performing	US REITs −4.60%	EM Equity −30.60%	Developed Asia Equity −25.40%	US Equity −25%	US Fixed Income 4.10%	Managed Futures 3.30%	Managed Futures 1.70%	US TIPs 0.40%	US REITs −15.70%	EM Equity −52.30%

Source: Author.

Chapter 2

Surfing Alternatives Waves

The purpose of this book is to enable people to understand alternatives and how one can use them to build better, more diversified portfolios (whether they are for institutional investors or for high-net-worth and/or retail investors). Navigating alternatives is not easy and requires a skill set similar to that of a world-class surfer riding waves in the ocean.

> Surfing is a tough sport to master. While the professionals often make it look easy, catching a wave and maintaining balance is difficult. Experienced surfers are typically judged by their ability to perform various maneuvers. But, as with any discipline, mastering the advanced moves requires learning the basics.[1]

Riding the perfect wave in the ocean is analogous to finding the right alternative for a portfolio and earning a handsome return. The alternatives space is vast like an ocean and will one day eclipse both the equity and fixed-income markets combined. Alternatives should be in everyone's asset-allocation model.

Making money is one thing, but losing it is another. No one likes to lose money. Alternatives, like any other security, carry risk. One of the central risks to investing in alternatives is timing. Buying an alternative at the wrong time is no different than being crushed by a wave or being thrown from your surfboard. In order to ride our alternatives waves, we must know everything there is to know about riding waves like a professional surfer. As the surfer Kelly Slater advised, "Your surfing can get better on every turn, on every wave you catch. Learn to read the ocean better. A big part of my success has been wave knowledge."[2] Understanding the alternatives marketplace is also imperative. A neophyte investor in alternatives is identical to someone who has never surfed before. I recall one of my best friends, Brad Leve, who attempted to teach me how to surf in Ocean City, New Jersey, when we were teenagers. The waves were huge, and I was terrified. Now that decades have passed and we are much older, I worry about things like water temperature, sharks, and skin irritation. I can honestly say there would be no way I would ever attempt to go surfing again without a good teacher or guide such as Brad. Otherwise, one is merely being reckless or ignorant of risk. Understanding alternatives, the risk and return characteristics, marketplace, correlation with other assets, advantages and disadvantages, and performance are all helpful in learning how to surf the alternatives waves.

Definition of Waves and Alternatives

Alternatives travel in waves. In order to understand Wave Theory, one first needs to understand the essence of a wave. In Robert Dinwiddie's *Ocean*, waves are defined:

> Waves are disturbances in the ocean that transmit energy from one place to another. The most familiar types of waves—the ones that cause boats to bob up and down on the open sea and dissipate as breakers on beaches—are generated by wind on the ocean surface. Other wave types include tsunamis, which are often caused by underwater earthquakes, and internal waves, which travel underwater between water masses. Tides are also a type of wave.[3]

According to *Merriam-Webster's Dictionary*, a wave can also be defined as:

- Moving ridge or swell on the surface of a liquid, open water
- Something that swells and dies away
- A rolling or undulatory movement or one of a series of such movements passing along a surface or through the air
- A disturbance or variation that transfers energy progressively from point to point in a medium and that may take the form of an elastic

deformation or of a variation of pressure, electric or magnetic intensity, electric potential, or temperature

- One complete cycle of such a disturbance
- An undulating or jagged line constituting a graphic representation of an action

There are distinct wavelike or cyclical patterns one can observe with alternatives. Investing in alternatives is not too different from riding a wave on which the alternative(s) can serve as a surfboard. The alternatives space is quite large and complex, reminiscent of an ocean or large body of water. Table 2.1 shows the explosion of various asset classes (including alternatives) over the last few decades.

Alternatives have grown in number, type, and size. The hedge fund space, for instance, has grown dramatically. Between 1990 and 2008, the industry's assets under management grew almost 50-fold, to nearly $2 trillion.[4] Similarly, the private equity space has grown. Vehicles in the alternatives space are making bigger investments and have become more important today. According to the Director of the McKinsey Global Institute, Diana Farrell, "Pension and insurance funds continue to be the major private investors, but other private and public players are increasing in importance. Hedge funds, private equity funds, central banks, sovereign wealth funds, government investment corporations, and government-controlled companies—all with different investment goals and strategies—are now prominent on the global landscape."[5]

History

Understanding the ocean is not an easy task. Many famous people have studied the ocean, including Benjamin Franklin, who noted the expediency of eastern travel versus western travel across the Atlantic because of the Gulf Stream. Shakespeare wrote quite a bit about oceans:

I have seen tempests, when the scolding winds
Have rived the knotty oaks, and I have seen
The ambitious ocean swell and rage and foam
To be exalted with the threatening clouds. . . .[6]

Table 2.1   Asset Classes

1970s
US Stocks
US Bonds
Cash
Gold

1980s
US Large Stocks
US Small Stocks
US Bonds
Real Estate
International Equities
Venture Capital
Gold

1990s

US Equities
- Large Cap Growth
- Lage Cap Value
- Mid Cap Growth
- Small Cap Growth
- Small Cap Value

International Equities
- Traditional
- Emerging

Bonds
- Long-Term
- Immediate
- High Yield
- Mortgage

Alternatives
- Real Estate Direct
- Real Estate REITs
- Private Placements
- Venture Capital
- Hedge Funds
- Gold

2000s

US Equities
- Large Cap Growth
- Large Cap Value
- Mid Cap Growth
- Small Cap Growth
- Small Cap Value

International Equities
- Traditional
- Emerging

Bonds
- Long-Term
- Immediate
- High Yield
- Mortgage

Alternatives
- Real Estate Direct
- Real Estate REITs
- Private Placements
- Venture Capital
- Hedge Funds
- Gold

- Principle Protected Indexes
- Indexes
- Exchange Funds
- Fundamental Indexes
- Structured products
- Timber
- Hedge Fund-of-Funds
- Commodities
- Tips
- Emerging Market Debt
- Bond Indexes
- IPOs
- Distressed Securities
- CDOs
- LBO Funds
- Managed Futures
- Reverse Conv. Notes

Source: Rebecca McReynolds, "Alternative Investments Are One Key to Outperforming the Market," *On Wall Street Magazine* (August 2007). Used with permission.

Similarly, Captain James Cook studied the ocean and was the first to describe surfboarding when he made the first documented European trip to Hawaii in 1778.

Comparable with the ocean's secret treasures, certain alternatives have been around for a long time. In fact, commodities have existed for centuries and stem back to the formation of the earth. In 1807, the English chemist Sir Humphry Davy established the existence of aluminum; lead was used in England in the thirteenth century. Uranium was discovered in 1789 by German chemist Martin Klaproth. Cocoa was found in 1000 BC by the Olmec, people who were from the Mexican Gulf Coast. Rice was a source of food back in 2000 BC.

Commodities have been around a long time, but ways of investing in them, like other alternatives, is more recent. For example, commodity indexes have only been recently established. The Commodity Research Bureau (CRB) was founded in 1986, the Goldman Sachs Commodity Index (GSCI) was founded in 1992, the Dow Jones–American International Group (DJAIG) was founded in 1998, and the Rogers International Commodities Index (RICI) was founded in 1998. The vast majority of vehicles to invest in alternatives are new. For instance, there is now an ETF for uranium.

Venture capital has also evolved. George F. Doriot was one of the first American venture capitalists. He founded the American Research and Development Corporation in 1946, which became the first publicly owned venture capital firm. Venture capital funds were not commonplace until the 1980s.

Similar to when venture capital was first formed, in the late 1940s, Alfred W. Jones started the first hedge fund in 1949. Hedge funds grew over time but really blossomed in the 1990s.

Wave Heights

Waves are generated by wind energy:

Wind energy is imparted to the sea surface through friction and pressure, causing waves. As the wind gains strength, the surface develops gradually from flat and smooth through growing levels of roughness. First, ripples form, then larger waves, called chop. The waves continue to build, their maximum size depending on three factors: wind speed, wind duration, and the area over which the wind is blowing, called the fetch. When waves are as large as they can get under the current conditions of wind speed and size of fetch, the sea surface is said to be "fully developed."[7]

Waves, like returns in the stock market, can be good or bad. Bad waves do not last forever nor do really good ones. Performance can vary dramatically from year to year. Extremely large waves have been observed from time to time. These unusual rogue waves are unprecedented and relentless. As William J. Board notes, "Enormous waves that sweep the ocean are traditionally called rogue waves, implying that they have a kind of freakish rarity."[8] The financial market in the second half of 2008 could be categorized as a rogue or killer wave; it was a dramatic financial storm. M. A. Donelan and A. K. Magnusson note that "Rogue waves are believed to be the consequences of focusing of wave energy."[9]

There was ample evidence for negativity in the 2008 performance of various markets worldwide. For instance, the year-to-date domestic market return as of October 24, 2008, was as follows: S&P 500 Index (−39.2%), S&P 100 Index (−36.9%), S&P 400 (−40.9%), S&P 600 (−35.7%), NASDAQ Composite Index (−41.1%), Dow Jones Industrial Average Index (−35.5%), Dow Jones Transportation Index (−23.8%), Dow Jones Utilities Average Index (−31.9%), Russell 1000 Index (−40.1%), and Russell 2000 Index (−37.8%).[10] Except for the Depression and the crash of '87, the United States has never witnessed such precipitous declines in equities as we viewed in the month of October.

Hurricanes and other storms do not usually travel to all corners of the Earth. The 2008 financial tempest was different. It was ubiquitous and moved with alacrity. Foreign markets were even worse for equities during 2008. Year-to-date (as of October 24, 2008) returns for the Non-U.S. Equities Indices were as follows: MSCI World (−43.9%), MSCI World ex. U.S. (−47.8), MSCI EAFE Index (−48.0%), MSCI Europe Index (−52.3%), MSCI Japan Index (−36.1%), MSCI Emerging Market Index (−61.2%), MSCI EM BRIC Index (−67.4%), MSCI Europe Index (−72.9%), MSCI EM Asia Index (−60.5%), and MSCI EM Latin America Index (−59.9%).[11] Globally, individual countries had the following performance in local currency terms, year to date through October 24, 2008: Brazil (−51%), Mexico (−43%), France (−43%), Germany (−47%), Australia (−39%), Hong Kong

(−55%), India (−57 %), Japan (−50%), Russia (−71%), South Korea (−51%), and Taiwan (−46%).[12]

Figures 2.1 and 2.2 are Bloomberg charts (11/06/87–10/31/08) for the S&P 500 and MSCI EAFE indices (respectively).

The year 2008 was a rogue wave of financial markets; it was massive, violent, uncontrollable, and devastating. The financial meltdown might be compared with a category 5 hurricane in which winds exceed 155 miles per hour.[13]

November 2008 was the third negative month in a row. This seldom happens with equity markets. From December 1987 until December 2008, the occurrence of three negative months in a row has seldom transpired.[14] There were five negative months in a row in 1990, three in 1999, three in 2000, four in 2001, and four in 2002. The year 2008 had the distinction of having two occurrences of large negative returns three months in a row with two negative months in between. More precisely, January 2008 showed a −6.12% change for the month; February 2008 showed −3.48%, and

Figure 2.1 S&P 500 10 Year

Source: Bloomberg. Used with permission.

MXEA   1453.44Y as of close   7/23   Index **G**

Figure 2.2   MXEA 10 Year

Source: Bloomberg. Used with permission.

Table 2.2   S&P 500 Monthly Returns (Typical Year)

Typical Year			
STANDARD & POOR'S INDEX SERVICES S&P 500 MONTHLY RETURNS			
Month of	Price Close	Price Change	1 Month % Change
Dec–06	1418.03	17.67	1.26%
Nov–06	1400.63	22.69	1.65%
Oct–06	1377.94	42.09	3.15%
Sep–06	1335.85	32.03	2.46%
Aug–06	1303.82	27.16	2.13%
Jul–06	1276.66	6.46	0.51%
Jun–06	1270.02	0.11	0.01%
May–06	1270.09	−40.52	−3.09%
Apr–06	1310.61	15.78	1.22%
Mar–06	1294.83	14.17	1.11%
Feb–06	1280.66	0.58	0.05%
Jan–06	1280.08	31.79	2.55%

March 2008 showed −0.60%. September 2008 showed a change of −9.08% for the month. October 2008 showed a return of −16.94%, and November 2008 showed a return of −7.49%. Not only were these dual sets of three months in a row negative returns, but they were extremely negative. For example, October 2008 had a −16.94% decline for the month. A total of 8 out of 12 months for 2008 were negative versus 2006, when there was only one negative month:

Table 2.3   S&P 500 Monthly Returns (Problematic Year)

Problematic Year			
STANDARD & POOR'S INDEX SERVICES S&P 500 MONTHLY RETURNS			
Month of	Price Close	Price Change	1 Month % Change
Dec–08	903.25	7.01	0.78%
Nov–08	896.24	−72.51	−7.49%
Oct–08	968.75	−197.61	−16.94%
Sep–08	1166.36	−116.47	−9.08%
Aug–08	1282.83	15.45	1.22%
Jul–08	1267.38	−12.62	−0.99%
Jun–08	1280.00	−120.38	−8.60%
May–08	1400.38	14.79	1.07%
Apr–08	1385.59	62.88	4.75%
Mar–08	1322.07	−7.93	−0.60%
Feb–08	1330.63	−47.92	−3.48%
Jan–08	1378.55	−89.81	−6.12%

The unusual market of 2008 was reminiscent of the rogue wave event at the Draupner oil platform on January 1, 1995, in the North Sea off the coast of Norway. Although no one actually witnessed the wave, it was recorded by a laser-based wave-height detector. This rogue wave was thought of as a freak or killer wave because of its unusual characteristics.

The wave recorded at Draupner was estimated to be around 27 meters, otherwise known as a 100-year wave. Another killer wave in a severe storm in December 1978 destroyed a boat headed to Savannah, Georgia. The boat, *Manchen*, was loaded with steel products. Waves for alternatives,

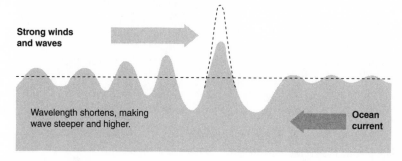

Waves and winds heading straight into powerful ocean currents may cause a surge of water to rise out of the deep.

Figure 2.3 Ocean Current

similar to waves found in the ocean, are erratic. There might be several big waves followed by a giant wave and then regular waves. Theoretically, any combination is possible. See Figure 2.3.

Riding Out the Storm

Hurricanes can cause vast amounts of damage. For instance, The USS *Monssen,* a 350-foot war vessel, was washed ashore en route to Newport, Rhode Island, because of the heavy seas caused by the Ash Wednesday Storm of 1962.[15] The year 2008 clearly demonstrated risks to all types of investing, including alternatives, and demonstrated that a global financial failure can be contagious. Articles like "No Place to Hide"[16] and "No Corner of the Earth Spared in October's Worldwide Sell-Off"[17] pointed out that "[I]nvestors have seen even 'safe' stock and bond funds get hammered. No wonder they're so spooked."[18] Equities and bonds were very much adversely effected in 2008. Alternatives were also effected and not invincible. Table 2.4 compares the S&P 500 with a number of alternative asset classes from 2000 to 2008. Alternatives lost money in 2008, including gold, which was −23.10%. However, the S&P 500 was −37%.

If one focuses on the negative year that 2008 produced, one might be inclined to overlook the compelling nature of alternatives. Only a year before (2007), the 10-year performance of alternatives was hard to beat.

Table 2.4   Alternative Asset Class Calendar-Year Returns

2000	2001	2002	2003	2004	2005	2006	2007	2008
Commodities 20.74%	Gold 22.63%	Gold 52.61%	EM Equity 55.92%	Infrastructure 42%	EM Equity 34.00%	Infrastructure 44%	EM Equity 39.39%	TIPS -2%
EM Income 16%	TIPS 8%	TIPS 17%	Gold 25.59%	Global Real Estate 38%	Gold 29.35%	Global Real Estate 42%	Commodities 31.35%	Market Neutral -6%
Market Neutral 15%	Market Neutral 7%	EM Income 14%	Infrastructure 43%	EM Equity 25.55%	Commodities 24.34%	EM Equity 32.17%	Gold 19.62%	EM Income -10%
Global Real Estate 14%	Floating Rate 4%	Commodities 11.72%	Global Real Estate 41%	Commodities 19.66%	Global Real Estate 15%	Gold 20.13%	Infrastructure 18%	Gold -23.10%
TIPS 9%	Alternatives 0%	Alternatives 10%	EM Income 29%	Alternatives 16%	Alternatives 15%	Alternatives 15%	Alternatives 12%	Alternatives -27%
Infrastructure 9%	EM Income -1%	Infrastructure 5%	Commodities 27.62%	EM Income 12%	EM Income 12%	EM Income 10%	TIPS 12%	Floating Rate -19%
Alternatives 8%	EM Equity -2.62%	Global Real Estate 3%	Alternatives 25%	TIPS 9%	Infrastructure 10%	Market Neutral 7%	EM Income 6%	Infrastructure -38%
Floating Rate -5%	Global Real Estate -4%	Floating Rate 2%	Floating Rate 10%	Floating Rate 5%	Market Neutral 6%	Floating Rate 7%	Market Neutral 5%	Commodities -45.31%
Gold -22.77%	Infrastructure -13%	Market Neutral 1%	TIPS 9%	Market Neutral 4%	Floating Rate 5%	Commodities 1.91%	Floating Rate 2%	Global Real Estate -48%
EM Equity -30.83%	Commodities -20.37%	EM Equity -6.17%	Market Neutral 2%	Gold -5.54%	TIPS 3%	TIPS 0%	Global Real Estate -7%	EM Equity -53.33%
S&P 500 Index calendar-year returns (as of 12/31/08)								
-9.10%	-11.89%	-22.10%	28.68%	10.88%	4.91%	15.79%	5.49%	-37.00%

Source: Alternative Asset Class Calendar-Year Returns, *Morningstar* (December 31, 2008). Used with permission.

Table 2.5, a JPMorgan "Alternative Investment Returns" chart, shows returns for hedge funds, real estate, and private equity over 10 years.

Storms pass. Just because one comes along every once in awhile, including the nasty of the nastiest (e.g., hurricanes, monsoons, cyclones, typhoons), one should not abandon setting foot on a beach or going for a swim in the ocean. For the last two centuries, there have been numerous financial storms and hurricanes. Most investors think of the Great Depression as the only negative period in financial markets. However, there were numerous financial storms similar to hurricanes. The first major depression transpired in 1837 and lasted 5 years. The Long Depression or Panic of 1873 lasted 65 months. The Great Depression of 1929 (which hit in two waves) lasted a total of 55 months. Recessions, like the one that started in 2007, are more regular but can be equally devastating. There were at least a dozen recessions over the past century. Recessions are not too dissimilar from hurricanes;

Table 2.5 Alternative Investment Returns

Hedge Funds (as of 12/31/07)	1 year	3 year	5 year	10 year
CSFB/Tremont HF Index	12.6%	11.3%	11.8%	9.2%
Multi-Strategy	10.1	10.7	10.9	9.4
Distressed	8.4	11.9	15.1	11.4
Convertible Arbitrage	5.2	5.4	6.2	8.4
Equity Market Neutral	9.3	8.8	8.0	10.0
Risk Arbitrage	8.8	6.6	6.9	6.9
Fixed Income Arbitrage	3.8	4.3	5.5	5.1
Global Macro	17.4	13.3	13.3	11.2
Real Estate (as of 12/31/07)	**1 year**	**3 year**	**5 year**	**10 year**
NCREIF Property Index	15.8%	17.5%	15.1%	12.9%
Apartment	11.4	15.7	13.8	12.5
Industrial	14.9	17.4	14.4	12.9
Office	20.5	19.7	15.2	13.0
Retail	13.5	15.6	17.3	13.6
Asset Class				
Private Equity (as of 9/30/07)	**1 year**	**3 year**	**5 year**	**10 year**
U.S. Venture Capital Index	23.1%	15.3%	9.1%	34.6%
U.S. Private Equity Index	29.9	29.7	23.6	14.2
Global (ex-U.S.) PE & VC	53.1	41.2	30.6	19.7

Source: JPMorgan, Alternative Investment Returns, *JPMorgan Asset Management: Market Insight Series,* 2007. Used with permission.

they range in size, duration, and frequency, and they can inflict damage. They are erratic but are guaranteed to happen.

Financial storms are nothing new. From 1901 until 2009, there have been 23 depressions, recessions, negative events, and/or market turmoil. During this same time, there were 28 hurricanes:

Table 2.6 Recessions (Negative Events and Market Turmoil) and Hurricanes

Dates of Market Peak	Dates of Market Trough	Percent Return	Duration	Crisis Events	Year of Hurricane	Category of Hurricane	Fatalities in Hurricane
May 10, 1837		N/A	60 months	Depression or Panic of 1837			
				Hurricane (situated in LA)	1856	4	400
				Hurricane (situated in SC/GA)	1893	3	1500
				Hurricane (situated in LA)	1893	4	1250
Oct. 1873	Mar. 1879	N/A	65 months	The Long Depression or Panic of 1873			
				Hurricane (situated in Galveston)	1900	4	8000
June 30, 1901*	Nov. 30, 1903	–0.44	29 months	Assassination of President William McKinley			
Oct. 30, 1906*	Nov. 30, 1907	–0.45	13 months	Roosevelt's antitrust movement, Boer and Russo-Japanese Wars			
				Hurricane (situated in FL)**	1906	3	164
				Hurricane (situated in MS, AL, Pensacola)	1906	2	134
				Hurricane (situated in LA)**	1909	3	350
Dec. 31, 1909*	Feb. 28, 1915	–0.29	62 months	WWI begins			
Nov. 30, 1916*	Dec. 31, 1917	–0.36	13 months	Germany started to attack US shipping (WWI)			
				Hurricane (situated in LA)**	1918	3	34
				Hurricane (situated in FL, TX)**	1919	4	287
Oct. 30, 1919*	Aug. 31, 1921	–0.44	22 months	Post-WWI recession, bursting of the first big tech bubble			
				Hurricane (situated in SW, US)**	1926	4	372
				Hurricane (situated in FL)**	1928	4	2500
Sep. 06, 1929	Jun. 01, 1932	–0.86	33 months	Germany Depression; stock market crash (Black Tuesday)			
Sep. 07, 1932	Feb. 27, 1933	–0.41	55 months	Germany Depression, Fed tightens credit			
				Hurricane (situated in TX)**	1932	4	40
				Hurricane (situated in TX)**	1935	5	408
Mar. 05, 1937	Mar. 31, 1938	–0.54	13 months	Roosevelt Recession (19% unemployment)			
				Hurricane (situated in New England)**	1938	3	256
				After-shock of stock market crash			
Nov. 11, 1938	Apr. 28, 1942	–0.45	41 months	Attack on Pearl Harbor (WWII)			
				Hurricane (situated in GA/SC/NC)**	1940	2	50
				Hurricane (situated in NE US)**	1944	3	64
May 29, 1946	Jun. 13, 1949	–0.3	36.5 months	Post-WWII Recession			
				Hurricane (situated in FL/LA/MS)**	1947	4	51
				Hurricane Hazel	1954	4	95
				Hurricane Diane	1955	1	184
Aug. 02, 1956	Oct. 22, 1957	–22%	8 months	Eisenhower Recession			
				Hurricane Audrey	1957	4	416
				Hurricane Donna	1960	4	50
				Hurricane Carla	1961	4	46
Dec. 12, 1961	Jun. 26, 1962	–28%	6.5 months	Vietnam War Recession			
				Hurricane Hilda	1964	3	38
				Hurricane Betsy	1965	3	75
Feb. 09, 1966	Oct. 07, 1976	–22%	8 months	Credit crunch			
Nov. 29, 1968	May 26, 1970	–36%	18 months	Nixon Recession			
				Hurricane Camille	1969	5	256
				Hurricane Agnes	1972	1	122
Jan. 11, 1973	Oct. 03, 1974	–48%	20.5 months	Oil Embargo Recession, Post-Vietnam War, Nixon's resignation			
Sep. 21, 1976	Mar. 06, 1978	–19%	17.5 months	Oil crisis, OPEC and Iran raise oil			
Nov. 28, 1980	Aug. 12, 1982	–27%	20.5 months	Iran/Energy Crisis Recession			
Aug. 25, 1987	Dec. 24, 1987	–34%	4 months	Stock market crash (Black Monday)			
Jul. 16, 1990	Oct. 11, 1990	–20%	3 months	Gulf War Recession			
				Hurricane Alberto	1994	Tropical Storm	30
Jul. 17, 1990	Aug. 21, 1998	–19%	1.5 months	Asian stock market crisis			
				Hurricane Floyd	1999	2	56
Mar. 24, 2000	Oct. 09, 2002	–49%	30.5 months	Tech Bubble, 9/11 Recession			
				Hurricane Alisson	2001	Tropical Storm	41
				Hurricane Ivan	2004	3	25
				Hurricane Katrina	2005	3	1500
Oct. 09, 2007	On-going	Unknown	Unknown	Subprime Meltdown & Credit Crisis			

The S&P 500 was not created until 1926, so the Dow is used for these numbers.
**Names were not used for hurricanes until the 1950's.*

Notation:
Recessions
Hurricanes

A stock market correction is measured in performance declines while hurricanes are measured in terms of categories or wave heights (Table 2.6). The similarities are strikingly uncanny. Hurricanes, like financial markets, move in waves. The Chicago Mercantile Exchange (CME) started trading futures contracts linked to the CME Hurricane Index (CHI). The CHI uses both wind speed and size to measure a hurricane's potential for damage. Hurricanes move with great speed. Contracts expire at the end of every hurricane season and offer protection or a way to measure against a hurricane such as Katrina. Even hurricanes not as destructive as Katrina can generate large waves: Hurricane Bill, energized by warm ocean temperatures, agitated the North Atlantic like a giant plunger, creating waves up to 28 feet near Bermuda, which could go as high as 47 feet in the open sea today according to officials.[19]

Indexes with hurricanes will enable investors a great deal of flexibility. Although the area is new, one could sell call options on the CHI and purchase natural gas as a hedge just like someone might short the Dow and go long gold. Services such as Bloomberg now help navigate hurricanes. Figure 2.4 depicts various Exxon Mobil assets along the Gulf of Mexico:

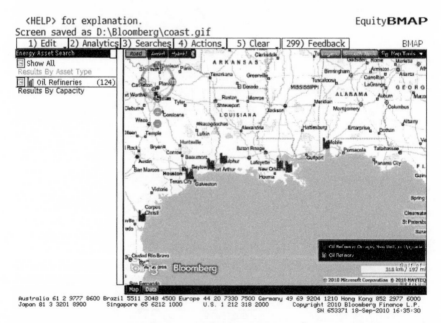

Figure 2.4 Exxon Mobil Assets in the Gulf of Mexico

Source: Bloomberg. Used with permission. © 2010 NAVTEQ. NAVTEQ map content is used with permission. Used with permission from Microsoft.

Figure 2.5 shows the technology now available to follow storm data and see what the impact would be on oil refineries such as Hurricane Ike.

It is interesting to note that these charts combine both financial waves and storm waves from a hurricane. In other words, the interactions between an alternative such as oil and a hurricane are now transparent. The wave metaphor with alternatives, in essence, becomes real with Bloomberg's tracking software. Hurricanes affect a variety of sectors, such as travel, resorts, and cruise lines. Real estate (both commercial and residential) can be adversely affected by hurricanes. Reports of hurricanes destroying real estate stem back to the 1920s when two pernicious hurricanes wrecked the real estate boom:

> Then, as journalist Frederick Lewis Allen recounted in his 1931 book *Only Yesterday*, "two hurricanes showed what a Soothing Tropical Wind could do when it got a running start from the West Indies." The first of these, known as the Great Miami Hurricane, made landfall between South Miami and Coral Gables on September 18, 1926.

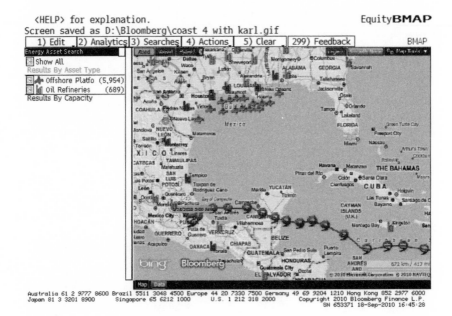

Figure 2.5 Hurricane Ike: Impact on Oil Refineries

Source: Bloomberg. Used with permission. © 2010 NAVTEQ. NAVTEQ map content is used with permission. Used with permission from Microsoft.

> It devastated what had been some of the most in-demand real estate in Florida. . . . The boom was over, not withstanding such brave talk as the claim of Miami's mayor that he saw "no reason why this city should not entertain her winter visitors the coming season as comfortably as in past seasons." Then, in September 1928, Hurricane San Felipe Segundo took a hit to the north, making a mess of Palm Beach, Jupiter Island and Lake Okeechobee. Shuttered real estate offices were now a common Florida sight.[20]

The paradox of investing during a financial storm is identical to surfing when there is a storm or hurricane because it might produce the best wave to ride in both scenarios. If you take one of the riskiest and illiquid alternatives, private equity, it might actually be the best performer (the antithesis of what the typical investor would believe to be true). Psychologically, it takes guts to ride a wave in a storm. Although it might seem like a dangerous time, riding a wave in a financial storm can be the most lucrative move.

Because valuations on private companies typically fall below their public counterparts because of a lack of liquidity, one might benefit even more from investing in private equity when the public markets are trading off (when the ocean is producing big waves).

Securities move in waves. According to seafriends.org, "Part of the irregularity of waves can be explained by treating them as formed

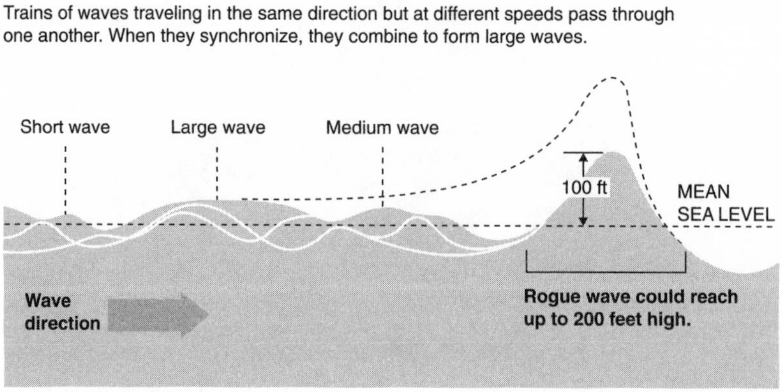
Trains of waves traveling in the same direction but at different speeds pass through one another. When they synchronize, they combine to form large waves.
Short wave
Large wave
Medium wave
100 ft
MEAN
SEA LEVEL
Wave
direction
Rogue wave could reach
up to 200 feet high.

Figure 2.6 Merging Waves

Source: From the *New York Times*, ©7/11/2006. All rights reserved. Used by permission and protected by the Copyright Laws of the United States.

by interference between two or more wave trains of different periods, moving in the same direction. It explains why waves often occur in groups."[21] See (Figure 2.6.) Sometimes they travel together, other times they travel separately or act different—not too dissimilar from waves in an ocean. "Most wave systems at sea are comprised of not just two, but many component wave trains, having generally different amplitudes as well as periods. This does not alter the group concept, but has the effect of making the groups (and the waves within them) more irregular."[22] It is feasible to see the correlation between asset classes, including alternatives.

In an ideal world, an investor will have securities that do not have a high correlation with each other. According to seafriends.org, "Anyone having observed waves arriving at a beach will have noticed that they are loosely grouped in periods of high waves, alternated by periods of low waves."[23] Table 2.7 shows correlations: 10-years.

If one examines the correlation between the large cap with foreign securities such as the EAFE Index, one will find a relatively high degree correlation of 0.92. However, there is a low degree of correlation between large cap and commodities. Alternatives typically have a low correlation with traditional asset classes, such as equities or fixed income.

The rate at which a wave moves is analogous to the volatility of the equity market. Bloomberg can be used to graph the Chicago Board Options Exchange's Market Volatility Index (VIX). Huge swings in the market caused by negative or positive news affect the VIX index. After 9/11, the stock market was closed for a week and then opened for a free fall. Huge volatility waves occurred. The tech bubble imploding from 2000, 2001, and 2002 was volatile but not as much as 2008–2009 with the real estate meltdown and credit crisis. Figure 2.7 shows the VIX Index from July 24, 2000 to July 22, 2009.

After 9/11, the VIX broke 40, which was four times a volatile day in the market. To put matters in perspective, the VIX passed 80 in the fourth quarter of 2008. This financial wave was a rogue wave not too different from the Draupner wave. The more one thinks about Wave Theory with alternative investments as it is applied to economics, the more it becomes clear that the price of an asset is not just affected by one variable but by many factors working at once.

Table 2.7 Correlations: 10 Years

	Large Cap	Small Cap	Value	Growth	EAFE	Bonds	EME	Hedge Funds	Real Estate	Eq Market Neutral*	Commodities
Large Cap	1.00	0.94	0.92	0.94	0.92	−0.37	0.87	0.73	0.23	0.36	0.33
Small Cap		1.00	0.90	0.87	0.86	−0.39	0.83	0.67	0.20	0.35	0.25
Value			1.00	0.74	0.88	−0.22	0.76	0.63	0.29	0.42	0.35
Growth				1.00	0.83	−0.44	0.86	0.74	0.14	0.26	0.29
EAFE					1.00	−0.27	0.90	0.77	0.20	0.45	0.44
Bonds						1.00	−0.30	−0.20	−0.17	0.14	−0.12
EME							1.00	0.77	0.13	0.32	0.43
Hedge Funds								1.00	0.28	0.48	0.50
Real Estate									1.00	0.32	0.32
Eq Market Neutral										1.00	0.49
Commodities											1.00

*Market Neutral returns include estimates found in disclosures.

All correlation coefficients calculated based on quarterly total return data for period 9/30/99 to 9/30/09.

This chart is for illustrative purposes only.

Source: Large Cap: S&P 500 Index; Small Cap: Russell 2000 Index; Value: Russell 1000 Value; Growth: Russell 1000 Growth; EAFE: MSCI EAFE; Bonds: Barclays Capital Aggregate; EME: MSCI Emerging Markets; Hedge Funds: SC/Tremont Multi-Strategy Index World; Real Estate: NCREIF National Property Index; Equity Market Neutral: CS/Tremont Equity Market Neutral Index; DJ UBS Commodity Index.

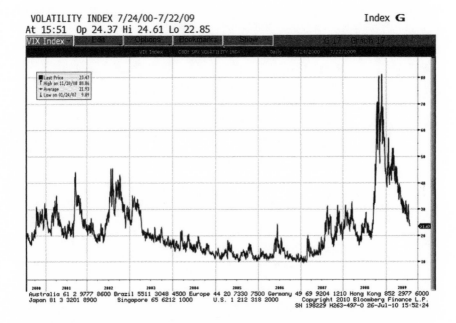

Figure 2.7 Volatility Index, July 24, 2000–July 22, 2009

Source: Bloomberg. Used with permission.

Weiser (2003) reports that commodity futures returns vary with the stage of the business cycle. In particular commodity futures perform well in the early stages of a recession, a time when stock returns generally disappoint. In later stages of recessions, commodity returns fall off, but this is generally a very good time for equities.[24]

Chapter 3

Wave Action, Reflection, and Mastery

Waves can cause mass destruction as they hit land, but they eventually calm down. Even without a storm, nature is at work slowing down waves. "The size of a wave depends on its fetch. The fetch is the distance a wave travels. The greater the fetch, the larger the wave. Wind also has a significant effect on the size of waves. The stronger the wind the larger the wave."[1] (See Figure 3.1.)

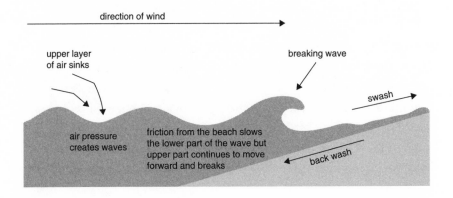

Figure 3.1

Source: "Wave Action," www.geographylearnontheinternet.co.uk. Retrieved July 15, 2009

Financial waves can be compared to waves hitting a beach. When waves approach a beach, they break. The break is caused by friction between the beach and the water. Financial waves have breaks as well. Seafriends.org tells us:

> Like sound waves, surface waves can be bent (refracted) or bounced back (reflected) by solid objects. Waves do not propagate in a strict line but tend to spread outward while becoming smaller. Where a wave front is large, such spreading cancels out and the parallel wave fronts are seen travelling in the same direction.[2]

Waves, of course, do not always reach the shore in a straight line and typically approach from an angle. Not all shorelines are flat but rather lined with rock. When waves hit rock, they bounce back. Financial storms can also be changed or reversed at times.

Waves can be very different from one another. According to Robert Dinwiddie, "Within the wave-generation area, the sea surface is usually quite confused—the result of groups of waves of different size and wavelength interfering with each other. Outside this area, the waves become sorted by speed to produce a more regular pattern, called a swell."[3]

While oil dropped in price after its massive run up, many alternatives prevailed and lost far less than traditional asset classes. They demonstrated the role they might play in a well-constructed, diversified portfolio. Ocean waves can vary in size just like the ones found with alternatives. Similar to the ocean, one can find small, medium, and large alternative waves. A multitude of factors can affect the prices of a particular class of alternatives. For example, West Texas intermediate crude from January 17, 2007 to July 21, 2009 had a huge run up and a perilous drop. Figure 3.2 highlights the precipitous drop in West Texas intermediate crude oil.

Currents

When used in association with water, the word *current* describes its motion. Like ocean currents, alternatives sometimes run together. In other words, it is possible to see various alternatives act similarly. From August 1999 to August 2009, a number of agricultural commodities acted

Figure 3.2 West Texas Intermediate Crude Spot, January 17, 2007–July 21, 2009

Source: Bloomberg. Used with permission.

similarly. Rice, soy, corn, and wheat all mimiced each other. The relevance is that an investor who selects certain agricultural commodities for diversification purposes might be unaware that there is little to no benefit of adding redundant commodities to a portfolio. Diversification means you are presumably investing in different asset classes that do not act the same. In this illustration (Figure 3.3), one could just add wheat to a portfolio without investing in rice, soy, or corn.

Surfboard Selection

Depending on the type of wave you intend to ride, you need the appropriate equipment: a surfboard. A surfboard can be constructed using different materials—not too dissimilar to an investor selecting one or more types of alternatives for a customized alternative portfolio. The portfolio is in essence a customized surfboard. The central alternatives covered in this book along with their advantages and disadvantages are as follows (Table 3.1):

10-YEAR COMMODITY PRICES 8/99-8/09   Equity**G**

Figure 3.3   10-Year Commodity Prices, August 1999–August 2009

Source: Bloomberg. Used with permission.

Table 3.1   Alternatives Advantages and Disadvantages

Alternatives	Advantages	Disadvantages
Hedge Funds[4]	–Diversification –Low correlation with traditional assets –Investment flexibility –Few restrictions –Talented managers –Often uncorrelated with broad stock market indices	–Typically high cost and high fees –Leveraging and other speculative investment procedures which can increase risk –Potential for overdiversification –Can withdraw money only once each quarter or even once a year –Must be an "accredited investor" due to Securities and Exchange Commission restrictions –Potentially high degree of risk
Hedge Fund-of-Funds	–Diversification across different hedge funds –Access to hedge funds with high minimums and restrictions –Failure or underperformance of one hedge fund will not ruin the whole –Rebalancing and portfolio constructing	–Illiquid –Tax risk potential –Transparency –Layering of fees

Alternatives	Advantages	Disadvantages
Managed Futures Funds[5]	−Potential for reduced portfolio volatility −Ability to earn profit in any economic environment −Possibility to reduce downside risk in times of crisis in traditional markets −Global diversification −Historically low to slightly negative correlation with traditional investments, including equities and bonds	−High degree of risk −Commodity markets are subject to temporary distortions or other disruptions −Highly speculative −No guarantee that an investment of this type will achieve its objectives −Involves the use of significant leverage that may increase the risk of investment loss −Illiquid −Commodity prices can be affected by a variety of factors at any time
Venture Capital[6]	−Historically enjoys the highest rate of return versus other asset classes −Reduces overall portfolio risk −Significant growth potential and the possibility of high returns −Offers institutional investors and high-net-worth individuals high returns (historically better than stocks) and strong diversification benefits from very low correlations with other asset classes −As companies in the portfolio go public or are sold, the investors realize their returns	−Because there are no short-selling mechanisms, venture capitalists, like a commodity investors, face potential overpricing −Valuation risk −An early-stage venture capital project may only be an idea −Long time frames −Lack of liquidity −High management fees −Restrictions on transferring interests in the investment −Absence of information that is typically replaced by publically traded companies to produce to shareholders: 10k, 10k annual report −Publically held, venture-backed companies do not have the same rules and regulations as public companies
Commodities[7]	−Negative correlation wtih stocks and bonds −Compelling returns −Provides strong diversification −A good hedge or diversifier in periods of turmoil −Price rises are result of increasing demand	−Price of virtually every commodity—agricultural, mineral, and energy—have fallen steadily throughout the twentieth century relative to wages −High degree of risk −Unsophisticated investors are at a disadvantage −The true value can be challenging to find −Difficult to sell

(Continued)

Table 3.1 Alternatives Advantages and Disadvantages (*Continued*)

Alternatives	Advantages	Disadvantages
Gold[8]	–Diversifying into gold during troubled times can provide long-term protection for a portfolio –There is greater liquidity in physical gold for large pools of capital. –Historically, gold has provided the best protection against financial catastrophe and upheavals	–Gold bugs and other speculating can drive up the price of gold –When gold becomes very valuable, gold coin usage is sometimes made illegal by governments or is so heavily taxed and constrained –Storage costs of physical gold can be expensive

Top Surfers and Alternative Managers

Mastering the art of surfing a wave takes time and a lot of practice. The best surfers have unique qualities. According to Drew Kampion in "What Makes a Surfer Great?," the best surfers have the following qualities: luck, uniqueness, boldness, creativity, discipline, intuition, endurance, and strength.[9]

Institutions continue to use alternatives; individuals are relatively new to the game. According to Rydex, "While forms of alternative investments have been available for centuries, recent decades have seen the rapid development and increased use of alternative investments among institutional investors, such as pensions and endowments, which have looked to alternative asset classes and strategies in an attempt to manage risk, improve diversification and provide more consistent returns.[10] The July 28, 2008, edition of *BusinessWeek* notes that "Endowments with some $1 billion in assets have had the best return and the most money in hedge funds and other alternative investments."[11] Endowments with more than $1 billion had 40% in alternative asset classes and had 21.3% average annual total return compared with endowments with less than $25 million, which had 6% alternatives and a 14.1% annual return. Moreover, as Figure 3.4 indicates, the top-200 U.S. defined benefit plans were invested as of January 2007 in the following manner.[12]

Institutions are the professional surfers of the alternatives world. However, high-net-worth individuals as well as retail investors are learning how to surf. Institutional plans offer traditional asset classes (domestic fixed income and equity, international fixed income and equity, and cash). For instance, the top-200 defined benefit plans utilize private equity and real estate equity as alternatives.

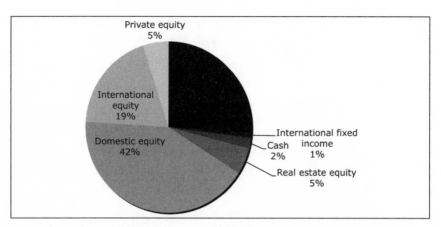

Figure 3.4   Capital Allocation Top 200 U.S. DB Plans

Source: "Top 200 U.S. DB Clients," *Pensions and Investments,* January 2007.

Hedge fund investment by defined benefit plans in the 200 largest U.S. employee benefit plans increased at least 69% to $50.5 billion in the year ended Sept. 30. . . . Of that total, $23.1 billion was invested directly in hedge funds, a 76% increase from the prior year, and $27.4 billion was invested through hedge fund-of-funds as of Sept. 30, a 63% increase.[13]

According to Rebecca McReynolds in "Think Like an Institution: Alternative Investments Are One Key to Outperforming the Market," institutions outperform equity investors: "Between 1995 and 2005—boundaries that include both the peak of the longest bull market in history and its bloody aftermath—the average institution outperformed the average equity investor by more than 300 basis points in average annual total returns." One might ask why such an extreme outperformance. McReynolds goes on to ponder the reasons behind this difference in performance: "Institutional investors had access to and made investments in alternative asset classes." While institutions usually invest more in alternatives, high-net-worth individuals are increasing funds to alternatives at a rapid rate:

The expectation is that by 2010, demand for alternatives by U.S. institutional investors will grow to 10.8% or $3.3 trillion out of total assets of $30.3 trillion, according to a report published by Freeman in 2004 based significantly on data from Pension & Investment's annual directory of the 200 largest U.S. pension funds. But the largest consumers of the alternative investments will be high-net-worth investors, who will hold an estimated $1.3 trillion in alternative investment strategies by the end of the decade, the report projects.[14]

Morningstar, Inc., a leading provider of independent investment research, and Barron's, a premier business and finance magazine, conducted a national survey among institutions and wealth managers regarding the "perception" and "usage" of alternatives:

"Our survey found that both institutions and advisors want alternative investment that are liquid, transparent, and regulated like traditional investments," said Steve Deutsch, director of separate accounts and collective investment trusts at Morningstar. "This demand is driving the convergence of traditional and alternative money management. We're seeing more alternative investment strategies in mutual funds and ETFs, higher prevalence of retail and alternative money managers competing for assets under management, and traditional money managers acquiring, merging with, or recruiting alternative investment expertise."[15]

Two of the best-performing endowments, Yale and Harvard, utilize alternatives. Marcia Vickers reports that "Swensen and Meyer have been pioneers in diversification: spreading their money over a variety of asset classes that do not move in sync with one another. The resulting portfolios tend to be less volatile than simple stock-and-bond mixes and produce better returns."[16]

Short-term fluctuations in the market can impair any asset class. However, alternatives tend to outperform traditional assets classes over time as evidenced by many of the endowments of the Ivy League schools:

The Ivies' results in the past 10 years have been very impressive. Harvard's endowment was up an average of 13.8% annually, bringing it to $36.9 billion as of June 30, tops in the academic world. Yale's endowment grew at an average annual pace of 16.3% in the same span, to $22.9 billion, making it second to Harvard in size.

Princeton's endowment rose at a 14.9% annual clip, to $16.4 billion. Stanford, in Palo Alto, Calif., also has shined; its endowment rose by 14.2% a year, to $20.4 billion.[17]

Barron's also provides tables (Tables 3.2 and 3.3) highlighting the allocations that each school implemented to the different type of alternatives as well as comparing their performance against that of the S&P 500.

Table 3.2   What Are Better Alternatives?

Asset	Yale	Harvard	Princeton	Stanford	Avg. Edu Endowment	Est. Return Since June 30♦
Hedge Funds	23%	18%	26%	18%	20%	−20%
Domestic Equity	11	11	9	37**	26	−25
Fixed Income	4	11	3	10	13	−5
Foreign Equity	15	22	16	N.A.	22	−37
Private Equity	19	13	25	12	7	−50
Real Assets*	28	26	19	23	10	−35
Cash	0	−3	1	N.A.	2	

♦Barron's estimates.
*Real estate, timber, oil and gas.
**Domestic and foreign stocks.
N.A., not available.
Source: School reports, Bloomberg.

Table 3.3   Straight-A Returns

Endowment	Size* (bil)	TOTAL RETURNS	
		1 year	10 year
Harvard	$36.9	8.6%	13.8%
Yale	22.9	4.5	16.3
Stanford	20.4	6.2	14.2
Princeton	16.4	5.6	14.9
MIT	10.1	3.2	13.2
Michigan	7.6	6.4	13.2
U. Penn	6.3	−3.9	N.A.
Cornell	5.4	2.7	8.7
Dartmouth	3.6	0.5	12.1
S&P 500		−13.1%	2.9%

*As of June 30.
N.A., not available.
Source: Barry, Andrew. "Crash Course," *Barron's*, November 10, 2008.

Yale University added many alternatives and had the best performance (+16.3% over the past decade).Yale had twice as many hedge funds as domestic equity. By owning hedge funds, the endowment improved their risk-return profits.

Just like surfers, alternatives managers are not all created equal. There is a wide spread between the top surfers and regular surfers, similar to alternatives managers. In other words, an investor must strive to hire the best alternatives manager. You want the best surfer money can buy. Professional surfers in alternatives are Swensen from Yale or Meyer from Harvard. They know all the right surfing maneuvers. Both surfing and investing in alternatives can be hazardous. As Raul Guisado states in *The Art of Surfing,* "It almost goes without saying that big-wave surfing can be extremely dangerous. . . . Depending on how you fall, you could easily head directly for the bottom, where contact with coral or rocks could result in serious injury, and even death."[18]

Every professional surfer or institutional investor in alternatives has a unique, individualized methodology. It is best to develop one's own strategy, but an investor might consider the following "Top-25 Alternative Surfing Maneuvers" list, the next section, when either buying or selling an alternative investment:

Top-25 Alternative Surfing Maneuvers

1. Buy points. After an alternative has corrected, wait until it is in the recovery phase before jumping right in and investing.

2. Patience is a virtue, a virtue is patience. Think long term, not short term. There is no rush to investing (ever), especially with alternatives. Time is on your side. It can take days, weeks, months, or even years for a sector to come back in favor. For example, if a particular alternative, such as real estate investment trusts (REITs), goes through a fierce correction, one should not run out and invest right away. Jumping in too early is like attempting to catch a falling knife. Alternatives can have corrections that last years.

3. Observe the smart money. Watch what the institutional investors are doing. Are they buying or selling? Institutions are pension funds, mutual funds, insurance companies, banks, hedge funds, and other investors.

They tend to move in packs like wolves and can move mountains. They have billions of dollars to deploy. For example, the top-15 hedge funds all bought billions of dollars worth of gold during 2008 and 2009. Many hedge funds own the same stocks. Large funds need to report what they own, and the information is readily available. However, one can lose a lot of money this way if the hedge funds or other institutions dump the securities before you do. Remember, hedge funds compete with each other. Unless you are Bill Gates, you are not the competition of a large institution. If a lot of sell orders hit the desks of large banks, who do you think will get out first: the hedge funds that generate millions in fees or your small trade? Institutions can drive prices in either direction rather quickly. One needs to be careful about trailing institutional investors. In other words, you do not want to buy what they are buying (much later after prices are way up). If institutions buy a particular commodity like oil and drive the price to $140, you would not necessarily want to be buying at the high or much higher than they did because they can sell quickly and use derivatives and other means faster and cheaper than a regular investor. You could end up holding the bag. One might conjure up the image of children playing Duck, Duck, Goose.

4. Market direction. Before investing in any security, one needs to pay attention to the overall market. Has it been going up or has it been going down? Is it a positive or bullish environment? Or are people jumping out of windows? For the most part, the best time to invest in alternatives (like many other investments) is when there is "blood in the streets." Never ever buy after a security or asset class has grown to the sky—you will invariably get crushed by a nasty wave like a sunbather sitting on the beach before a tsunami hits land.

5. Abandon emotions. One does not invest in alternatives to make friends. Your goal should be to make money. Do not fall in love with any alternative or manager, no matter what. Do not keep an investment because it was inherited. Many naïve investors trusted Bernie Madoff because of a relative. Do your own due diligence or suffer the consequences. Emotional people are horrible investors. Certain attributes are guaranteed to help one fail: being in denial, acting impetuously, being obstinate, or being outright delusional.

6. Trust yourself. Often with alternatives, one needs to use innate intelligence and go with their gut feeling. If you feel something is too good to be true, it is. Those who were impressed with Bernie Madoff's year-after-year 11% returns should have questioned him. How did he do that? A vague answer or cryptic answer should not suffice. Many alternatives are unregulated. Unfortunately, good goes hand-in-hand with evil. Investing in alternatives is a learning experience, and so is trusting others.

7. Greed will kill you. If a person brags about particular investments, run, do not walk. People are full of it. Most investors typically buy at the wrong times. Many times they get swept up in the greed factor like the days of the Internet bubble. Obscene returns caused investors to believe the Internet would control everything. Hundreds of Internet companies went public. Shares sold at nosebleed levels. I had a client flip an initial public offering (IPO) the same day to make a $200,000 profit and never even got a thank-you. Investors (both retail and institutional) could not get enough. Just because there is an open bar does not mean you close the place and drive home drunk using your nose instead of your hands to steer.

8. Diversify, diversify, diversify. Do you eat only McDonald's food for breakfast, lunch, and dinner, 365 days a year? I like McDonald's but would not eat the food every day. Too much of anything will kill you. Same thing with investing in alternatives. If you load up on too much venture capital or any other alternative, you might harm yourself. One needs to diversify. Ask those who invested all their money with a single hedge fund, Bernie Madoff. Diversify using alternatives, but own others as well, such as stocks and bonds. It is possible to buy too many securities, which will ultimately ruin any chances of a good return. Do not overdiversify. One does not need to own 1,000 stocks or 500 mutual funds. Also, be careful that the securities you select are not too similar in nature. Just like with equities, one should not buy a broad equity index such as the S&P 500, an equity mutual fund with 500 stocks, and then select 100 different individual equities. Such a portfolio is redundant and does not offer diversification. Mix it up.

9. Buy the best. If you select an active manager (for example, a leveraged buyout [LBO] manager like Bain or Carlyle Group) as opposed to an index, attempt to buy the best manager you can afford. Alternatives managers range from horrendous to awesome.

10. Be cognizant of price, not obsessed. If you are innately frugal, do not let being cheap ruin a good opportunity. I have observed clients spend 20% on tips for dinner but fight tooth and nail over a 2% fee. When is the last time you stuffed your face in a restaurant and had someone pay you when you left the restaurant? If a wealth manager earns an investor 20% on $1 million, why haggle over a 2% fee? Do not nickel and dime your financial expert. Alternatives managers can be quite expensive, especially the really good ones. Sometimes, you get what you pay for in life. Frugal investors typically harm themselves and miss fantastic opportunities. Investment professionals deserve to earn a living just like anyone else. One thing is certain: if they do not make money, you will not either. Be a good or important client. Unless it is a courtesy or favor, no respectable wealth manager, private banker, financial advisor, and/or consultant charges less than 1–2%.

11. Performance matters. A negative year does not mean you should not invest with a manager or company in the alternatives space. The relevance is how they did or how the company performed compared with its peer group and the market over time. Generally, 1, 3, and 5 years should give one an idea as to the capability of the manager or company.

12. Do your homework. Think back to high school and college. Some of us did not study, but most did. Taking standardized tests like SATs, GMATs, or LSATs requires studying. *Not* studying increases your failure rate. Would you walk into an important test like this without studying? No. Same thing applies to investing in alternatives. If you invest in a particular alternative, do your homework. Know everything there is to know about the alternative you are contemplating buying. If you invest in gold, examine your investment options. Do you want to own a gold brick? An exchange-traded fund (ETF)? Futures? A company involved with gold like a mining company? A gold mutual fund? Where is gold on the wave chart? Are you entering at a good time or will you be crushed by a nasty wave?

13. History repeats itself. Markets and securities (including alternatives) all move in waves. Was the recent real estate collapse anything new? No. Did it happen before? Yes. Again and again. Recessions are not new either. They happen again and again. Recession. Recovery. Recession. Recovery. All alternatives move in waves. Follow the waves.

14. Look before you leap. Are there distribution days or signs that the indexes are fading or heading south? Where are you buying? Where is the wave you are going to ride? Is the smart money heading for the exit? Will you be the last guest to the party? As stated in an *Investor's Business Daily* article, "The clearest signal that a market uptrend is in distress is the buildup of distribution days. When a major index drops more than 0.2% in higher volume than the previous session, that's a distribution day. It suggests institutional investors are selling their holdings."[19] Examine the fund or security you are considering investing in with others. How does it compare?

15. Sector rotation. The market consists of various sectors, such as consumer, technology, health care, energy, and others. Sectors rotate. According to Alan R. Elliott, "Research has found that 37% of a stock's price move is linked to its industry group."[20] If you are investing in an alternative that is tied to a sector, pay attention to whether it is in or out of favor. Elliott also notes: "While some defensive sectors have weakened, others indicative of an economic rebound have rallied. This is sector rotation: Some go from leaders to laggards, and others from laggards to leaders."[21]

16. A dog is great if you can pet it, not if it's a security. If a hedge fund manager, venture capital fund, or CEO of a private company loses your money, wait until they make you whole again. Do not give them more money for doing a poor job. Nine times out of ten they will lose your money again. Do not throw your money away! A polite response might be, "I will consider giving you more money if and when things improve." The old adage is applicable, "Don't throw good money after bad."

17. Jump ship if necessary. Cut your losses short. If feasible, set a stop loss. Many alternatives are illiquid, and this might not be an option. However, if the option exists, use it. For example, place a stop loss on a publicly traded master limited partnership (MLP) for protection for energy. If one invested in private real estate, one could also short a publicly traded real estate index. Whether it is an index like USO (oil index) or equity like Exxon Mobil, sell it if it drops more than 10%. A 10% loss can be made back. On the other hand, a 70% loss will be very difficult to earn back. Losses are easy to get. Gains are harder to achieve.

18. Knowledge is power. Information on the Internet is plentiful. Traders are even using Twitter for information. You can track hurricanes and use Google maps. One can follow oil in Russia and plot it against gross domestic product. Table 3.4 lists a number of informative Web sites with information that is useful on many topics helpful for analyzing waves.

Table 3.4 Useful Financial Web Sites

Financial Information	
Briefing	www.briefing.com
Stock Picking Secrets	www.easystock.com
Market Trak	www.markettrak.com
Market Watch	www.marketwatch.com
Horses Mouth	www.horsesmouth.com
Edgar Online	www.edgar-online.com
Zacks	www.zacks.com
Investtools	www.investtools.com
Red Herring	www.redherring.com
Smart Money	www.smartmoney.com
Publications	
Wall Street Journal	www.wsj.com
Investor's Business Daily	www.investors.com
BusinessWeek	www.businessweek.com
Forbes	www.forbes.com
Bloomberg	www.bloomberg.com
Economist	www.economist.com
The Street	www.thestreet.com
New York Times	www.nytimes.com
Washington Post	www.washingtonpost.com
News	
CNN	www.cnn.com
MSNBC	www.msnbc.com
FOX News	www.foxnews.com
CBS	www.cbsnews.com
ABC	www.abcnews.com
USA Today	www.usatoday.com
ESPN	www.espn.com

Source: Author.

As an example of how to use these Web Sites, visit *Investor's Business Daily's* Web site or read the newspaper version. There exists a section from *Investor's Business Daily* on commodities called "Key Commodity Futures." Figure 3.5 charts all show recent waves and their development.

19. Maximize returns. Knowing when to take a profit is important. Minimize risk and maximize returns. Focus on both. Investors frequently think the winner will go on forever and never go down. When an alternative begins to break down after a long run up, that is the time to reduce or eliminate a position. Many refuse to take a gain because there will be a tax consequence or they are just plain stubborn. Never let taxes get in the way of taking a profit. With alternatives (private equity and real estate), it is

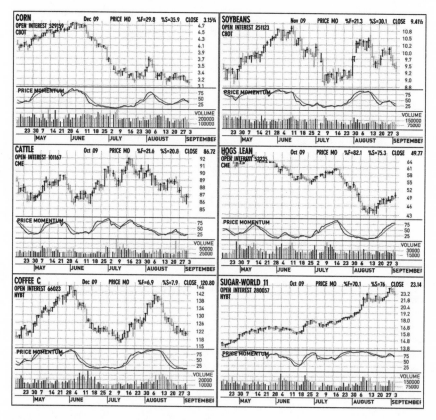

Figure 3.5 Key Commodity Futures

Source: Key Commodity Futures, *Investor's Business Daily* (September 4, 2009). Used with permission.

possible to defer taxes by rolling a sale (with a gain) into another like investment. In other words, one could sell a private equity investment (with a large gain) and roll it within a certain time frame into another private company. One should, of course, consult with a tax attorney or knowledgeable accountant. Also, be careful that you do not sell too early. If there is no good reason to sell, do not depart with the investment.

20. Utilize ongoing monitoring. You would not landscape your yard then never touch it again. Any investing requires ongoing monitoring of your portfolio. Should you be adding or selling? Are you paying attention to the winners and losers? Are there waves that are going to crash or ones that you can surf? What is your mix of alternatives? What percentage of your overall portfolio is invested in alternatives? Is the weighting too high or too low? These questions should be asked by every investor whether institutional or not. Harvard, like many other colleges and universities, was overweighted in alternatives and ran into liquidity problems with their endowment.

21. Buy when there is a market rally. Ideally, buy in the beginning of a new market rally. One can clearly see when a market rally is about to begin; there is no mysticism. Do not deploy all your capital at once (in case you are wrong). Test the waters before yelling the rallying cry for riders of the surf: *Kowabunga!* Putting a toe in the water to test the water before jumping in is only prudent.

22. Ignore the media. News media invariably lead investors to make the wrong decisions. Do not listen to hype or get caught up in the pessimism! The grossly exaggerated or hyped news regarding the Internet harmed many investors. Howard Kurtz describes the media hype in *The Fortune Tellers: Inside Wall Street's Game of Money, Media, and Manipulation*.[22] On December 9, 1974, the cover of *Time* magazine had the caption "Recession's Greetings."[23] At the time, the Dow Jones was 579.94. Ten years later, a $10,000 investment would have been $200,660. On December 3, 1984, *Time*'s cover read "America's Banks Awash in Trouble."[24] The Dow Jones was 1182.42 at the time. Ten years after that, the Dow Jones was at 3745.62. A $10,000 investment would have been worth $31,680. On January 13, 1992, the cover of *Time* read "How Bad Is It?"[25] At the time, the Dow Jones was 3185.60. Ten years later, it was

Table 3.5 Time Headlines Over 30 Years and Dow Jones Performance

Time Issue	Cover Title	Dow Jones	Dow Jones (10 Years Later)	Initial Investment	Return on Investment
July 2, 1979	The Energy Mess	834.04	2440.06	$1,000	$2,926
July 9, 1979	The World Over a Barrel	852.99	2487.86	$1,000	$2,917
August 27, 1979	The Topsy-Turvy Economy	885.41	2732.36	$1,000	$3,086
October 22, 1979	The Squeeze of '79	809.13	2689.14	$1,000	$3,326
March 2, 1981	The Ax Falls	977.99	2909.90	$1,000	$2,975
February 8, 1982	Unemployment: The Biggest Worry	833.43	3225.40	$1,000	$3,870
May 8, 1982	Interest Rate Anguish	860.92	3369.41	$1,000	$3,914
March 5, 1984	The Monster Deficit: America's Economic Black Hole	1165.02	3832.30	$1,000	$3,229
December 3, 1984	Awash in Troubles	1182.42	3745.62	$1,000	$3,168
April 14, 1986	Good News! Cheap Oil! . . . Bad News! Cheap Oil!	1805.31	5532.59	$1,000	$3,065
November 10, 1986	Is It Good for America?	1892.29	6219.82	$1,000	$3,287
November 2, 1987	The Crash	2014.09	7442.08	$1,000	$3,695
November 15, 1990	High Anxiety	2545.05	10707.60	$1,000	$4,207
January 13, 1992	How Bad Is It?	3185.06	9987.53	$1,000	$3,135
September 28, 1992	Is There Light at the End of the Tunnel?	3276.26	7701.45	$1,000	$2,351
September 14, 1998	Is the Boom Over?	7945.35	9310.99	$1,000	$1,172
January 8, 2001	How to Survive the Slump	10621.35	N/A	$1,000	N/A
March 26, 2001	Looking Beyond the Bear	9687.53	N/A	$1,000	N/A
September 14, 2001	September 11, 2001	8920.07	N/A	$1,000	N/A
March 26, 2008	Surviving the Lean Economy	12479.63	N/A	$1,000	N/A

Source: Author, *Time* magazine.

9987.53. A $10,000 investment would have been worth $31,350. Table 3.5 shows 30 years of *Time* titles.

While there are dozens of such titles from *Time*, others were far more pessimistic, especially on television.

23. Skin in the game. Having skin in the game means that one has their own money at risk. Any manager you entrust your money with should not be afraid to have their own money or "skin" invested in the fund, company, or security you are contemplating buying. If you buy an alternative, how much of the company or fund does the CEO or manager own? If you lose, they lose. Managers that have nothing to lose or CEOs that will not share the pain deserve a pass from you.

24. Illiquidity is not one of the seven deadly sins. A number of alternatives are illiquid, but this is not necessarily a bad thing; it is commonplace. Private equity—equity not publicly traded like venture capital or LBO— offers compelling risk-versus-return characteristics. If a portion of one's portfolio can be illiquid, one should consider alternatives. Children sometimes are reluctant to try fruit, but when they do, they tend to like it. Alternatives can be sweet. If, however, you cannot feed your dog and/or need liquidity, shy away. A number of alternatives require periodic payments (draw downs), which you should factor in before investing. Because alternatives are illiquid investments, I have witnessed some investors sell liquid securities (i.e., stocks) at precisely the wrong time. They take huge losses and never recover. They could not sell their illiquid alternatives, which could end up providing handsome returns, helping offset their nervous trigger-happy reaction to a market decline. In other words, the illiquidity with alternatives can save an investor from doing something fatal like selling at the wrong time.

25. Try it, you might like it. Alternatives are a lot like sampling a new food that you have never tried before. It is foreign, unknown, and might make one uncomfortable at first but end up being delicious. I recall someone offering me calamari. I resisted at first, but now it is a favorite of mine. What might be out of your comfort zone with alternatives might actually perform the best and help one build a better, more diversified portfolio— that is, you might like alternatives once you invest in them.

Risks and Returns

Investing in alternatives carries as much risk as surfing. Both have sharks. The ocean is full of them. In fact, the "Ten Best Surf Towns in America" all have had shark attacks, according to Surfing.com:

Although I might be inclined to surf in New Smyrna Beach, I think I would rather have a beer than go in the water. (See Table 3.6.) The alternatives ocean is also filled with sharks. One of the most pernicious killer sharks of all time (pertaining to alternatives) is former hedge fund manager Bernie Madoff. Bernie owned a home in Florida as well as a boat.

Table 3.6 Ten Best Surf Towns in America

	City	Reported Shark Attacks
1.	Santa Cruz, CA	6 (since 1926)
2.	Haleiwa, HI	34 (in Oahu County since 1828)
3.	Encinitas, CA	10 (in San Diego County since 1926)
4.	Paia, HI	35 (in Maui County since 1828)
5.	San Clemente, CA	1 (in Orange County since 1926)
6.	Kill Devil Hills, NC	10 (in Dare County since 1935)
7.	Malibu, CA	5 (in Los Angeles County since 1926)
8.	Montauk, NY	5 (in the State of New York since 1670)
9.	New Smyrna Beach, FL	210 (in Volusia County since 1822)
10.	Ocean City, NJ	17 (in the State of New Jersey since 1670)

Source: "Ten Best Surf Towns in America," *Surfer Magazine* (July 2009).

Besides sharks, there are dangerous tropical storms. In fact, there are so many hurricanes, there is actually a 6-year rotating list. Here is one of the lists of names for tropical storms, which will be rotated every 6 years: Ana, Bill, Claudette, Danny, Erika, Fred, Grace, Henri, Ida, Joaquin, Kate, Larry, Mindy, Nicholas, Odette, Peter, Rose, Sam, Teresa, Victor, Wanda.[26] If a hurricane causes enough damage to be entered in the history books, the name will be taken off the list.

Surfing has its risks as depicted by various expressions:

- **Grubbing:** Falling off your board while surfing.
- **Hammered:** When a big wave breaks right on top of you, you get hammered.
- **Thrashed:** What happens when a wave pounds you. Synonym: Worked.

- **Slammed:** The result of when a wave comes down hard, knocks you off your board, and drills you deep.
- **Rinse cycle:** To get caught in the whitewater boil after a wave breaks.

Just as surfing has gained in popularity along with new exotic surfing destinations and risks, the alternatives ocean has experienced a shift in risk versus return. Each asset class or alternative carries its own unique risk-versus-return characteristics. When the market collapsed in October 2008, managed futures performed well (+12.58%) while U.S. equities were down −36.09% and Europe was down −48.01% (See table 3.7). Hedge funds had a return of −16.89% (October 2008) with low risk or standard deviation of 8.91%. By way of comparision, U.S. equity had a standard deviation of 20.34% and Europe had a risk of 26.04%. Hedge funds have better returns and lower risk or standard deviation than equities with only a little more risk than U.S. Treasury notes over 1, 3, 5, 10, and 15 years (ending October 2008).

There are risks to alternatives just like surfing. In other words, there are nice returns or positives for both alternatives and surfing. An astute person might ask why surfing is expanding to all sorts of exotic destinations. The answer is it is rewarding. Riding a wave in San Diego's Black Beach, South Africa's Cape Town, or Australia's Cyclops is a once-in-a-lifetime opportunity. One might ask why alternatives have grown so much in size and popularity. The answer lies in attractive rates of return. Alternatives offer attractive returns and typically have low correlations with stocks and bonds. Says Rebecca McReynolds: "By adding asset classes that are not correlated to the public markets, portfolio managers can achieve the dual benefit of lowering overall risk while improving returns."[27]

Wave Properties and Performance

Robert Dinwiddie tells us:

A group of waves consists of several crests separated by troughs. The height of the waves is called the amplitude, the distance between successive wave crests is known as the wavelength, and the time between successive wave crests is the period. Waves are classified into types based on their periods. They range from ripples, which have

Table 3.7 Rolling Year Returns and Risk
One Year, Three Years, Five years, Ten Years, and Fifteen Years (ending October 2008)

Asset Class	Index	Rolling 1 Year (Nov. 07 - Oct. 08) CAGR%	Standard Deviation	Rolling 3 Years (Nov. 05 - Oct. 08) CAGR%	Standard Deviation	Rolling 5 Years (Nov. 03 - Oct. 08) CAGR%	Standard Deviation	Rolling 10 Years (Nov. 98 - Oct. 08) CAGR%	Standard Deviation	Rolling 15 Years (Nov. 93 - Oct. 08) CAGR%	Standard Deviation
Equity											
U.S. Equity	S&P 500	-36.09	20.34	-5.22	14.95	0.25	12.67	0.39	15.15	6.93	14.86
Non-U.S. Equity											
Europe	MSCI Europe Index	-48.01	26.04	-4.29	20.24	4.44	20.24	1.53	17.59	6.77	16.41
Fixed Income											
U.S. Treasury Note	U.S. Treasury 10-Year Note	7.75	6.71	5.47	5.29	4.54	5.8	4.58	6.93	5.39	6.93
Alternative Investments											
Real Assets	Handy & Harman Spot Gold Index	-9.90	26.30	16.08	20.28	13.27	17.92	9.24	16.09	4.49	14.40
Hedge Funds	HFRI Fund Weighted Composite Index	-16.89	8.91	2.79	7.51	5.18	6.46	8.52	7.24	9.79	7.22
Managed Futures	Barclays CTA Index	12.58	7.13	8.06	6.42	5.90	6.49	5.57	7.44	6.47	7.88

Source: Author.

periods of less than 0.5 seconds, up to tsunamis and tides, whose periods are measured in minutes and hours (their wavelengths range from hundreds to thousands of miles).[28]

Figure 3.6 illustrates these properties of waves. Wave properties are apparent with alternatives. No country, sector, or publicly traded security was left untouched by the financial storm that commenced in 2007, but alternatives did quite well considering the circumstances. Alternatives are

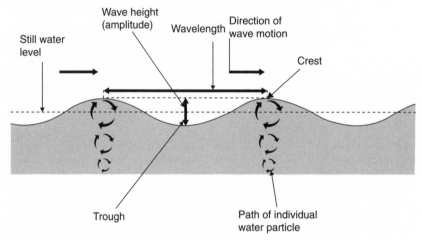

Figure 3.6 Wave Properties

Source: Robert Dinwiddie, *Ocean: The World's Last Wilderness Revealed* (New York: Dorling Kindersley Publishing, 2008), 76.

not invincible, but they held up relatively well in a volatile market—arguably one of the worst in U.S. history. From January 2008 to November 2008, alternatives produced the following returns: Cambridge Associates US Venture Capital −1.3%, HFR Fund of Funds Index −19.1%, Commodity Research Bureau Total Return −30.7%, Barclay CTA +12.4%, and Handy & Harman Spot Gold −1.9%. By way of comparison, the S&P 500 had a −37.7% return and the MSCI had a −46.6% return.

Before 2008, how did alternatives perform over 1, 3, and 5 years as of 11/30/08 (See Table 3.8)? Returns over 5 years (December 2003–November 2008) were Handy & Harman Spot Gold (+15.5%), CTA Commodity Trading Advisors (+6.4%), HFR Fund Weighted Composite Hedge Fund Index (+4.4%), HFR Fund of Funds Index (+2.8%),

Table 3.8 Equities and Fixed Income Total Returns versus Alternatives, 11/30/08

	Total Return % Change				
	1-Month Return (Nov. 08)	YTD 2008 Return (Jan. 08- Nov. 08)	1-Year Return (Dec. 07- Nov. 08)	3-Year CAGR (Dec. 05- Nov. 08)	5-Year CAGR (Dec. 03- Nov.08)
US Equity Index					
S&P 500	−7.20%	−37.70%	−38.10%	−8.70%	−1.40%
Non-US Equity Index					
MSCI EAFE Net	−5.40%	−46.60%	−47.80%	−7.80%	2.00%
Fixed Income Index					
Barclays Capital					
Aggregate Index	3.30%	1.50%	1.70%	4.60%	4.10%
Alternative Investment Indices					
Cambridge Associates US					
Venture Capital	N/A	−1.30%	4.70%	13.30%	11.30%
HFR Fund Weighted Composite					
Hedge Fund Index	−1.40%	−17.70%	−17.30%	1.30%	4.40%
HFR Fund of Funds Index	−1.60%	−19.10%	−18.70%	0.10%	2.80%
Commodity Research Bureau					
Total Return	−8.70%	−30.70%	−26.60%	−4.50%	2.50%
Barclay CTA (Commodity					
Trading Advisors)	1.30%	12.40%	13.80%	7.70%	6.40%
Handy & Harman Spot Gold	12.90%	−1.90%	4.40%	18.40%	15.50%

Source: S&P 500, MSCI EAFE; Barclays Capital Aggregate; Cambridge Associates U.S. Private Equity Index; HFRI Fund Weighted Composite Hedge Fund Index; Barclay CTA (Commodity Trading Advisors) Index; DJ UBS Commodity Index; Handy & Harman Spot Gold Price.

and Commodity Research Bureau Total Return (+2.5%). During this same period, bonds returned +4.1%), S&P 500 −1.4%, and MSCI +2.0%.

The year 2002 was considered a negative year for equities, whereas 2003 was robust. The S&P 500 was −22.1% during 2002 but delivered a healthy +28.70% for 2003. The MSCI EAFE lost −15.9% in 2002 but gained +38.6% in 2003. The Barclays Capital Aggregate was up +10.3% in 2002 versus +4.1% in 2003. By way of comparison, venture capital returned −31.8% in 2002 and −2.5% in 2003, hedge fund −1.5% and 19.6%, hedge fund-of-funds 1.0% and 11.6%, Gold 24.8% and 19.4%, Commodity Trading Advisor (CTA) 12.4% and 8.7%, and CRBT 33.5% and 24.2%. (See Table 3.9.)

Table 3.9 Annual Returns for Equity and Fixed Income versus Alternatives, 11/30/08

	Total Return % Change										
	1998	1999	2000	2001	2002	2003	2004	2005	2006	2007	2008 YTD
US Equity Index											
S&P 500	28.60%	21.00%	−9.10%	−11.90%	−22.10%	28.70%	10.90%	4.90%	15.80%	5.50%	−37.70%
Non-US Equity Index											
MSCI EAFE Net	20.00%	27.00%	−14.20%	−21.40%	−15.90%	38.60%	20.30%	13.50%	26.30%	11.20%	−46.60%
Fixed Income Index											
Barclays Capital Aggregate Index	8.70%	−0.80%	11.60%	8.40%	10.30%	4.10%	4.30%	2.40%	4.30%	7.00%	1.50%
Alternative Investments Indices											
Cambridge Associates US Venture Capital	26.70%	280.10%	21.60%	−39.10%	−31.80%	−2.50%	15.10%	8.30%	17.90%	16.20%	−1.30%
HFR Fund Weighted Composite Hedge Fund Index	2.60%	31.30%	5.00%	4.60%	−1.50%	19.60%	9.00%	9.30%	12.90%	10.00%	−17.7
HFR Fund of Funds Index	−5.10%	26.50%	4.10%	2.80%	1.00%	11.60%	6.90%	7.50%	10.40%	10.30%	−19.10%
Commodity Research Bureau Total Return	−27.20%	31.80%	31.90%	−21.80%	33.50%	24.20%	18.20%	23.00%	−2.90%	22.20%	−30.70%
Barclay CTA (Commodity Trading Advisors)	7.00%	−1.20%	7.90%	0.80%	12.40%	8.70%	3.30%	1.70%	3.60%	7.70%	12.40%
Handy & Harman Spot Gold	−0.30%	−0.10%	−5.50%	2.50%	24.80%	19.40%	5.50%	17.90%	23.20%	31.00%	−1.90%

Source: S&P 500, MSCI EAFE; Barclays Capital Aggregate; Cambridge Associates U.S. Private Equity Index; HFRI Fund Weighted Composite Hedge Fund Index; Barclay CTA (Commodity Trading Advisors) Index; DJ UBS Commodity Index; Handy & Harman Spot Gold Price.

David Swensen believes alternatives provide smarter diversification. Andrew Barry says, "Swensen was pushing asset allocation further than other endowments, gradually moving more money to hedge funds, private equity and real assets, which include real estate, timber and energy. In these assets classes, Swensen reasoned, inefficiencies allowed good managers to add value and, because of the greater diversification he'd achieved, to do so with less risk."[29] More recently, Barron's "Crash Course" cited:

> Reflecting the philosophy of David Swensen, its influential endow-ment director of the past 23 years, Yale has 70% of its endowment invested in three categories: hedge funds, private equity and "real" assets, including timber, real estate and oil-and-gas properties—one of the most aggressive allocations among major endowments. Princeton similarly has 70% in hedge funds, private equity and real assets, while Harvard has 57% in those groups.[30]

Similarly, Harvard's Jack Meyer has achieved impressive results using alternatives. The target asset allocation for Harvard in 2004 was as follows: domestic equity 14%, foreign equity 14%, private equity 17%, fixed income 5%, real assets (real estate and commodities) 25%, and absolute return 25%. According to the New York Times, "The endowment of Harvard University, among the most watched in the country, said Friday that it had earned an 8.6 percent return for the fiscal year that ended June 30 and Harvard said the endowment outperformed its internal benchmark and that its return compared favorably with those reported by the Trust Universe Comparison Services. The endowment said that it outperformed 95 percent of the 165 large institutional funds that the trust sector measures." Some of this stellar performance was attributed to alternatives: "Its emerging market holdings and private equities holding exceeded their benchmarks by about 3 percent and its real assets—liquid–liquid com-modities, timber, and land and real estate—beat the benchmarks by nearly 3 percent."[31] Barron's "Crash Course" discusses further the performance of Harvard, Yale, and Princeton's endowments:

> They've been trendsetters over the past decade, generating superla-tive returns from an asset-allocation mix that looks nothing like what

individuals typically maintain. These schools are light on U.S. stocks and bonds, and heavy on illiquid assets, such as private-equity, real-estate and commodity holdings, and hedge funds.[32]

At the time, there was a lot of misleading information that the more alternatives an institution possessed, the better the returns they would achieve. Endowments worth more than $16 million in assets had the most money in alternatives. Coincidently, the bigger endowments had the best performance. (See Figure 3.7.)

Alternatives should be considered for those seeking a well-diversified port-folio, especially in difficult markets. Managed futures tend to do well in really bad markets. But having no alternatives in a portfolio might be as unwise as owning 100% alternatives. Alternatives can lose money just like any other asset class. "However," says Shefali Anand of the *Wall Street Journal*, "individuals should be cautious about jumping head-long into these and other alternative investments. For one thing, many of the funds that bet against stocks haven't been around long enough for advisors to make con-clusions about their risk or return patterns."[33] How many or what percent-age of alternatives one should own depends on a number of variables.

Any investor can become overweighed in a particular type of alternative or have too much of their portfolio in alternatives. Even institutions can make mistakes, as did Yale, Harvard, and Princeton universities. All three

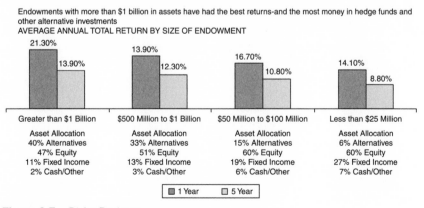

Endowments with more than $1 billion in assets have had the best returns-and the most money in hedge funds and other alternative investments
AVERAGE ANNUAL TOTAL RETURN BY SIZE OF ENDOWMENT

	Greater than $1 Billion	$500 Million to $1 Billion	$50 Million to $100 Million	Less than $25 Million
1 Year	21.30%	13.90%	16.70%	14.10%
5 Year	13.90%	12.30%	10.80%	8.80%

	Greater than $1 Billion	$500 Million to $1 Billion	$50 Million to $100 Million	Less than $25 Million
Asset Allocation	40% Alternatives	33% Alternatives	15% Alternatives	6% Alternatives
	47% Equity	51% Equity	60% Equity	60% Equity
	11% Fixed Income	13% Fixed Income	19% Fixed Income	27% Fixed Income
	2% Cash/Other	3% Cash/Other	6% Cash/Other	7% Cash/Other

☐ 1 Year   ☐ 5 Year

Figure 3.7   Risky Business

Source: Ray Vella, "Endowments Soar, but Colleges Keep the Purse Strings Tight," *BusinessWeek* (January 28, 2008). Used with permission.

schools had a heavy weighting toward alternatives. Although one can maintain that endowments should have a long-term view, one should not ignore the illiquidity of alternatives, nor should they neglect examining waves associated with alternatives. Loading up on alternatives at the wrong time will likely produce poor results, even if you have a long-term view. Craig Karmin reports: "Harvard University has predicted the asset value of its endowment, the nation's largest, would drop as much as 30%. Yale University and Princeton University have projected declines of about 25% each."[34]

One might consider adding a small position (such as 2%–5%) to an alternative before making a larger commitment until one learns more about waves. Do not sell all your all your municipal bonds and CDs in order to rush out and buy alternatives. Walk before you run. One needs to allocate properly depending on age, risk tolerance, net worth, current allocation, liquidity, income needs, and other variables.

PART 2

VENTURE CAPITAL

RIDING THE WAVE

Chapter 4

Defining Venture Capital

I was born in 1966, the year Digital Equipment went public. Digital Equipment was one of the first venture-backed initial public offerings (IPOs). Digital Equipment helped propel the venture capital market. Many of the most successful companies in the world were started with venture capital. Before Starbucks went public, it raised $30 million in 1990 through a private placement. Starbucks now has revenue in excess of $17 billion. Private placements (equity or debt) grew in popularity. According to Allen, Brealey, and Myers, "In 1980 private placements accounted for about one-fifth of all new corporate debt issues, but by 1989 this proportion had expanded to almost one-half."[1] Alex. Brown helped many emerging growth companies raise money with venture capital. Investors would line up for Alex. Brown IPOs like small children on the beach in Avalon, New Jersey, on a hot summer day waiting for ice cream. The allure of venture capital for investors is simply high returns:

> Part of the attraction of venture capital investing lies in the option-like character of individual investments. Downside losses cannot exceed the amount invested. Upside gains can multiply the original stake manifold. The combination of limited downside and substantial upside produces an investor-friendly, positively skewed distribution of outcomes.[2]

Alex. Brown Private Equity Group, for example, from June 30, 1991, to June 30, 1997, had an average internal rate of return of +33.31% versus

DJIA +21.3%, venture capital funds +21.0%, S&P 500 +9.8%, Russell 2000 +17.7%, and T-Bills +4.6%.[3]

At the time, I introduced many of the most successful private placements to Alex. Brown. For example, I brought in a company called CDNow (arguably the first business-to-consumer company) as well as placed tens of millions in deals with high-net-worth clients looking to diversify. CDNow raised $10 million in August 1997. Private placements are simply a private round of financing for a company led by an investment firm or bank. Private placements are generally purchased by institutions such as venture firms and high-net-worth individuals. The investments are a minimum of $100,000 to $500,000 and illiquid. Private equity—unlike the other alternatives—where an investor can become liquid in a reasonably short period if not immediately—are illiquid for a long time.

In the 1990s the only thing better than a hot IPO was receiving shares before the company went public: pre-IPO shares. Private placements were the hot ticket of the alternatives world. They were the vehicle that allowed access to pre-IPO shares. Wealthy clients could not get enough. I remember advising one client in particular to invest in one of the best private placements ever. In February 1999, I recommended Cobalt Networks, which was priced at $3.70 per share with a minimum of $3 million to invest. Cobalt went public in November 1999 at a price of $22. The stock reached a high of $158. The Dow Jones News Wire reported this IPO to be the third-best IPO ever. Putting aside any kind of lockup, this investment hypothetically would have been worth $117,567,567.51. Cobalt Networks was a high-risk, high-return investment. Even the name of the company was alluring. Surfers have a term that can be used to describe such a lucrative investment: *amped*. Amped means getting excited while surfing or really looking forward to surf.

There are few things in life as exhilarating as watching an investment you made go public be such a screaming success. Right before a company goes public, the underwriters have a clear idea of how "hot" the IPO is or if it will be mediocre. A lackluster IPO is frequently referred to as a dog. A hot IPO, on the other hand, will be oversubscribed, such as the Boston Beer Company, another hot IPO I introduced to Alex. Brown. Even if you hated the taste of beer or Samuel Adams, one appreciated the buildup before the IPO as more and more investors wanted a finite amount of shares. The venture capitalists that funded the company did quite well. The Boston Beer Company was the lead microbrewery to go public in September 1995, and no other microbrewers were public at the time. A hot IPO like the Boston Beer Company will typically open "up" and keep on going. Because of its success, other microbreweries went public, such as Pete's Brewery Co., maker of Pete's Wicked Ale. Watching a company go public is exciting. The rush is tantamount to driving 150 miles per hour in a Porsche or winning the lottery. Adrenaline courses through your veins. Your heart races. Your palms sweat. You can even feel faint not knowing where the stock will close the first day.

Because Alex. Brown was ranked the number-one firm for taking venture-backed IPOs public, I had exposure to a lot of venture capital funds. There are certain venture funds an investor would want to avoid like the plague, whereas others are like running into Taylor Swift in an airport (assuming you like country music). I helped run a small $30 million venture fund for partners of Alex. Brown called Momentum. The fund had many success stories derived from investments in fast-growing health-care and technology companies. For example, we invested in the first Linux company called Andover.net, which ultimately became part of VA Linux. We contributed to a private round of funding (totaling $7 million) on November 1, 1998, for Andover.net, which eventually led to an IPO on December 8, 1999, and was worth $82,800,000. The first-day return on Andover.net when it went public was +252.08%. Andover.net was then acquired by VA Linux Systems on February 3, 2000, for a total of $950,000,000.

Personally, I have invested in many fast-growing companies. A good money manager will taste his own cooking. I have never recommended a security or company that I would not purchase myself. The best money managers are invested in their own funds. Advisers and managers that do not put their own money where they invest others' money typically do not have as good performance. While I experienced many success stories, I also invested in a few companies that made going camping with Freddy Krueger or Jason Voorhees look like a good time; I have invested in both good and bad companies. Anyone investing in venture capital should study the waves and examine whether they are entering or leaving at a good time. Often the worst of times presents the best of times to invest in venture capital. Venture capital is high risk, high reward, and should be carefully studied. Investing blindly in venture capital is ill-advised. An investor should not be in the dark. As James Joyce said in *A Portrait of the Artist as a Young Man*, "He saw the sea of waves, long dark waves rising and falling, dark under the moonless night."[4] Do not surf in the dark.

While venture investing is not for the faint of heart and many things can go askew, the rewards are quite compelling. Benchmark Capital's $6.7 million investment in eBay mushroomed into $6.7 billion or a 1,000-times return, qualifying it as "the valley's best-performing venture investment ever."[5] Then came Google. Andy Bechtolsheim, a founder of Sun Microsystems who invested in early-stage companies, helped start Google with $100,000.[6] On September 7, 1998, Google Inc. was finally incorporated. Sequoia Capital and Kleiner Perkins Caulfield and Byers funded a $25 million round at a valuation of $100 million in June 1999.[7] On April 29, 2004, Google filed an S-1, the formal public offering document for an IPO, and stated that they would sell $2,718,281,828 worth of shares. On December 10, 2007, Google's market capitalization was $173.6 billion.

Venture capital can go one of two ways: up or down. One either makes a lot of money or loses it. Over time, returns of venture capital are quite compelling. If one chooses to add venture capital to a portfolio, it is prudent to really do your homework. Google was not the first search engine. There were many search engines at the time, such as Lycos, Infoseek, and AltaVista. However, not all search engines use the same algorithm, and none were as successful as Google. Venture capital investors need to be careful as to the sector they choose but also selective among the companies in that particular area. The industries in which venture capital is invested covers primarily technology, consumer, media, health care, environmental, and transportation. A me-too or copycat company is not the same as the original or leader of the pack. Venture capital is one of the most challenging of all the alternative investments but is by far the most lucrative.

Defining Venture Capital

According to Wright and Robbie, "Venture capital is typically defined as the investment by professional investors of long-term, unquoted, risk equity finance in new firms where the primary reward is in an eventual capital gain, supplemented by dividend yield."[8] Generally, there are two groups involved with venture capital: general partners and limited partners. The general partner manages the fund, and the limited partners are the investors. Venture capital involves early-stage investing in the equity of privately owned companies with the potential for rapid growth. Venture funds require accredited investors. Federal securities laws define the term *accredited investor* in Rule 501 of Regulation D as follows:

1. a bank, insurance company, registered investment company, business development company, or small business investment company;
2. an employee benefit plan, within the meaning of the Employee Retirement Income Security Act, if a bank, insurance company, or registered investment adviser makes the investment decisions, or if the plan has total assets in excess of $5 million;
3. a charitable organization, corporation, or partnership with assets exceeding $5 million;
4. a director, executive officer, or general partner of the company selling the securities;
5. a business in which all the equity owners are accredited investors;
6. a natural person who has individual net worth, or joint net worth with the person's spouse, that exceeds $1 million at the time of the purchase;
7. a natural person with income exceeding $200,000 in each of the two most recent years or joint income with a spouse exceeding $300,000 for those years and a reasonable expectation of the same income level in the current year; or
8. a trust with assets in excess of $5 million, not formed to acquire the securities offered, whose purchases a sophisticated person makes.[9]

Venture capital is one of a number of investment strategies under the private equity umbrella. Within the venture capital space, investors can encounter companies that are just beginning and require seed capital. Venture capital entails investing mainly in early (but can also involve later-stage) growth companies that are private.

Parents, friends, college roommates, or neighbors might initially "seed" a company or help form it. They are also commonly referred to as "angel" investors. Angel investors typically provide seed capital to get the ball rolling or put money into start-ups with the hope of the investment turning into a fast-growing, profitable company down the road. Investors who prefer early-stage investing are most commonly known as angel investors. *Early Stage VC* or *start-up* refers to a company that is newly formed, analogous to a builder framing a house, whereas seed investing might be compared with the cement or foundation being poured. Venture financing in start-ups typically is devoted to a product or for designing a prototype. As a company grows, it requires additional funds.

Growing companies can consume tremendous amounts of capital. Venture capital firms will most likely then enter the picture to invest in mezzanine or expansion rounds. In some cases the investment takes the form of a loan or might even include an "equity kicker" or some other component in order to entice an investor. As the company continues to grow and nears an IPO, it will often require more capital. Late-stage investing, as this is known, is popular among investors because much of the risk is diminished. There are also opportunities between venture rounds called bridge rounds, in which an investor puts money in to help ensure that the company has enough capital to get to the next round. Private equity is a

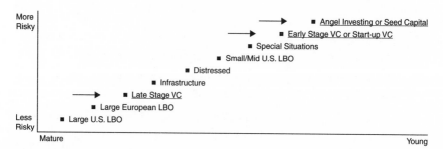

Figure 4.1 Private Equity Spectrum (Venture Capital)
Source: Author.

broad-based alternative asset class comprising a number of different areas, as seen in Figure 4.1.

Venture capital is illiquid and involves equity in private companies or ones not publicly traded on an exchange. Private equity strategies might include leveraged buyout, distressed investments, mezzanine capital, and growth capital. Venture capital can be viewed as a component of private equity. A general partner runs the venture fund, and limited partners invest in the fund. Venture capital is invested in limited partnerships that are usually 10 years in duration. The companies are neither mature nor traded on any stock exchange. Venture capital seeks companies that show promising new technologies or concepts that are not necessarily proven. Funds are raised either using bonds or equity. Private placements are "the direct sale of bonds to lenders by the debtor company, bypassing an underwriter for the offering."[10] Private placements can also involve equity that is sold to high-net-worth investors, companies, or institutions, such as venture capital firms. Venture capital firms take a stake in these companies by purchasing equity in the company. Normally, there is a lead investor who contributes the most money but also helps dictate the terms. Companies typically raise between $10 million to $80 million and use the money for expansion, development, or going public.

One fallacy about investing in venture capital is that an investor cannot buy into great companies in bad markets. When the going gets tough, Americans get innovative. "Americans are adept at finding opportunity in adversity."[11] Some of the best companies in America were started in the worst of economic times:

> History shows that great companies are often built during bad times. In 1939, at the tail end of the Great Depression, two engineers started Hewlett-Packard in a garage in Northern California. Silicon Valley itself was largely created during the nasty recession of the mid–1970s. During that decade, entrepreneurs laid the groundwork for the boom of the 1980s, building companies that pioneered three new industries: Atari in the video game business, Apple in personal computers, and Genentech biotechnology.[12]

Many great companies were built using venture capital. Venture capital plays a vital role in the U.S. economy, funding the launch and success of a variety of industries inspired by innovations in technology, transportation, and pharmaceuticals, among others. The direct role of venture capital investment has gone to research and development expenses, and, more important, to hiring hundreds of thousands of new personnel to oversee those roles. That is, venture capital creates jobs. Jobs get eliminated in both good times and, especially, bad times. However, venture capital helps fill the void. According to the *Economist*, "Even in boom times, 15% of American jobs disappear each year. Their places are taken by new ones created by start-ups and expansions. This dynamism remains evident [in a post-recession world]—the most crushing economic conditions most businesses have encountered."[13] In the first decade of the twenty-first century, tens of millions of Americans were either starting or running small businesses:

> The annual study by Babson College and London Business School, released Thursday, covers 34 countries with a combined labor force of 566 million. It is the largest annual measure of entrepreneurial activity worldwide. Babson, based in Wellesley, Mass., is seen as a leader in the study of small businesses. The study estimates that 73 million adults are either starting a new business now or managing a young business they own.[14]

Many of these businesses require some form of outside funding, and contrary to what one would think, the overwhelming amount of funds for venture capital comes from individuals, not venture firms. according to *Investor's Business Daily*'s study of the Babson report, "Fewer than one in 10,000 new startups get their initial funding from venture capitalists."[15] Friends, neighbors, family, colleagues, relatives, and former classmates are typical investors in venture capital. In fact, according to *the same* report, 99.9% of start-ups rely on funding from everyday investors, who have collectively contributed about $105 billion (versus $20.4 billion from venture capital firms) to help get new businesses of the ground.[16] The bulk of financing (on average about $50,000 to start a business) is from entrepreneurs themselves.

Venture Capital and Entrepreneurs

Venture capital is based on investing in fast-growing companies run by entrepreneurs. Robert E. Wright notes, "At its most basic level, financial history is the story of the competition between different means of linking the savings of investors to the spending of entrepreneurs."[17] If you have a great concept, you will need someone competent and driven to build on that idea and turn it into a company. Companies that are immensely successful were built by entrepreneurs. McDonald's was built by Ray Kroc. "Under his leadership, the company exploded from one store in the mid–1950s to more than 8,300 locations at the time of his death in January 1984. . . . From its IPO in April 1965 to when Kroc died, shares surged 1,014%."[18]

According to the Edward Williams and Albert Wapier in *Essentials of Entrepreneurship*, "All [entrepreneurs] have common roots in economics, economic/growth, and the creation of wealth.... The origin English word *entrepreneur* comes from the French word *entreprendre*, which can be translated to mean 'to do something' or 'to undertake'."[19] An entrepreneur is a creative, hard-working, charitable, motivated individual with an idea for a unique product or service that he or she turns into a viable growth company that will improve the lives of others and add to society. The definition of an entrepreneur varies widely:

> To an economist, an entrepreneur is one who brings resources, labor, materials, and other assets into combinations that make their value greater than before, and also one who introduces changes, innovations, and new order. To a psychologist, such a person is typically one driven by certain forces—needs to obtain or attain something, to experiment, to accomplish, or perhaps to escape authority of others. … To a Communist philosopher, the entrepreneur may be a predator, one who usurps resources and exploits the labor of others. The same person is seen by a capitalist philosopher as one who creates wealth for others as well, who finds better ways to utilize resources and reduce waste, and who produces jobs others are glad to get.[20]

Many successful entrepreneurs give back to society either with foundations or other philanthropic giving. Table 4.1 provides a chart of philanthropic entrepreneurs.

Table 4.1 Philanthropic Entrepreneurs

Name	Background	Causes	Estimated Lifetime Giving (millions)	Net Worth (millions)	Giving as a % of Net Worth
Bill and Melinda Gates	Microsoft cofounder	Global health and development, education	$40,780	$59,000	48%
Gordon and Betty Moore	Intel cofounder	Environment, science San Francisco Bay area	7,404	4,500	165
Alfred Mann	Medica devices	Biomedical education and research	1,735	2,200	79
Ted Turner	CNN founder	Environment	1,500	2,300	65
Larry Ellison	Oracle CEO	Research on aging and diseases	808	26,000	3
Jeff Skoll	Founding president of eBay	Social entrepreneurs	744	3,500	21
Bernard Marcus	Home Depot cofounder	Jewish causes, health, free enterprise, children	700	2,000	35
Pierre Omidyar	eBay chairman and founder	Unleashing human potential	657	8,900	7
Irwin Jacobs	Qualcomm cofounder	Education, arts	627	1,600	39
Thomas Siebel	Siebel Systems founder	Education, meth prevention Meth Project, community	386	1,900	20

Source: "The 50 Top American Philanthropists," *BusinessWeek,* 2008; "The 50 Top American Philanthropists," *BusinessWeek,* 2009. Used with permission.

True entrepreneurs are heroes. Many have made huge sacrifices (financial, personal, emotional, and familial) to build their dreams. The reward for an entrepreneur should be great because it is no easy feat:

In sharp contrast, an IPO is the pinnacle of a long chain of new money invested in a highly risky venture. It typically begins with an entrepreneur tapping into personal savings to develop an idea. Later, the entrepreneur persuades wealthy private investors or even a venture capitalist that the business has intriguing growth prospects, and they seed the startup with somewhere between $100,000 and $1 million. The money can come from the traditional venture-capital industry, which is made up of more than 500 venture-capital funds that invest between $3 billion and $4 billion a year in some 3,000 companies or the invisible venture-capital industry, drawn from some 2 million self-made high-net-worth individuals who conservatively invest between $10 billion and $20 billion a year in more than 30,000 ventures.[21]

The companies that entrepreneurs build create jobs. A total of 243,421 employees from Apple, Microsoft, Yahoo, Oracle, and Google alone would be unemployed in 2009 if the entrepreneurs behind them could not have raised capital when they were in their infancy:

> Over the past 60 years the money and the expertise provided by venture firms has led to the creation of thousands of companies, including Intel, Genentech, FedEx, and Google. A study by the National Venture Capital Assn. found that US venture-backed companies generated 10 million jobs and 18% of the nation's gross domestic product from 1970 to 2005.[22]

Venture capital helps companies grow into large-cap companies, which employ millions of people in a variety of industries. Joseph Schumpeter viewed entrepreneurs as agents of historical change. Venture capital gets deployed into a number of industries. However, technology is one of the biggest, and, not surprisingly, a huge source of jobs in the United States. Figure 4.2 is a chart of the number of employees at various technology companies.

When one includes other sectors in addition to technology, such as health care, venture capital creates a massive number of jobs. Guy Fraser-Sampson reports: "Research suggests that even by the end of 2000,

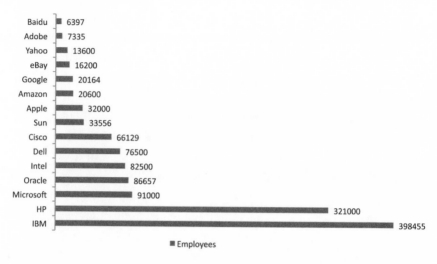

Figure 4.2 Number of Employees at Major Technology Companies

Source: Royal Pingdom, "The Size of IBM Makes Microsoft and Google Look Like Tiny Startups," http://royal.pingdom.com/2009/05/04/ibms-size-makes-microsoft-and-google-look-like-tiny-startups/, accessed May 4, 2009. Used with permission.

venture capital had directly created about 8 million new jobs in the USA (roughly equivalent to one job for every $36,000 of investment), and that if one added into the mix the jobs created indirectly in supporting and related businesses then the total rose to a staggering 27 million."[23] Whether the economy is good or bad, entrepreneurs are building companies and, in turn, hiring. Many talented and terrific employees lost jobs in a variety of industries when the market crashed. Recessions lay off workers, who then become marketable and sought after by entrepreneurs. Recruiting talented employees becomes easy, as well as obtaining office space. Americans, for the most part, are hard working and industrious:

> Such is the nature of human beings to strive to get more output from a given amount of input. All people want to be productive so that they can enjoy more wealth and more leisure. Not all people, however, have access to institutions that make increased levels of productivity possible. The mere desire to be more efficient is insufficient to drive productivity to higher levels because efficiency comes with start-up costs. Those costs will eventually be repaid many times over, but the initial cost of increased productivity is often a barrier that thwarts the introduction of innovations or reforms.[24]

The American culture admires those who work hard and are successful with their endeavors as opposed to those who are idle and complacent. The *Economist* reports: "A Pew poll released on May 21st found that 76% of Americans agree that the country's strength is 'mostly based on the success of American business' and 90% admire people who get rich by working hard."[25] Many successful companies were created during challenging times in the United States:

> Since its inception after World War II, venture capital has had a little-known but profound impact on the U.S. and world economy. It has played a catalytic role in the entrepreneurial process: fundamental value creation that triggers and sustains economic growth and renewal. In terms of job creation, innovative products and services, competitive vibrancy, and the dissemination of the entrepreneurial spirit, its contributions have been staggering.[26]

Five of America's Top Entrepreneurial Companies

1. **Zippo Manufacturing Co.** Zippo Manufacturing Company was founded in 1932 by George G. Blaisdell. Zippo has flourished from a $10-a-month room over a garage with two employees in the early twentieth century to a multimillion dollar business that employs 570 people based in Bradford, Pennsylvania, along with an office in London and a joint venture company in Paris that generates revenues upward of $155 million.[27] Zippo lighters are sold in more than 120 countries and have become a household name. The firm expects to sell its 500 millionth Zippo in 2010.

2. **Kraft Cheese.** Kraft Foods, Inc. was founded in Chicago in 1903 by James Lewis Kraft. "With just $65 in capital, a rented wagon pulled by a horse named Paddy and a never-say-die attitude, Kraft, 29, started a business peddling unpackaged cheese wholesale to local merchants."[28] Kraft's first year was a nightmare, and he went $3,000 into debt. Now the Kraft brand is the largest food and beverage company in the United States and the second largest in the world, after Nestlé. Kraft's 2008 revenues were $42.201 billion and net income was $2.901 billion for 2008.

3. **Goodyear.** Goodyear would not be possible without Charles Goodyear's vulcanization process, which was developed in 1839. Before vulcanization, rubber products could not withstand hot and cold weather. Goodyear's process could be one of the most significant developments of the nineteenth century. Charles Goodyear was determined to succeed and even spent time in debtor's prison. His accomplishment paved the way for tires and life rafts as well as a plethora of other products that revolutionized the industry.[29]

4. **Eli Lilly.** Eli Lilly founded Eli Lilly and Company and fought for the north in the American Civil War. Eli's company was founded in 1876 and primarily focused on the manufacturing of drugs. He then marketed them wholesale to different pharmacies across the nation. Two medical advances he pioneered were the creation of gelatin capsules that hold medicine fruit flavoring for liquid medicines. Today, Eli Lilly and Co. is the tenth-largest pharmaceutical company in the world with a market cap of $38.56B.[30]

5. **Smith & Wesson.** Smith & Wesson was founded in 1852 in Norwich, Connecticut, by gunsmiths Horace Smith and Daniel B. Wesson. Their aim was to produce a "lever action repeating pistol that could use a fully self-contained cartridge." After two financial setbacks, one of which forced them to sell their venture to Winchester in 1854, they created "the first successful fully self-contained cartridge revolver available in the world."[31] With their patents, Smith & Wesson grasped market superiority and emerged as the world leader in handgun manufacturing.

There are quite a few examples of entrepreneurial companies in the United States, as discussed in the sidebar below:

Venture Capital and National Security

Venture capital plays a large role in the national security of the United States. The United States was an innocent bystander to the diabolical terrorist event on September 11, 2001, but venture capital has helped prevent further attacks from happening. Besides making the United States the leader worldwide in medical and technology advances, venture capital has also assisted the U.S. government with security. Long before September 11th, the Central Intelligence Agency (CIA) set up its own venture firm known as In-Q-Tel. The fear was that the United States was falling behind with the Internet and national security. "'For many years, our intelligence technical capabilities were the standard of the world,' U.S. Senator Bob Graham (D. Florida), chairman of the Senate Select Committee on Intelligence, told reporters on the day of the attacks. 'We have fallen behind, and we need to close the gap and reassert our leadership.'"[32]

Originally, In-Q-Tel was set up as a nonprofit by the CIA in 1999 with an annual budget of $30 million to improve its Web prowess. The focus of the fund was "Information organization, access management, search, link analysis, Internet privacy, self-protecting data, threat detection, location information."[33] An example of a company that In-Q-Tel invested in was SafeWeb, which allows one to roam the Internet without a trace. Another high-tech company the CIA invested in is called Stratify. "Stratify is among a handful of companies that can find important tidbits of 'unstructured data'—information scattered throughout organizations in word-processing files, e-mails and databases, for example—and put them together in a way that makes sense."[34] In-Q-Tel's investment in Stratify fostered the development of technology that the government felt would directly aid them in the War on Terror.

The former head of Alex. Brown, A. B. "Buzzy" Krongard, was appointed executive director and helped with the CIA's information technology. Table 4.2 provides a list of companies that the In-Q-Tel invested in for the CIA.

Not surprisingly, security investing became even more popular following September 11th for national security as Thompson's Venture Economics showed:

> Indeed, while security accounts for just a slice of overall venture capital, the pace of investing in the sector is up 50% since 1998, Venture Economics data show. Security accounted for about 5%, or $1.2 billion, of $21.2 billion total venture-capital investing in 2002.[35]

Table 4.2 In-Q-Tel's Investments

Company	Product	$ Amount
SafeWeb	Software that allows users to browse Web sites without being detected	$1.0 million
Intelliseek	Software for searching across multiple, disparate sources and managing search results	$1.4 million
Mohomine	Software for managing unstructured data	<$1.0 million
Graviton	Wireless and sensor technology that monitors and adjusts remote functions	$1.0 million
Open GIS Consortium	Develops standards for presenting geographical information on the Web	$1.1 million
MediaSnap	Security software that controls access to individual documents	$1.3 million
Digital Data Development*	Identifies potentially fraudulent	Undisclosed
SRA International	Advanced search engine that mines data	Undisclosed
Twisted Systems	Software for sharing and archiving information	$350,000
Science Applications International Corporation	Software that repels denial-of-service attacks and shores up security	$3 million
Browse3D	Software for visualizing linked Web pages	Undisclosed
TecSec	Strong encryption software	$55,000
TruSecure	Internet security services	$500,000

*A subsidiary of Systems Research and Development.

Source: Justin Hibbard, "Mission Possible," *Red Herring* (December 10, 2001).

From 1999 until 2007, the CIA venture fund reviewed thousands of business plans and invested hundreds of millions of dollars:

> Since In-Q-Tel was founded in 1999, the firm has reviewed more than 6,300 business plans for everything from identity recognition software to nano-sized electronic circuits. Many proposals come in via its Web site. In-Q-Tel has put about $200 million into more than 100 companies, beating traditional VC investors to technologies such as the mapping software that's become Google Earth.[36]

A critic might fret about taxpayer dollars going toward a government venture fund, but the government has actually had quite a few home runs with its investments (besides keeping the United States in the forefront of

Table 4.3 In-Q-Tel Successes

Company (technology)	Date
@Last Software (3-D modeling)	Jul–04
Decru (data production)	Aug–01
Keyhole (3-D Earth satellite visualization)	Feb–03
Mohomine (text search tool)	Apr–01
Spotfire (information management)	Sep–01
SRD-NORA (data mining)	Jan–01
Visual Sciences (visual data analysis)	Mar–04

Source: Kameiz Foroohar, "Spy Funds," *Bloomberg Markets,* December 2007.

national security). The CIA's foray into venture capital has been profitable, ultimately saved taxpayers money, and protected the United States.

Although the U.S. government has made many terrible investments, the CIA had many companies that filed IPOs or were acquired. Table 4.3 shows a number of In-Q-Tel success stories. Astute venture capital investors would note that 9/11 was going to develop or create a new area of focus for venture capital firms. War usually leads to increased defense spending (public or private companies), and the malicious attack on U.S. soil would most likely result in increased military spending. Hundreds of successful security and defense companies were started. For example, In-Q-Tel partnered with Kleiner Perkins to invest $12.5 million into Arc-Sight, a security management software company. On September 1, 2007, ArcSight, Inc. filed an S–1 to sell shares in a $74 million initial public offering.

Chapter 5

The History of Venture Capital

The concept of venture capital is nothing new. It has existed for more than a century. "In the first quarter of the nineteenth century, New England manufacturing was 'hot'. . . . Mill profits created an ample supply of venture capital, with activist investors prospecting for opportunities. The most talented young men perceived that a flair for machinery could be a fast track to financial independence."[1] However, venture capital has evolved and is currently changing again:

> Initially, the venture capital industry grew out of the search by wealthy families for new investments. After World War II John Hay Whitney invested $10 million to form J.H. Whitney & Company. Other families active in the venture capital business were the Rockefellers, Rothschilds, Phippes, Paysons, Rosenwalds, Hillmans, and Bessemers. These wealthy families had an interest in public welfare. They felt they could help humanity by nurturing new ventures. Although personal gain also influenced their decisions to establish venture capital firms, they were driven primarily by a desire to build persons and companies to benefit society.[2]

Investing in oil companies or railways back then was not too different from investing in Internet companies today. Ron Chernow, in his biography of John D. Rockefeller, Sr., writes of the elite Wall Street banker's preference "to finance railroads and government," and goes on to say that they "regarded oil refining as risky, untested business, nothing short of outright gambling. Mindful of the extreme fire hazards and the specter of the oil running dry, only a few intrepid souls dared to wager on it."[3] New industries get created over time, and if you are lucky enough to be born during those periods, vast investment opportunities are available to those who can identify them.

Venture capitalists can be classified into three broad categories. In surfing terms, a "Gandalf" is an older, experienced surfer who is wise in the ways of the wave. The first category, the Gandalf venture capitalists, are the classic surfers of venture capital waves:

> Some historians mark the beginning of venture capital to the 1930s and 1940s, when wealthy families, such as the Vanderbilts, Rockefellers, and Bessemers began private investing in private companies. These so-called angel investors have a following still. One of the first venture capital firms, J.H. Whitney & Company, was founded in 1946 (J.H. Whitney n.d.). They are still in business today, having raised their sixth outside fund, for $750 million, in 2005.[4]

The second category of venture capitalists might be called "Core." A Core is a dedicated surfer who goes out in all conditions, no matter what the air or sea temperature is or how good the waves are. The typical Core surfer is often someone who has been at it a long time and is more often than not quite a good surfer because of his dedication. These would be the modern venture capitalists. The third category of venture capitalists are "Groms." The Groms are the younger surfers who really rip, as a surfer would say.

Gandalf Venture Capitalists

1. Benjamin Franklin (1706–1790). America is the land of opportunity. One of the first true entrepreneurs was Benjamin Franklin. Thousands of entrepreneurs followed Franklin's entrepreneurial footsteps over the years, exemplifying that the United States is a breeding ground for innovation. Benjamin Franklin was a printer, publisher, philanthropist, scientist, and politician. As an entrepreneur, he borrowed money in order to fuel the growth of his printing house. Conscientious of incurring debt, Franklin paid it down. One might view Benjamin Franklin not just as an entrepreneur, but as a serial entrepreneur or one who builds numerous businesses. Franklin was creative enough as an entrepreneur to build additional lines or businesses. For instance, he used his successful printing company for a lucrative newspaper he ran: "My business was now continually augmenting, and my circumstances growing daily easier, my newspaper having become very profitable, as being for a time almost the only one in this and the neighboring provinces. I experienced, too, the truth of the observation, 'that after getting the first hundred pound, it is more easy to get the second,' money itself being of a prolific nature."[5]

2. Thomas Edison (1847–1931). Thomas Alva Edison was born on February 11, 1847, in Milan, Ohio. With only three months of formal education, he became one of the greatest inventors and industrial lenders in history. Edison obtained 1,093 U.S. patents, the most issued to any individual. Edison's greatest contribution was the first practical electric lighting. He not only invented the first successful electric light bulb, but also set up the first electrical power distribution company.[6]

3. Andrew Mellon (1855–1937). One of the godfathers of venture capital was Andrew Mellon. Mellon might have contributed the most of all historical figures in creating the concept of modern-day venture capital:

> He was thought to possess exceptional powers of judgment, both of the character and capacity of the men who sought help and of the feasibility and potential of the schemes which they presented—and he was especially open to the commercial possibilities of emerging science and technology.[7]

Mellon understood growth. In fact, he would take profits and reinvest them back into a company to grow it. He also knew when to exit an investment, such as the Union-Sharon merger, in which he turned a $1 million investment into $42 million plus profit. Today, a 42x (or 42 times your investment) is phenomenal. Railroads, steel companies, and companies were the equivalent of today's technology or Internet companies like Netscape. Mellon also diversified his investments. "This outlook and

activity inspired the accumulation of an unusually diverse and widely dis-
tributed fortune: Mellon was in this sense a forerunner in the now commonplace practice of portfolio diversification."[8] Just like modern-day
venture capitalists, Mellon financed various companies and provided an
array of useful services. "He was required not only to devise and oversee
so many complex and varied deals, but also to provide funding packages,
management assistance, and even technological advice for numerous
companies."[9] He identified opportunity and helped mentor companies
that showed promise:

> The Pittsburgh Reduction Company was the first significant benefi-
> ciary of what would prove to be…Andrew Mellon's extraordinary gift
> [was] for spotting and nurturing outstanding individuals with prom-
> ising ideas — though in this case, as in others, it would be some time
> before the promise was abundantly redeemed, both for them and for
> him. But Mellon was prepared to wait, riding out losses if need be
> (especially in the early 1890s) and plowing back profits when they
> came (during the company's first decade dividends were paid out
> only twice).[10]

Mellon was cognizant of venture capital waves, which helped him
become extremely rich. Although involved with many types of businesses, Mellon best capitalized on his acknowledgment of waves within
the market through his two most recognized deals, Alcoa and Gulf Oil,
which yielded an estimated $128 million in combined profits. Mellon
invested in these oil companies at the beginning of a very long and
lucrative oil wave.[11] His biographer notes this awareness going back
almost two decades before it paid off handsomely on his two key oil
investments:

> By the late 1900s and early 1910s, Andrew Mellon's varied business
> activities had settled into a recognizable pattern that had been devel-
> oping since the early 1870s: a slump, weathered with difficulty but
> determination, then a recovery; burgeoning profits for the banks, the
> Union Trust Company, and many of his companies; one or two
> undertakings performing below par but with long-term prospects of

growth and profit; and one or two just performing below par. To that extent, the years 1907–14 were business as usual, consistent with this latest phase of the economic cycle.[12]

As Secretary of the Treasury, Mellon also made tax cuts that propelled growth. He was a visionary for venture capital. As stated by Lerner and Gompers in *The Venture Capital Cycle,* "Decreases in the capital gains tax rates are associated with greater venture capital commitments."[13] Many fail to see the relationship between taxes and venture capital. Lower taxes are beneficial to small companies. Although he was prescient and correct about his views, Mellon was blamed and prosecuted for tax evasion when the market collapsed.

4. Laurance Rockefeller (1839–1937). Mellon and Rockefeller passed away the same year. Rockefeller was adept at finding and procuring large investors, which is what the most successful venture funds do today. There were others dabbling in what is known today as venture capital, but none took it to the level that Laurance Rockefeller and his decedents did:

> The Rockefeller family, the Whitney family, and the Phipps family were among the first to establish separate venture capital programs. Laurance Rockefeller provided the initial spark in the 1930s. His interest in aviation and his access to capital helped him finance two seminal businesses: Eastern Air Lines and McDonnell Aircraft.[14]

Later, the family set up Venrock to invest in entrepreneurs in a variety of industries. For instance, in 1969, Venrock invested in Intel. Venrock continues the eight-decade Rockefeller tradition of funding entrepreneurs and establishing successful, enduring companies. Having invested $2.5 billion in 442 companies resulting in 125 initial public offerings (IPOs) and 128 merger and acquisition (M&A) exits over the past 41 years, Venrock's investment returns place it among the top-tier venture-capital firms that have achieved consistently superior performance.[15]

5. Henry Phipps (1839–1930). Henry Phipps, one of Andrew Carnegie's partners, founded Bessemer Trust in 1907 to manage his family's wealth.

Bessemer was named for the process he developed in 1856 to convert large amounts of iron into low-cost steel, which he and Andrew Carnegie made a mint using. Bessemer is still active in the venture capital world.

6. Andrew Carnegie (1835–1919). According to J. Bonasia, "The tycoon Andrew Carnegie made a fortune licensing Bessemer's breakthrough in America."[16] Carnegie took an existing technology and leveraged it. He was both innovative and creative. In addition, he was one of the first to arrange a joint venture:

> He [Carnegie] had recapitalized his original sleeping car investment, reorganized two iron companies into the Union Iron Mills, and organized the Keystone Bridge Co. During a nine-month world tour in 1865 — part of his continuing quest for social polish — he encountered processes for putting steep caps on iron rails, and when he came home, started a company to experiment with the new Bessemer steel (unsuccessfully at this point). As competition between his sleeping car company and the interloper George Pullman heated up, he negotiated a tricky joint venture for a major Union Pacific contract, settled a contentious patent dispute, and merged the two companies in 1870.[17]

Today's Internet has much in common with the initial construction of railroads in the nineteenth century. Jeff Bezos with Amazon is a modern-day Carnegie; he used the Internet and leveraged it selling books through Amazon. Amazon sells many items today, not just books. Bezos launched the revolutionary Kindle in 2007, which might change the way people read books. Both had explosive growth and created new opportunities. As with modern-day venture funds, Carnegie had venture partners until he went out on his own. In doing so, he took the lessons that his mentors had taught him and applied them:

> Only invest in companies you have investigated yourself; only invest in companies about which you have insider knowledge; only invest in companies that sell goods or services for which demand is growing; never invest as an individual, but always with a group of trusted associates who together will own a controlling or dominant interest in the company.[18]

Core Venture Capitalists

1. George Doriot (1899–1987). There were a number of legendary entrepreneurs and venture capitalists after Franklin and Edison, but it was the industrious French immigrant Georges Doriot who pioneered venture capital from Boston with his venture capital firm, American Research and Development (ARD). ARD was very supportive of the company. Among other things, they helped find board members similar to modern day venture firms. Eventually, ARD went the route of an IPO. As evidenced by many successful IPOs backed with venture capital, Digital continued to prosper. "By the summer of 1967, Digital shares hit $80, and in October ARD's stock reached a record of $152, its stake in Digital now worth more than $200 million. Digital was the venture capital industry's first home run, proving that venture capitalists could generate wealth by backing a hot new business."[19] As the godfather of venture capital, Doriot helped finance many growth companies.

> During its 26-year existence, ARD financed 120 companies. Although it was acquired by Compaq Computer in 1998, Digital's rise allowed Doriot to accomplish his ultimate goal of forging a nationwide movement of entrepreneurs. "Doriot was the first one to believe there was a future in financing entrepreneurs in an organized way.… He [and ARD] really created the venture capital community."[20]

Doriot taught and influenced countless entrepreneurs while at Harvard. In fact, a number of the most successful venture capitalists were his students.

2. Edgar F. Heizer, Jr. (1929–2009). According to Trevor Jensen, "Edgar F. 'Ned' Heizer Jr. was a seminal figure in the history of the venture capital industry, whose ability to see beyond the horizon led to successful investments in fledgling companies in fields from computers to pancakes."[21] Edgar Heizer, founder of Heizer Corp., is most famous for backing Amdahl Corp., a database and server production company that is now owned by Fujitsu. He also helped back Federal Express and the International House of Pancakes.

3. Jon Hay Whitney (1904–1982). John Hay Whitney's obituary states: "He founded J.H. Whitney & Company in 1946 as a venture capital company, and its first major investment of $1.25 million in the Spencer Chemical Company doubled in a year."[22] Some have tried to justify Mr. Whitney as the first venture capitalist. He was definitely a shrewd investor with diverse business interests:

> The organization of the venture fund J. H. Whitney & Co. by John Hay (Jock) Whitney in February 1946 is arguably the official starting point of private venture capital in the United States. At the time, Whitney was considered one of the richest men in America, a champion polo player, a horse breeder, and a frequent backer of Broadway shows and Hollywood movies, including *Gone with the Wind*. The idea to raise a private pool of venture capital for venture investing was Whitney's, but it was the execution by Benno Schmidt in his role as managing partner that made the fund the most significant of its time.[23]

Whitney owned Whitney Communications, which owned newspapers, televisions stations, radio stations, Aviation Corporation of America, and other investments.

4. Peter Brooke (1925–). Many venture pioneers learned from Doriot, including Peter Brooke, who helped form TA Associates back in 1968. "In 1973, Brooke—who always had an interest in international affairs—brought the VC model to Europe with the founding of Paris-based Sofinnova SA. And in 1974, Brooke left TA Associates to form Advent International."[24] When Brooke started his career, the venture capital market was quite different. Early on, the industry was more localized and not as regulated:

> Today the industry that Brooke helped define is entrenched, global, and the subject of much discussion about possible regulation. To Brooke's thinking, if lawmakers were to move forward with regulation, then they should move forward cautiously. Large private equity investors who can't police their own industry and rely too heavily on debt should be called to account. But over-regulating early-stage venture capitalists—who more than anyone else have the capacity to identify promising companies, move the economy along and create jobs—would be disastrous, he said.[25]

Advent International was originally founded in Boston as a divestiture from TA Associates.

5. Arthur Rock (1926–). Arthur Rock was another venture capital legend. He was involved with starting Fairchild Semiconductor, Teledyne, Intel, and Apple. In 1961 Rock moved to California and formed a partnership with Tommy Davis known as Davis & Rock. Davis & Rock invested $5 million and returned $100 million to investors.[26] Later, he founded Arthur Rock & Company in 1969 to help fund one of the most lucrative companies ever, Apple. In 1975, Arthur Rock invested $1.5 million in the start-up Apple computer, which reached a value of $100 million after the IPO in 1978.[27] As of November 20, 2009, Apple's market cap was approximately $180.3 billion.

6. Eugene Kleiner (1923–2003) and Tom Perkins (1932–). Eugene Kleiner and Tom Perkins are best known for their prowess in the technology space. In 1972, the two launched one of the industry's most successful venture capital organizations, now known as Kleiner Perkins Caufield & Byers.[28] Kleiner Perkins Caufield & Byers's portfolio consists of many leaders such as AOL, Amazon, Genentech, Intuit, Google, and Sun Microsystems. Kleiner Perkins has excellent timing as to when to invest in growth companies and when to exit. Many venture firms were not active in 2009, but Kleiner Perkins appeared to be one of the most active. The firm is a leader with regards to investing in Cleantech. Venture-capital firms are dedicating enormous amounts of money to green companies. Kleiner Perkins serves as a benchmark for anyone investing in venture capital.

7. Richard Kramlich (1935–). New Enterprise Associates (NEA) was founded in 1978 by Dick Kramlich, with approximately $16.5 million. One of NEA's most notable deals was in 1986 with Silicon Graphics, which went public in a $22 million IPO. Ten years later they had UUnet, which went public at $415 million in the IPO and was acquired shortly after by Worldcom for $2 billion. Offices were set up in Washington, Baltimore, and Menlo Park, California. Baltimore was selected as a location partially because of its proximity to Alex. Brown, which took many technology companies public, including Microsoft, America Online, Amazon, and eBay. NEA worked with Alex. Brown, which was the number-one venture-backed IPO firm out of every investment firm or bank on Wall Street for many years. In 2000, NEA closed its tenth fund at $2.3 billion, which made NEA the largest-funded, early-stage venture-capital firm nationwide.

8. Don Valentine (1943–). One of the most legendary venture capitalists of all time is Don Valentine. Valentine is the founder and general partner of Menlo Park, California–based Sequoia Capital. Valentine is not just a wave rider, he is the equivalent of the individual who invented the surfboard. Sequoia invested $2.5 million in Cisco in 1987, the year the market crashed. Like many successful venture capital deals, Cisco did quite well after it received funding in a dismal market: "Valentine became deeply involved at Cisco, serving as chairman from 1986 to 1995. In mid–1988 he brought in John Morgridge as CEO, and in two years the stock started on its 81,900% stratospheric ride." He also helped finance Oracle, Apple, LSI Logic, Electronic Arts, and many others. Early in his career, he met Gordon Moore and Robert Noyce, who later founded Intel. Sequoia was started by the Capital Group. Capital Group manages American mutual funds. According to Reinhardt Krause, "Capital wanted in on the venture capital business. With its help, Valentine in 1972 started Capital Management, a forerunner of Sequoia."[29]

Grom Venture Capitalists

1. Trae Vassallo (1973–). Trae Vassallo is a venture capitalist with Kleiner Perkins Caufield & Byers. Her main areas of interest are green technology and consumer Internet services. She has helped back a variety of companies in these fields, such as Altarock Energy and Aggregate Knowledge. Before joining Kleiner Perkins, she "learned to program when she was 7 and at 28 cofounded a wireless e-mail company that Motorola bought for $550 million."[30]

2. Sky Dayton (1971–). Sky Dayton founded EarthLink, cofounded eCompanies, and is the founder and current chairman of Boingo. Early in his career as an entrepreneur, Dayton owned a pair of trendy Los Angeles coffeehouses. In 1994, he started EarthLink. EarthLink became a huge player in voiceover Internet protocol (VoIP), which allows users to make telephone calls across the Web. Dayton originally got his funding through angel investors:

In 1994 I got the idea for EarthLink and scraped together $100,000 from a couple of angel investors. The commercial Internet was just beginning, I hadn't heard the words *venture* and *capital* in the same sentence, and I actually believed that $100,000 was a *ton* of money. Today EarthLink has a billion-dollar market cap, $600 million in the bank, nearly 5 million customers, and 6,500 employees.[31]

EarthLink went public on January 22, 1997, selling 2 million shares to raise $26 million. eCompanies began as a way to start and develop Internet companies. Privately held, it struggled for several years until it successfully launched companies like LowerMyBills.com.

3. Samir Kaul (1974–). Samir Kaul is a founding general partner at Khosla Ventures and "the right-hand man of Vinod Khosla."[32] He focuses primarily on clean technology and life sciences companies. He has backed companies such as Austra and Great Point Energy. Furthermore, "Samir Kaul led the effort to effort to sequence the genome of the Arabidopsis plant and then built three life sciences companies from scratch."[33]

4. Elon Musk (1971–). Musk was a cofounder of PayPal, an online payment service launched in 2002. He sold PayPal to eBay for $1.5 billion. Musk is now chief executive of Space Exploration Technologies, a company he founded with $100 million of his own cash. Musk is now working with solar power company SolarCity, which makes solar products. Musk is also well known for his involvement in Tesla motors, makers of the high-performance electric sports car, the Tesla Roadster. Musk is also well known for his pet project, SpaceX, a company that makes space-launch vehicles. It is Musk's ultimate goal to put a greenhouse on Mars.[34]

5. William "Bo" Peabody (1970–). Along the way, one of the entrepreneurs I became very acquainted with regarding venture capital was Bo Peabody. I met Bo in the late 1990s. We both like to invest in venture capital. Our learning experience revolved around venture capital, and the trials and tribulations we experienced were not too different from those in college or graduate school. Before becoming a venture capitalist, Bo founded a company named Tripod in 1992, which was bought by Terra Lycos. Basically, Tripod gave individuals the ability to publish their own "personal homepages." In the mid–1990s, NEA invested $3 million into the company. A couple of years later, Bo was made an offer he could not refuse. As Bo summarized in *Lucky or Smart? Secrets to an Entrepreneurial Life*: "On December 31, 1997, I agreed to sell Tripod in exchange for $58 million in stock of a publicly traded company named Lycos, which at the time was an internet company only slightly more stable than Tripod."[35] Bo now runs Village Ventures which is based in Williamstown, Massachusetts. According to Bo, in an interview with the author, "Village Ventures is a venture capital firm specializing in seed and early stage investments. The firm typically invests in consumer media and retail, health care, and financial services companies based in the United States. For early-stage investments, it invests in companies with revenues less than $10 million and within seed investments, the firm invests in companies with no revenues."

6. Peter Thiel (1967–). Thiel provided funding to PayPal in 1998. In October 1999, PayPal was launched, an online person-to-person payment provider. PayPal was backed by Sequoia Capital, Nokia Venture Partners, and Clearstone Venture Partners (formerly Idealab Capital). Thiel was the chief executive officer and helped PayPal go public:

> That March, as the NASDAQ Composite Index roared its way to a record 5048, Thiel set out to raise money from venture capital investors. Dot-com fever was running high, and VCs valued the money-losing PayPal at $500 million. "Everyone thought that wasn't high enough," Sacks says. Everyone except Thiel. He looked at the NASDAQ frenzy and concluded the dot-com bubble was about to pop. He seized the opportunity. Based on the $500 million valuation, Thiel raised $100 million, more than his colleagues had planned, and closed the deal in three weeks, on March 31, 2000. He was just in time. The next day, the NASDAQ began a plunge that would eventually send it tumbling 67 percent in 18 months. "If he hadn't made that call, the company wouldn't be around today," Howery says of Thiel.[36]

After selling PayPal to eBay for $1.5 billion, Thiel founded Clarium Capital Management, LLC, a combination hedge and venture fund based in San Francisco.[37] Thiel is a wave rider.

Forbes 400 Members and Venture Capital

Quite a few of the wealthiest individuals in the United States have made fortunes from investing in companies and/or building them using venture capital. Figure 5.1 features a list of Forbes 400 members involved with alternatives (including venture capital).

The Formation of Venture Capital Waves

Although there were various forms of venture capital before this time frame, the venture capital industry truly solidified in the United States in the 1960s:

> Venture economics has data on the U.S. venture capital industry that goes back to the late 1960s. By accessing that historical data and tracking new data as the industry evolved throughout the 1950s, we were able to analyze longitudinal data sets spanning 20 years. Over that period the industry went from being red-hot at the end of the 1960s to almost an ember by 1974; it rekindled in the late 1970s until it was white hot by 1983; then from 1987 it began to cool off.[38]

As data began being collected in the late 1960s and 1970s, it is evident there were venture capital waves even from the industry's infancy. Venture activity peaked in 1969 when the market reached a high and was followed by a 5-year bear market (see Figure 5.2).

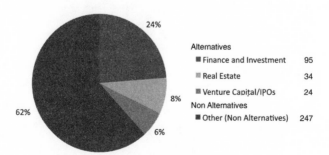

Figure 5.1   Forbes 400 Richest by Investment Type

Source: "The 400: 2009 Edition," *Forbes 400* (October 27, 2008). Used with permission.

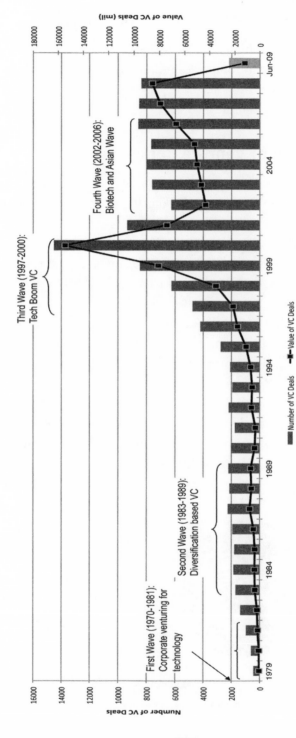

Figure 5.2 30 Years of Global Venture Capital Activity

Source: Author.

The first real wave of venture capital was started in 1970 and lasted until 1981 with corporate venturing for technology (shown in Figure 3.8). Venture capital did well in the 1970s after the capital gains tax was reduced. A standard legal form of venture capital funds evolved called the 10-year partnership. The 10-year partnership offered both a tax-friendly structure and enough longevity to attract institutional investors for longer-term commitments.[39] As a result of the 10-year partnership, pension funds and other institutional investors commenced buying venture capital.

It was really at this point that the modern concept of venture capital began. According to *BusinessWeek*, "The modern VC industry started in a partnership format in the 1970s and '80s."[40] As one can plainly see in Table 5.1, the idea of venture firms commenced in the 1960s and early 1970s.

Government Involvement

Over the years, venture capital has been at the mercy of government changes. Like all alternatives, investors must be cognizant of the investment climate at the time they are considering making an investment. Government actions can propel or chill investments in venture capital overnight, and the outcome can last over a decade. According to Scott Denne, "Increased regulations imposed on public companies, such as the Sarbanes-Oxley Act of 2002, have made going public a much less attractive option for venture-backed companies."[41] Figure 5.3 depicts a few of the major legislative changes that affected venture capital.

Here are some of the key moments of Figure 5.3 in detail:

1. 1958 Small Business Investment Company (SBIC) Act. Venture capital began with wealthy families, but changed after the Small Business Investment Company Act (SBIC) was created. The Small Business Administration (SBA) helped fuel venture investing by making attractive loans.

2. 1978 Revenue Act. The 1978 Revenue Act reduced the capital gains tax at the time from 49.5% to 28%. As a result, venture capital investing flourished.

3. 1979 ERISA ("Prudent Man") Rule. Government invention can be beneficial to venture capital as evidenced by the 1979 Employee Retirement Income Security Act (ERISA) Rule. The 1979 ERISA "Prudent Man" Rule

Table 5.1 History of Venture Firm Formation

1960s		1970s		1980s		1990s	
Name	Year	Name	Year	Name	Year	Name	Year
Sutter Hill Ventures	1964	Sequoia Capital	1971	Accel Partners	1983	Benchmark Capital	1995
Greylock Partners	1965	Kleiner Perkins	1972	Advent International	1984	Polaris Venture Partners	1996
Warburg Pincus	1966	NEA	1978	Edison Venture Fund	1986	Silver Lake	1999
TA Associates	1968			Sandler Capital	1988		
Venrock	1969			Hummer Winblad	1989		
Arthur Rock & Co.	1969						
The Mayfield Fund	1969						

Source: Author.

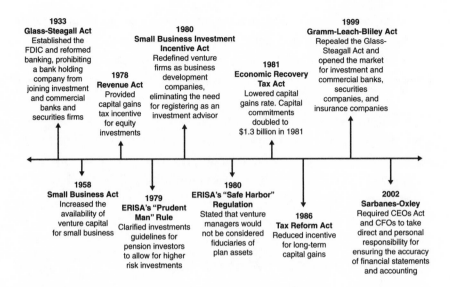

Figure 5.3   Legislative Impact on Venture Capital Investment

Source: Author.

governing investment guidelines for pension-fund managers was revised and clarified to allow for higher-risk investments, including venture capital arrangements.[42]

4. 1980 Small Business Investment Incentive Act. The SBII Act categorized venture capital firms as business development companies, which meant they need not register as investment advisors with the Securities and Exchange Commission (SEC).

5. 1980 ERISA "Safe Harbor" Regulation. The 1980 ERISA "safe harbor" regulation allowed venture capital firms to manage pension assets without becoming fiduciaries, which ultimately reduced their risk for accepting these new limited partners. People managing or investing funds do not like clients who are likely to sue them. Given this positive change, assets flowed into venture capital.

6. 2002 Sarbanes-Oxley Act. Government intervention can also be negative for venture capital as seen with Sarbanes-Oxley. The Sarbanes-Oxley Act of 2002 has had a dramatic effect on public companies. Sarbanes-Oxley, which became law on July 30, 2002, was the first comprehensive federal legislation to impose significant corporate governance requirements on public companies and to address the responsibilities of corporate executives and board members.[43] Chairmen, CEOs, board members, officers, auditors, legal council, and even banks have new regulation to contend with as a result of the act. New regulation was needed after events such as Tyco, Enron, and Worldcom, in which there was definitely too little regulation. However, Sarbanes-Oxley went far enough in the other direction to the point that it is now considered excessive. Both the New York Stock Exchange (NYSE) and National Association of Securities Dealers Automated Quotations (NASDAQ) adopted new listing standards focused on heavy corporate governance.

Effect of Politics on Venture Capital

Surfers use the phrase "raked over," which means to be hammered by incoming waves while paddling out. Sarbanes-Oxley ("Sarbox") hammered a lot of CEOs as well as investors. A negative effect of Sarbanes-Oxley is dramatically higher accounting and legal costs for compliance. Going public, in other words, became extremely expensive for a small, fast-growing company. Some companies even need to raise venture capital for these added expenses. A general rule of thumb is a company should have approximately $10 million in the bank before pursuing an IPO today. Murray Beach, managing director of TM Capital, describes the venture capital market in the aftermath of Sarbanes-Oxley:

> Where the IPO was the favored choice for entrepreneurs and their investors when raising growth capital in the 80's and 90's, most managers and boards of successful young privately held companies today are opting to stay private and raise money from venture and private equity funds or have decided to enter the M&A market and sell their business to larger companies. The cost, burden, and risk of being a public company is now too high. Investors are not interested in the risks associated with stock in a small public company, and the professionals and institutions which have the expertise in creating public companies have abandoned this part of the market and moved to other segments.[44]

Ironically, the U.S. government did a 180-degree turn with venture capital. Precisely one decade before Sarbanes-Oxley, the SEC helped companies prosper. The SEC adopted rules in August 1992 intended to make it less costly and burdensome for small- to medium-sized growth businesses to raise capital. Government intervention often is extreme. One minute a company has loosey-goosey regulations (1992), and the next minute they are as tight as a steel drum (2002). Somewhere there is a happy medium. The approach of letting growth companies have a free-for-all and then strangling them with red tape does not seem rational. While politicians debate back and forth, investors can take advantage of these extreme waves in the meantime. Pay particular attention as to when and where you are considering investing in venture capital.

Government actions can also affect exit strategies for venture capital. Each government is different regarding how they view small businesses. For instance, the SBA assists entrepreneurs with 500 or fewer employees. A business must be a certain size to qualify for federal grants or be given government contracts. The SBA Web site has a classification system and defines which businesses are considered small businesses. Historically, there have been certain times the U.S. government is favorably inclined toward small businesses and other times it is not. In 2009, the National Venture Capital Association was quoted in response to the economic meltdown of the late 2000s: "This is a time the country should be supporting venture capital firms because we're in the business of creating new companies and new jobs, which is what the country needs right now."[45]

Initial Public Offerings

The governments of Israel, Singapore, and China value venture capital. These nations have made huge strides toward creating environments that are favorable toward venture capital. What is the tax structure for venture-backed companies? How does the IPO market look? What kind of exchanges exist for publicly traded companies? What does the M&A market look like? Delbert Smith, senior partner at the global powerhouse law firm Jones Day, advises, "Companies looking to go public or merge, need to examine venture waves as well as trends in the IPO or M&A market places."[46] IPOs are a primary exit for venture capital. According to Wright and Robbie, authors of *Management Buy-Outs and Venture Capital,* "Historically, IPOs have been the preferred means to exit venture capital. The most important determinant, by far, of the health of the venture capital industry is the condition of the IPO market. All other factors pale in comparison."[47] *Investor's Business Daily* says, "A strong IPO market is key to venture capital investors, who depend on the public markets to cash out of their investments."[48] Without a robust IPO market, the exit strategyfor a venture capital firm is reduced to just M&A (the other central exit strategy). According to George M. Taber, "An initial public stock offering has long been the epitome of success for a startup company. It's also the ultimate liquidity event because the company stock is freely traded on one of the stock exchanges."[49] When a company is public and the lockup expires, venture capital investors can sell at their leisure; the shares are freely tradeable.

Figure 5.4 uses a chart to show 30 years of U.S. initial public offering activity.

Venture capital moves in waves, and so does its main exit strategy, the IPO. When the IPO market is robust, venture capital funds can exit quickly and make a profit. According to Wright and Robbie, "Successful timing of a venture-backed IPO provides significant benefits to venture capitalists in that taking companies public when equity values are high minimizes the dilution of the venture investor's ownership stake."[50] Any seasoned venture capital expert will be cognizant of venture capital and IPO waves. Years ago, I met Ed Mathias, who runs the venture arm of the Carlyle Group, and I remember his advice on venture capital from his decades of observations. He best describes the cyclical nature of venture capital and the IPO market this way:

> Venture capital again peaked in terms of fundraising in 1987 following the bull market and ensuing IPO boom. Performance is historically followed, with a delay, by money into venture capital. Coincident with the '87 market peak, the venture industry raised $4 billion. For perspective, and as further testimony to the historic cyclicality, fundraising declined to $1 billion in 1991 as performance of the mid-'80s funds lagged. There was virtually no IPO market, with the cumulative amount of IPOs from 1988 to 1990 being less than was done in 1986 alone. I believe after the crash in 1987, there was only one deal done for the balance of the year.[51]

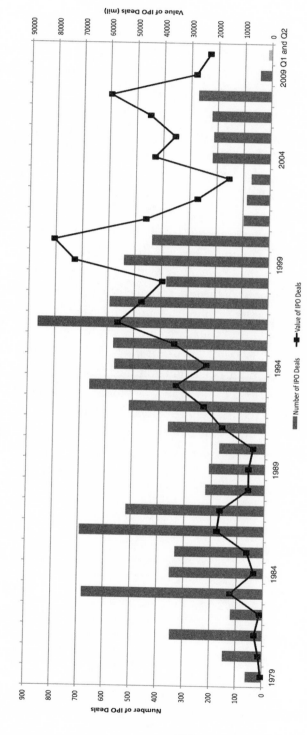

Figure 5.4 30 Years of U.S. Initial Public Offering Activity.

Source: Author.

These cycles, patterns, or trends occur on a regular basis. Table 5.2 shows a number of banner as well as lackluster IPO years.

Waves can be identified in shorter periods with venture capital. There are years when venture capital is perfect to surf with a robust market and plenty of IPOs (1968–368, 1969–780, 1970–358, 1971–391, 1972–562, 1973–105). Venture capital firms are adept at taking portfolio companies public at peak periods. According to Wright and Robbie, "Seasoned venture capitalists appear to be particularly good at taking companies public near market peaks, though of course this does not necessarily mean that such timing is appropriate from the point of view of the company itself."[52] When an investor sees a lot of venture-backed IPOs in a certain area all going public, it usually means the potential for upside investing in a private company in this area is limited because the ride is almost over or ending shortly. By the time the company is ready to go public (unless it is really different or superior to all the other competitors in the area in which it filed to go public), investors can lose a lot of principal.

Other times, you want to put your surfboard away when the IPO market slows to a crawl (1974–9, 1995–12, 1976–26, 1977–15, 1978–20, 1979–39, 1980–75). If one was observant, one might note the last 3 years were steadily rising (from 1978–20, 1979–39, and 1980–75). Based on this trend, would 1981 be a good year for venture capital? Probably. In fact, 1981 provided 197 IPOs, indicating that the IPO market was very much improving. Waves keep on moving. They will never end. Bygrave and Timmons state,

Table 5.2

Year	Number of IPOs
1961	435
1966	85
1969	780
1974	9
1983	521
1990	112
1996	687
2003	68
2004	186
2008	21

Source: Author.

"Historically, the ability to harvest an investment depended heavily on a hot new issues market."[53] In 1983, there were a huge number of IPOs, totaling 521 new issues (see Table 5.2). Until 1986, the IPO market was robust. But all good things must come to an end. On October 19, 1987, the stock market crashed, and IPOs dwindled again.

During my career, I helped place funds for at least 1,000 private companies and IPOs. Certain top-quality IPOs can do well in bad markets. It is not unreasonable, therefore, for select private companies to do the same—there are always good buys. Rosetta Stone is a good example of a private company going public in a terrible market. Rosetta Stone was priced at $18.00 on April 16, 2009, and reached a high of $32.97 soon after. The years 2000, 2001, and 2002 were negative years for the equity market. As evidenced time after time, venture capital trails public equities. The year 2003 was terrible for IPOs. However, venture-backed IPOs did well in 2003. Venture capital investing picked up in 2004 in terms of amount invested and number of deals (compared with 2003).

Venture capital trailing the IPO market is nothing new, as evidenced by Ernst & Young's report, "3Q'09 Venture Insights,"[54] which claims there were 6,351 deals with a record amount invested in venture capital for 2000. Figure 5.5 illustrates this wave:

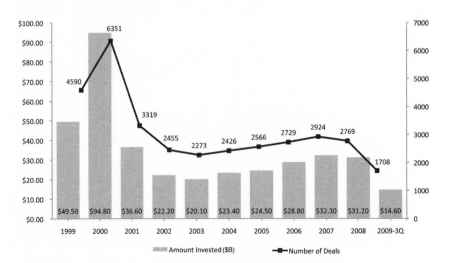

Figure 5.5 Annual Deal Flow and Equity into Venture-Backed Companies

Source: Ernst & Young, "3Q'09 Venture Insights," 2009. Used with permission.

The year 2000 was when the tech bubble burst. Yet it was a record year for venture capital. Incidentally, Figure 5.5 also shows waves of both number of deals and amount invested for venture capital. These waves move in sync. Following the IPO market, venture capital started doing well after 2003. A total of 85 companies came to market in 2003 raising $15.77 billion, followed by 249 U.S. IPOs in 2004 raising $48.12 billion, versus 385 companies raising $60.63 billion in 2000.[55] As evidenced in the past, venture capital followed the IPO market with increased number of deals and amount invested until the 2007 recession. IPOs can be quite lucrative, as seen in Table 5.3, which details various IPOs released in 2005 and 2006.

The years 2005 and 2006 were good years to go public. Because the IPO market is a way for an investor or fund to exit their investment in a private company, one needs to be cognizant of where one is with

Table 5.3 Initial Public Offerings

Company	Ticker	Issue Price	Date of IPO	High	% Gain	High
Lazard Ltd	LAZ	$25.00	05/04/05	$55.75	123%	05/02/07
XenoPort	XNPT	$10.50	06/02/05	$65.86	527%	01/18/08
Focus Media Holding	FMCN	$17.00	07/13/05	$65.10	283%	11/06/07
Adams Respiratory	ARXT	$17.00	07/20/05	$60.01	253%	01/24/08
Genco Shipping	GNK	$21.00	07/21/05	$84.00	300%	05/16/08
CF Industries	CF	$16.00	08/10/05	$169.62	960%	06/17/08
WebMD Health Corp	WBMD	$17.50	09/28/05	$61.35	251%	10/10/07
Intercontinental Exchange	ICE	$26.00	11/15/05	$194.50	648%	12/26/07
SunTech Power	STP	$15.00	12/13/05	$88.35	489%	12/26/07
Altus Pharmaceuticals	ALTU	$15.00	01/25/06	$25.25	68%	03/17/06
Chipotle Mexican Grill	CMG	$22.00	01/25/06	$152.36	593%	12/26/07
NightHawk Radiology	NHWK	$16.00	02/08/06	$26.99	69%	12/20/06
Alexza Pharma	ALXA	$8.00	03/08/06	$15.21	90%	03/26/07
CTC Media	CTCM	$14.00	05/31/06	$31.75	127%	02/27/08
Omniture Inc.	OMTR	$6.50	06/27/06	$36.81	466%	10/30/07
WNS Global Services	WNS	$20.00	07/25/06	$35.43	77%	02/08/07
InnerWorkings Inc.	INWK	$9.00	08/15/06	$18.69	108%	10/09/07
Ehealth	EHTH	$14.00	10/12/06	$35.99	157%	11/16/07
Hansen Medical Inc.	HNSN	$12.00	11/15/06	$38.87	224%	10/31/07
First Solar Inc.	FSLR	$20.00	11/16/06	$311.14	1455%	05/16/08
Spirit Aerosystems	SPR	$26.00	11/27/06	$40.50	56%	07/19/07
Affymax	AFFY	$25.00	12/14/06	$40.87	65%	02/12/07

Source: Author.

regards to IPO waves. When the broad market tanks, IPOs dry up and venture capital follows. Buying IPOs during an overheated market or top of the market might be as reckless as throwing money into venture capital during the same period. IPOs will likely plunge as hard if not more than the broad-based market, and private valuations might implode. Private companies need a lot of fuel, which is difficult to get in bear markets. In fact, many private companies go bankrupt in difficult times because they cannot get financing. Low valuations for private companies as well as increased costs for going public due to Sarbanes-Oxley, weaken the entire venture capital market. In Figure 5.6, one can see the number of venture capital deals from 1994 skyrocket to 2000.

The year 2000 shows IPOs falling off a cliff while the number of venture capital deals reached an all-time high. The reason for this is that public markets (including IPOs) move very fast, unlike venture capital, which is private. Deals that were restricted or cash committed to venture-backed companies take a while to register. Likewise, when the market finally picks back up, as depicted by the line representing the number of IPO deals from 2003–2004, venture capital will follow, as seen by the bar charts from 2003–2004 as investors start putting money back into venture capital.

The venture capital wave charts combined with IPO waves can be very helpful in decision making when an investor contemplates when to exit an investment in a private company. In some cases, if you invested in a private company (and it filed for an IPO), it makes sense to exit your investment when the company goes public. Other times, one might hold the IPO shares (if the IPO market appears to be doing well). In one case, I held my shares after an IPO and the stock did extremely well. I realized a much better return on my investment. Both the IPO market as well as the general market were in an uptrend. Further, the company continued to have positive news and improved financials. Letting winners run can be beneficial. One can also have an attractive company but the venture capital and IPO waves look ominous. In other scenarios, I sold some shares on the IPO and kept some shares in order to hedge my bet. The stock proceeded to crater. My error

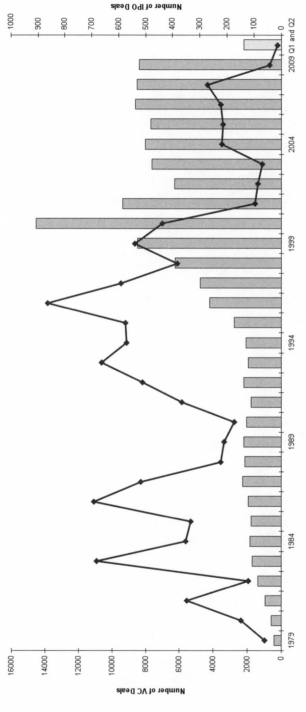

Figure 5.6 30 Years of Global Venture Capital versus U.S. Initial Public Offering Activity

Source: Author.

was that I should have sold all the shares at the offering because the handwriting was on the wall with the direction the waves were heading. My warm relationship with the CEO clouded my judgment and I forgot an important rule: Never fall in love with an investment. Invest to make money, not friends.

Mergers and Acquisitions

Besides IPOs, the other main exit for venture capital is mergers and acquisitions. Before the tech bubble bursting, it was not out of the ordinary for venture-backed companies to go public in 2 to 3 years. After Sarbanes-Oxley, the exit horizon greatly expanded to 7 to 10 years. While the IPO market was slammed, M&A activity continued to prosper. According to the *Boston Business Journal,* "The number of initial public offerings by venture-backed companies has decreased so far this year compared with the same period last year. Prevailing conditions in the stock market and a healthy acquisitions market have made public offerings a less tempting exit strategy for venture capitalists."[56] In Figure 5.7, one can see the number of M&A deals (the bars) has steadily increased from 2001 until 2008. Because the exit for venture capital saw one of its primary exit strategies (IPOs) vanish, M&A became much more popular. Richard A. Silfen, M&A attorney and senior partner at Duane Morris, LLP, states, "the M&A wave picked up since the IPO market declined. Timing is everything in M&A."[57] M&A waves are affected by a number of variables, which are evident by the value of M&A deals (the line) as shown from 1995 to 2000.

Figure 5.8 shows that although the size of deals might have decreased, M&A activity remains high, especially with venture capital. The *Wall Street Journal* noted 404 acquisitions of venture-backed companies ($31 billion in value) in 2006, with similar figures for 2005 (401 acquisitions at $30 billion).[58] One can also see from the chart (looking at 2000–2002) that as venture capital deals slow, M&A deals do as well. Valuation becomes more of an issue between buyer and seller because of public comparables.

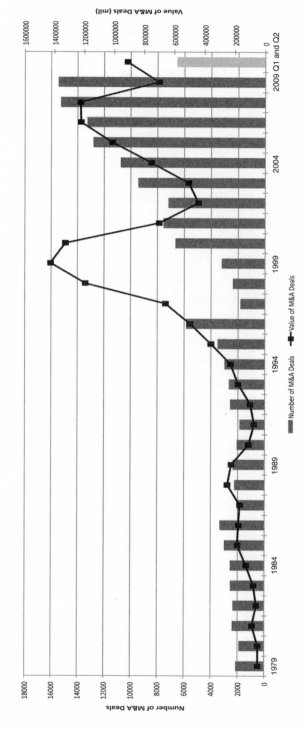

Figure 5.7 30 Years of Global Mergers and Acquisitions Activity

Source: Author.

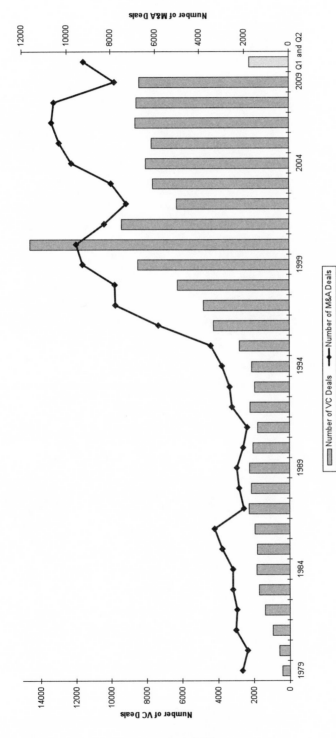

Figure 5.8 30 Years of Global Mergers and Acquisition versus Venture Capital Activity

Source: Author.

Chapter 6

Venture Capital
Market Dynamics

The venture capital market experienced one of the most brutal investment climates during 2008 and 2009 since Andrew Mellon struggled with his investments during the Great Depression. CalPERS (the California Public Employees' Retirement System), the largest pension in the United States, is a big investor in venture capital. CalPERS explained the decline in venture capital in the June 2009 *Alternative Investment Management Program Quarterly Review*:

> In the second quarter of 2009, venture capital activity decreased in dollar amount and in the number of companies receiving funding compared to the second quarter of 2008. According to Venture Economics, 2,615 companies received $21.8 billion in venture funding in 2009 compared with 4,352 companies that received $52.4 billion in the second quarter of 2008.[1]

CalPERS is not perfect (no investor is), but they have a good pulse on the venture capital, market and reports such as this are worthwhile. Only 10 venture-backed companies went public in 2009; there were just six in 2008. The real estate market collapse and credit crises affected all areas of finance both public and private. Venture capital did not escape. Investors flocked to gold and cash. Illiquid investments were shunned, causing a number of well-known venture capitalists (particularly those of retirement age) to hang up their hats. Employment at venture capital firms typically has low turnover, but in June 2009, the *Boston Business Journal* reported that New England had already experienced nearly double the turnover rate for the year from 2007 and 2008, including nearly a dozen senior-level venture capitalists.[2] However, many employees were fired or quit, and some even switched firms. A number went on to pursue other opportunities unrelated to venture capital.

The initial public offering (IPO) market evaporated and was the worst anyone had seen for 30 years. Institutional investors walked away. Further, certain endowments, like Harvard, ran into cash flow problems and put billions of private equity up for sale. Venture capitalists fortuitous enough to stay and fight focused on helping their strong companies weather the storm while letting weaker players fail. Venture capitalists increased allocations to later-stage companies. Some experienced difficulty raising new funds. The *San Francisco Business Times* reported that "Most venture capitalists agree the industry is contracting. Some VCs won't be able to raise new funds. Those that do say they don't expect as lucrative returns as they achieved in years past. And the outlook for IPOs and acquisitions, while improving, is still relatively bleak."[3]

Whether it be Boston or Minneapolis, early stage or late stage, many venture capital deals are either tech or health care. Table 6.1 provides a sampling of Boston top-funded startups in 2008.

Table 6.2 provides a list of Minnesota venture capital deals in 2009.

These two sectors (on any given year) are favorites with venture capital firms. According to *Barron's*, "Venture-capital funding plummeted after the dot-com bubble burst, but current levels represent a more sustainable base of investment. Technology and health-care companies continue to raise the largest sums."[4] Figure 6.1 provides a chart that shows information technology as the largest area for venture capital in 2005.

In a 2009 analysis of the trends generated by each sector, *Investor's Business Daily* noted that "For the first time since the National Venture Capital Association and others started tracking these data in 1980, biotech surpassed software as the largest single category of venture investment."[5] Health care as a whole is also a large part of venture capital and almost equal to information technology. Figure 6.2 gives greater detail of investment allocation in venture-capital industries.

Table 6.1 Boston Top-Funded Startups in 2008

Company	Business	Amount Raised ($)	Venture Firms and Individual Investors
1366 Technologies	Alternative energy production	12,500,000	Individual investors, North Bridge Partners, Polaris Venture Partners
Agios Pharmaceuticals	Biotechnology	20,000,000	ARCH Venture Partners, Flagship Ventures, Third Rock Ventures
Alnara Pharmaceuticals	Biotechnology	20,000,000	Bessemer Venture Partners, Frazier Healthcare Ventures, Third Rock Ventures
Artemis Health Inc.	Diagnostic equipment	20,000,000	Alloy Ventures, Mohr Davidow Ventures, Sutter Hill Ventures
Auraria Networks	Business software	10,000,000	Matrix Partners, Pilot House Ventures Group
Aveksa	Network software	12,000,000	Charles River Ventures, First Mark Capital, FTVentures
BitWave Semiconductor	Specific integrated circuits	10,000,000	Apex Venture Partners, eCentury Capital Partners, TVM Capital
Blueshift Technologies Inc.	Integrated circuit production	12,000,000	Atlas Venture, Intel Capital, North Bridge Venture Partners
Boston-Power Inc.	High-tech	45,000,000	Gabriel Venture Partners, Venrock Associates
Codon Devices	Medical devices	37,000,000	Alloy Ventures Inc., Flagship Ventures, Highland Capital Partners Inc., Khosla Ventures, Kleiner Perkins Caufield & Byers

Source: Boston Top-Funded Startups in 2008, *Boston Business Journal* (November 28–December 4, 2008). Used with permission.

Table 6.2   Minnesota Venture Capital Deals in 2009

Name	Stage	Amount Raised	Investors
Industry: Medical Devices			
Anulex Technologies Inc.	Later	$10.2 million	Affinity Capital Management, Delphi Ventures, MB Venture Partners, New Enterprise Associates, SightLine Partners, Split Rock Partners
CoAxia Inc.	Later	$21.5 million	Affinity Capital Management, Baird Venture Partners, Canaan Partners, Johnson & Johnson Development Corp., Prism VentureWorks, Sofinnova Partners
Inspire Medical Systems Inc.	Early	$17 million	Kleiner Perkins Caufield & Byers, Medtronic Inc., Synergy Life Science Partners, U.S. Venture Partners, and an undisclosed firm
Orasi Medical Inc.	Early	$3.5 million	CentreStone Ventures Inc., PrairieGold Venture Partners
Torax Medical Inc.	Later	$22.1 million	Accuitive Medical Ventures; Kaiser Permanente Ventures; Sanderling Ventures; Thomas, McNerney & Partners
Wound Care Technologies	Early	$460,000	Rain Source Capital

Source: Andrew Conry-Murray, "Startup City," *Information Week* (April 13, 2009), http://www.informationweek.com/blog/main/archives/2009/04/introducing_inf_2.html, accessed April 20, 2009. Used with permission.

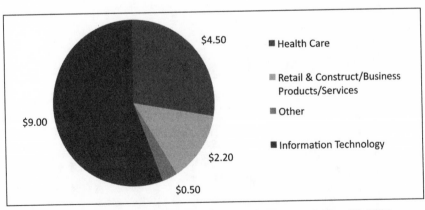

Figure 6.1   Venture Capital Equity Investments ($bil) through Sep. 30, 2005

Source: Russ Garland and Brian Gormley, "Grooming the Next IPOs," *Barron's* (January 9, 2006).

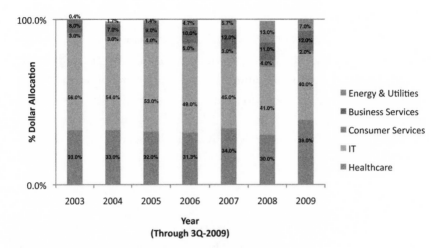

Figure 6.2 Investment Allocation by Industry Group

Source: Ernst & Young, "3Q 2009 Venture Insights," 2009, 8. Used with permission.

Global expansion and mega funds fell by the wayside in the Great Recession. Mergers and acquisitions of venture-capital companies experienced problems because of the credit crisis. As Bo Peabody of Village Ventures explains, "It is much harder to get good exits when credit is tighter which makes it harder for big companies to be flexible."[6] The market declined in 2008 and 2009 as the result of a credit crisis. Because public valuations dropped (the Dow went from 14,164 to 6,469), valuations of private companies also plummeted. Entrepreneurs believe their companies are worth more than competitors, but public companies with cash (possible buyers) struggled with buying a business when the valuation was hard to justify. Companies have been hoarding cash to record levels. Cash is king, as they say.

The Sarbanes-Oxley Act

As small, fast-growing companies look to grow and head toward an IPO, Sarbanes-Oxley, which held CEOs and CFOs accountable for the accuracy of their company's financial statements, has turned into a hindrance, not a help. Sarbanes-Oxley is about as useful as surfing with a two by four and as helpful as throwing a heavy anchor to a surfer washed out to sea by a sudden, vicious storm. The intention might have been good—to help the surfer—but it was not done the right way, and the expenses have thwarted many fine companies from going public. Moderation would be more helpful with venture capital. On one hand, you do not want to red-tape and restrict-to-death growth companies. On the other hand, you do not want a free-for-all. Companies that want to go public in the United States are now looking abroad to markets in Europe or Asia where restrictions are not as stringent nor costs as high. Sarbanes-Oxley costs small public companies a lot of money to comply. Not a lot of companies have extra funds to throw around.

Taxes

As noted with Andrew Mellon, when taxes on capital gains are increased, it adversely affects venture capital. The contrapositive is true: lower capital gains taxes is beneficial for venture capital. Lower capital gains tax rates propel businesses to grow and not wither on the vine. Entrepreneurs are more inclined to start companies in favorable tax environments. Paul Gompers and Josh Lerner discussed this relationship in their book, *The Venture Capital Cycle*:

> The relation between capital gains taxes and venture capital commitments... is clearly negative. In the 1970s high capital gains tax rates were associated with low levels of venture capital fund-raising. Increases in the capital gains tax rates in 1988 were followed by reductions in venture capital commitments, while the reduction of capital gains for long-held investments in 1993 was followed by a rise in venture fund-raising. This negative relation between venture capital funds levels and capital gains tax rates is clearly only suggestive, because the influence of multiple factors needs to be examined.[7]

Besides entrepreneurs themselves, investors tend to invest more in venture capital when taxes are lower. Any investor contemplating making an investment in a novel medical device company that saves lives might be doing it not just because they are altruistic but also because they are looking to generate a profit. Venture capital either does really well or very poorly, and seldom is there a middle-of-the-road result. If an individual investor risks capital for a company, most people think they should be rewarded. However, the threat of removing the 15% capital gains tax greatly increases an investor's risk. Why risk your money if there is reduced potential for a healthy return? Steve Goodman, senior partner at Morgan Lewis and one of the most experienced venture capital attorneys in the country, views venture capital in 2009 as "the worst it has ever been" and believes the venture capital industry will take "many years to recover."[8]

Michael J. Heller, chair of business law development at Cozen O'Connor, echoes the sentiment: "The only reason a company will go public in today's environment is a need for either liquidity or access to capital. It will be a long time before tech IPOs come back in vogue. If a tech company is before its time it will need at least 5 years of capital."[9] Similarly, a report by Foley & Lardner states that "virtually no emerging company executives surveyed (3%) plan to test the IPO market. Further, respondents expect the IPO market to continue to lag, with 81% predicting a stagnant IPO market over the next to years."[10]

The Market Moving Forward

At this point, one might turn to a different chapter or even hide in a bomb shelter. One might come to the false conclusion that venture capital is not worth it and write off the asset class altogether. Although this is easy to do, it is my belief that the years following the recession from 2007 to 2009 have yielded an environment in which the venture capital industry is extremely attractive, and the time to buy will be optimal as long as that environment holds. If an investor finds the appropriate vehicle to invest in venture capital, understands the risk, and performs the appropriate due diligence, the possibilities are limitless.

The market for venture capital is constantly moving and evolving. The structure of venture capital firms has even changed over time to include areas outside of venture capital. Years ago, venture capital, hedge funds, and leveraged buyout (LBO) firms stuck to their own knitting and did not enter into each others' backyards. More recently, venture capital firms have morphed into other areas like hedge funds and LBO firms. For instance, venture capital funds are moving into the LBO area. Silver Lake Partners does both venture capital and LBO. Besides Jim Davidson and Dave Roux, one of the other partners, Roger McNamee, is a top venture capital and hedge fund manager. Glenn Hutchins previously worked at the LBO firm Blackstone Group. Likewise, many of the LBO funds like Bain Capital have set up venture funds. The Carlyle Group, a Washington, D.C.–based LBO firm, created a venture area led by Ed Mathias, who also helped set up New Enterprise Associates (NEA). Jay C. Hoag of Technology Crossover Ventures does venture capital and LBO. Last, hedge funds have moved into venture capital. Thus, venture capital has cross-pollinated with hedge funds and LBO firms.

Well-Known Venture Capitalists Who Were Previously Entrepreneurs

1. **Ann Winblad.** Originally a programmer, Ann Winblad cofounded Open Systems in 1976 with a $500 investment. Open Systems, Inc., was an accounting software company. She operated the firm profitably for 6 years, later selling it for more than $15 million. Her venture fund, Hummer Winblad Venture Partners, is software only (a specialty fund). Hummer Winblad Venture Partners was founded in 1989. It was the first venture capital fund to invest primarily in software companies. She was named the 2007 Financial Woman of the Year by the Financial Women's Association.

2. **Mitchell Kapor.** Mitchell Kapor was a pioneer in the personal computing space and has been involved with information technology for decades as an entrepreneur, software designer, and angel investor. Before Accel Partners, he created Lotus 1-2-3 and founded Lotus Software Company in 1982. He was president and chief executive officer from 1982 to 1986. In 1983 the company went public. Kapor was a founding investor in UUNET, Real Networks, and Linden Research. He also created the virtual world Second Life.

3. **Mike Farmwald.** Mike Farmwald is an entrepreneur at heart. He started back in 1986 and founded numerous companies: Rambus, Inc., Chromatic Research, Epigram, FTL, and Matrix Semiconductor.

Farmwald has a superb track record. In 1990 Farmwald cofounded the semiconductor company Rambus, then went on to start three more chip companies, including Epigram, which he sold to Broadcom for $316 million. He is now a general partner at Skymoon Ventures, based in Santa Clara, California. This venture capital firm focuses on semiconductors and telecommunications infrastructure. It also helps entrepreneurs with business plans and with building their companies.

4. **Josh Kopelman.** As an undergraduate at the Wharton School at the University of Pennsylvania, Kopleman and Marvin Weinberger founded Infonautics, which introduced the online research service for libraries. Kopelman left Infonautics in 1999 to launch Half.com Inc. the following year. At the time, Half.com was a Web site that enabled buyers and sellers to exchange used items for less than half the original price. To advertise the start-up, Kopelman convinced the town of Halfway, Oregon, to change its name to Half.com. In the same year it was launched, Kopelman sold his e-commerce company to eBay Inc. for a deal valued at more than $312 million.[11]

5. **David King.** Before joining Quaker BioVentures, David King had nearly three decades work experience with life sciences. He first started as a lawyer at Morgan Lewis. Then he became CEO of Principia Pharmaceutical Corporation, which was acquired by Herman Genome Sciences, Inc., for $135 million in 2000. Next he became president of Delsys Pharmaceuticals Corporation in 2001, which was acquired by Ekon Corporation. He then founded BioRexis Pharmaceutical Corporation and served as the CEO. BioRexis raised $38 million in venture capital to finance its operations in 2002. BioRexis was Quaker BioVentures's first investment. BioRexis's main product was protein and peptide therapeutics. BioRexis was sold to Pfizer, Inc., in 2007. For his next phase, David joined Quaker BioVentures as a venture partner, where he invests and helps portfolio companies involved in life sciences. Quaker BioVentures invests in companies at all stages of development, from early stage to public corporations, and has $700 million under management.

Serial Entrepreneurs

There are a number of entrepreneurs who have taken multiple companies public or sold them for substantial amounts of money. I call these entrepreneurs "serial entrepreneurs" because they are extremely successful in building fast-growing companies that are immensely attractive to the marketplace. The pattern is always the same. They build the company to a point where it's large enough, they turn it over to someone experienced with managing such a large company, and they start a new one. The following are serial entrepreneurs:

1. **Jim Clark.** Jim Clark, the legendary Silicon Valley entrepreneur and the founder of Silicon Graphics, Netscape, and Healtheon—as well as a man deeply rooted in the culture of venture capital firms— has cast doubt on the necessity of a formal structure for corporate venturing. "If you have a team that has done good stuff before, they can take even a mediocre idea and make a good company," he once said. Yet his confidence in the ability of talented and experienced individuals to be the primary driving force of a venture overlooks a critical fact about corporations: Most do not have people with extensive experience launching new businesses. Many have never worked outside the corporate bubble, much less for a start-up. It is precisely this absence of experience that makes a formal structure for the corporate venturing process so necessary.[12]

    When asked about the IPO market, Clark responded:

    > The IPO market is fueling the innovations that are transforming the U.S. economy into the world's productivity powerhouse. The driving force behind the technological revolution changing the way we live and work is the maverick, the risk-taker—in other words, the entrepreneur. And backing the entrepreneur is the most sophisticated capital market in the world.... Without IPOs, you would not have any startups.... IPOs supply the fuel that makes these dreams go. Without it, you die.[13]

2. **Alfred Mann.** During the Depression, Alfred Mann sold lemonade and magazines door to door. Since the 1950s, he helped grow 10

companies. In the 1960s, he sold aerospace companies Spectrolab and Heliotek. A *Forbes* profile noted, "He was just 30 when he started Spectrolab in 1956, and he turned it into the leading maker of solar-powered systems for spacecraft. Mann switched to medicine with remarkable results at the age of 42. He invented the first rechargeable pacemaker for the heart, forming Pacesetter Inc. Mann sold his interest in the company in 1985 for $150 million to Siemens AG."[14] Mann is a lifelong inventor and entrepreneur who has helped fund a number of immensely successful upstart biomedi-cine companies that include:

- MiniMed (external and internal insulin pump)
- Advanced Bionics (cochlear implants, neurosimulators)
- Pacesetter Systems (rechargeable pacemakers)
- MannKind Corp. (inhalable insulin medication)
- Second Sight (implantable device to restore vision for retinal degeneration)
- Bioness (medical devices to help recovery from neural injuries)
- PercuPort (pharmaceutical delivery applications)

One of his greatest success stories was MiniMed, which he sold to Medtronic for more than $3 billion. MiniMed held a dominant share of 75% to 80% of the U.S. market for insulin infusion pumps. Currently, Mann's main focus is Mannkind. The company went public in 2004 and demonstrated Mann's ability to know how to ride IPO waves. At the time, he read the market correctly and postponed his IPO for Mannkind in April 2002 until the market was better. "We met with bankers and they told me that, because of my track record with companies and my reputation, that we could go public now. But I don't believe the market is ready," Mann said.[15] Mann is an experienced wave rider.

3. **Steve Case.** Steve Case became CEO of America Online, Inc., in 1993. I knew Steve Case's brother, Dan Case, who ran H&Q. My old firm Alex. Brown took AOL public. AOL became one of the largest and most profitable Internet companies in history. At AOL's peak, in early 2000, Case acquired TimeWarner in order to create

an online media conglomerate. The acquisition was at the peak of the tech bubble and valued the company around $290 billion. In early 2003, Case launched Revolution LLC. Revolution LLC is a private holding company that has interests primarily in health care, but also wellness and resorts. In 2005, Revolution LLC acquired and launched 11 companies. Revolution Health, a subsidiary of Revolution LLC, merged with Waterfront Media in 2008 for $300 million, which gave both companies strong positioning to compete with online medical giant WebMD.[16] On November 24, 2009, Time-Warner released AOL shares on a when-issued basis.

4. **Marc Andreessen.** Andreessen developed Netscape 15 years ago with Ben Horowitz, which he sold to AOL in 1999, becoming AOL's chief technology officer. In the past 15 years, he and Horowitz have started three companies, including software company Opsware, which was sold to Hewlett-Packard for $1.6 billion in 2007. His latest Internet venture, Loudcloud, provides software infrastructure services to accommodate the increasing complexity of networks of servers for Internet businesses. Along with his partner, Andreessen started a venture capital firm called Andreessen Horowitz. Their strategy with this fund is to invest in young, small companies, testing the traditional theory that "smaller funds making smaller investments in very young companies will yield higher returns."[17] For someone who recognizes venture capital waves, Marc Andreessen knew that 2009 was the time to start a new fund. In a recent interview, Andreessen noted, "If you look at the history of venture capital, which tends to be seven years of feast followed by seven years of famine, most of the really good investments have been made during that famine period."[18] Andreessen is a wave rider. According to a *Fortune* magazine profile:

> In some ways Andreessen has already put his money where his mouth is. He invested in LinkedIn partly because he believes employees won't be hired through jobs listings and resumes but through myriad connections. He built Ning because he feels people will move narrow aspects of their social lives onto the Net, convening online in groups specifically for, say, beagle owners.

Raising venture money in bad equity markets is hard to do, but those who can do it are funds worthy of exploring. The fact that Andreessen was able to raise money in a difficult time is a testament to his entrepreneurial savvy. Many venture funds with excellent track records struggled to raise money during this time. Few (if any) new funds were able to raise funds. When the going gets tough, the tough get going.

5. **David Levison.** Levison was president of Oncology Therapeutics Network, which was sold to Bristol-Meyers Squibb in 1996. Previously, he was CFO of Oncology Therapeutics Network's parent company Axion. He later founded iScribe, which focused on health-care technology. Levison then sold iScribe to AdvancePCS (now Caremark) in 2001. Levison knows about waves. As he says, there is a "need to see beyond historical trends."[19] He has also worked at various venture firms, including Texas Pacific Group, Mohr Davidow Ventures, Intel Capital, and Pappas Ventures, and was interim CEO at XDx. In early 2005, Levison founded CardioDx, a diagnostic test developer, with three rounds of about $50 million financing from Kleiner Perkins Caufield & Byers, TPG Biotech, Mohr Davidow Ventures, Intel Capital, and Pappas Ventures.[20]

Venture Ideas

Venture ideas can come from a variety of sources. Many such ideas come from former companies where an employee comes up with a new or better idea leaves to start a new company. Venture ideas can also be started through science, for example, when a doctor or scientist discovers an idea for a new biotech company. Table 6.3 lists the top-10 places where venture ideas are devised:

Table 6.3 Top 10 Places from Which Venture Ideas Emanate

Previous companies	Self-employment
Friends	Practical use/necessity
Family	Travel
Hobbies	Health care
College or graduate school connections	Purely accidental

Source: Author.

Supply and Demand

Venture capital revolves around supply and demand. Venture capitalists are the ones supplying the capital; entrepreneurs and companies are the ones demanding the capital. In other words, the demand is the desire of the company or entrepreneur for growth capital. When the equity market corrects or crashes, the supply of venture capital in the system significantly decreases, which makes it more difficult for early-stage companies and entrepreneurs to obtain funds. The investing process becomes advantageous to the venture capitalist and/or investor. But when the market is at an all-time high, it is much easier to get capital (supply), and the entrepreneur benefits, not the venture capitalist and/or investor.

When the equity and IPO markets are good and there are new venture capital entrants to the market and a lot of cash sloshing around, it is not the best time for investors. The reason is that the case revolves around supply and demand. Venture capital firms will need to compete more and ultimately pay higher prices for companies. It is good news for entrepreneurs because they can extract higher prices from venture capital firms, but it ultimately will lead to lower returns for investors. One can easily find out how much money is moving into venture-backed companies. Various firms such as VentureOne track theses statistics. The following excerpt is from the *Wall Street Journal:*

> In 2006, 56 venture-backed companies went public in the U.S., raising about $3.7 billion, according to data from research firm VentureOne and New York accounting firm Ernst & Young LLP. While that exceeded the 42 venture-backed IPOs in the U.S. that raised $2.3 billion in 2005, it is down from the 67 venture-backed IPOs of 2004 that raised nearly $5 billion.[21]

Fundraising

Although 2009 was a great time to invest in venture capital, investors were still leery. Venture funds have difficulty raising new funds when markets correct because investors are traumatized by the market. As 2009 drew to a close, the *Wall Street Journal* looked back at the venture-capital data for the year:

This year, 435 venture-capital funds have hit the road to raise money, compared with 452, for all of 2008 and 445 in 2007, according to research firm Preqin. Out of that field, just 134 new venture-capital funds had completed their fund raising and closed to investors as of early November, down from the full-year totals of 309 funds in 2008 and 363 in 2007. The new combers raised just $20.4 billion in total capital down 65% from $58.2 billion in all of 2008, according to Preqin.[22]

Fundraising for venture capital firms has steadily declined from 2007 to 2009. Similarly, there are a large number of funds on the road trying to raise capital.

Market Trends

Venture capital is trendy. What was hot in 1994–1996 (microbreweries) was quite different from 2007–2009 (cloud computing, cleantech, solar, and Smart Dust). As described in Cendrowski, Martin, Petro, and Wadecki's 2008 book *Private Equity*:

> VC has always been a lumpy business for returns, with huge ups and large downs. Venture is currently looking for its next wave of cutting-edge technology to help buoy its returns: In the early 1980s, it was venture's assistance in the personal computer market that drove such high returns; in the late 1990s, venture's—and the overall market's—obsession with Internet-based technologies caused returns to sky-rocket. Right now, venture investors are searching for that next bit of breakthrough technology to bolster their returns and help the industry regain some traction.[23]

Figure 6.3 depicts trends in venture capital from the early 1990s. As discussed, venture capital helps start whole industries (e.g., railroads, personal computers, microbreweries, Internet, and cleantech). At the time that these nascent industries formed, they seemed unrealistic, futuristic, or impossible to imagine. Looking back (hindsight is always 20/20), it seems obvious. If one sat in a saloon with Carnegie, Mellon, and Rockefeller (at the time) and told people you had a vision to put railroad tracks made

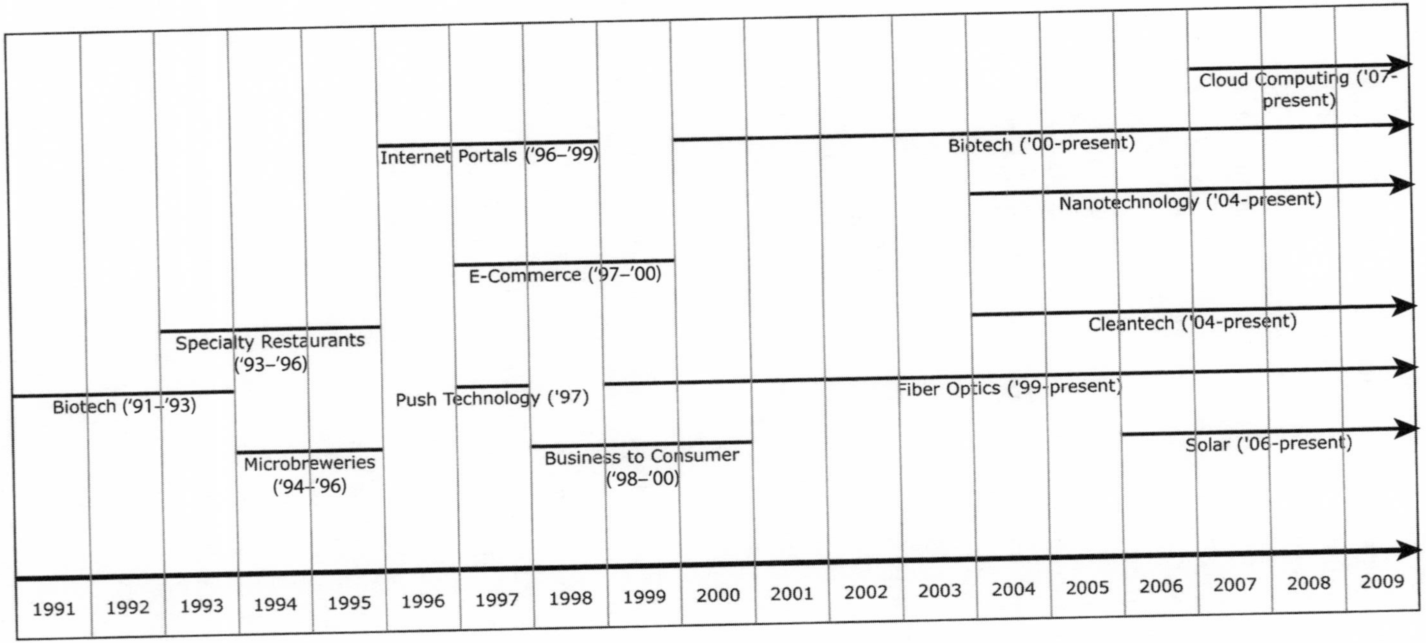

Figure 6.3 Venture Capital Trends

Source: Author.

of steel across the country with trains so you could ship goods and people, it would seem novel. Today, we take railroads for granted. The objective for any investor or venture capitalist is to try to identify the next new thing. Although there are others, the sectors profiled below highlight three venture capital trends worth following in the opening decades of the twenty-first century.

Nanotechnology

Nanotechnology started in 2004. It is basically the science of making things smaller. A nanometer is one billionth of a meter. Consumers frequently desire smaller objects. Television sets used to be massive and heavy. Now they feature flat screens and are much lighter. Even fabric can be made so that clothing is spillproof. The area is vast and growing. One area that appears to be growing within nanotechnology is Smart Dust. *Investor's Business Daily* characterizes Smart Dust as being "based on microelectromechanical systems, or MEMs. These tiny computer chips can measure temperatures, vibrations, or surface pressures. Smart sensors relay signals back to a command computer, which then compiles the data to give feedback to plant managers."[24]

Smart Dust has a variety of uses: tiny, wireless networks of sensors can be used to change pharmaceutical, security, space-exploration, environmental, technology, and oil industries. One specific health-care use might be for a patient with cardiovascular disease to swallow a pill and, as Smart Dust roams through their bloodstream, be able to pinpoint or identify a problem likely to occur. Adds *Investor's Business Daily*, "Or tiny robotic chips drifting through a human artery to locate, and eradicate, a hidden clot."[25] Smart Dust can aid industrial companies as well. Companies like Crossbow offers industrial applications such as semiconductor, mining, and pharmaceuticals. Dust Networks assists oil and gas industry technology. DataDot Technology makes "microdots" for car parts as a security against theft.

Cleantech

Cleantech or "clean" technology goes by different names. Sometimes referred to as "green technology," "green investments," or "alternative energy," the names all apply to efficient energy such as solar, wind power, biofuels industrial technologies, energy efficiency, energy stage, or other renewables. The field also applies to pollution control, recycling, and other "environmentally friendly" developments. According to *Investor's Business Daily*, "In 2008, cleantech VC funding rose 42% from 2007, to $4.6 billion."[26] Despite the market collapse in 2008, a record amount of venture capital was raised for cleantech, with more than $2 billion in funding invested in cleantech start-up companies during the second quarter—a new record that worked well to ease concerns about the overall health of venture capital during the recession.[27] Cleantech continues to attract capital from VCs especially after the federal stimulus bill, with over $12 billion in allocations to "green" cleantech projects.[28]

One of the largest and well-known venture capital firms, Kleiner Perkins Caufield & Byers, is committed to cleantech. Table 6.4 highlights the top-five venture firms committing capital to cleantech. Two of the more visible partners, Vinod Khosla and John Doerr, favor cleantech. Vinod Khosla worked with John Doerr at Kleiner Perkins but went on to form Khosla Ventures. However, both independently invest in cleantech. According to *BusinessWeek*, "Kleiner is the established giant. The firm has raised a total of $5.9 billion since its founding in 1972 and in, addition to Doerr's hits, helped launch America Online and Genentech. Still, the firm is a relative newcomer to green investing. Khosla has been dabbling in such details since he started his outfit in 2004."[29] Khosla recently raised another $275 million for a seed fund to invest primarily in cleantech and information technology.[30]

Table 6.4 2009 Venture Capital Firms Investing in Cleantech

Name	Amount Invested
NGP Energy Technology Partners	$496 million
Nth Power	$420 million
Kleiner Perkins Caufield & Byers	$300 million
Khosla Ventures	$300 million
Draper Fisher Jurvetson	$143 million

Source: Author.

Billions of dollars have flowed into many new technologies stemming from cleantech such as smart grids. Smart grids are electric meters that provide two-way communication. These grids could help consumers determine ideal usage times to avoid peak costs and cut back during peak usage times. The start-up Silver Spring builds smart grids. Silver Spring raised $200 million in 2009.

Algae is another area of focus coming into play with cleantech. Reports Elizabeth Millard: "Algae can be farmed into biofuels, much like other sources. It's expensive to do so, but proponents say the yield is much higher and algae farming doesn't have the water-quality issues that have cropped up around corn-based ethanol production."[31] Despite a banner year in 2008, investing in cleantech slowed during the first half of 2009; however, it came back with strong interest during the second part of the year with $1.9 billion invested over 112 deals during the third quarter (up from $1.2 billion over 85 deals in the second and $836 million over 59 in the first).[32] Solar power proved to be the leading segment of the cleantech sector. Cleantech appears to have a bright future. Deloitte Touche Tohmatsu and the National Venture Capital Association polled 775 venture capital firms in 2009 and came to the conclusion that clean technology will see the biggest increase in venture capital funding over the next three years.[33] Most likely, cleantech will become a whole new industry and a major sector to invest with indexes, mutual funds, and other investment vehicles.

Cardiovascular Disease

Cardiovascular disease is the number-one killer in the United States for both men and women. According to the Centers for Disease Control and Prevention (CDC), "Every 33 seconds, one American dies of some form of heart disease or of stroke." Part of the reason health-care costs are so high in the United States is due to cardiovascular disease, not to mention the billions lost when workers are ill or suddenly die. According to the CDC:

Heart disease and stroke are among the most widespread and costly health problems facing our nation today, yet they are also among the most preventable. Cardiovascular diseases, including heart disease and stroke, are the first and third leading causes of death for both men and women in the United States. They account for more than one-third (35.3%) of all U.S. deaths…more than 1 in 3 (80 million) U.S. adults currently live with one or more types of cardiovascular disease.[34]

The estimated direct and indirect cost for cardiovascular disease in the United States for 2008 is $448.5 billion. Ironically, the U.S. government spends very little on cardiovascular disease despite its widespread complications, the severity of the disease, and the exorbitant costs to the health-care system. The next wave of venture capital appears to be heading toward cardiology and companies devoted to heart attacks. The smart money knows that heart attacks are the number-one killer of both men and women worldwide, and it's getting worse. The *Wall Street Journal* reported in 2009 that "Heart disease is projected to rise by 16% each decade, and deaths from stroke are expected to double from 2000 to 2032."[35]

Despite being in its infancy, more research is being devoted to plaque, which could be deemed as the "next big thing." Plaque is hard to measure and most people are unaware of how much plaque they actually have. Plaque clogs arteries. Plaque can also burst, killing a person instantly. According to Dr. Kevin Williams at Temple University School of Medicine, "Atherosclerosis kills roughly half of individuals living in Western countries and 30% of people worldwide, making it easily the most deadly human disease." Williams's research may be found in *The Journal of Clinical Investigation* 2008; 118:3247–3259.

There are many new companies, both private and public, devoted to cardiovascular disease, which I call "cardiocompanies":

Volcano Corp is a company devoted to plaque and which is now publicly traded. The company has stated that it "sees opportunities in diagnosing and detecting vulnerable plaques."[36]

CardioDX, a diagnostic test developer, run by serial entrepreneur David Levison. CardioDx is Levison's fourth Kleiner Perkins Caufield & Byers–backed company. Levison believes that molecular diagnostics and personalized medicine offer an immense opportunity. His company should reduce health-care costs and is being positioned for an IPO. The market is challenging, but

Levison was successful enough to raise $50 million. Although the lackluster IPO market might dissuade some CEOs, Levison feels that one "needs to see beyond the historical trend" and that the best returns often are "when there are few exits available."

CVRx, a med-tech start-up based in Brooklyn Park, Minnesota, raised $200 million in financing to develop a device to treat high blood pressure, one of the risk factors for cardiovascular disease.

Kardia Health Systems Inc., started in Rochester, Minnesota, raised $15.1 million in venture capital for developing software for cardiology clinics. The software can be accessed online for doctors to review medical records and images remotely.

Resverlogix Corporation raised $25 million for new treatments for plaque reduction and other vascular disorders. The focus of Resverlogix's program is to develop normal small molecules that enhance ApoA-I, which helps build HDL or good cholesterol.[37]

diaDexus, which offers the PLAC Test, which helps identify hidden risk for heart attack and stroke;

Cardiorobotics Inc., which received $11.6 million in a Series A funding led by Eagle Ventures. The company has built several generations of snake robot platforms, which are highly articulated multi-link catheters allowing minimally invasive procedures.

Boston Heart Lab, which makes a diagnostic test for heart disease that was funded by eight angel investment groups; and

CardiAQ Valve Technologies, which raised $6.5 million with Broadview Ventures. Technology is a Transcatheter Mitral Valve Implantation system designed to be an effective alternative to open-chest surgery.

Imricor Medical Systems raised $3 million with a private placement for developing imaging technology.

InfraReDx, Inc. was granted clearance by the FDA to market IVUS Coronary Imaging System, a medical device for cardiologists to help identify plaques linked to heart attacks after a patient is given stents. According to the company, the system is the "first cardiac catheter to combine intravascular ultrasound and near-infrared spectroscopy."

Global Markets

The venture world is becoming far more global and a number of countries are gaining traction, unlike the United States. Presently, the United States has 60% of the world market but is losing ground as China and India gain momentum.

China

According to the Organization for Economic Development, China's spending on research and development surpassed Japan's in 2006, putting it second in the world, behind the United States.[38] *Investor's Business Daily* reported China's growth potential:

> ChiNext, also known as the Growth Enterprise Market of GEM, is a secondary board of the Shenzhen Stock Exchange in southern Guangdong province. Unlike the big government enterprises mostly found on other mainland exchanges, the newly listed firms on ChiNext provide a window into China's entrepreneurial laboratory. … ChiNext is also expected to give a strong boost to China's venture capital and private equity markets. Listed shares in promising start-ups now offer such investors a way to cash out of these investments once they've matured.[39]

ChiNext could be a hotbed of activity. ChiNext raised more than $2 billion from the 28 firms that went public and by the second day of trading, had a combined market value of almost $19 billion.[40] Figure 6.4 was compiled by *Red Herring*, a magazine that focuses on new technologies; hosts conferences for venture capitalists, entrepreneurs, and technologists; and breaks down the global market share, of which China has 8%.

India

Like China, India is making progress with growth companies. Figure 6.5 is a chart by Deloitte expressing the anticipated level of investment in India.

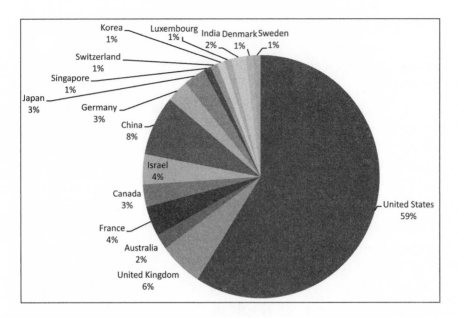

Figure 6.4 2009 Red Herring 100 Global VCs

Source: Red Herring staff, "Top 100 Global Venture Capitalists," *Red Herring* (September 11, 2009),
http://www.redherring.com/home/26206, accessed September 11, 2009.

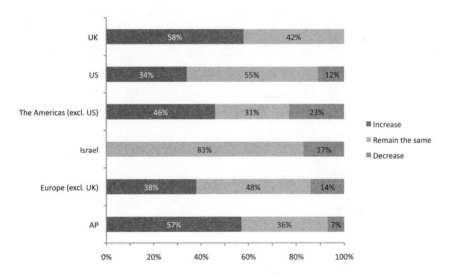

Figure 6.5

Source: Deloitte Touche Tohmatsu, "Weathering the Storm: New Strategies for Global Economic Condition,"
Global Trends in Venture Capital 2009 Global Report 2009, 7. Used with permission.

According to Deloitte, if you have a small venture fund, you tend to have big aspirations for future fundraising. However, if you already have a really big fund, there tends not to be such a need. This concept is highlighted in Figure 6.6.

The venture world is becoming far more global. One of the most dramatic developments over the past 10 years has been the global growth of venture capital to more than $80 billion by 1990. In 1979, venture capital was virtually nonexistent outside the United States. The venture capital market is still dominated by the United States. A 2008 survey by the National Entrepreneurial Assessment for the United States of America concluded that "the United States continues to be at or near the top of the group of innovation-driven economies in terms of early-stage entrepreneurial activities."[41] However, new entrants are gaining market share.

Investors in Venture Capital

Sting has a song called "Murder by Numbers." The same philosophy of the song title can be applied to venture capital. Institutions have far more money than individuals, but when you pool or aggregate the individual investors, the numbers are quite large and meaningful.

The typical high-net-worth investor became interested in alternatives in the late 1990s. Private equity was an area many found to be intriguing and in fact was the leading response in a poll conducted by *Ticker*, in which participants were asked which area they wanted to learn more about (Table 6.5).

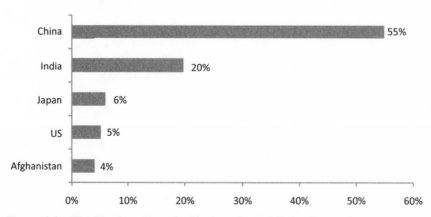

Figure 6.6   Top Five Locations for Venture Capital Going Forward

Source: Deloitte Touche Tohmatsu, "Global Trends in Venture Capital," 2009 Global Report.

Table 6.5   What Do HNWs Want?

Percentage of high net worth investors very interested in learning more about certain products

Private equity	45.10%	U.S. taxable bonds	8.2
Annuities	33.9	U.S. equity	8
Wrap accounts	30.1	U.S. municipal bonds	7.8
Hedge funds	28	Life insurance	6.7
Funds of funds	26.7	Int'l equity (developed countries)	6.4
Collectibles	23.7	Int'l bonds (developed countries)	6.4
Offshore accounts/companies	21.2	Int'l equity (emerging markets)	4.4
Derivatives	14	Int'l bonds (emerging markets)	4.2
Precious metals	12.2	Custody accounts	0.6
Real estate	11.1	Money market accounts	0

HNWs, high net worths.

Source: Jackie Day Packet, "High Life," *Ticker*, March 1998, 37.

Pensions are large players in the venture world. Pension funds have the ability to put billions into an asset class. Table 6.6 lists funds among the top 200 with defined benefit assets in venture capital from *Pensions & Investments*:

Table 6.6   Funds Among the Top 200 with DB Assets in Venture Capital

Assets in millions as of Sept. 30, 2008	
Fund	Assets
California Public Employees	$2,609
New York State Common	$1,848
Pennsylvania Employees	$1,538
Verizon	$1,423
California State Teachers	$1,324
Washington State Board	$1,295
Colorado Employees	$1,160
Michigan Retirement	$958
Massachusetts PRIM	$901
New York State Teachers	$842
Ohio State Teachers	$819
Total	$14,717

Source: Pensions and Investments, January 26, 2009.

Table 6.7 Venture Investors: Past and Present

Former Venture		Current Venture
1. Pension funds		1. Pension funds
2. Foundations		2. Foundations
3. University endowments		3. University endowments
4. Angel investors	⟶	4. Angel investors
		5. Foreign investors
		6. Corporations
		7. State-back venture funds
		8. Entrepreneurs/mentors
		9. Government (CIA)

Source: Author.

Besides venture funds, there are a growing and evolving number of new investors in venture capital, detailed in Table 6.7.

Private Versus Public Markets

The market is vast when it comes to private companies. In 1997, there were approximately 71,118 domestic companies with revenues of $10 million or more. Only 5,846 or 8.2% were public.[42] Private companies far exceed public companies. In 2003, there were 124,568 companies with revenues between $10 million and $15 million. Another 32,040 have revenue greater than $50 million. With the epic downturn in the market in 2008–2009, thousands of new companies will emerge.

Wave Riders

Finding great companies to invest in is neither an art nor a science. It takes a little from each. When it comes to identifying good companies, some skills can be learned, whereas others are innate. Ideally, an investor in venture capital (if it is a company and not a fund) is betting on two things: the company and the CEO. Envision placing a wager on a surfer and his surfboard during a surfing contest. The more you know about the surfer and his/her board, the better off you will be. Financials in the venture world can be completely and utterly unreliable. Pixar and Netscape are two classic examples in which the entrepreneurs made a world of difference despite the balance sheets, as detailed in *BusinessWeek*:

> Pixar Animation Studios, the computer animation company controlled by Steven P. Jobs, was initially to be priced at $12 to $14 a share. Demand was so strong that it went public on Nov. 29 at $22 and closed at $39. Jobs's 80% stake at the end of day one: $1.1 billion. Netscape Communications Corp., a maker of software for navigating the Internet, went public at $28 a share last August. Its stock price was up to $171 on Dec. 5, making Chairman James H. Clark a Netscape billionaire.[43]

Jobs and Clark know how to surf the alternative waves.

Contrarian View

Like many alternatives, the best time to invest in venture capital appears to be when the equity market is at its worst. Valuations are low, and many new companies are formed by entrepreneurs. According to Ernst & Young in 2009, "The firms that managed to close their most recent funds in the last 6–18 months will likely see the best opportunities in years to come since valuations have come way down and entrepreneurs are forced to build their ventures in a capital-efficient manner."[44] It is possible to locate a diamond in the rough like Google. Good companies can raise money in any environment. Google did well after the tech bubble burst and the market was horrible over 3 years (2000–2002).

Google might have grabbed a lot of attention, but there are plenty of smaller companies that rode out the storm, perhaps some that many investors have never heard about, such as Digital River. When I met the CEO of Digital River, years before the S–1 was filed, the company was very small and was not even called Digital River. People I know invested in the company when it was private. Hypothetically, if an investor purchased shares of the company when it was private, the December 1996 income statement looked terrifying, with $111,000 in sales and $689,000 in net losses. When financials are too early to judge, one is left with the CEO, the technology, and projected sales, cash flows, and/or earnings. When there are little to no financials to examine, a numerical projection or pro forma financial statement is used to render a decision of whether to invest. Justin Camp, author of *Venture Capital Due Diligence*, describes the decision-making process this way:

> Pro forma financial statements are of critical importance to venture capitalists. The projections in such statements constitute one of the fundamental bases on which venture capitalists make their investment decisions. Pro forma financial statements provide venture capitalists with black-and-white pictures of companies' business models and of what those models might look like over subsequent years.[45]

Investors who took the time to understand the business model and to get to know the CEO of Digital River, Joel Ronning, were well rewarded. Joel is a first-class CEO. By December 2008, revenue was $394 million with $63 million net income. The stock performed well during two market crashes, one of which was technology related. The financials for Digital River from December 1996 to 2008 are detailed in Table 6.8.

Finding great private companies requires time and effort. Numbers are important but they should not be the sole criteria. Otherwise, one could miss the next Digital River.

Exit Strategies

Investing in venture capital has two primary exits: mergers and acquisitions and IPOs. Today, however, there is a third area developing that might make it more difficult for individual investors to participate in private equity or venture capital unless they have $100 million to invest. The third leg of the stool is Rule 144A securities. Unlike IPOs, Rule 144A equity

Table 6.8 Digital River Income Statement Over Time (in Millions USD)

	Dec–96	Dec–97	Jun–98*		Dec–05	Dec–06	Dec–07	Dec–08
Sales	0.111	2.472	5.746	→	220.41	307.63	349.27	394.23
Net Income	−0.689	−3.485	−5.523		66.42	67.60	73.91	71.57

*August 1998 initial public offering.

Source: Author.

offerings are pre-IPO (PIPO) and not subject to Sarbanes-Oxley rules. According to a *Forbes* article, "In the two years before Sarbox went live in 2002, there were only two PIPO deals. Since then there have been 83, raising an average $282 million."[46] Rule 144A might be defined as follows:

> Rule 144A, adopted by the SEC in 1990, permits companies to issue their securities without registration provided that all the purchasers are "qualified institutional buyers," i.e., sophisticated institutional investors such as hedge funds, insurance companies investment companies, and investment advisors with at least $100 million under management.[47]

What exactly is the reason for this explosive growth? The Committee on Capital Markets Regulation, an independent and nonpartisan research organization dedicated to improving the regulation of U.S. capital markets, completed a survey on February 13, 2009. The survey was directed to legal counsel representing a number of the largest Rule 144A offerings in 2007. They revealed five reasons for this growth: "more developed home markets and increased liquidity outside the U.S.; the burdens imposed by the Sarbanes-Oxley Act; the risk of securities class actions; compliance with US GAAP; and liquidity of Rule 144A market."[48] Rule 144A has evolved from convertible debt offerings to companies trying to raise money but not file for an IPO.[49]

One of the most visible Rule 144A equity offerings was for Oaktree Capital Management:

> In a groundbreaking deal closed in May 2007, Oaktree Capital Management LLC, a leading private U.S. hedge fund advisory firm, sold a 15 percent equity stake in itself for $880 million. The deal is groundbreaking because it was not structured as an initial public offering (IPO), traditionally the only option for an equity offering of this size by a private company. Instead, it was structured as a private placement under Rule 144A of the Securities Act of 1933, which enables a company to market and sell securities through an underwriter to institutional investors without registering the offering with the Securities and Exchange Commission.[50]

Using Rule 144A basically enabled Oaktree Capital Management not to have to comply with the regulatory requirements typically found with an IPO because the platform is designed for investors with assets greater than $100 million, it will exclude quite a few investors.[51]

Essentially, there are now two primary exchanges:

- **Portal Alliance.** In September 2009, NASDAQ OMX and nine banks formed the Portal Alliance. The Portal Alliance is a group of private exchanges that work together to trade offerings by both United States and foreign-based companies. Originally, NASDAQ OMX and the banks announced the exchange in 2007 but put it on hold. The Portal Alliance consists of various broker-dealers (BofA Merrill Lynch, Citi, Credit Suisse, Deutsche Bank, J.P. Morgan, Morgan Stanley, UBS, and Wells Fargo) trading restricted stock as well as a trading platform, Goldman Sachs's GS TRuE.[52] The NASDAQ Web site describes the Portal Alliance as "an open, industry-wide platform to facilitate over the counter trading of 144A equity securities."[53] According to *Investor's Business Daily*, "NASDAQ OMX, investment banks, venture capital firms and foreign companies are all zeroing in on the 144A market, in which private placements of company shares are sold mainly to institutional investors."[54]

- **SecondMarket (formerly Registered Stock Partners).** Launched in 2004 by Barry Silbert, SecondMarket is a brokerage that runs a platform for alternative asset classes. The pool of illiquid-asset buyers is limited to people with a minimum net worth of $1 million and to institutions managing $100 million or more. Among secondary-market players, SecondMarket serves as the intermediary for the broadest range of illiquid assets, from auction-rate securities to limited partnerships to private-company stock. Facebook and Tesla Motors are two companies that trade on the exchange. *Investor's Business Daily* interviewed Eleazer Klein, a partner at the law firm Schulte Roth & Zabel, who characterized the value of SecondMarket, saying "VCs and private equity firms today are looking at nontraditional ways to monetize the positions that they have and find liquidity."[55] SecondMarket holds auctions among investors using a 3,500-member database. SecondMarket is a broker-dealer but does not take positions in any transactions. They charge from 2% to 4% of the sales price.

The development of exchanges to help investors to buy and sell private placements or investments in companies that are not traded on a public exchange is monumental. Typically, an investors would have limited exit strategies and a long period to wait. The private exchanges have the potential of becoming quite large and game changing for venture capital.

Venture Fund Size and Shape

In the past, venture funds normally covered a much broader, diversified array of portfolio companies. A fund could have companies dispersed geographically or be in multiple sectors. Today, many have a niche like health care or technology. Some invest in early-stage and others in later-stage companies. Some venture firms invest for the short run, whereas others invest for the long run. Operationally, venture firms have needed to become far more focused. It's a bigger industry with a lot more competition, so you have to specialize. Still funds expand with size, as illustrated in Figure 6.7:

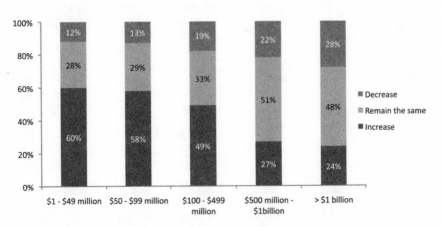

Figure 6.7 Projected Fund Size Compared to Current Fund (by Assets Under Management)

Source: Deloitte Touche Tohmatsu, "Weathering the Storm: New Strategies for Global Economic Condition," *Global Trends in Venture Capital 2009 Global Report 2009,* 12. Used with permission.

But the desire to have a large fund is not just a domestic issue. Other areas around the world appear to have a greater desire for bigger venture funds. Fees might play a role in the desire to have many large funds. One should always ask what the goal is and the type of opportunity the venture firm is seeking. Venture funds all have a good idea of how they want to invest the money.

Venture-Backed IPOs

Table 6.9 shows that from 1980 to 2009, there were 7,456 IPOs. From 1980 to 1989, there were 2,065 IPOs. By way of comparison since Sarbanes-Oxley (2001–2008), there have been only 920 IPOs, a dramatic drop. Besides Sarbanes-Oxley, Glass-Steagall changed Wall Street forever when Bankers Trust was allowed to acquire Alex. Brown.

Table 6.9 Percentage of Initial Public Offerings with VC Backing

Year	# IPOs	# VC-backed IPOs	% VC-backed IPOs	Year	# IPOs	# VC-backed IPOs	% VC-backed IPOs
1980	73	24	33%	1998	284	73	26%
1981	197	56	28%	1999	477	267	56%
1982	80	21	26%	2000	381	239	63%
1983	449	115	26%	2001	79	29	37%
1984	178	45	25%	2002	66	14	21%
1985	185	38	21%	2003	62	24	39%
1986	397	78	20%	2004	174	78	45%
1987	291	69	24%	2005	160	45	28%
1988	102	33	32%	2006	157	53	34%
1989	113	40	35%	2007	160	65	41%
1990	110	44	40%	2008	21	9	43%
1991	287	111	39%	2009	41	12	29%
1992	412	139	34%	1980–89	2,065	519	25%
1993	509	172	34%	1990–94	1,722	598	35%
1994	404	132	33%	1995–98	1,891	641	34%
1995	458	183	40%	1999–00	858	506	59%
1996	675	259	38%	2001–09	920	329	36%
1997	474	126	27%	1980–09	7,456	2593	35%

Source: Jay R. Ritter, Cordell Professor of Finance, University of Florida, "Some Factoids about the 2008 IPO Market," research report, July 27, 2009, 6.

Table 6.10 is a *Forbes* review of the biggest underwriters. Out of ten underwriters for IPOs, only two exist today (Morgan Stanley and Goldman Sachs). Goldman Sachs and Morgan Stanley become bank holding companies. Lehman went bankrupt.

H&Q, Alex. Brown, Montgomery, and Robertson Stephens were four underwriters known as the "Four Horsemen" that catered to small- to medium-sized companies going public. The four underwriters served a viable purpose in that they created supply and fed demand. Big banks seldom want to swim downstream and take a small company public, which is why a number of small to mid-sized investment banks are prospering today: Oppenheimer, R.W. Baird, Stifel, Jefferies, Cowen, Raymond James, Janney, and others.

Prolonged reduction in IPOs or new companies being created in the United States will have dire consequences if not addressed sooner than later. Murray Beach, managing director at TM Capital, appraised the situation:

The long term implications of the reduced number of IPOs are significant. The lack of funding options for the fastest growing companies points to a chronic weakness in the capital formation process in

Table 6.10 The Biggest Underwriters: 1996

| Underwriter | Number of Issues | % of Issues That | | Cumulative Performance | | |
		Went Up	Beat the Market	Actual (%)	Rel to S&P 500 (%)	Total Offer Value ($mil)
Goldman Sachs	159	76	55	196	169	$25,287
Morgan Stanley	147	71	59	229	205	15,949
Merrill Lynch	172	65	42	94	115	15,066
Smith Barney	122	69	52	76	123	8,775
Donald Lufkin Jenrette	109	60	44	57	109	8,706
CS First Boston	95	64	48	65	110	7,793
Salomon Brothers	66	61	41	94	121	7,339
Alex Brown & Sons	217	70	54	219	188	7,004
Lehman Brothers	78	68	49	98	144	5,996
Robertson Stephens	121	67	52	121	141	4,080

Source: Linda R. Killian, "The New Game in New Issues," *Forbes*, June 17, 1996.

the United States relative to its past history as well as to the rest of the world. Whereas the U.S. market has seen a sharp decline in IPOs the European and Asian markets have seen precisely the opposite trend, with IPOs in the UK, India and China setting records in both number and amount of capital being raised. The access to inexpensive capital is fundamental to economic growth, innovation, and high quality job formation. In the new global economy with hyper-competition in so many industries and markets, the need for capital is critical to best position U.S. businesses for the next decade. Losing its historic advantage in the capital formation process is a strategic mistake for the United States.[56]

According to Dealogic, issues on the Hong Kong/Mainland Exchanges raised $52 billion compared with only $26.5 billion in IPOs in the United States. Because larger deals bring more banking fees, it is unlikely that large banks will want to focus on small IPOs in the future. While Goldman Sachs focuses on large-cap IPOs, it did take a small company, Synchronoss Technologies, public in 2006. Synchronoss ended up being one of the hottest IPOs of the year. There will be exceptions, but small IPOs will most likely not be an area of focus for big banks. Middle market investment firms, on the other hand, will likely have the best IPOs going forward because it is an area of focus and can be profitable for them.

Five Venture Deals and the Entrepreneurs Behind Them

1. **Twitter.** Twitter is a free communication site launched in 2006 by Biz Stone, Evan Williams, and Jack Dorsey. Twitter allows users to post brief updates called "tweets." The social networking space has mushroomed in recent years. Aside from the growing number of social networking sites—including Twitter, LinkedIn, Facebook, and MySpace—the number of users on each of these services has been growing quickly. The *Economist* reported the following regarding registered participants in mid–2009: "Facebook, one of the biggest networks along with News Corporation's MySpace, has seen membership

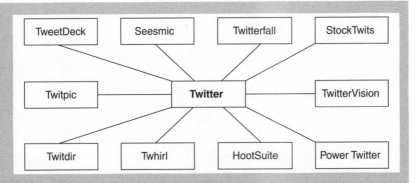

Figure 6.8

Source: Author.

leap from 100m in August 2008 to some 250m today."[57] Twitter, the youngest of these services, already has about 23 million users. The company raised $35 million in February and then $100 million in September. Twitter is growing the fastest. According to *Financial Advisor Magazine*, citing Nielsen.com: "Twitter is growing more than five times as fast as the second-fastest growing social networking site. … In February 2009, Twitter had a user growth rate of 1,382%, while Zimbio had growth of 240%, followed by Facebook with growth of 228%.[58] Many new innovative companies are being started that revolve around Twitter, detailed in Figure 6.8.

2. **Avid.** Avid is a molecular-imaging company. A recent profile described Avid's proprietary targeting agents as being able to "allow radiologists to image amyloid plaques, and the company is currently testing these compounds in clinical trials for the detection of Alzheimer's disease…. Avid's pipeline of imaging compounds has the potential to dramatically alter the clinical course of Alzheimer's disease, dementia, Parkinson's disease, and diabetes."[59] The company's CEO and president, Daniel Skovronsky, MD, PhD, established Avid as a spin-out from his graduate school, the University of Pennsylvania. Skovronsky began his work on the project in 1999, while he was still a student, then moved to the Science Center in 2005. Skovronsky knows how to ride waves and raised venture capital despite market uncertainties. At the time Skovronsky was raising

money, he felt the future was quite uncertain. Nevertheless, his company was doing well, and he raised $34.5 million in a Series D financing on May 21, 2009, arguably one of the toughest times ever to raise money for a private company. As Skovronsky related to the author, "Business cycles come and go." Because the valuation of his company was flat and he considered it a bargain, Skovronsky invested some of his own money in the deal. He had skin in the game. As he describes it, "Flat is the new up 40%" (meaning that ordinarily it would be an up round, but due to market conditions, the round was flat). Existing investors put more money in as well, which is always a good sign for a company raising money.

3. **Tengion Inc.** Tengion was founded by Dr. Steven Nichtberger in 2003. The *Philadelphia Business Journal* called it "a platform for regenerative medicine that truly changes lives by creating neo-organs and tissues for patients in need of transplants."[60] In 2006, the company began its first phase II clinical trial for FDA approval of a bladder neo-organ, targeted specifically for children with spina bifida. Since its founding, Tengion has raised $123 million from private investors in addition to funding from institutional investors, including Bain Capital, Johnson & Johnson Development Corp., Deerfield Partners, Quaker BioVentures, Oak Investment Partners, HealthCap, and L Capital Partners. As the IPO market reached an historical low, Nichtberger followed Wave Theory and filed an S–1 to go public.

4. **Groupon.** One of the fastest growing Internet companies, Groupon, was a simple but brilliant idea for a Chicago based start-up. Andrew Mason, who started this company with the help of angel Eric Lefkofsky (InnerWorkings), grew the company to have 15 million subscribers in 30 countries. Groupon combines the word "group" with "coupon" and offers online customers various services or products at steep discounts. The catch is that there is a time limit, and a certain number of customers must buy the same item on the same day. Groupon will sell anything from tickets to the King Tut exhibit in New York's Time Square to the Gap which had an $11 million day.

Though a music major from Northwestern, Mason learned computer code and persuaded Lefkofsky to invest $1 million as an angel investor in his concept. His idea caught on like lightening. Groupon received $135 million in venture capital in April, 2010 to make acquisitions of competitors, from a number of investors including NEA and the Moscow investment fund Digital Sky Technologies.

5. **Energy Recovery Inc.** Energy Recovery Inc. (ERI) is a cleantech company started in 1992 by Leif Huage, an inventor. Huage's invention that served as the foundation of ERI's clean technology was inspired by his brother's Norwegian farm. The brothers wanted to pump water from an adjacent fjord up about 100 feet to circulate around vegetable storage areas to keep the produce cool. However, Huage realized that it takes a lot of energy to pump water up 100 feet, which is wasted when it runs back down. He discovered that the "energy can be recovered in a pressure exchanger,"[61] a device he later marketed to desalination plants through his start-up ERI. Huage knows how to ride the venture capital waves.

Chapter 7

Private Equity: Venture Capital Advantages and Disadvantages

In the previous chapters, we detailed the history and dynamics that make venture capital a viable sector of the alternatives market. Now we will maneuver the discussion toward providing investors with what they will need to both understand and surf the waves ahead.

Advantages

In surfing venture capital waves, here are ten compelling advantages for investors:

1. Unique Investment Opportunities

The emerging nanotechnology, cleantech, and cardiovascular trends discussed in the previous chapter capture the essence of the unique opportunities venture capital investment has to offer. As discussed, venture capital firms' investments in cleantech have increased dramatically. Cleantech companies are likely to become a vast new industry like the railroads or the market (see Figure 7.1). John Cassidy, author of *dot.com: The Greatest Story Ever Told*, puts these types of waves in a familiar perspective, focusing on the Internet and comparing it with the American gold rush of the nineteenth century. "The discovery of gold on the Internet can be dated, with some precision, to

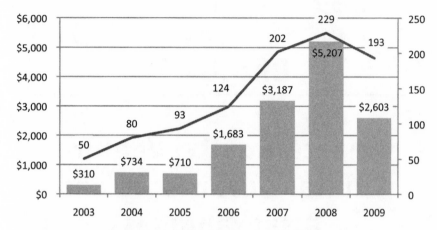

Figure 7.1   Cleantech Venture Capital Investments United States

Source: Ernst & Young, "Cleantech Investment and Trends," 4Q'09 Venture Insights, Dow Jones Venture
Source, 12.

August 1995, when Netscape, the maker of Netscape Navigator Web browser, held its initial public offering (IPO). Like the strike in the Sierra Nevada, the Netscape IPO attracted a host of prospectors..."[1] Cleantech, cardiovascular, or all three areas might very well be the next gold rush.

2. Distributions

Funds or individual companies will make distribution in cash, as seen in Table 7.1, which shows a sample venture fund schedule of distributions since inception through June 30, 2009. Investors like receiving periodic payments. Unlike a bond, venture capital payments vary in amount and are unpredictable.

3. Vintage Year

Vintage year can be the most important determinant of private equity returns as evidenced during the 1975–2005 period where the best vintage years have tended to be those in which funds were able to invest in the immediate aftermath of a capital markets dislocation.[2] Similar to wine, venture capital has its vintage years. Every year will not be a banner year, and vintage years frequently occur after very bad periods, which is why one might hear of either a bad or good year for wine such as a Bordeaux. Each year wine writers head to Cercle Rive Droite to taste new wines such as the

Table 7.1   Sample Schedule of Distributions

	Date of Distribution	Total Amount ($)	Per $1 Million Investor $
Initial distribution (final close)	22-Aug-01	448,125.00	2,508
Second distribution	10-Jun-02	2,714,545.00	15,367
Third distribution	15-Apr-03	3,646,404.00	20,642
Fourth distribution	22-Dec-03	8,878,635.00	50,525
Fifth distribution	27-Jan-05	10,263,779.00	58,102
Sixth distribution	30-Nov-05	8,000,000.00	45,287
Seventh distribution	10-Apr-06	8,000,000.00	45,545
Eighth distribution	14-Aug-06	4,000,000.00	22,773
Ninth distribution	22-Dec-06	5,973,081.00	33,809
Tenth distribution	19-Mar-07	11,993,800.00	67,896
Eleventh distribution	17-Jul-07	14,018,723.00	79,358
Twelfth distribution	03-Dec-07	6,500,000.00	36,796
Thirteenth distribution	18-Mar-08	7,461,426.00	42,238
Fourteenth distribution	30-Jan-09	4,282,346.00	24,242
Total amount distributed as of June 30, 2009:		96,175,864.00	545,085
Percentage of total commitment distributed:		61.80%	61.80%

Source: Author.

2009 Bordeaux en primeur. En primeur or "wine futures" is a way to purchase wine while a vintage is still in a barrel. Some vintages are better than others. The best venture capital firms are adept at selecting vintage years, which enables them to raise money even in troublesome markets:

> The newcomers raised just $20.3 billion in total capital down 65% from $58.2 billion in all of 2008, according to Preqin. David Sze, a general partner at Greylock Partners, says the San Mateo, Calif., firm allotted more time than usual to fund raising because of the uncertain market, but ended up raising money for a new $575 million fund in four to six weeks.[3]

4. Professional Management

By selecting a venture fund, one can hire a top-quartile venture professional who is experienced negotiating valuations that your typical investor might not be able to negotiate for themselves. Venture firms also have the expertise to ferret out the best deals.

5. High-Compound Annual Growth Rates over Long Periods

There are times when venture capital does not do well, such as investing at the peak of a bull market. However, venture capital annual growth rates (both in nominal and real returns) tends to outpace publicly traded equity over longer periods of time covering multiple market cycles. As a market recovers, investments in venture capital can even lead to substantial outperformance.

6. Low Correlation

Venture capital has a low correlation of returns with other asset classes. Part of the reason for this low correlation is that venture capital is private and not public. The *Wall Street Journal* article detailed the benefits of low correlation by reporting that "a strength of venture capital is that its investments are held for many years, so the valuations are not as important on a short term basis with returns being realized only when assets in the portfolio are sold or go out of business."[4]

Venture funds invest in unique and often first-of-a-kind or new areas that are not publicly traded. The largest and most well-known microbrewery, Sam Adams (Boston Beer Company), accepted venture capital. Even after the Boston Beer Company went public, it was different from the other beer companies in that it was the only microbrewery.

7. Access to Pre-IPO Companies

Good IPOs are difficult to get unless you know someone or are extremely wealthy. Investing in venture capital not only gives one access to the IPO market when the company files to go public, but it is financially rewarding; the valuation and share price will most likely be lower before the IPO. If the private company performs well, the IPO shares are often set at a higher price.

8. Lower Fees and/or Carried Interest

The management fee is the carried interest for a fund. Carried interest is derived from profits taken when a venture-backed company is sold or taken public. Fees on carried interest range from 20% to 30%.

Venture firms are becoming more competitive with carried interest. Battery Ventures, for example, lowered their carried interest in 2009. Battery Ventures is incorporating a performance hurdle into their new $750 million venture capital fund, which will charge a carried-interest fee of 20% (down from the previous 25%) until it returns three times its capital, whereby, the fee will climb to 30%.[5] Venture funds can be very expensive but typically offer lower expenses in bad markets, enabling attractive or far better terms than normal. Fees vary but usually are around 2%. Greylock Partners recently offered investors the ability to approve a yearly budget instead of paying a 2% fee. Draper Fisher Jurvetson, which backed hits such as Skype and Hotmail, sent a letter to prospective investors that said the firms would charge a premium carried-interest fee only if their new $400 million fund met certain performance targets.[6]

9. Access

A top-tier venture fund will see deal flow that an ordinary investor will not see. If a technology company needs venture funding, they will turn to the best possible venture firm they can find. The venture capitalists who took Google public see a huge number of business plans. Your typical investor will never see such volume nor have the opportunity to see the best companies.

10. Performance

Depending on the investment(s) as well as the vehicle used, venture capital has the potential for huge returns. The upside is virtually unlimited.

Disadvantages

Here are some of the disadvantages to investing in venture capital:

1. Illiquidity

Financial venture capital waves are difficult to measure and explore because one is dealing with private companies and the information is not readily available. Venture capital is not as easy to invest in as a large growth mutual fund; you are dealing with private companies, not public ones.

2. Timing Is Difficult

A number of venture firms put money into companies at the peak of the market before the tech market blew up. Perhaps they will learn from their mistakes. The market was low but not at the bottom. Some venture capital firms invested heavily but the market was not at its low. The market corrected for two more years.

It is impossible to time when you will find a great company or idea, nor can you even tell if you will be able to invest in one if you ultimately find one. Wave Theory is based on trying to find the best possible time to invest. If a venture capital firm, high-net-worth individual, or institution were going to invest after the tech correction, they should examine where the venture capital waves and the broad market are at the time. Venture capital waves are difficult to measure and explore because you are dealing with private companies, and the information is not readily available. Even professionals can make mistakes.

3. Unfair Advantages

To an extent, both entrepreneurs and venture firms have the upper hand over an individual investor. Hypothetically, if an individual investor invests $100,000 in a $20 million round for a private company versus a venture firm that takes half the round and puts in $10 million, the individual will not have much say in anything. The individual will most likely not be given a board seat and will be more or less a passive investor.

Like any industry, nothing is perfect. That is, not all venture capital firms act in the best interest of their investors. Venture capitalists look out for their investments, and they do everything they can to protect them. Based on today's legal system, it is costly should a dispute rise. A venture firm might shut down a company, wipe out your investment, and then move the assets to another company they own, sell it, and make money while you have already been wiped out. Unfair? Yes. Real world? Yes. Sad? Yes.

For instance, a number of investors felt mistreated by S.R. One. A report on the troubles surrounding the company recalled the following events:

> The venture-capital arm of British pharmaceutical giant Glaxo-SmithKline PLC has been sued by 21 investors who claim it cheated

them out of their stake in Herndon, Va., software company Clareos. The lawsuit, which was filed Feb. 9 in U.S. District Court in Alexandria, Va., accuses S.R. One Ltd. of West Conshohocken of defrauding 21 investors in Clareos Inc. It seeks at least $400 million from S.R. One—$100 million in compensatory damages and $300 million in punitive damages.[7]

If you do not know the other investors (like those who knew each other in Clareos), one could file his or her own lawsuit, but it is not very cost-effective. The venture capital firm might have $20+ million at stake and will commit more than you can in legal fees. If the investor put in $100,000, he or she could fly through legal fees and spend far more than the original investment.

Just like one can encounter a disreputable venture firm, one can find a bad CEO. Charles Goodyear admonished those who merely sought to make money rather than grow a company:

Life should not be estimated exclusively by the standard of dollars and cents.... I am not disposed to complain that I have planted and others have gathered the fruits. A man has cause for regret when he sows and no one reaps.[8]

Have there ever been any CEOs that went to jail? Yes. Enron. Worldcom. Adelphia. Tyco. There are hundreds of cases involving CEOs of publicly traded companies in which there was wrongdoing. Are all CEOs of publicly traded companies morally bankrupt? Absolutely not. There are 10,000+ honest, hardworking CEOs, but that does not mean it cannot happen. A few bad apples can spoil the whole bunch. Risk will increase with an investment in a small, privately held company because private companies are not regulated like publicly traded companies. Most entrepreneurs are honest and hardworking, but not all of them.

What happens if a dispute arises with an entrepreneur running a private company you invested in? One would refer to the huge pile of legal documents you signed, such as an investor's agreement. Justin Kline, a securities lawyer and senior partner at Ballard Spahr, told the author, "If you are not a securities lawyer, odds are you might not know what you are signing." Blindly signing these documents would be about the same as surfing naked without sunscreen at a crowded resort. Protect your investment and have a good attorney who knows security law. In the passage below, the *Boston Business Journal* describes exactly what can go wrong with a poorly worded agreement:

> Venture capitalists investing in later rounds will often require changes to the terms of the preferred stock issued in earlier rounds. Typically, the preferred stock issued in the earlier rounds is protected by provisions requiring the company to obtain the consent of the holders of a requisite percentage of such stock before any changes are made to the terms of the stock. Poorly drafted protective provisions can be insufficient to preclude change to an existing preferred stockholder's essential economic, voting and other rights.[9]

If an investor disagrees with something the entrepreneur did, he or she can take legal action. According to author Karl Vesper, "Some ventures are legally frauds, whereas others may be more morally than prosecutably fraudulent."[10] However, there is a huge disadvantage to the investor. In essence, the investor is spending money to protect his/her rights via legal fees. Ironically, you are also paying the legal fees of the entrepreneur because you invested your money in the company. The entrepreneur will not be using his/her own money. He or she will be taking it from the company that you invested in. Ever shoot yourself in the foot? You do not get very far. The vast majority of venture capitalists and entrepreneurs fly straight, but not all of them.

4. Capital Calls/Additional Rounds

If you elected to invest in either a venture fund or a single company, there will most likely be capital calls. Few funds take all the money up front today. As the venture fund identifies new opportunities, they will call on their investors to put more money into the fund (draw down). Because these calls are random and over long periods (years), it can be burdensome to an investor. Should the investor (for whatever reason) decide not to invest, there are normally severe penalties. For example, if a client commits $1 million, there will be an initial call and subsequent ones of varying amounts over time. Table 7.2 displays a sample schedule of capital calls with calls since inception through June 30, 2009:

Table 7.2 Sample Schedule of Capital Calls

	Date of Call	Total Amount ($)	Per $1 Million Investor $
Initial capital call (final close)	01-Feb-01	52,995,000.00	300,000
Second capital call	22-Aug-01	17,665,000.00	100,000
Third capital call	10-Jun-02	17,665,000.00	100,000
Fourth capital call	15-Apr-03	17,665,000.00	100,000
Fifth capital call	22-Dec-03	6,427,232.00	36,384
Sixth capital call	28-May-04	8,516,083.00	48,209
Seventh capital call	27-Aug-04	8,516,083.00	48,209
Eighth capital call	27-Jan-05	5,204,851.00	29,464
Ninth capital call	30-Nov-05	15,669,592.00	88,704
Tenth capital call	22-Dec-06	2,938,749.00	16,636
Eleventh capital call	19-Mar-07	1,477,147.00	8,362
Twelfth capital call	17-Jul-07	988,887.00	5,598
Total amount called as of June 30, 2009:		155,728,624.00	881,566
Percentage of total commitment called:		91.40%	91.40%

Source: Author.

If an investor puts money into a single company as opposed to a fund, there is a distinct possibility that the company will need more money and require future capital. The investor can choose to participate and maintain his/her pro rata share. If he/she declines, he/she will be diluted (depending on valuation and series or number of rounds) and own less of the company because new investors are buying more shares.

5. Down Rounds

What happens when you miss the wave for venture capital? If one throws money into a private company or venture fund without paying attention to the wave, he or she could be investing at a bad time or an all-time high. According to *Business 2.0*, "Some Silicon Valley VCs estimate that as many as 80% of all financings in 2001 were down rounds, meaning that the VCs had slashed their estimate of a company's value since its previous funding round."[11] What happens to your money? The funds you invested in a company or companies (if it is a fund) will be worth less, similar to a publicly traded company declining in value. For example, if a publicly traded medical device company is worth less since its stock price dropped in a market downturn, a comparable private medical device company will likewise have a lower valuation. Private shares are frequently valued less than public shares because of illiquidity. The value might actually even be less than public comparables.

Private companies will also require more money to grow over time. Raising more money is not necessarily a bad thing. Racing cars need fuel. If your company raises a subsequent round of financing (after your initial investment), the company will ask you to invest more money in this down round (a round of financing done at a lower valuation than the last round). If one is given a pro rata share of company ownership, he or she can maintain ownership. However, the decision is immensely tricky. Envision putting a $100,000 into a start-up or early-stage private company. The market turns on you. What looked like a brilliant idea now looks like a grotesque nightmare you cannot escape.

Back in 1999, the tech bubble was on fire. Hundreds of Internet companies were going public. When the bubble burst, 800 to 900 Internet companies went bankrupt. The ones that did not, struggled like the passengers who scrambled after life preservers as the *Titanic* sank. Unless a company raised a lot of cash (to get through the storm), it needed to raise more funds. Your investment in the last round has a fair market value (according to the new round being raised) of $20,000. Essentially, your $100,000 investment lost $80,000. You are given the chance (according to a several-inch-high legal packet sent to you by the company's attorneys, which, incidentally, you paid for) to invest more money.

The amount one can invest will depend on what you put in the last round. An investor will be given a chance to invest a pro rata amount. Hypothetically, you might be given the opportunity to invest $10,000 (a pro rata amount), but the valuation of the company is now far less. If you elect to invest, you will own more illiquid shares of the company but at a lower valuation. Instead of investing $100,000, your new, combined total investment is now $110,000. You own two different baskets of stock, one higher valuation and one lower. The company will need to do really well going forward to make a return. However, if it does not, you will lose all or part of your money. Only once can I recall breaking even. Venture capital is normally two directional: up or down. The decision to put more money into a down round is extremely complex. If you decide not to invest in maintaining your pro rata share, your investment will be worth a lot less because other investors (who came in after you) are buying company shares at a much more attractive valuation than you and will own a lot more of the company.

Another complication might arise and that is that the company might need more than one financing round. In other words, a company can have multiple rounds of financing (e.g., Series A, Series B, Series C, Series D). I invested in a private company in 1999. It is now 2009. Godot might show up before I actually get any money out of the deal. The company had numerous management changes and went through two market declines. I invested in some rounds and passed on others. To date, the company is still struggling to grow. My investment remains illiquid and the CEO refuses to give any inkling as to valuation or exit strategy. Given the history, I am waiting for another opportunity to invest in another down round by the same company. Down rounds are problematic.

6. Exit Strategy

Venture capital is fast paced, and there never is a dull moment. One of the areas within venture capital that changes is how an investor can exit or become illiquid. Figure 7.2 charts the changes in exit strategy that the venture world has seen over time.

As one can see from Figure 7.3, one of these strategies is not like the other.

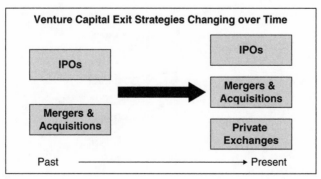

Figure 7.2

Source: Author.

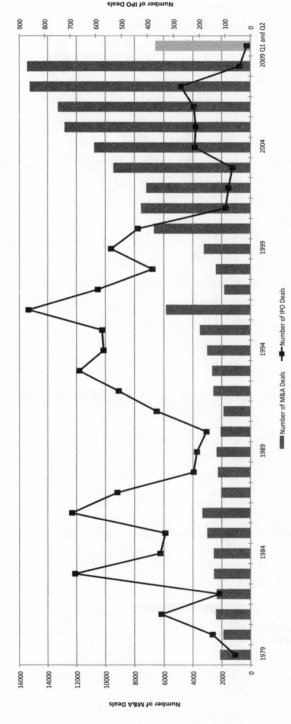

Figure 7.3 30 Years of Global M&A versus U.S. IPO Activity

Source: Author.

Rarely does the mergers and acquisitions (M&A) world equal the IPO market in activity and vice versa. Usually, one does better than the other. From 2000 until mid–2009, M&A far exceeded the lackluster IPO market. The 1990s, however, had an abundance of IPOs. It is important to observe exit strategies in the marketplace because that is the only way you will get your money back.

7. Restricted Securities

According to the Securities and Exchange Commission (SEC), restricted securities are defined as the following:

> Restricted securities are acquired in unregistered, private sales from the issuer or from an affiliate of the issuer. Investors typically receive restricted securities through private placement offerings, Regulation D offerings, employee stock benefit plans, as compensation for professional services, or in exchange for providing "seed money" or start-up capital to the company. Rule 144(a)(3) identifies what sales produce restricted securities.[12]

If the private company that you invested in goes public and does extremely well during its first day trading, it might be a moot point. The reason why it is irrelevant is because your shares are "locked up" or restricted unless you elected to sell shares at the IPO price. If an investor desires to sell restricted shares, a number of steps need to be taken. First, there is a holding period:

> Before you may sell any restricted securities in the marketplace, you must hold them for a certain period of time. If the company that issued the securities is subject to the reporting requirements of the Securities Exchange Act of 1934, then you must hold the securities for at least six months. If the issuer of the securities is not subject to the reporting requirements, then you must hold the securities for at least one year. The relevant holding period begins when the securities were bought and fully paid for. The holding period only applies to restricted securities...[13]

Second, an investor must remove the legend from the certificate. Transfer agents remove the legend after receiving consent of the issuer or an opinion letter from the issuer's counsel. Removing a legend is not instantaneous, and you are at the mercy of the lawyer removing the legend as well as the transfer agent. Even if an investor works for a bank, the process can be arduous if not frustrating. In some cases, an investor might even need to hire an attorney if the issuer's counsel is burdensome. Other investors will want to sell as well, and you might not be of any importance to them—that is, there could be foot dragging or stonewalling.

I once ran into an in-house counsel who tried to charge investors a legal fee for removing the legend. Although the in-house counsel maintained it was in the company's right, many investors (who backed the company) were affected. I am not certain, but I believe the real reason was that the lawyer owned shares (he was employed by the company) and did not want to see the stock decline in value because of a lot of investors wanted to sell. Investors were finally able to sell and, not surprisingly, the company had bad earnings and the stock crashed. For the most part, the issuers' counsel is courteous and helpful. Complications can happen, but the SEC will not intervene:

> If a dispute arises about whether a restricted legend can be removed, the SEC will not intervene. The removal of a legend is a matter solely in the discretion of the issuer of the securities. State law, not federal law, covers disputes about the removal of legends. Thus, the SEC will not take action in any decision or dispute about removing a restrictive legend. If the company that issued the securities is subject to the reporting requirements of the Securities Exchange Act of 1934, then you must hold the securities for at least six months. If the issuer of the securities is not subject to the reporting requirements, then you must hold the securities for at least one year. The relevant holding period begins when the securities were bought and finally paid for.[14]

IPOs in the mid- to late 1990s were the favored exit strategy for private companies. But from 2000 to 2009, M&A was the dominant strategy. IPOs started coming back in 2009, but it is far too early to tell if this is an enigma or a new wave.

8. Herd Mentality

Frequently, venture capital firms move in packs. Monkey see, monkey do. Venture funds invest all the time, which might not be prudent. Yet, certain funds have better timing than others. Table 7.3 relays a number of investments from venture firms (from March 2000–February 2001) as the market started to break down.

No one could have foreseen September 11th, which put the market into another vicious downturn. Quite a few venture-backed companies in 1999–2000, later collapsed due to the market. The stock market did poorly until 2003. Market bottoms are extremely difficult to judge even for the smart money, which is why an investor might want to deploy assets piecemeal and not all at once.

9. Size Matters

With regards to venture capital, size plays a significant role or determinant with private equity returns because if the venture firm is too small, they might not be able to ride through the storm. In other words, larger venture

Table 7.3 Top Investors in Early-Stage Venture Investments (March 2000–February 2001)

Company	Investments
Bessemer Venture Partners	$ 38 million
St. Paul Venture Capital	32
Austin Ventures	32
Atlas Venture	31
Chase Capital Partners	29
New Enterprise Associates	29
3i Group	27
Polaris Venture Partners	26
Goldman Sachs Group	24
Draper Fisher Jurvetson	24
Accel Partners	23
Crescendo Ventures	23
Advent International	23
Battery Ventures	23

Source: Lark Park, "Where the Seed Money Is," *The Industry Standard* (February 26, 2001).

firms tend to be better capitalized. Further, larger venture firms will be more diversified and have multiple types of funds or series of funds. Regardless, the investor should be cognizant of when they are investing.

10. Long-term Investments

Whether one is investing in a private company, a venture fund, or a private-equity fund-of-funds, your money will most likely be tied up for 8 to 10 years or longer. Although a single investment might be shorter in duration (and the odds are better for a faster liquidity event with an individual company), one cannot count on it. Illiquidity for such a long time is far different from buying liquid securities, such as stocks or index funds.

11. Management

Part of the risk of investing in venture capital is putting faith and money behind an entrepreneur. A lot can go wrong. Bo Peabody, author of *Lucky or Smart?: Secrets to an Entrepreneurial Life*, summed it up this way:

> There are entrepreneurs who start fundamentally silly, morally bankrupt, and philosophically negative companies.... These destined-to-self-destruct companies are, first and foremost, about the entrepreneur trying to make a million dollars rather than about doing anything interesting or valuable.[15]

With that in mind, it is imperative that an investor in venture capital find an entrepreneur that he or she both likes and trusts.

12. Government Action

Depending on government action, venture capital can do extremely well or languish. The National Federation of Independent Business states that for many, a "major concern is the level of uncertainty being created by government, the [usual] source of uncertainty for the economy."[16] Before investing, attempt to get a read on government policies:

Government policies can have a strong impact, both by setting the regulatory stage, and by galvanizing investment during downturns. ... Many governments have begun to recognize the benefits of venture capital and have made efforts to fund startup businesses. Government spending on venture capital may hinder the development of a private venture capital sector. Furthermore, many are skeptical about the government's ability to appropriately target healthy ventures.[17]

13. Unreliable Benchmarks

Unlike mutual funds, money managers, hedge funds, and other asset classes in which there are clear or well-defined benchmarks, venture capital does not have easy to access data. There are a number of services, such as PricewaterhouseCoopers Money Tree, Thomson Reuters (VentureXpert), Cambridge Associates, and Dow Jones Venture Source. Performance data are extremely unreliable because of private entities, which might view the value of their investments differently from others. In other words, it is hard to set a valuation on a private company. Even with publicly traded companies and securities, valuation can be inaccurate, as we witnessed in 2008–2009 when various securities markets froze.

Chapter 8

Venture Capital Performance

Depending on the manager or particular investment, venture capital can have compelling risk/reward characteristics. As of March 31, 2009, the U.S. Venture Capital Index outperformed the U.S. Private Equity Index in 1-, 3-, and 10-year periods, as seen in Table 8.1.

Compared with other alternatives and asset classes, such as equity and fixed income, the U.S. Venture Capital Index has done remarkably well especially in bull markets, as illustrated in Table 8.2.

The Cambridge Associates U.S. Venture Capital Index shows −4.1% for 2008 as opposed to −37.0% for the S&P500; therefore, one might be tempted to buy a lot of venture capital. However, months later (when more accurate numbers are recorded for valuations stemming from the market collapse), the venture capital area did not do as well.

Venture capital managers face an uphill battle to retain their place in investors' portfolios, as the subasset class is rocked by lousy returns and the weakest fundraising in more than a decade. Venture capital returns were negative 20.9% for the year ended Dec. 31, falling close

Table 8.1 Private Equity (as of 3/31/09)

	1 Year	3 Year	5 Year	10 Year
U.S. Venture Capital Index	−17.5%	1.3%	5.8%	26.2%
U.S. Private Equity Index	−24.2%	0.3%	9.7%	7.9%
Global (ex-U.S.) PE & VC	−39.6%	1.4%	11.2%	10.1%

Source: JP Morgan, "Market Insights, Q4 2009, Guide To The Markets," (September 30, 2009).

Table 8.2 Asset Class Investment Performance: 1999–2008

| | Total Returns in U.S. Dollars | | | | | | | | | |
Asset Class Indices	1999	2000	2001	2002	2003	2004	2005	2006	2007	2008
U.S. Equity Indices										
Standard & Poor's 500 Index	21.0%	−9.1%	−11.9%	−22.1%	28.7%	10.9%	4.9%	15.8%	5.5%	−37.0%
Non-U.S. Equity Indices										
MSCI EAFE Net Index	27.0%	−14.2%	−21.4%	−15.9%	38.6%	20.3%	13.5%	26.3%	11.2%	−43.4%
Fixed Income Indices										
Barclays Capital U.S. Aggregate (Taxable) Bond Index	−0.8%	11.6%	8.4%	10.3%	4.1%	4.3%	2.4%	4.3%	7.0%	5.2%
Alternative Indices										
NAREIT (Real Estate Investment Trusts) Index	−4.6%	26.4%	13.9%	3.8%	37.1%	31.6%	12.2%	35.1%	−15.7%	−37.7%
HFRI Fund Weighted Composite Hedge Fund Index	31.3%	5.0%	4.6%	−1.5%	19.6%	9.0%	9.3%	12.9%	10.0%	−18.3%
Commodity Research Bureau Total Return Index	31.8%	31.9%	−21.8%	33.5%	24.2%	18.2%	23.0%	−2.9%	22.2%	−35.0%
Cambridge Associates U.S. Venture Capital Index	280.1%	21.6%	−39.1%	−31.8%	−2.5%	15.1%	8.3%	17.9%	16.2%	−4.1%

Source: U.S. Equity S&P 500 Index; MSCI Barra; Barclays Capital U.S. Aggregate (Taxable) Bond Index; NAREIT Index; HFRI Fund Weighted Composite Hedge Fund Index; Reuters Jefferies CRB Total Return Index; Cambridge Associates U.S. Private Equity Index. Used with permission.

to 19 percentage points from the 12-month period ended Sept. 30, according to the most recent return data from the National Venture Capital Association and Thomson Reuters. Plus, the second quarter saw the lowest number of venture capital funds raised since the mid–1990s, according to the NVCA and Thomson Reuters.[1]

As Figure 8.1 plainly shows, venture capital did very well before 2000. Since the tech bubble, venture capital has experienced negative waves. As time goes on, 10-year numbers will not look as good because the stellar performance during 1999 will be too old.

The softening stance follows the venture-capital industry's decade of poor returns. The average return for venture-capital funds fell to 14% for the 10 years ended June 30, down from 34% for the 10 years ended June 30, 2008, largely because the venture returns generated in the first half of 1999 dropped out of the calculation, according to research firm Cambridge Associates LLC.[2]

Pensions use different benchmarks for private equity. Some pensions even make comparisons with the S&P 500. For instance, in 2009 the

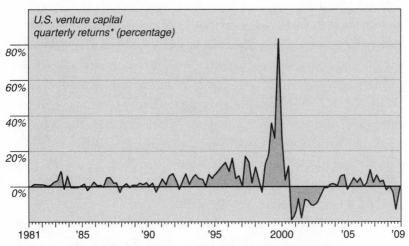

Figure 8.1 Venture Capital's Wild Ride

Source: Adam Lashinsky, "Sequoia Branches Too Far," *Fortune* (November 9, 2009). Cambridge Associates LLC. Used with permission.

Washington State Investment Board performance report, "private equity return for the 3rd quarter was 7.8%. It underperformed its benchmark, S&P 500 plus 500 basis points (lagged one quarter) for the quarter and 1 year, yet outperformed it for all other time periods."[3] As of June 30, 2009, its venture capital fund managed $4,133,345,130 with an internal rate of return (IRR) since inception of 10.5%.[4]

The California Public Employees' Retirement System (CalPERS) has as part of its investment program the Alternative Investment Management program (AIM). The AIM program had 11% exposure to venture capital as of June 30, 2009:

> Since inception to June 30, 2009, the AIM Program generated a net IRR of 6.7%. At June 30, 2009, the public market ten-year rolling average return for the CalPERS' Custom Wilshire 2500 Index plus 380 basis points was 2.9%. As of June 30, 2009, the weighted average age of all the current investments in the AIM portfolio was 3.9 years. Consequently, a large portion of the portfolio is in the early state of its investment life, when payment of feeds has not been offset by young investments that are held at cost.[5]

Venture capital performance is extremely difficult to measure and fraught with complications. Valuation, cash flow, J-curve, benchmarks, duration, transparency, and other factors make it challenging to know how well or not an investment performed. Some believe it is pointless to try to measure performance. "Private equity is different in so many ways, but most importantly it is the only asset class where (1) annual returns are meaningless, invalid and irrelevant and (2) true returns can only be measured many years in arrears."[6] In a perfect world, one invests in a private company, and it gets sold for cash within a year. The return is simple to calculate. However, the private company might not be sold and may be in limbo for ten years or more with no exit strategy.

If an investor selects a venture fund, a group of companies, a fund-of-funds, or a combination of difficult investments, the situation can be more troublesome to measure. One should not buy into a fund or company based on past performance. There is no guarantee that past performance will continue in the future. The odds of someone you know inviting you to fund the next Google are slim. Likewise, a fund might have done well 10 years ago (when everyone did well) but that does not necessarily mean that performance will be replicated.

Cash flow with venture capital is somewhat unreliable and unpredictable. Initially, the general partner draws down money to invest the fund into venture capital deals. An investor will have no idea of when or how much capital will be called down. Normally, the money is invested in the first 3 to 4 years. The period when there are negative cash flows as monies are being invested in the early stages of the investment is known as the J-curve:

> Briefly, the J-curve is produced by looking at the cumulative return of a fund to each year of its life. In other words, the first entry will represent the IRR of the fund for the first year of its life. The second entry will represent the IRR of the fund for the first two years of its life, the third the IRR for the first three years, and so on.[7]

The shape of a J-curve can vary but usually is lower during the first few years because funds are being invested into venture capital and there is no return on capital. The early stage is described well in *Inside Private Equity* (Bachman, Kocis, Long, and Nickels): "The downward portion of the IRR series is typical of the start-up phase of the fund. Capital is called, often taking the form of fees that do not contribute appreciably to the valuation."[8] Figure 8.2 is an example of what a J-curve might look like:

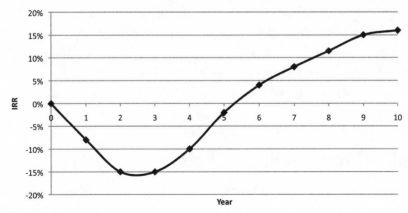

Figure 8.2 J-curve

Source: Author.

However, quite a few funds never accept all the committed capital because the fund(s) sometimes start paying back investors before all the money is invested. For example, on a $1,000,000 commitment, a venture firm could call $300,000 in the first year, $200,000 in year two, $400,000 in year three, and return $40,000 in year four. Although every investment scenario is different, funds can call all the money or most of the money. If the market is good, an investor might start getting paid out earlier rather than later, but this is also unpredictable and depends on the status of the individual company that was invested in, the market for initial public offerings (IPOs), or other exit strategies.

The reason why capital calls vary is that there is no guarantee the venture fund manager will be able to make the investment or how much he will be able to invest; therefore, the manager cannot promise an investor an exact dollar amount. For example, a company looking for venture capital might allow the venture firm only to invest $6 million. It is irrelevant how big the venture fund is or how much the venture fund manager wants to invest or how much the investors would like to invest if the amount promised by the company is $6 million. It is a finite amount. The size of the venture fund, depending on the allocation they get, will vary. Measuring cash flows with venture capital is an arduous task. Nevertheless, investors use a variety of methods to attempt to figure out cash flows.

Internal Rate of Return

When valuing projects, one of the most common methods is based on the IRR of the project. "The internal rate of return (IRR) method…is defined as that discount rate which forces the present value of a project's expected cash inflows to equal the present value of the project's expected costs."[9] IRR is the dominant method of measuring performance. "For better or worse, the IRR is looked on as *the measure* of private equity performance."[10]

Modified Internal Rate of Return

Different types of projects will have different cash-flow structures. These scenarios can produce multiple IRRs. In this case, a method to alleviate this issue and determine whether a project might be accepted is called "modified IRR." Eugene Brigham and Joel Houston, authors of

Fundamentals of Financial Management, describe it as "the discount rate at which the present value of a project's cost is equal to the present value of its terminal value, where the terminal value is found as the future value of the cash inflows."[11] Modified IRR might give a clearer picture of a project's true rate of return with reinvestment. The reason modified IRR might be more helpful to use than regular IRR is that "it assumes that cash flows from all projects are reinvested at the cost of capital whereas the regular IRR assumes that the cash flows from each project are reinvested at the project's own IRR."[12]

Net Present Value

Regarding a project, net present value (NPV) is the present value (the discounted value of future cash flows) minus the initial investment.

Time-Weighted Returns

Time-weighted returns are calculated as the geometric mean of all the funds' annual percentage returns. According to Guy Fraser-Sampson, "IRRs are often referred to as 'dollar-weighted' returns within the private equity industry in order to distinguish them from 'time-weighted' returns."[13]

Manager selection is important when selecting alternatives. According to William D. Bygrave and Jeffry A. Timmons, "Overall returns from venture capital are typically below 20% with only brief spikes above 30%. However, the top-quartile funds perform much better, with returns above 20% in nine out of sixteen years, above 30% in four of those years, and above 40% one year."[14] A review of top-quartile venture capital managers easily beat the bottom-tier venture capital managers from 1981 to 2008, as seen in Figure 8.3.

There is a big difference with performance, as Figure 8.3 clearly illustrates. Similar to venture capital, hedge fund performance varies dramatically between managers (including either individual hedge funds or hedge fund-of-funds). The manager matters.

Waves

Can waves be found with IPOs? Yes. In 1961 there were 435 IPOs. In 1966, there were 85. History repeats itself with IPOs. Table 8.3 gives a sampling of public offering totals from key years.

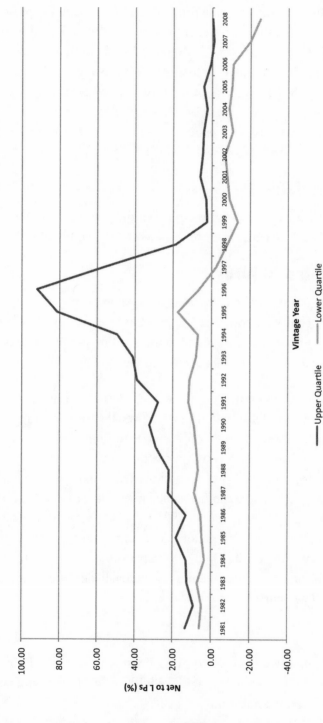

Figure 8.3 Top-Tier versus Bottom-Tier Manager Performance 1981–2008

Source: Cambridge Associates LLC U.S. Venture Capital Index and Selected Benchmark Statistics (December 31, 2009), 5. Used with permission.

Table 8.3	Number of Initial Public Offerings
Year	Number of Offerings
1961	435
1966	85
1969	780
1974	9
1983	521
1990	112
1996	687
2003	68

Source: Jay R. Ritter, "Some Factoids about the 2008 IPO Market," http://bear.warrington.ufl.edu/ ritter/IPOs2008Factoids.pdf (July 27, 2009), 10. Used with permission.

An inquisitive investor in venture capital might ask whether investment bankers could use Wave Theory for public markets as well as private markets (alternatives). The answer is that a form of Wave Theory is used by bankers to set a share price or valuation for a private company that is slated to go public. Bankers use a number of methods. First, they examine broad market waves, such as the Dow Jones. Second, waves of money flowing into or out of equity mutual funds are examined. Third, waves of IPO pricing statistics are observed (IPOs priced above/within/below filing ranges). Fourth, waves with IPO volume are explored as seen in Figure 8.4, a Bear Stearns' "IPO Volume Slows" chart:

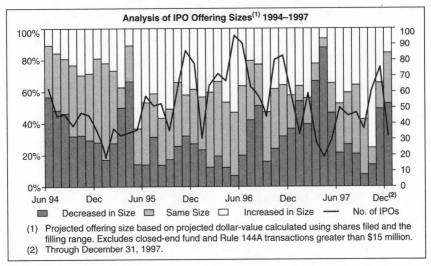

Figure 8.4 Larger Offering Sizes

Source: Securities Data Company, IPO Volume Slows, Bear Stearns, 1998. From a presentation to the Institute for International Research, "IPOs: The Pros and Cons of Taking Communications and Media Companies Public," 44.

Fifth, waves of offering sizes are noted. As an illustration of a Bear Stearns analysis of IPO offering sizes, Figure 8.4 is an analysis of IPO offering sizes from 1994 to 1997.

These five waves are part of an overall analysis to see at what price or even if it is advisable for a company to go public. Going public at the wrong time can be devastating. Entrepreneur William Loftus states:

> Trying to fight against the wave can be devastating. Building in protections at the height of a wave, when you have the capital, will help you weather bad times as the wave crashes. Conversely, becoming aggressive after a wave has crashed can help accelerate growth as the wave rises. As we battled the tech dot-com downturn, a better perspective on that wave would have helped save many good companies, including ours. Not understanding the wave properly cost many venture capitalists, investors, and consequently employees dearly.[15]

Wave Theory pertains to cycles, patterns, or trends with alternatives, including the venture capital market. The IPO or public markets have historically been a main exit for venture capital. There are now enough data to observe these trends with venture capital to help decide whether it is advisable for an investor to put money into a private company or venture fund.

Wave I: Trough to Peak (1970–1973) and Peak to Trough (1973–1974)

There were a record number of IPOs in the late 1960s. The stock market and phenomenal performance of IPOs at the time helped lure investors into venture capital at precisely the wrong time. Based on the euphoria in the market, investors were deceived. They were about to experience a very nasty wave. Imagine surfing for the first time and simultaneously getting attacked by a shark, surfing into a piling, and being struck by lightning.

Wave II: Trough to Peak (1975–1987) and Peak to Trough (1987–1991)

Although the 1970s did not have an abundance of venture funds, performance was quite good. Bygrave and Timmons discussed these periods in their 1992 book, *Venture Capital at the Crossroads*:

The 1977 to 1979 vintage, which comprises seven funds, performed spectacularly, with a median rate of return peaking 35% in 1983, then gradually declining to 24% by 1989. Funds formed after 1979 did not perform well. For example, at the end of 1985, the average returns of the 1981, 1982, 1983, and 1984 vintages were all lower than 10%, with the 1984 vintage being slightly negative. By 1989, even post–1979 vintage was returning less than 10%, and, what's worse, all post–1980 vintages were below 5%.[16]

Venture capital cycles, patterns, or trends are reoccurring. Wright and Robbie discuss these trends in *Management Buy-Outs and Venture Capital*. The two authors look at cycles from the mid- to late-twentieth century, stating that "the industry went from being red-hot at the end of the 1960s to almost an ember by 1974; it rekindled in the late 1970s until it was white hot by 1983; then from 1987 it began to cool off."[17] One possible explanation of the second wave was the creation of many new venture funds in the 1980s. Wright and Robbie go on: "The total number of portfolio companies receiving venture capital dropped from 1,740 in 1987 to 792 in 1991. The drop in the number of new portfolio companies—that is, companies receiving venture capital for the first time—was more steep; 712 in 1987 compared with 173 in 1991."[18]

Wave III: Trough to Peak (1991–1992) and Peak to Trough (1992–1993)

Wave III was short lived. The early 1990s witnessed a surge in venture capital deals, but the equity market quickly turned, taking venture capital with it.

Wave IV: Trough to Peak (1993–2000) and Peak to Trough (2000–2002)

The venture market from 1993 to 2000 looked like a hockey-stick curve; it went straight to the sky. In discussing this period, Wright and Robbie note that "Venture capital returns from 1992 through 1995 confirmed what we had observed in the 1970s and 1980s. When the IPO market for small-cap stocks is robust, venture capital returns are healthy."[19] The *Red Herring* in November 1999 described how heated the venture capital market was at the time:

> Venture-backed investments in the second quarter of 1999 reached a record level of $7.7 billion, obliterating the previous record of $4.3 billion in the first quarter of 1999, according to the PricewaterhouseCoopers MoneyTree survey. Investment levels rose 104 percent over the $3.8 billion recorded in the second quarter of 1998. Venture capitalists are putting their money to work like never before.[20]

As discussed previously, no alternative grows to the sky. There is bound to be a correction. Waves have crests, and the end of the 1993–2000 period was no different. A January 2006 *Barron's* article reflected on what happened when the good times came to an end: "As the dot-com market of the late 1990s gathered momentum, venture capitalists stood as the nexus of hope and hype. In 2000, they poured nearly $95 billion into mostly young, untested companies, some no more than ideas, expecting to reap rich rewards by later selling many of these outfits to the public. But the bubble burst…"[21]

Wave V: Trough to Peak (2002–2006) and Peak to Trough (2008–June 2009)

Wave V clearly shows the concept of Wave Theory. *Forbes*, in a 2005 article, observed its rise as it approached a peak:

> IPO investors fared best in the depressed year of 2002, which reinforces the notion that in hard times underwriters bring only the best companies to market. Just 68 companies had offerings in 2002, but the group showed an average gain of 76% from their IPO prices to the end of May 2005.[22]

Even though there are fewer IPOs in tough times, these IPOs historically have done quite well. Markets move quickly, and one can easily miss a new opportunity. In either case, venture capital follows the IPO market.

In a 2005 piece, *Investor's Business Daily*, citing research firm Venture-One, noted that "In 2004, 67 venture-backed U.S. companies completed initial public offerings, just one fewer than in the 1998 bubble year and at least 45 more than in any of the last three years. These 2004 IPOs raised $4.98 billion versus $1.41 billion for 22 IPOs in 2003."[23] Venture capital, as we have seen, trails the IPO market: 93 venture-backed companies raised $11.1 billion through new stock offerings in 2004, which was more than the total for 2001, 2002, and 2003 combined for 94 venture-backed companies (that raised $8 billion), but less than the $21.5 billion for 239 venture-backed companies in 2000.[24]

Similar to the robust IPO market, the mergers and acquisitions (M&A) market prospered as well: a 2005 *Investor's Business Daily* piece notes that "the number of mergers and acquisitions involving VC-backed companies also rose. The 376 M&A deals in 2004, for a total value of $22.6 billion, surpassed the 2003 tallies of 335 and $12.9 billion."[25] Momentum continued into 2006 but showed the IPO market and venture capital slowing down. A *Wall Street Journal* piece picked up on the signals at the time and suggested to investors that they should be cautious:

In 2006, 56 venture-backed companies went public in the U.S., raising about $3.7 billion according to data from research firm Ven-tureOne and New York accounting firm Ernst & Young LLP. While that exceeded the 42 venture-backed IPOs in the U.S. that raised $2.3 billion in 2005, it is down from the 67 venture-backed IPOs of 2004 that raised nearly $5 billion. It also pales compared with IPO activity of the tech-boom heyday in 2000, when 202 venture-backed companies completed IPOs, raising a total of $19.2 billion.[26]

After the long run up from 2002 to 2008, the epic market collapse in 2008 reversed the wave. IPOs dried up. Venture capital was affected and fell 39% in the fourth quarter of 2008 (compared with the same period in 2007) and was down 47% in dollars and 37% in number of deals compared with the previous quarter.

Waves I through V with trough to peak and peak to trough graphs can be seen in Figures 8.5 through 8.9:

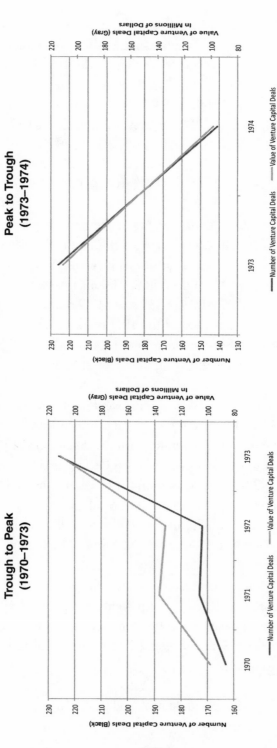

Figure 8.5 Wave I Value of Global Venture Capital Deals

Source: Data from Thomson Reuters. Used with permission.

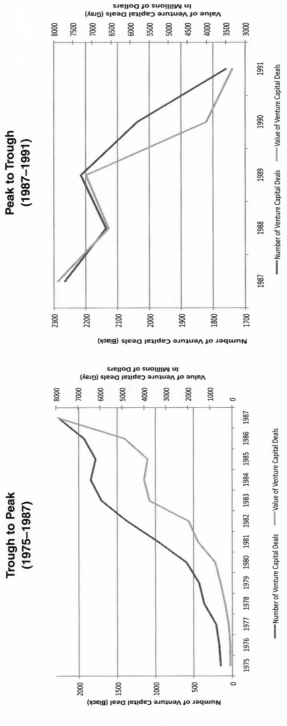

Wave II   Value of Global Venture Capital Deals

Figure 8.6   Wave II Value of Global Venture Capital Deals

Source: Data from Thomson Reuters. Used with permission.

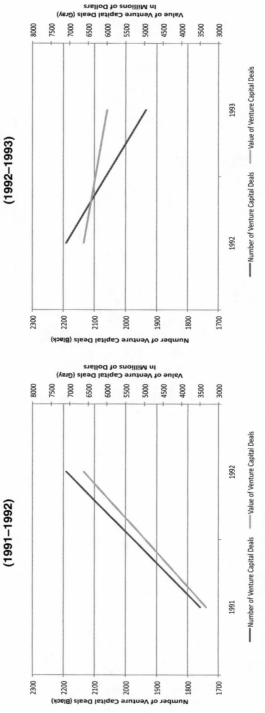

Figure 8.7 Wave III Value of Global Venture Capital Deals

Source: Data from Thomson Reuters. Used with permission.

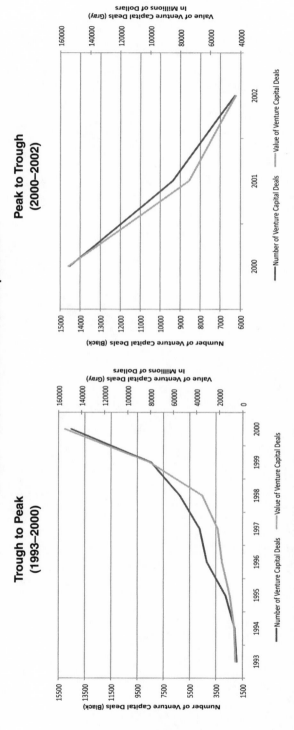

Figure 8.8 Wave IV Value of Global Venture Capital Deals

Source: Data from Thomson Reuters. Used with permission.

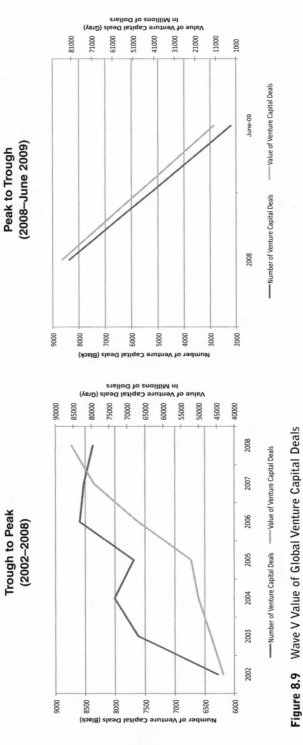

Figure 8.9 Wave V Value of Global Venture Capital Deals

Source: Data from Thomson Reuters. Used with permission.

Chapter 9

Venture Capital
Investment Vehicles

As with all alternative investments, one needs to consider which way the market is headed before investing. There is no guarantee that past performance will continue into the future or that waves will duplicate themselves. Figure 9.1 provides a possible guide to riding waves with venture capital:

Figure 9.1 Venture Steps (When to Surf)

Source: Bloomberg Terminal. Used with permission.

Venture Steps: When to Surf

Section A: This uptrend is a positive indicator of a market in recovery (early on) and is usually what leads to the highest returns. Recoveries follow recessions. (See Figure 9.1).

Section B: This bull market or ascendant stage is the next step on its way to being the high of the index. If one is investing in funds or individual companies (and there may be none available), one might ladder the investments or wait a little. Spread out your venture capital investments. Sometimes one can get in too early and the market goes into a downturn again.

Section C: When the market spirals to the sky and investors become irrational, you enter the danger zone. Investing after the market has shot to the sky is like showing up at your friend's surprise birthday party as they pull in the driveway at the same time and you wreck the surprise. In other words, you are late to the party. Investing at market peaks with venture capital can wipe out your investment. On the NASDAQ chart, because venture capital takes a while to invest, you will be investing at the peak of the market. Unless the company or fund you select can convert seawater to tap water, you will most likely lose a lot of money. Going down steps can be tricky as well. Ever teach a small child who just learned to walk to go down a flight of stairs? It can be problematic if you are not watching out.

Section D: Past the peak is another danger zone. As the market begins to go into a free fall, buying venture capital can be a bad idea.

Section E: Once the steep drop off the peak has passed, the risk associated with this stage depends on when the money is actually invested and how careful the venture fund is with your money. It can enable an investor in venture capital to put money at or near the bottom. Many very experienced wave riders got crushed in Section E when September 11th, Enron, and other events unfolded, all of which fooled those investors who thought that the market had bottomed—but it had not.

Section F: The settling after the peak is the ideal spot to invest in venture capital because the market already hit bottom and should recover.

While many investors do not have a Bloomberg (which offers a plethora of data and is immensely useful) to help decide on an investment such as venture capital, quite a few newspapers and magazines offer such information. *Inc.* magazine, for example, is devoted to small businesses and entrepreneurs. Information they provide can be helpful to investors. Figure 9.2, for example, graphs venture investments and shows the tide turning for venture capital.

With a publicly traded company or fund, you can invest at a precise time in the market. After the market has bottomed and is in a confirmed rally, one can enter the market. With a private company or venture fund, you can invest only if the company is looking for money or there is a new venture fund at the time. If you invest in a venture fund, there is no telling how quickly or slowly it will take the general partner of the fund to make investments. Some venture funds have better timing than others. Also, entrepreneurs might not want to accept low valuations. The *San Francisco Business Times* described this process further in a July 2003 piece that presented the results of a Market4Demand survey of local entrepreneurs:

> Low valuations have discouraged many startups and pushed some to scrap VCs as a source of capital. According to a survey released this month by marketing services firm Market4Demand, 63 percent of entrepreneurs are considering funding alternatives in addition to

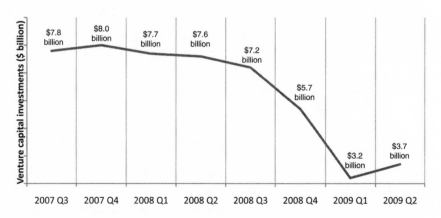

Figure 9.2 Why Your Idea Needs to Be Better Than Ever

Source: National Venture Capital Association. Used with permission.

private equity placement, with the majority opting for small business loans or bootstrapping the company by tapping their personal savings, family, and friends. The survey polled 240 Bay Area entrepreneurs, of which 65 percent were from companies with revenue less that $1 million and 9 percent were from startups generating between $1 million and $5 million.[1]

Types of Investments

There are a number of alternative investments options:

1. Venture funds. If one wants to invest in venture capital, an investor can either invest directly into a particular company or give a venture firm money to invest. Select the best fund money can buy. A 2009 *Forbes* report followed a 30+ year analysis of venture fund returns and reported that the "median return for the top-quartile firms was 28%."[2] Venture funds can add significant value and bring a lot to the table. William Bygrave and Jeffry Timmons highlighted the benefits of venture capital firms in their book *Venture Capital at the Crossroads*:

> Venture capital firms seek to add value in several ways: identifying and evaluating business opportunities, including management, entry, or growth strategies; negotiating and closing the investment; and tracking and coaching the company; providing technical and management assistance; attracting additional capital, directors, management, suppliers, and other key stakeholders and resources…[3]

What makes a venture capital firm successful? The list is quite long, but connections, fundraising ability, negotiating skills, operational experience, and entrepreneurial experience are most helpful. Venture funds are not inexpensive but they have the ability to add significant value.

For instance, a venture firm might be able to negotiate warrants as part of the investment. Warrants are contractual rights that can be exercised over time to purchase various amounts of equity at predetermined prices. Warrants can be viewed as icing on the cake; a sweetener for the deal. Warrants typically are over a 3- to 4-year period. The typical investor might not know about warrants, let alone how to negotiate for them. There are also different types of warrants, such as preferred stock warrants or common stock warrants.

One should also attempt to procure a fund with top-quartile performance. Table 9.1 is a list of some of the top venture capital firms in the United States.

2. Individual companies. Venture capital neophytes frequently make the colossal mistake of investing in the same types of companies without diversifying. Hypothetically, if you had invested solely in privately held storage companies in 2000–2001, you would have ended up with the portfolio illustrated in Table 9.2.

Although there were two companies that were acquired (see present status column in Table 9.2), the story could have been much worse. Investing $100,000 into five similar companies is extremely risky. If you are investing in individual investment companies, diversification is crucial. Table 9.3 provides a list of different types of sectors one might consider to create a well-diversified venture capital portfolio. Venture capital sectors move in waves.

3. Angel investors. Throughout the nation, there are angel investors. According to *Inc.* magazine, citing the University of New Hampshire's Center for Venture Research, "In 2007, 258,200 angels pumped $26 billion into 57,120 companies, making these wealthy individuals the single largest source of start-up capital."[4] Many of these angels join associations or organizations devoted to angel investing, such as the CommonAngels. According to the *Boston Business Journal,* since 1998 "CommonAngels has funded 39 companies with more than $43 million from Common-Angels and over $200 million from co-investors."[5] Another similar organization is the Tech Coast Angels. While the CommonAngels are based on the East Coast, the Tech Coast Angels are situated on the West Coast in Southern California. The Tech Coast Angels is the largest angel investor network in the United States. Table 9.4 provides a list of U.S. angel investor networks.

4. Fund-of-funds. Many venture funds do not make their performance visible to the general public. Venture capital funds have been successful

Table 9.1 2009 Top Venture Capital Firms

Name	AUM (mm)	Preferred Industries	Name	AUM (mm)	Preferred Industries
Advent International Corp.	$1,900	Financial, consumer, industrial	New Enterprise Associations	$8,500	Health care, IT, energy
Battery Ventures LP	$298	IT, clean tech, digital media	Oak Investment Partners	$8,400	Communication, medical devices, clean energy, Internet
Clearstone Venture Partners	$662	Technology	Palomar Ventures	$525	Software, networking and telecom infrastructure
Coral Capital Management	$500	IT, communications, digital media	Quaker BioVentures	$600	Telecom, software, financial services, materials
Cross Atlantic Capital Partners	$575	Life sciences	Rustic Canyon Partners	$975	Software, semiconductors, services
Draper Fisher Jurvetson	$6,115	Mobile services, IT	Sequoia Capital	$1,800	Energy, financial, health care, technology
Edison Venture Fund	$650	IT, pharmaceuticals	Split Rock Partners	$2,067	Health care, software and Internet services
GRP Partners	$650	Restaurants, tech, financial services	Summit Partners	$1,000	Technology, financial services, health care
HarbourVest Partners LLC	$440	Technology, generalist	TA Associates	$1,650	Technology, financial services, business services, health care
Kleiner Perkins	$5,000	IT, clean energy	TL Ventures	$1,400	Communications, IT
Menlo Ventures	$4,000	IT, Internet	Vesbridge Partners	$500	IT networking

AUM, assets under management; IT, information technology.

Source: Author.

Table 9.2 Privately Held Storage Companies

Company	Founded (Year, City)	CEO (2001)	# of Employees	Web Site	Funding and Status (2001)	Present Status (2009)
3Pardata	1999, Fremont, CA	David Scott	115	www.3pardata.com	Not profitable. Raised a $16 million second round in April 2000. Raised a $100 million third round in June 200. Total capital raised: $121.1 million.	Still around
DataCore Software	1998, Ft. Lauderdale, FL	George Teixeira	200	www.datacore.com	Not Proftable. Raised a $6 million first round in December 1998. Raised $35 million second round in July 2000. Total capital raised: $41 million.	Still around
DataPlay	1998, Boulder, CO	Steven Volk	175	www.dataplay.com	Not profitable. Raised a $55 million fourth round in July 2001. Total capital raised: $119 million.	Bankrupt; technology purchased by DPHI
LeftHand Networks	1999, Boulder, CO	Bill Chambers	35	www.lefthandnetworks.com	Expects to be profitable by first quarter 2002. Raised a $13 million first round in 2001. Total capital raised: $13 million.	Acquired by Hewlett-Packard
Storability	2000, Southborough, MA	Matthew Westover	150	www.storability.com	Expects to be profitable by first quarter 2002. Raised an $18.5 million first round in July 2000. Raised a $30 million second round in June 2001. Total capital raised: $13 million.	Acquired by StorageTek, which was then acquired by Sun Microsystems

Source: *Red Herring*, September 15, 2001.

Table 9.3 Venture Capital Sectors

Software
Life Sciences
Wireless
Hardware
Infrastructure
Security
Telecom
Services
Content
Cleantech

Source: Author.

Table 9.4 Leading U.S. Angel-Investor Networks

Name	Typical Investment	Number of Investors	Web Site
Investor's Circle	$300,000–$600,000	225	investorscircle.net
Keiretsu Forum	$250,000–$2 Million	750	k4forum.com
The Tribe of Angels	$250,000–$500,000	2,732	tribeofangels.com
Common Angels	$500,000–$1 Million	75	commonangels.com
Hub Angels Investment Group	$250,000–$750,000	75+	hubangels.com
Launchpad Venture Group	$100,000–$500,000	60+	launchpadventuregroup.com
New York Angels	$250,000–$750,000	65+	newyorkangels.com
Silicon Garden Angel Investor Group	$20,000–$250,000	100+	njangelsnet@aol.com
Alliance of Angels	$500,000–$750,000	100+	allianceofangels.com
Oregon Angel Fund	$400,000–$600,000	62	oen.org/programs_oaf.aspx
The Desert Angels	$300,000	70	edesertangels.com
New Mexico Angels	$250,000–$800,000	75+	nmangels.com
Band of Angels	$500,000	131	bandangels.com
Pasadena Angels	$500,000–$1 Million	110	pasadenaangels.com
Sand Hill Angels	$500,000–$2.5 Million	70	sandhillangels.com
Sierra Angels	$250,000–$750,000	50	sierraangels.com
Tech Coast Angels	$300,000–$1 Million	250	techcoastangels.com
Central Texas Angel Network	$25,000–$1.5 Million	55	centexangels.com
Houston Angel Network	$250,000–$300,000	100	houstonangelnetwork.net
IMAF-Triad	$250,000	75	imaftriad.com

Name	Typical Investment	Number of Investors	Web Site
New Vantage Group	$250,000–$500,000	55	newvantagegroup.com
Piedmont Angel Network	$500,000	150	piedmontangelnetwork.com
Springboard Capital	$350,000–$800,000	50+	springboardcapllc.com
Triangle Accredited Capital Forum	$200,000–$300,000	About 100	capital-forum.com
BlueTree Allied Angels	$350,000	50	bluetreealliedangels.com
Mid-America Angels	$250,000–$500,000	100+	midamericaangels.com
Ohio TechAngels	$425,000	218	ohiotechangels.com

Source: "Angel Investing 2009," *Inc. Magazine*, January/February 2009.

lobbying to change several states' open records laws so that pension funds and university endowments can refuse to disclose key details about investments.[6] In fact, various funds have clashed with pension funds over this topic. Sequoia Capital refused to allow the University of Michigan to make future investments in their funds because they did not want performance disclosed to the rest of the world.[7] Venture capitalists do not share a lot of performance data with fund-of-funds either. Venture funds can be selective because they do not need the assets. As a result, there are not nearly as many venture capital fund-of-funds as with hedge funds. A good venture capital fund-of-funds (providing an investor can locate a good one) will be expensive but offer a lot of diversification if the manager is prudent. Access to the best venture capital funds might be problematic, so an investor should inquire what is under the hood. Learn about the portfolio companies that the fund-of-funds selects. Table 9.5 lists the top managers of private equity.

Each organization is different. Some will offer private placements to invest in individual companies, whereas others have fund-of-funds or access to nonproprietary fund-of-funds involving venture capital.

5. Venture-backed IPOs. If you buy venture capital–backed IPOs, you will tend to do better than non-venture–backed IPOs. Assuming an investor can get them (good IPOs are not easy to get), venture-backed IPOs are a liquid, inexpensive way to gain exposure to companies backed by venture capital. IPOs during bad markets can be extremely volatile and lose a lot of value. Good IPOs in bad equity markets tend to do well when public markets

Table 9.5 Top Managers of Private Equity as of December 31, 2008

Manager	Total Assets	Domestic Assets	Int'l Assets	Manager	Total Assets	Domestic Assets	Int'l Assets
Neuberger Berman	$10,343	$10,343	–	Brown Brothers Harriman	$655	$655	–
Goldman Sachs Group	$7,600	–	$7,600	Amalgamated Bank	$643	$643	–
JPMorgan Asset Mgmt.	$7,593	$7,593	–	Fort Washington	$570	$570	–
Oaktree Capital	$4,122	$2,803	$1,319	Legg Mason	$316	$6	$310
DuPont Capital	$3,797	$3,797	–	Columbia Partners	$291	$291	–
UBS Global Asset Mgmt.	$3,345	$3,275	$70	New York Life Inv. Mgmt.	$227	$227	–
Abbott Capital	$1,634	$1,634	–	Federated Investors	$156	$156	–
Mesirow Financial	$1,541	$1,541	–	TCW Group	$41	–	$41
GE Asset Mgmt.	$1,453	$1,067	$386	Prudential Financial	$20	$20	–
Morgan Stanley	$1,346	–	$1,346	Fortis Investments	$5	$5	–
Invesco	$1,195	$1,195	–	**TOTAL**	**$47,760**	**$36,688**	**$11,072**
Congress Asset Mgmt.	$867	$867	–				

Source: "The Top Managers of Private Equity," *Pensions & Investments,* May 18, 2009.

improve. IPOs that were not attractive to begin with seldom recover. Buying IPOs is not the same as buying venture capital.

6. Indexes. As can be expected, venture capital (because it is private) lags the public markets. Although it is impossible to time the market (as it is also difficult to know when you will discover a great company), one should not be the first in the water. The venture capital market trails the public market. In 1999, NASDAQ reached its all-time high. Not until the following year did venture capital reach its peak. Figure 9.3 compares venture capital and NASDAQ activity over a 30-year period.

One could use another index, like Dow Jones or MSCI EAFE (Europe, Australia, Far East), but NASDAQ more closely resembles the venture capital market. Most venture-backed IPOs are on NASDAQ, not the New York Stock Exchange (NYSE) or some other exchange. There is no venture capital index that is publicly traded, but one is likely to be created as

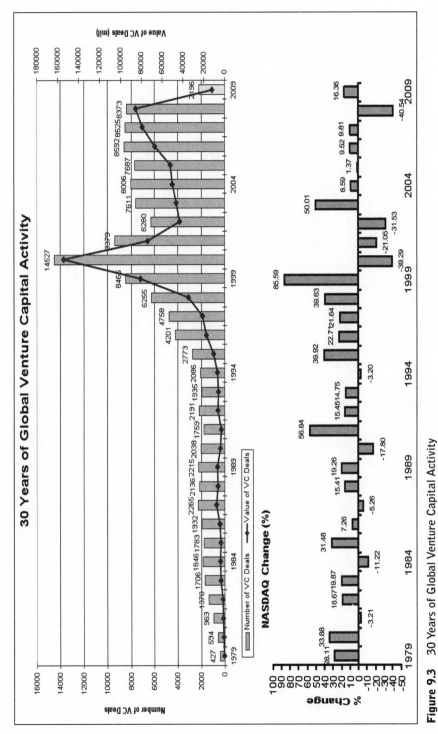

Figure 9.3 30 Years of Global Venture Capital Activity

Source: Data from Thomson Reuters. Used with permission.

Table 9.6 VC-Backed Deals Perform Better

IPOs from 1980–2006 Categorized by Venture Capital Backing					
			Avg. 3-year Buy-and-Hold Return		
VC-Backed or Not	#IPOs	Avg. First-day Return	IPOs	Market-adjusted	Style-adjusted
VC-backed	2,465	28.10%	24.90%	−12.90%	2.60%
Non VC-backed	4,629	12.70%	20.40%	−23.90%	−10.70%
ALL	7,094	18.10%	22.00%	−20.10%	−6.00%

Source: Jay R. Ritter, "Some Factoids about the 2008 IPO Market,"
http://bear.warrington.ufl.edu/ritter/IPOs2008Factoids.pdf (July 27, 2009), 16. Used with permission.

the alternatives space grows. However, a good many IPOs are venture backed, as illustrated in Table 9.6.

Because data on venture capital are hard to obtain and not easy to chart, I found another method one might consider (among many others). NAS-DAQ contains many technology companies as well as health-care companies. There are new indexes of IPO companies that one could use for diversification if they had to have a liquid investment that covers IPOs at the time—for instance, the FTST Renaissance Capital IPO Composite Index. In lieu of trying to find a venture company or new fund at the bottom of the market collapse, one could invest in such a fund. The benefits are you can move quickly and it is cost-effective and liquid. One could also short this index if you realized you invested in venture capital at a market peak and you needed insurance or protection from a weakening market. Figure 9.4 charts the NASDAQ versus the First Trust US IPO Index Fund.

Many exchange-traded funds (ETFs) and indexes are appearing that focus on venture-type investments. A few sector ETFs that are now publicly traded are listed in Table 9.7.

Investments for venture capital can be made through either venture firms or individual companies. If an investor elects to invest in a fund instead of individual companies, there are different stages as well as sectors they can select. Suzanne King from NEA states, "We are usually classified as the largest early-stage fund."[8] An investor should ask the question,

Figure 9.4 NASDAQ versus First Trust U.S. IPO Index Fund

Source: Bloomberg. Used with permission.

What angle is the venture firm coming from? King adds, "We always look at the management team and the market opportunity."[9] Certain venture capitalists seek the public route as an exit strategy, whereas others prefer mergers.

Table 9.7 Sector ETFs

Fund Name	Ticker	Intraday NAV	Index Ticker
First Trust US IPO Index Fund	FPX	XPT	IPXO
First Trust NASDAQ Clean Edge Green Energy Index Fund	QCLN	QCLNI	CELS
First Trust NASDAQ Clean Edge Smart Grid Infrastructure Index Fund	GRID	GRIDIV	QGDX
First Trust NYSE Arca Biotechnology Index Fund	FBT	EBT	BTK
First Trust ISE Global Wind Energy Index Fund	FAN	FANIV	GWE

Source: Author.

San Francisco–based Hummer Winblad Venture Partners is an early-stage software investment venture capital firm. When the *Boston Business Journal* interviewed Ann Winblad, the firm's cofounding partner, to discuss their investing philosophy, she said "We don't fund companies to be acquired; we hope to build companies that are considerable in scale and will be around forever."[10] Ann Winblad has a specific type of company she looks for but also focuses on a particular sector: software. Each venture capital fund is different. The Mayfield Fund and Canan Partners both make technology and health-care investments. Accel Partners, on the other hand, invests in both technology and telecommunications companies.

Before investing in a small, fast-growing private company, it is prudent to ask questions. The following is a list of sample questions an investor might ask an entrepreneur:

Top-20 Questions to Ask Entrepreneurs before Investing in Their Companies

1. **Competitive advantage.** How is your product or service better than your competitors? Find out why or how there is a unique advantage. Have the entrepreneur name their biggest competitors. A typical response is "We do not have any: we are better." Ask for more detail. Everyone has a competitor. Is the competition public or private? Domestic or foreign? Google might have had plenty of competitors in its early days: Infoseek, Lycos, Altavista, AOL, Netscape, Microsoft. An answer Google might have as to why they are better is simply that they have a superior algorithm over the competition.

2. **Future.** What are your long-range goals, and where do you see the company 5 to 10 years from now? Public or private? Solo or part of a bigger company? Where did you work before? What is your educational background? Find out if the CEO is credible. Your view of the CEO is crucial. Do you trust him? Is he CEO material? How would he appeal to other investors? Some CEOs are brilliant but have terrible people skills. Can he sell? Does he tell a good story? How would he do on a road show speaking with potential investors? Is he a spendthrift or frugal? First impressions are important here!

3. History/track record. Tell me about your background. How did you start this company? If the entrepreneur has successfully run other companies, it is a major plus for the investor. Has he ever run a company before? Does the entrepreneur have a past of selling successful businesses and taking them public? Serial entrepreneurs are the best to invest in because they are experienced. A serial entrepreneur might be defined as one who has a history of taking numerous companies public or selling them; he has a success record for growing companies. A frequent mistake with a first-time entrepreneur is he dramatically changes the business model and does not focus. The person you invest in needs to stay focused.

4. Management. What is your management structure? Management should be solid. Frequently, start-ups or early-stage companies do not have a savvy CFO because of finances. However, as the company grows, hiring an experienced CFO is imperative. The CFOs would have prior experience taking companies public. Certain CFOs are better at numbers than articulating the company's story. Ideally, a fast-growing company needs a CFO with both skills.

5. Target market. What is your target market? Learn where the company intends to market their services or products. Are they regional, national, or global? Certain companies can become global brands, such as Starbucks, whereas others stay regional. Wawa convenience stores have been on the East Coast as long as In-and-Out Burgers have flipped burgers on the West Coast. It is unclear whether either will ever expand. Expansion can be difficult.

6. Revenue. How do you intend to increase revenues? Internal growth or acquisitions? Review the company's balance sheet (see sample in Table 9.8). Are revenues increasing?

7. Expenses. What is your burn rate? How much money is the company "burning" through at the end of the month? After expenses are subtracted from revenues, is the company's net income positive? If not, is the company heading toward positive net income? When will the company become profitable?

8. Cash. How much cash does the company have at the moment? How long will this amount keep the company out of trouble? Find out if and when the company might need more financing.

Table 9.8 Inktomi Operations Data (in Thousands)

Statement of Operations Data	Historical Information		Projected Information (year ended September 30)		
	2/02/1996 to 9/30/96	FY Ended 9/30/97	1998	1999	2000
Total revenue	$530	$5,785	$17,953	$53,482	$103,138
Gross profit	291	4,273	11,827	43,832	90,638
Operating income (loss)	−3,431	−8,466	−14,801	−1,701	15,253
Net income (loss)	−3,534	−8,662	−15,049	−962	16,762

Source: Inktomi Corporation, Placement Memorandum (January 12, 1998), 6.

9. Venture firms. Who are your investors, and who is leading the round? How much are they investing? Are venture firms investing? The relevance is that a venture capitalist will be able to control the CEO and you will not. The old adage comes to mind, "Misery loves company."

10. Valuation. What is being raised for this round? What is the valuation both pre- and post-money valuation? It is important to ask both. Also, is it an up round or down round?

11. Board. Who is on your board, and how do they help you? In an ideal world, there will be seasoned, experienced board members who can give good advice to the CEO. You do not want the CEO's college roommate and sister guiding the company.

12. Legal and accounting. What law firm and accounting firms do you utilize? These firms should be responsible entities, not the ones used by Bernie Madoff nor ones connected or related to the CEO. Any conflicts of interest should be avoided.

13. Growth. Companies should have long-term growth in excess of 30%.

14. Earnings visibility. When will you be earning money? The earnings might be negative, but they should have some hope of turning positive. For example, Synchronoss Technologies, Inc., raised money privately. Their revenues were small but fast growing. In the year ending December 31, revenues (in thousands) were $16,550 in 2003 with negative net income of $1,044. By 2005, revenues were $54,218, and net income was positive $12,429.

15. Uniqueness. How is your product unique? See if there are value-added products. Does the company have a unique or strong market position? Look for a substantial consumer base with a technology edge, a company with strong or rapidly growing market share, and high barriers to entry.

16. Documents to obtain. Stock purchase agreement, form of articles of amendment and restatement, stockholder list, form of amended and restated stockholders agreement, form of registration rights agreement, legal opinion, stockholder listing, registration rights agreement, consent and amendment agreement, officer's certificate, and secretary's certificate.

17. Leader. How do you lead? Find out the entrepreneur's view on leadership. He will be managing people. He will be raising more funds. He will be selling and getting new business. Does he have what it takes to run a company?

18. Investor presentation. Do you have an investor presentation on the company? Often a venture company will have a presentation book they give to prospective investors for their road show. A "road show" can be defined as the period between the preliminary filing and the offering (IPO) during which the issuer (company) and the securities by the managing underwriter and syndicate members are marketed. The road show consists of information/marketing meetings in different geographic areas throughout the country designed to place or "sell" the company and the offering to financial advisors and institutional investors.

19. Investor updates or reports. What kind of updates will you be providing to investors? These updates should cover good and bad things that happened each quarter. Reports should include an income statement and/or balance sheet.

20. Charitable giving. What charitable organizations are you invested with and why? There are certain entrepreneurs who are the real deal who give back to society, and then there are those who are just quick-buck artists. Find the real deal.

There are various stages that a growth company enters. It is important to identify how early or late a stage a company is before investing in it. Table 9.9 provides a roadmap to start-ups along with their stages.

Table 9.9 Startup "Roadmap"

I. Concept Stage ⟶	II. Planning Stage ⟶	III. Implementation Stage
**Venture idea research **Begin patent notebook 1. Personal goals evaluated 2. Own strengths, weaknesses identified 3. Outside help needs identified 4. Consumer needs identified 5. Product identified **Physical feasibility studied **Physical prototypes made 6. Market identified 7. Future market identified 8. Target market identified 9. Personal investment capacity determined 10. Return on investment goals defined 11. Profit goals defined 12. Ballpark of costs estimated 13. Sales goals defined 14. Timing evaluated 15. Legal constraints evaluated **Patent search **Patent applications 16. Review and revision performed	**Demonstration prototype constructed **Prototype tried on buyers 17. Sales tactics defined 18. Make or buy issues assessed 19. Manufacturing needs defined 20. Engineering and design needs 21. Technical people needs defined 22. Locations evaluated 23. Supply needs defined 24. Supply sources availability assessed 25. Distribution system defined 26. Salesperson needs defined 27. Management information system 28. Administrative people needs defined 29. Management people needs defined 30. Outside help needs finalized 31. Organization structure defined 32. Operating plan and budget 33. Capital needs defined 34. Capital needs for buying going concern defined (if needed) 35. Buyout versus startup choice made 36. Overall policy finalized 37. Review and revision performed	38. Incorporation completed 39. Whether to market test decided 40. Whether to subcontract decided 41. Market test completed 42. Capital obtained 43. Management people hired 44. Sales campaign begun 45. Salespeople hired and trained 46. Sources of supply found 47. Make or buy decision made 48. Supply sources selected 49. Location selected 50. Technical people hired and trained 51. Management information 52. Manufacturing plant set 53. Administrative people hired and trained 54. Production people hired and trained 55. Materials inventory purchased 56. First product made 57. First sale and delivery made

Source: Koul H. Vespe, *New Venture Strategies*, Prentice Hall, 1990, 101.

Asset Allocation and Diversification

One might walk before running with venture capital. In other words, it might be prudent to use a core/satellite approach in which an investor purchases either a fund-of-funds or individual venture fund before making individual investments in private companies. Venture capital is very complex and extremely risky if one does not do any homework. One needs to make sure that they are properly diversified and do not own all the same types of funds or companies. If an investor is too heavily weighted in the same types of venture deals, his or her risk will be magnified.

Private equity has a high degree of correlation with the equity market but has better returns, as seen in an article by Ben Warwick titled "Buying When There's Blood in the Streets: The Logic Behind Private Equity Is More Compelling Than One Might Think."[11] Because private equity is purchased at a discount to public comparables, it frequently has the potential for attractive returns. Also, there is an advantage to owning private companies in that the investment is not traded on an exchange. Kieran Beer notes that "Private equity has enjoyed returns of a higher magnitude than traditional equity and fixed income investments, and for good reason. Private equity firms have time on their side."[12]

If one invests in venture capital, they should have a 10-year horizon in mind. Short-term performance and worrying about the market on a daily basis (if you are a Nervous Nellie) becomes a moot point. Some of my clients have 80% in municipal bonds and 20% venture capital because they dislike equities and short-term volatility. They have a long-term view and do not want to worry about market volatility on a day-to-day basis. Just with selecting a good equity or fixed-income manager, selection among various managers is crucial. Two of the best-performing endowments in the country focus on asset allocation as well as manager selection when investing in alternatives such as venture capital: Yale and University of Pennsylvania. Having the appropriate asset allocation is imperative and should be based on a number of variables such as risk tolerance, age, liquidity needs, income, and other factors.

Before the Great Recession, David Swensen was known as the steward of Yale University's endowment and outperformed his peer group of endowment managers. Before 2006, Swensen averaged 16.1%. These impressive returns were accomplished with alternatives. Private equity, hedge funds, real estate, and other alternatives all played a role in Swensen's allocation. Yale's $15.2 billion endowment fund had the following asset allocation targets for 2005: hedge funds 25%, real assets 25%, private equity 17%, domestic stocks 14%, foreign stocks 14%, and domestic bonds 5%.[13] David Swensen defines asset allocation as "the long-term decision regarding the proportion of assets that an investor chooses to place in particular classes of investments."[14] Proper asset allocation is crucial, as *On Wall Street* magazine discussed in a 2007 piece:

> Forget picking stocks or trying to get ahead of the next market cycle. According to the groundbreaking work of Gary Brinson dating back

to 1986, 93.6% of performance differential between investment portfolios comes from asset allocation, not investment selection. Institutional investors, particularly endowments, have been applying the science of asset allocation for years, [Jim] Crotty says, and racking up the returns to prove the theory. Consider the Yale Endowment. Over the 10-year period ending June 30, 2006, the endowment posted an average annualized 17.2% return, net of fees, putting it in the top one percent of large institutional investors. A significant portion of that outperformance comes from the fund's target allocation of 44% of its assets to alternative investments, primarily real estate and private equity. Of course, institutions also have more access to these investment classes than the vast majority of retail investors.[15]

Yale had superior rates of return using alternatives. However, Swensen might have overdone it with the use of alternatives. Too much of any one thing can be bad for you. As the market reached new highs and alternatives hit absurd levels, Swensen continued aggressively adding alternatives (see Table 9.10 for a breakdown of the 2008 Yale endowment).

By the end of the fiscal year, June 30, 2008, Swensen had 74.5% of Yale's endowment in alternatives. Likewise, Harvard had a lot of funds directed toward alternatives. Harvard's endowment chief, Jane Mendillo, attempted to sell Harvard's alternatives at the absolute rock-bottom of the market. Fortunately for Jane Mendillo, she could not find buyers, and Harvard did not make the ill-fated mistake of selling at the low of the market.

Table 9.10   Yale Endowment, 2008

Absolute Return	25.10%
Domestic Equity	10.1
Fixed Income	4.0
Foreign Equity	15.2
Private Equity	20.2
Real Assets	29.3
Cash	−3.9

Source: Author. Yale Endowment, Endowment Highlights, Yale University, 2008.

Ironically, the illiquid nature of some of the alternatives that Harvard invested in saved the school from losing money because they could not be sold at the bottom of the market. The result was that Harvard's endowment went up with the recovery of the market. Liquidity turned out to be a dilemma for many Ivy League schools because they invested in too many illiquid securities and failed to think about liquidity needs. Schools that had appropriate asset allocation models (in which there were no extremes, such as an overweighting to illiquid securities or heavy equity exposure) fared the best. Schools with suitable asset allocation models were positioned to take advantage of those forced to sell at distressed prices. Whether you are running an endowment or investing in alternatives for yourself or your family, liquidity needs must be contemplated. Investors should ask themselves the question, "How much of a portfolio needs to be liquid or illiquid?"

Unlike Mendillo, Swensen did not rush to dump his alternative investments at the bottom of the market and appears to have done well holding them through the storm.

Kristin Gilbertson, chief investment officer at the University of Pennsylvania, had one of the better-performing endowments. According to *The Philadelphia Inquirer*, "For the fiscal year 2009, ending June 30, Penn's return on its endowment fell 15.7%—a hefty loss, but still much better than the rest of its Ivy League peers."[16] As one can see from the University of Pennsylvania associated investment and asset allocation (Table 9.11), Penn decreased equities from 50.8% to 19.7% while increasing private equity from virtually nothing to 6.1%.

Chief investment officer Kristin Gilbertson recently told the *Wall Street Journal* that in early 2008 she started reducing the portion of the endowment in public equities to 43% from 53% and put about 15% in Treasuries, which turned out to be prescient.[17] Gilbertson outperformed her peers: Yale was down 24.6% on its $16.3 billion endowment; Princeton fell 23.7% on its $12.6 billion endowment; Harvard was down 27% on its $26 billion endowment; Cornell, Dartmouth, and Brown also saw losses of greater than 20%.[18] A combination of prudent asset allocation, timing, investment selection, and manager selection all helped surpass her peer group's performance.

Table 9.11 University of Pennsylvania Associated Investment Fund Asset Allocation (by Percentage)

	1998–99	1999–00	2000–01	2001–02	2002–03	2003–04	2004–05	2005–06	2006–07	2007–08
Domestic Equity	50.8	41.1	42	43.3	36.8	34.1	24.6	22	24.1	19.7
International Equity	10.1	11.1	11.1	12.4	16.7	19.3	24.6	28	26.9	21.1
Emerging Mkt. Equity	4.9	6.3	4.4	0	0	0	2.5	4.8	5.2	4.9
Absolute Return	2.1	5.4	8.8	12.1	14.4	17.4	18.2	17.5	17.9	25.7
Private Equity	N/A	1.4	2.3	2.3	2.8	3.3	3.9	4.1	4.6	6.1
Real Estate	6.8	5.2	4.9	4.8	4.3	3.6	3.9	3.6	3.5	5.4
Natural Resources	0	0	0	0	0	0	0.3	0.7	0.9	1.6
Fixed Income	14.9	19	21.1	20.4	20	20.5	20.3	18	16.9	15.5
High Yield	8.6	8.3	5.4	4.7	5	1.8	1.7	1.3	0	0
Cash	1.7	2.2	0	0	0	0	0	0	0	0
Other	0.1	0	0	0	0	0	0	0	0	0

Sources: Author. University of Pennsylvania, *1998–2008 Financial Report.*

Outlook/Conclusion

More than a century ago, two entrepreneurs, Frank Skiff and Frank Ross, were building the Jewel Tea Company by selling tea, coffee, and other goods door to door. By 1910, Jewel had 100 delivery routes generating $1 million in annual sales ($23 million in today's dollars), and only 5 years later, it had mushroomed to 850 routes and $8 million in sales ($177 million today).[19] Investors realized the potential of Jewel Tea, which became a hot IPO. The company's shares skyrocketed 377% over a 122-week period from 1923 to 1927.[20] If one changed the name or substituted it for Starbucks, there are uncanny similarities. The central difference between the two immensely successful companies is time. Both companies did the same thing—grew rapidly—but were created 100 years apart: Jewel Tea was established in 1899 and Starbucks made its debut with a private placement in 1990. History can repeat itself, as evidenced by Wave Theory.

As the venture capital market began to develop in the late 1960s and early 1970s, distinct waves appeared. Cycles, patterns, or trends became quite apparent with venture capital around this time. Wave Theory is based on trying to find the best possible time to invest. Distinct patterns, trends, or cycles can be seen with venture capital, as demonstrated in Figure 9.5:

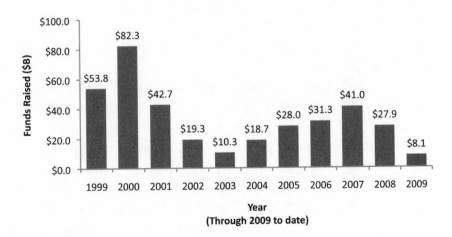

Figure 9.5 Commitments to Venture Capital Funds

Source: Ernst & Young, "3Q'09 Venture Insights," 2009, 14.

These waves happen again and again. If a venture firm or high-net-worth individual were going to invest after the tech correction, they should examine where the venture capital waves are heading at the time. Like other alternatives, it would be prudent to examine the waves up close, such as storage companies, as well as the big picture with the overall venture capital market. Venture capitalists directed $2.2 billion into 107 storage companies from the start of 2000 to the end of the second quarter 2001, and they continued to be bullish on just about every storage sector.[21]

Sector waves are also transparent with venture capital where a particular area moves in and out of favor, such as technology or health care. Venture capital waves exist today and will be around tomorrow. Ten years ago, Internet companies were all the rage. Then they were hated after the Internet bubble burst and the equity markets dropped from 2000 to 2002. The overall stock market recovered, but the 2008–2009 market crash put everyone on the edge of an abyss. The major exit strategy for venture capital, IPOs, virtually shut down. An IPO drought hit during the summer of 2008, and no companies backed by venture capitalists went public via an initial public offering in the United States, which was the first time that has happened since 1978.[22]

Investors witnessed money markets "breaking the buck." Others lost faith in municipal bonds and questioned whether U.S. treasuries were even safe. What sector attracted venture funding and had IPOs in 2009, when the equity markets started to recover? Against all odds, the Internet became popular once again with investors. Social networking sites such as Twitter, Facebook, and LinkedIn attracted new money. Only a handful of companies went public in 2009, but Ancestry.com was one of them—an Internet company. Waves exist with venture capital.

One will probably look back at 2009–2010 as a good time to invest in venture capital. According to the president of the National Venture Capital Association (NVCA), "The stability of seed and early stage deals as a percentage of total deal volume suggests that venture capitalists are continuing to fund very young companies…giving credence to the philosophy that an economic downturn is a time ripe with opportunity."[23]

Where are the wave riders heading? Similar to the last market correction with the tech bubble, the wave riders are seeking new opportunities. As Jonathan Flint of Polaris Venture Partners said in the *Industry Standard*, "It's down cycles when you make money."[24]

At the bottom of the venture capital market in 2009 (as opposed to the high of the market in 2007, in terms of number of deals and dollars raised), one of the most respected names in venture capital, Vinod Khosla, who helped found Sun Microsystems, was busy raising new funds. Why? Because the circumstances presented what may have been one of the best buying opportunities for anyone interested in the space. Buy low, sell high. In the summer of 2009, Khosla's firm, Khosla Ventures, announced two new funds, both with money from outside investors. According to the *San Francisco Business Times*, these funds included a $250 million vehicle for early-stage investments and a $750 million fund for larger deals.[25]

Josh Kopelman, another wave rider, was eager to take advantage of the low valuations in the market for venture capital. Kopelman invested heavily in start-ups as the financial world seemed to crash around him, with venture capital investment at its lowest level since 1997.[26]

What are the best venture firms (who are experienced surfers through both good and bad markets) doing? They are shopping. According to an October 2009 *Pensions & Investments* report: "Some 33 venture capital funds raised $5.5 billion..."[27] Venture capital moves in waves, and valuations seen in Q1 and Q2 of 2009 are extremely compelling. Smart money is getting deployed by the wave riders or experienced venture capital firms such as NEA, Rho Ventures, and Kleiner Perkins Caufield & Byers. For instance, Sequoia just raised a $400 million fund. Similarly, the founders of Google launched a venture capital fund called Google Ventures at the absolute bottom of the equity market on March 31, 2009. The fund will be around $100 million dollars and is dedicated to investing in cleantech, health care, and other areas. Greylock Partners also launched a new fund, Greylock XIII. San Francisco–based Azure Capital Partners raised a third fund, which was approximately $250 million dollars. Boston–based Highland Capital Partners raised $400 million.

Where is the smart money or the institutional money headed? The majority of the most astute institutions are buying and getting bargain-basement deals. Domestically, the smart money is buying. According to Christopher Ailman, chief investment officer of the CalSTRS (California State Teachers' Retirement System), Sacramento, "CalSTRS allocates 10% to 20% of its $14.6 billion private equity portfolio to venture capital. System officials expect to keep their venture capital investment about the same, investing opportunistically."[28]

At the same time, another massive institution, Texas Teachers, is buying alternatives. Looking at the $83 billion teacher retirement system of Texas, *Pensions & Investments* reported that the group is "a little more than halfway toward its goal of increasing alternative investments to 29% of plan assets in the second year of the fund's portfolio makeover."[29] Wealth managers, private banks, and financial advisors are all exploring the alternatives space. Reports have shown that these advisors intend to recommend more alternatives—such as venture capital—to clients rather than less alternatives. Globally, the smart money is going to work:

> The $25 billion Korea Investment Corp., Seoul, is preparing to invest approximately $2.25 billion in private equity, real estate and hedge funds, the KIC's first move into alternative investments, said Scott E. Kalb, chief investment officer. Private equity strategies will include LBO, mezzanine, distressed, growth capital and venture capital, according to the fund's 2008 annual report.[30]

Likewise, the Norwegian Government Pension fund ($423.7 billion) might allow the fund to move into alternative investments. Billions and billions of dollars are flowing into alternatives at a rapid rate.

Government regulation can thwart ingenuity. The original intent of the Sarbanes-Oxley Act was respectable. However, Sarbanes-Oxley needs to be changed and made less stringent. It was a quick solution at the time, but needs to be improved.

> Sarbanes-Oxley, passed in 2002, overhauled the financial reporting requirements for public companies, making the process lengthier and more complicated with the goal of creating more accountability. The rules also made the act of going public much more expensive, while many investors and company executives say it effectively barred small to mid-cap companies, the bread and butter of venture capitalist exits, from filing for public offerings.[31]

Sarbanes-Oxley is too restrictive. Adding more stringent regulation will most likely destroy innovation in the United States. According to Noel Francisco, partner at Jones Day, "Sarbanes-Oxley is a classic example of governmental overreach that drives American business out of the country. There is now an inverse ratio with more IPOs abroad and less domestically."[32] Sarbanes-Oxley has done far more damage than good for the country and increased government regulation will be problematic. The greatest companies in the United States raised venture capital when the market was bad. However, the majority prospered during periods with less restrictive government intervention and lower taxes. Does history repeat itself? It has again and again with venture capital.

Entrepreneurs build businesses. It is no surprise that the best companies tend to be run by former entrepreneurs. Entrepreneurs also tend to be charitable. The most successful entrepreneurs are very charitable and give back to society. For instance, Henry Kaiser was arguably one of the greatest and most well-known health-care entrepreneurs. His personal net worth was estimated at $2.5 billion, or $16 billion today.[33] Kaiser essentially set up the first health maintenance organization. According to *Investor's Business Daily*, "Today, Oakland, Calif.-based Kaiser Permanente is the largest nonprofit health delivery system in the country, serving 8.6 million members in nine states and the District of Columbia."[34] A good many of the most successful entrepreneurs (who rose to the top) give back to society with foundations; even when they are deceased, they are giving back to society. What is going to happen with venture capital? Nothing is certain, but a number of trends are emerging. Several of these trends have occurred in the past and might be short term or possibly longer term this time around.

Twelve Emerging Venture Capital Trends

1. **Angel investing will increase.** James Geshwiler, managing director of CommonAngels, forecasts a bullish view on angel investing. In an interview with the *Boston Business Journal*, he said, "I think there's a general consensus around CommonAngels that there's never been a better time to invest. I have more members writing more checks, so the total dollars are going up. . . . Single investors are far less likely to make investments (now). Groups are in it through thick and thin, and are more likely to invest in hard times. Good times don't breed angel groups"[35]

Geshwiler also is founding chairman of the Angel Capital Association, which is a trade association dedicated to supporting angel investment groups is North America. As of September 2008, ACA had 165 member angel groups, funds approximately 700 new companies each year, and has an ongoing portfolio of more than 5,000 entrepreneurial companies.[36]

2. University involvement. Universities will become more focused on producing new companies like Avid and the University of Pennsylvania. Universities that historically have not focused on this area will enter the picture. Brigham Young University is an example. A December 2009 *BusinessWeek* article noted that the Provo (Utah) university now ranks first in the country in the number of start-ups, licenses, and patent applications per research dollar spent, and its technology led to the creation of nine new companies.[37] Similarly, the University of Minnesota has a medical-device center fellows program for new medical technologies, such as AUM Cardiovascular, which makes a high-tech detection device for coronary artery disease. Historically, Stanford has had a large budget and helped nurture some of the most notable start-ups in the country.

3. Corporate venture arms. There is a distinct movement by companies to set up their own venture arms to acquire new technologies or products. Cisco is an example of a company with corporate venturing. In the first decade of the twenty-first century, it acquired more than 65 start-ups using a stringent system for appraising, acquiring, and developing technology companies.[38]

Corporate venturing is not new. Large corporations, such as Intel, had venture arms in the past. The purpose of large companies having venture arms is to expand into new areas or build complementary technologies for existing business lines.

4. Private exchanges. There will be a new exit strategy or third leg to the stool: private exchanges. Private exchanges are a viable alternative to either IPOs or a sale.

The *San Francisco Business Journal* tracked the declined rate of public offerings in the lead-up to the Great Recession:

> For all of 2008, six venture-backed companies made their public debut, the worst showing since 1977 when there were also just six VC-backed companies that went public. Preliminary figures show

only 260 M&A transactions last year, the first year since 2003 that were less than 300 venture-backed acquisitions. Last year had two quarters with no venture-backed IPOs. The last time that occurred was in 1975, when both the first and fourth quarters had no IPOs, even though the Dow soared 35 percent, starting the year at 632.04 and ended at 852.41. By dollar volume, last year's IPO proceeds totaled $470.2 million, the lowest since 1979, when IPOs raised $339.7 million.[39]

Likewise, the mergers and acquisitions (M&A) market was adversely affected in the third quarter 2008, as marked here in a *Pensions & Investments* write-up:

Venture capital investments in the quarter dropped 7% to $7.1 billion from the end of the second quarter, the largest decline in five years, according to the MoneyTree Report by PricewaterhouseCoopers and the National Venture Capital Association based Thomson Reuters data. The investments are 9% less than the year-earlier quarter. The number of deals also dropped, to 907 deals in the quarter ended Sept. 30, down 14% from the second quarter.[40]

In the future, there might be ways to invest in private equity (venture capital) that existed mainly for institutional investors, venture capitalists, or employees of the company. That is, a sophisticated and accredited investor might easily be able to buy or sell shares in a private company. There are several new "online stock bazaars" or bulletin board or market places to buy or sell private shares of companies.

SecondMarket is one of the leaders gaining traction in this space. In a 2009 report, Reuters observed the passing of the $1 billion mark for the face value of traded securities on SecondMarket (doubling its face value of only 5 months prior) and called it "the world's largest marketplace for illiquid assets."[41]

Investors are expected to purchase a staggering amount of private-company stock, somewhere in the neighborhood of $10 billion this year, up from $5.7 billion last year and $850 million in 2005.[42]

5. Boutique banks. Most likely Wall Street will see the emergence of boutique banks reminiscent of Alex. Brown, Hambrecht & Quist, Robertson Stephens, and Montgomery Securities. These firms (along with others) were gobbled up by larger financial institutions. Megabanks such as Citigroup failed miserably in virtually every conceivable manner. Large banks seldom have interest in smaller IPOs because of economics. They need bigger deals and bigger fees to support their infrastructures. Oppenheimer, Stifel, Jefferies, R.W. Baird, Leerink Swan, Raymond James, Janney Montgomery, and Cowen are a few boutiques emerging that are focused on fast-growing companies. There is definitely a need for such firms because there are both investors seeking venture capital deals and IPOs and entrepreneurs building emerging growth companies.

6. New entrepreneurs and innovation. Unlike all the other alternative investments, venture capital is an investment in human nature—that is, you are investing in people. Bo Peabody, author of *Lucky or Smart?: Secrets to an Entrepreneurial Life*, notes that "There is nothing more authentic in business than a fundamentally innovative, morally compelling, and philosophically positive company whose mission has been crafted carefully and communicated with charisma and passion."[43]

When you invest in people, you are betting that the person you are giving your money to will earn you a handsome return. You believe that person will make you a lot of money by growing a business. If one invests in commodities, one is investing in inanimate objects: gold, silver, wheat, copper, or coffee. Hedge funds are investments in a variety of securities. A new breed of entrepreneurs is emerging who are better trained and equipped to dealing with financial crises. Innovative ideas for funds will occur, such as Bo Peabody's fund, which invests in entrepreneurs based in any geographic location and not just large cities. Peabody points out that "Village Ventures, the venture capital firm I co-founded in 2000, makes money by taking advantage of the supply and demand imbalance that results from the concentration of venture capital in only a few large cities."[44]

Another innovative fund is the Fireman Capital Partners Fund, launched by the former chairman and CEO of Reebok International Ltd, Paul Fireman. According to the *Boston Business Journal*, in March 2009 "the firm invested approximately $30 million in California premium denim company Hudson Jeans."[45] Paul Fireman has structured this fund to invest in the retailing space. Not only does he provide funds but he has a wealth of knowledge and experience to mentor companies in the retail space. The Dow Jones VentureSource credits consumer goods start-ups with taking in $206.8 million nationally, noting that historically they have been shunned by venture capitalists on account of their high distribution costs. New England alone raised $31.6 million through consumer goods start-ups over this same period.[46]

7. Industry creation. Many talented employees were unemployed as a result of the financial carnage in 2008–2009. Tens of thousands of highly educated employees from firms such as Lehman or Bear Stearns are starting or joining new companies. Americans are creative and entrepreneurial. A lot of employees have started companies in market downturns. The pond is filled with more fish than ever. As Karl Vesper writes in his book, *New Venture Strategies*, "Most venture ideas come from former jobs held by the entrepreneurs."[47] The next big thing is out there. Finding it will be immensely rewarding whether you are a venture capitalist or an individual looking for the next big thing.

In the health-care sector alone, there were massive layoffs in 2009, resulting in 59,000 workers in that sector now searching for new avenues of employment.[48] The layoffs in the health-care sector might lead one to believe it is an ominous sign for investments in health-care venture capital. However, it is the polar opposite. Following the layoffs, investments in health-care venture capital were at a high of about 39% of all venture capital. A number of great new health-care companies will be born.[49]

8. Compelling valuations and lower fees. The best valuations are found after a market correction, not at the peak. Quite a few investors put money into venture capital at the peak of the market. For example, Pennsylvania Public School Employees Retirement System trustees decided to invest hundreds of millions in venture capital (according to its Web site) in the first half of 2008. Venture capital is not as easy to invest in as a mutual fund, which focuses on large growth. First, you are dealing with private companies. Second, it is impossible to time when you will find a great company or idea, nor can you even tell if you will be able to invest in one if you find one. Because it is more difficult to attract funds in a bad market, venture funds typically lower fees in order to make it more attractive for investors. Therefore, the best time to invest regarding valuation is also the most cost-effective. As *Pensions & Investments* notes:

> Some managers have seen the writing on the wall. TA Associates Inc., Boston, cut its carried interest to 20% from 25% on the $4 billion TA XI, which closed Aug. 12, said Brian J. Conway, managing director. TA Associates began raising TA XI in December, but lowered fees, including management fees, in the first quarter.[50]

9. Financial Darwinism. As a result of the market, many venture funds closed, and turnover was at an all time high. Although there are 866 venture firms in the industry—down slightly from 943 firms in 2001—it is the top tier of the industry leaders that are getting most of the best deals right now, many investors and entrepreneurs say.[51]

Financial Darwinism moved rapidly through the market and some in Silicon Valley say the number of venture firms, 741 at last count, could shrink by the hundreds before things pick up.[52] In Foley & Lardner's annual survey on emerging companies, Darwinism can be witnessed in the venture capital world. "Due to dismal returns, we're seeing a fallout in the number of VCs who will survive. The top VC funds are continuing to aggressively raise money, whereas the rest are choosing to walk away."[53]

However, venture capital will not fade away. The strong will become stronger. The weak will go bankrupt. Even a number of the older venture capitalists are slowing down; the last two downturns were extremely trying on venture capitalists. During the last stock market correction, the market was low but not at the bottom; the market was still falling. The market was off for two more years. Now we have experienced an even greater calamity, staring into the abyss. Only the real wave riders of the venture capital world will prevail.

10. Specialization. When markets turn ugly, there is a tendency among venture capital firms to retrench and stick to their knitting, as they say. Around the time of the tech bubble, venture firms were expanding everywhere (early to late stage across the country) and investing in areas beyond their areas of expertise. After the blowup, the firms that survived focused on areas they knew best. This time around, venture capital firms were expanding globally and branching into new areas such as leveraged buy-outs (LBOs) or hedge funds. The result will be the same in that venture capital will move back to its origin. Venture capital will most likely become highly specialized again. Specialization became popular in the last downturn and appears to be recurring.

11. Global prowess. For the near future, venture capital will flourish outside the United States, especially Asia. *Investor's Business Daily* reported in 2006 that venture firm investments for the year would reach a 5-year high of $32 billion (before the Great Recession) and that China's investments alone would mark an all-time high for that country.[54] Venture funds and entrepreneurs who want to ride the wave will explore opportunities abroad, and Asia will be the fastest-growing region for venture capital. China's high watermarks of 2006 were surpassed the following year, with a record number of IPO launches and $34.6 billion raised by mainland China firms through IPOs. On top of that, $12.4 billion was raised in Hong Kong by other firms.[55]

12. Longer exits. Traditional exits (IPO as well as M&A) will take longer. Already it is taking much longer to take a venture capital–backed company public. As *Forbes* magazine noted in the fall of 2009: "The exit ramp used to be a little faster: A company was ready for a public offering six years after getting VC money. Now the harvest comes after 10 years."[56]

These movements are happening in the venture world in 2009, but they might change in a few months and look very different from today. Venture capital changes on a day-to-day basis and will always be high risk, high return. As with all alternatives, the more you learn, the easier it is to become an experienced wave rider. For those who take the time to learn how to surf the venture capital waves, it can be a very rewarding experience.

Recommended Reading and Web Sites

Web Sites

www.federalreserve.gov
fis.dowjones.com/products/vc.html
punctuative.com/vcdb/
www.nvca.org/
www.reuters.com/finance/deals/mergers

www.privateequity.com/
www.privateequitycouncil.org/
www.pewnews.com/
www.iijournals.com/
www.reuters.com/finance/deals/mergers
venture-capital.alltop.com
www.fiercebiotech.com/

Books

Dermot Berkery, *Raising Venture Capital for the Serious Entrepreneur*

Justin J. Camp, *Venture Capital Due Diligence: A Guide to Making Smart Investment Choices and Increasing Your Portfolio Returns*

Harry Cendrowski, James P. Martin, Louis W. Petro, and Adam A. Wadecki, *Private Equity: History, Governance, and Operations*

Guy Fraser-Sampson, *Private Equity as an Asset Class*

David and Laura Gladstone, *Venture Capital Handbook: An Entrepreneur's Guide to Raising Venture Capital, Revised and Updated Edition*

Ulrich Grabenwater and Tom Weidig, *Exposed to the J Curve: Understanding and Managing Private Equity Fund Investments*

Chris Hale, *Private Equity*

Arthur Laffer, William Hass, and Shepherd G. Pryor IV, *The Private Equity Edge: How Private Equity Players and the World's Top Companies Build Value and Wealth*

Josh Lerner, *Venture Capital and Private Equity: A Casebook*

Kenneth H. Marks, Larry E. Robbins, Gonzalo Fernandez, and John P. Funkhouser, *The Handbook of Financing Growth: Strategies and Capital Structure, 2nd ed.*

Andrew Metrick, *Venture Capital and the Finance of Innovation*

Thomas Meyer and Pierre-Yves Mathonet, *Beyond the J Curve: Managing a Portfolio of Venture Capital and Private Equity Funds*

Stefan Povaly, *Private Equity Exits: Divestment Process Management for Leveraged Buyouts*

PART 3

COMMODITIES

RIDING THE WAVE

Chapter 10

Commodity Overview

O ver my career, I learned quite a bit about commodities. I discovered that you can make a ton of money or you can lose your shirt. Years ago, I suggested adding commodities to a conservative client's portfolio for diversification, to which he promptly asked whether I had lost my mind. The client was a high-powered attorney at a prestigious law firm. At first, I cringed and melted into the huge leather chair in his office overlooking the Capitol in Washington. Extreme doubt entered my mind. The silence was deafening to the point of awkwardness. I felt faint and slightly dizzy. Before exploding into a tirade and lambasting me, he quietly asked the question, "Why would anyone ever own commodities?" I was convinced in my view toward commodities as a means of further diversifying a client's portfolio but was being challenged.

Thinking quickly, I decided the best way to convey my point was to respond with a question. I asked him in rapid succession what he put on his cereal; what he filled his car tank with; what he used to heat his home; the type of petroleum used to fly the plane he took the day before; if he ever bought his wife silver, gold, or platinum; if he ever wore anything with cotton; the energy source for his barbeque grill; how much copper was used in the construction of his house; if he ever ate bread, pasta, beef, chicken, pork, or drank either coffee, milk, or orange juice. The client smiled at me. He understood my meaning. In the end, he invested and did very well. The reality is that commodities lower risk and increase return for any portfolio consisting of equities and fixed income. My client's fear of commodities was also reduced when I showed him the waves or patterns that commodities exhibit on an ongoing basis.

Waves can be found with commodities just like other alternatives, but you need to pay careful attention. As Ernest Hemingway wrote in *The Old Man and the Sea*, "If there is a hurricane you can always see the signs of it in the sky for days ahead, if you are at sea. They do not see it ashore because they do not know what to look for."[1] Often what appears to be the worst time to invest in commodities is actually the best time to invest. Commodities are a significant and growing segment of alternatives. According to a 2008 article in *The Economist*, "Some $260 billion is invested in commodity funds, 20 times the level of 2003."[2] Wave Theory has proved quite useful as the alternatives market grows in size.

Contrary to popular belief, Wall Street is heavily regulated, and so is the commodities industry. The Commodity Futures Trading Commission (CFTC) regulates commodities. In 1976, the entire futures market for oil and other commodities was approximately $4 billion. As of 2007, the market reached $4.78 trillion. Yet the total market (including the value of commodity derivatives traded off-exchange and outside CFTC regulation) has reached almost $10 trillion as of December 2007. The commodity space is large and includes gold, silver, platinum, zinc, copper, lead, nickel, soybeans, wheat, corn, cocoa, sugar, coffee, oil, natural gas, uranium, and many others on a variety of global exchanges. Despite the rogue wave that terrorized the financial markets in 2008, institutions will likely be committing additional funds to alternatives such as commodities.

Numerous studies have shown that it is prudent to add commodities to a portfolio. One in particular, by John Lintner, the late Harvard economist, found that "portfolios that combined stocks, bonds and managed futures showed 'substantially less risk at every possible level of expected return' than those without managed futures."[3] Individual investors will most likely increase or add commodities to their asset allocation mix because commodities outperformed equities.

Demand, supply, and market equilibrium are crucial to observe when investing in commodities and managed futures. Regardless of whether an investor has a penchant toward fundamental analysis over technical analysis (or vice versa), both should be reviewed before an investment. For instance, the supply of gold might include not just bullion and coins but even companies purchasing gold to melt down. Is the stock market soaring and investors leaving gold investments? Supply would include not just the existing amount of gold but gold obtained through mining. Is gold production declining? The supply of gold is global. How is gold doing in other countries? What is the demand? What is the supply? Unlike certain commodities that can be destroyed or are perishable like wheat, gold is quite durable and does not perish.

Commodities can be elastic in demand. Elasticity is defined as:

> A characteristic of commodities which describes the interaction of the supply, demand, and price of a commodity. A commodity is said to be elastic in demand when a price change creates an increase or decrease in consumption. The supply of a commodity is said to be elastic when a change in price creates change in the production of the commodity. Inelasticity of supply or demand exists when either is relatively unresponsive to changes in price.[4]

If you were to walk around your supermarket and into the meat and dairy aisles, basic items like beef, poultry, milk, and eggs would be seen as having a constant demand, thus inelastic. Consumers may not be happy about price increases with any of these dietary staples, but for the most part those increases will not drastically affect shopping behavior. Walk across the store to the fruit section, and you will find rows of elastic items that can be easily substituted (either for each other or entirely). If apples get too expensive, there are plenty of substitutes.

Besides fundamental analysis, there is technical analysis. Technical analysis attempts to determine the future price action of a given commodity by studying its price history. Technicians use statistical methods when analyzing commodities.

Commodities tend to do well when the stock market does poorly. Returns are inversely affected by business cycles. For investors to protect themselves against long periods of decline in the stock market, they could turn to commodities as a hedge. As Bjornson and Carter explain:

> Commodities may act as a hedge against business cycles, as commodities and capital assets are affected differently by macroeconomic

factors. Part of the reason is that stocks and bonds are affected by long-term expectations of future cash flows whereas commodities are influenced primarily by short-term shocks. Therefore we would expect commodities and capital assets to perform much different at different point in the business cycle. Additionally, we may expect some commodities to exhibit positive demand effects in response to economic growth.[5]

Commodities have moved in waves for the last century. In Jim Rogers's *Adventure Capitalist*, the author notes that "there have been long periods when stocks did well while raw materials did horribly—the late 1980s and 1990s, say. The late 1960s and the 1970s saw the reverse. From 1906 to the early 1920s stocks did nothing while commodities boomed."[6] As shown with other alternatives, if one catches a commodity wave at the right time, one can make a fortune. According to the 2009 CRB Commodity Yearbook, "the Continuous Commodity Index (CCI) in 2008 peaked at a record high of 615.04 in July 2008, bringing the 2001–08 bull market to a post-war record of +236.4%. The CCI index was driven to that high by weakness in the dollar and speculative fever."[7] More recently, commodities had exceptional performance: 2002 +23.0%, 2003 +8.9%, 2004 +11.2%, 2005 +22.5%, 2006 +13.5%, 2007 +20.6%. A wave is fun to ride, but when the wave crashes, the fall can be significant. The CCI ended 2008 down –23.7%, as a result of the global financial crisis in 2008. "All of the six CCI futures sub-sectors closed lower in 2008: Meats –2.7%, Softs –7.5%, Metals –19.0%, Grains –20.2%, Energy –46.1%."[8]

The CRB commodity index (from September 28, 1956 to July 31, 2009) highlights the 2008 turmoil with commodities, as illustrated in Figure 10.1.

Similar to other asset classes, commodities were affected by the rogue wave in 2008. The precipitous drop took the index backward 30 years to the 1970s. Yet commodities performed better over the last decade (1998–2008) than traditional asset classes, as illustrated in Figure 10.2.

Over the same period, managed futures (commodities) returned 153.69% versus 72.95% for Barclay's Aggregate Bond, 8.28% for the MSCI EAFE Index, –12.99% for the S&P 500, and –28.08% for the NASDAQ.

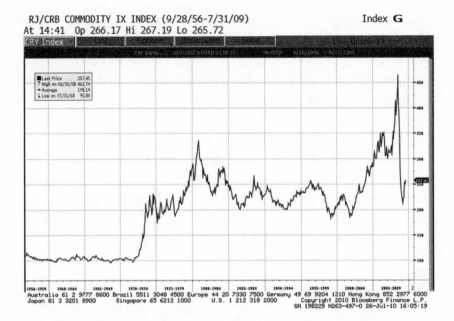

Figure 10.1 RJ/CRB Commodity Index (9/28/56–7/31/09)

Source: Bloomberg. Used with permission.

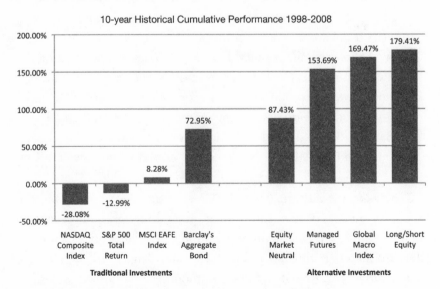

Figure 10.2 Traditional Investments versus Alternative Investments

Source: Ascentia Capital Partners, Data Source: Per Track.

There are many benefits to owning commodities, including beating inflation. *Forbes* magazine notes that during the last great inflation, "From 1977 to 1982 it tacked 68% onto the price of goods while the price of silver doubled and both oil and gold tripled."[9] Commodities tend to do well when the economy is growing.

Certain metals, such as gold or silver, tend to do well in economic uncertainties or major market disruptions such as a rogue wave or depression. Other commodities, like oil and livestock, respond positively to inflation, whereas corn and coffee tend to lag under the same circumstances.[10] Some commodities react differently to various economic variables: they make suitable diversification agents and as a result might be contenders for many asset allocation models.

Defining Commodities

The definition of a commodity, according to the Commodity Exchange Act, is as follows:

> The term "commodity" means wheat, cotton, rice, corn, oats, barley, rye, flaxseed, grain sorghums, mill feeds, butter, eggs, *Solanum tuberosum* (Irish potatoes), wool, wool tops, fats and oils (including lard, tallow, cottonseed oil, peanut oil, soybean oil, and all other fats and oils), cottonseed meal, cottonseed, peanuts, soybeans, soybean meal, livestock, livestock products, frozen concentrated orange juice, and all other goods and articles, except onions as provided in Public Law 85–839 (7 USC 13–1), and all services, rights, and interests, in which contracts for future delivery are presently or in the future dealt in.[11]

Commodity is a very broad term that covers virtually everything on earth except for onions. (Onion futures were traded in 1942, but because of onion growers' concerns about speculation and volatile prices, Congress later prohibited trading of onion futures in August 1958.[12]) In *Hot Commodities*, Jim Rogers defines commodities as "the raw materials," "natural resources," "hard assets," and "real things" that are the essentials of not just your life but the lives of everyone in the world.[13] Thus, a commodity is anything natural found on Earth.

Commodities futures can be broken down into three central areas: agriculture, metals, and energy. There are essentially two main agricultural commodities: first, grains and oilseeds (corn, soy, wheat, canola, and rice); second, softs (cocoa, coffee, cotton, orange juice, and sugar). Metals can be broken down into two primary areas: industrial metals (steel and iron, copper, aluminum, lead, nickel, tin, and zinc) and precious metals (gold, silver, platinum, and palladium)—all elements that can be found on the periodic table. The third main commodity, energy, can be subdivided into oil (crude oil, bent crude oil, gasoline, heating oil, and gas oil), natural gas, coal, ethanol, and uranium.

All commodities portray waves, but this book will highlight the most prevalent category: metals (gold). There are many commodities in the market, but gold is one of the most recognizable and highly traded, even though other commodities are gaining traction, such as platinum or sugar. Although these smaller players are intriguing and offer opportunity, we will cover gold in more detail. If one can master riding a wave with one commodity, they should be able to surf any commodity. Practice makes perfect.

Commodities futures are grouped together differently on almost every exchange; each exchange is different. Most major exchanges that trade commodity futures group them in a similar fashion to the list I devised (See Table 10.1).

Investors frequently confuse commodities and managed futures. According to Jenson, Johnson, and Mercer, "Managed futures can be characterized as investment funds in which managers invest in futures on a discretionary basis."[14] Managed futures involve professional trading managers called commodity trading advisors (CTAs) who use leverage and various credit strategies. Commodities generally encompass agricultural products, metals, energy, and other resources that are traded on an exchange. A futures contract is a binding agreement on an exchange to buy or sell a commodity or financial instrument in the future. A commodity is an "article of commerce or it can be a product that can be used for commerce."[15]

An investor with stocks, bonds, and cash can improve the risk/return characteristics by adding commodities and/or managed futures. Countless studies have shown that it is prudent to add commodities and/or managed

Table 10.1 U.S. Commodity Futures

Metals	Energy	Agriculture
Precious Metals	**Oil**	**Grains and Oilseeds**
Gold	*Crude Oil*	*Corn*
Silver	Bent Crude Oil	Soy
Platinum	Gasoline	Wheat
Palladium	Heating Oil	Canola (Rapseed)
	Gas Oil	Rice
		Oats
Industrial Metals	**Gas**	**Softs**
Steel and Iron	Natural Gas	Cocoa
Copper		Coffee
Aluminum		Cotton
Lead		Orange Juice
Nickel		Sugar
Tin		
Zinc		
	Other Energy	**Livestock**
	Coal	Cattle
	Ethanol	Hogs
	Uranium	

Source: Author.

futures to a portfolio. Managed futures, for instance, can further diversify a portfolio, especially when one considers their low correlation to stocks, bonds, and cash. Also, as Harry Kat advocated for the International Security Management Association (ISMA), "investing in managed futures can improve the overall risk profile of a portfolio far beyond what can be achieved with hedge funds alone. Making an allocation to managed futures not only neutralizes the unwanted side effects of hedge funds but also leads to further risk reduction. Since managed futures offer an acceptable expected return, all of this comes at quite a low price in terms of expected return foregone."[16] In addition, managed futures "offer institutional investors actively managed exposure to a truly global and diversified array of liquid, transparent instruments."[17]

Similarly, research has shown that commodities can lower risk and increase returns. According to Büyüksahin, Haigh, and Robe, "There is little evidence of a common long-term trend between investable commodity and equity indices and no evidence of secular strengthening of any such trend. An implication of this is that passive investors are likely to achieve gains over the long-run by diversifying portfolios across the two asset classes."[18]

History

Many people think that options and futures are recent inventions. However, options have a long history, going back to Ancient Greece. Aristotle wrote about the first futures trade with commodities. The account of Thales of Miletus reveals a futures trade. The philosopher bought up access to all of the olive presses in the winter because he divined that there would be a great olive harvest; when the harvest came, he alone controlled access to the presses as demand for them soared.[19]

Commodities have a rich history in every country around the world, especially American cotton. In fact, the serial entrepreneur Eli Whitney invented the cotton gin, which propelled America's economic boom in the late 1700s. At this time, the United States had an abundance of cotton that was in great demand in Europe. Whitney solved the dilemma of separating seeds from cotton. Once this issue was resolved through Whitney's cotton gin, exports mushroomed. *Investor's Business Daily* notes that in 1796, Americans shipped 6 million pounds of cotton to Europe; this was up from 190,000 pounds just 2 years earlier. In 1800, the United States produced 35 million pounds of cotton.[20] Commodities are prevalent and even more so today as evidenced through emerging markets — those markets being the primary beneficiary of a United Nations estimated 40% rise in global population, up from 2010 levels of 9 billion, anticipated over the next 40 years.[21]

Commodities move in waves. One type of wave, the Elliot wave, uses Fibonacci numbers to link waves with commodities. A Fibonacci sequence is one in which every number is the sum of the previous two (0,1,1, 2,3,5,8,13,21,34,55,89,144,233).[22] Traders use Fibonacci for investing in commodities, searching for patterns that might indicate future values.[23]

Even the World Bank has depicted these trends, patterns, or cycles over the years, as illustrated in Table 10.2.

According to the World Bank, there were four central growth periods for commodities. Although one could claim 1915–1917 and 1950–1957

Table 10.2

Common Features	1915–17	1950–57	1973–74	2003–08
Rapid global real growth (average annual percent)	–	4.8	4	3.5
Major conflict and geopolitical uncertainty	World War I	Korean War	Yom Kippur War, Vietnam War	Iraq Conflict
Inflation	Widespread	Limited	Widespread	Limited second round effects
Period of significant infrastructure investment	World War I	Postwar rebuilding in Europe and Japan	Not a period of significant investment	Rapid buildup of infrastructure in China
Centered in which major commodity groups	Metals, agriculture	Metals, agriculture	Oil, agriculture	Oil, metals, agriculture
Initial rise observed in prices of	Metals, agriculture	Metals	Oil	Oil
Preceded by extended period of low prices of investment	No	World War II destroyed much capacity	Low prices and a supply shock	Extended period of low prices
Percent increase in prices (previous trough to peak)	34	47	59	131
Years of rising prices prior to peak	4	3	2	5
Years of declining prices prior to trough	4	11	19	–

Source: World Bank, "The Commodity Boom: Longer Term Prospects," in *Global Economic Prospects 2009: Commodities at the Crossroads*, New York: World Bank Publications, 2008, 55.

were commodity waves, there were far fewer ways to invest in commodities during those years. Yet commodity waves seen over the last century are likely to occur again because of economic cycles. Fortunately, there are more alternative vehicles to invest in today than a century ago.

Market

The data featured in Figure 10.3 are from the Commodity Research Bureau's 2009 Commodity Yearbook. It represents the total volume of contracts traded during 2008.

Commodities are traded with futures. A futures contract is defined as a contract to buy a commodity or security on a future date at a price that is fixed today. Table 10.3 shows the top-25 United States futures contracts (volume) during 2008.

Exchanges exist all over the world, as shown in Bloomberg's Contract Exchange Menu (Figure 10.4).

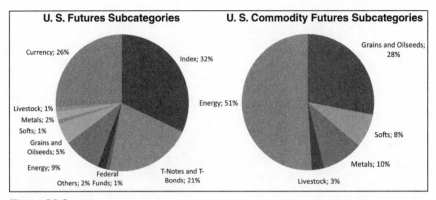

Figure 10.3

Source: Commodity Research Bureau, "The Commodity Price Trend," in *CRB Commodity Yearbook 2009*
(New York: Wiley, 2009), 6T. Used with permission.

Table 10.3 Top 25 U.S. Futures by Volume 2008

Rank	Contract	Exchange	2008 Volume	% of Total Volume
1	E-Mini S&P 500 Index	CME	633,889,466	24.44%
2	Eurodollars (3-month)	CME	596,974,081	23.01%
3	T-Notes (10-year)	CBT	256,770,689	9.90%
4	T-Notes (5-year)	CBT	168,127,469	6.48%
5	Crude Oil	NYMEX	134,674,264	5.19%
6	E-Mini NASDAQ 100	CME	108,734,456	4.19%
7	T-Bonds (30-year)	CBT	89,464,546	3.45%
8	T-Notes (2-year)	CBT	79,311,002	3.06%
9	Corn	CBT	59,957,118	2.31%
10	Mini ($5) D.J. Industrial Index	CBT	55,348,312	2.13%
11	Euro FX	CME	53,652,590	2.07%
12	E-Mini Russell 2000 Index	CME	46,065,655	1.78%
13	Natural Gas	NYMEX	38,730,519	1.49%
14	Gold (100 oz.)	COMEX (NYMEX)	38,377,367	1.48%
15	Soybeans	CBT	36,373,096	1.40%
16	Japanese Yen	CME	32,844,404	1.27%
17	Henry Hub Swap	NYMEX	31,401,575	1.21%
18	Sugar #11	NYBOT	27,019,704	1.04%
19	Gasoline, RBOB	NYMEX	20,522,571	0.79%
20	British Pound	CME	20,497,378	0.79%
21	Heating Oil #2	NYMEX	19,583,052	0.75%
22	Federal Funds (30-day)	CBT	19,434,295	0.75%
23	Wheat	CME	19,011,928	0.73%
24	Soybean Oil	ICE	16,928,361	0.65%
25	S&P 500 Index	CME	16,763,071	0.65%

Source: Commodity Research Bureau, "The Commodity Price Trend," in CRB Commodity Yearbook 2009
(New York: Wiley, 2009), 6T. Used with permission.

<HELP> for explanation.   N090c ComdtyCEM
Enter # <Go> for a list of contracts.
                    CONTRACT EXCHANGE MENU
        Sort By: ▓ Geographic   Page 1/3
North America   20) PHL NASDAQ OMX PHLX
 1) AMX American Stock Exchange   21) NCP NYMEX Clearport
 2) CBF CBOE Futures Exchange   22) NYM NYMEX Exchange
 3) CBT Chicago Board of Trade   23) NGE NYMEX Green Exchange
 4) CBO Chicago Board Options Exchange   24) NYL NYSE LIFFE U.S.
 5) CCX Chicago Climate Futures Exchang 25) OCG OneChicago
 6) CME Chicago Mercantile Exchange   South America
 7) CMX COMEX division of NYMEX   26) BMF Bolsa De Mercadorias & Futuros
 8) ELX ELX Futures   27) BOV Bolsa de Valores de Sao Paulo
 9) WCE ICE Futures Canada   28) CDE Colombia Derivatives Exchange
10) FNX ICE Futures US Currencies   29) SBA Merc. de Valores Buenos Aires
11) NYF ICE Futures US Indices   30) MBA Mercado a Termino Buenos Aires
12) NYB ICE Futures US Softs   31) MAE Mercado Abierto Electronico
13) ISE International Securities Exchan 32) RFX Rosario Futures Exchange
14) KCB Kansas City Board of Trade   Europe
15) MDX Mercado Mexicano de Derivados   33) ADE Athens Derivative Exchange
16) MGE Minneapolis Grain Exchange   34) BNF Bluenext
17) MCE Montreal Climate Exchange   35) MIL Borsa Italiana (IDEM)
18) MSE Montreal Exchange   36) BTS Bucharest Stock Exchange
19) NFX NASDAQ OMX Futures Exchange   37) BSE Budapest Stock Exchange
        Type CEPR <GO> for the FUTURES AND OPTIONS EXCHANGE DIRECTORY
Australia 61 2 9777 8600 Brazil 5511 3048 4500 Europe 44 20 7330 7500 Germany 49 69 9204 1210 Hong Kong 852 2977 6000
Japan 81 3 3201 8900   Singapore 65 6212 1000   U.S. 1 212 318 2000   Copyright 2009 Bloomberg Finance L.P.
                                                            G368-938-0 06-Aug-09 10:14:40

Figure 10.4   Bloomberg Futures and Options Exchange Directory

Source: Bloomberg. Used with permission.

The United States leads in volume of commodities futures contract being traded. The CME and NYMEX are two of the largest. Table 10.4 looks at the volume traded for the top-10 exchanges in the United States:

Table 10.4   U.S. Futures Exchanges by Volume 2008

	Exchange	2008 Contracts	% of Group
1	CME Group	2,438,142,653	85.53
2	New York Mercantile Exchange (NYMEX)	338,455,289	11.87
3	InterContinental Exchange (ICE)	63,433,647	2.23
4	OneChicago	4,012,281	0.14
5	Kansas City Board of Trade (KCBT)	3,778,266	0.13
6	Minneapolis Grain Exchange (MGE)	1,361,067	0.05
7	CBOE Futures Exchange (CFE)	1,161,397	0.04
8	Chicago Climate Exchange (CCFE)	370,505	0.01
9	Green Exchange	35,523	0.00
10	U.S. Futures Exchange	22,955	0.00
	Total	2,850,773,583	100.00%

Source: Commodity Research Bureau, "U.S. Futures Volume Highlights," in *CRB Commodity Yearbook 2009* (New York: Wiley, 2009), 36T.

Exchanges exist all around the world and vary in contract size, from Germany being the largest to Japan being one of the smallest exchanges by volume in 2008. Table 10.5 looks at the volume traded for the top-10 global exchanges:

Table 10.5   Top 10 Worldwide Futures Exchanges by Volume 2008

Exchange	2008 Contracts	% of All Futures
1 EUREX, Frankfurt, Germany	1,146,081,579	21.07
2 Euronext, LIFFE, UK	544,395,261	10.01
3 South African Futures Exchange, SAFEX, Africa	475,051,729	8.73
4 National Stock Exchange of India	428,167,428	7.87
5 Bolsa de Mercadorias & Futuros (BM&F), Brazil	323,770,173	5.95
6 Dalian Commodity Exchange (DCE), China	313,217,957	5.76
7 Zhengzhou Commodity Exchange (ZCE), China	222,557,134	4.09
8 ICE, UK	152,322,268	2.80
9 Shanghai Metal Exchange, China	140,263,185	2.58
10 Osaka Securities Exchange (OSE), Japan	131,028,334	2.41

Source: Commodity Research Bureau, *The CBR Commodity Yearbook 2009* (New York: Wiley, 2009), 36T.

The CFTC oversees U.S. futures exchanges but not the over-the-counter (OTC) market or foreign exchanges. Pension funds, commodity companies, and hedge funds can make large trades off an exchange through the swap market. Although bank OTC trading rooms have taken a large portion of derivatives, exchanges still have many contracts. Exchange-traded futures contracts are readily available in energy, agriculture, and metals. A number of mergers and acquisitions have take place with exchanges, but the following are some of the largest and more well known.

CME Group

The CME Group is listed on the NASDAQ under the symbol CME and offers one of the largest ranges of futures and options products available on any exchange. The CME offers futures and options based on interest rates, equity indexes, foreign exchange, energy, agricultural commodities, metals, and alternative investment products, such as weather and real estate.[24]

New York Mercantile Exchange

The New York Mercantile Exchange, Inc., is the world's largest physical commodity futures exchange and trading platform for energy and precious metals. NYMEX provides markets for the trading and clearing of crude oil, gasoline, heating oil, natural gas, electricity, propane, coal, uranium, environmental commodities, softs, gold, silver, copper, aluminum, platinum, and palladium.[25] The exchange offers many different types of options.

Chicago Board of Trade

The Chicago Board of Trade (CBOT) was formed in Chicago in 1848 by a group of 25 businessmen for the grain market because farm prices were ruled by boom and bust cycles.[26] The CBOT offered farmers a way to get a guaranteed price for goods ahead of time with contracts or futures. Today, the CBOT is one of the largest commodities exchanges in the world with more than 3,600 members, who trade almost 50 different futures and options products such as U.S. Treasury bonds, soy beans, wheat, or the Dow Jones Industrial Average futures.

Intercontinental Exchange Futures

The Intercontinental Exchange is publically traded on the New York Stock Exchange under the ticker ICE. In January 2007, ICE acquired the New York Board of Trade (NYBOT) now known as ICE Futures U.S.[27] In May 2000, IntercontinentalExchange (ICE) was established, with its founding shareholders representing some of the world's largest energy companies and global banks with a goal to transform OTC energy markets by providing an open, accessible, around-the-clock electronic energy marketplace to a previously fragmented and opaque market. ICE developed an electronic marketplace for energy commodities, along with the leading electronic trade confirmation platform.

World commodity output in 2008 as a percentage of global gross domestic product (GDP) was $9.4 trillion, 15% of the total global GDP of $60.7 trillion. At these levels, commodities are clearly integral to the global economic infrastructure.

Chapter 11

Commodity Investing

In the previous chapters we walked through an overview of commodities. Now we will address the logistics and considerations tied to investment. We will begin by looking at the advantages and disadvantages inherent in the asset class, then discuss the waves that have emerged over the years, and conclude by offering profiles of the various investment vehicles available.

Advantages to Commodities Investing

Advantages to investing in the commodities market include low correlation to equities, diversification, and nonconventional markets.

Low Correlation to Equities

Over the past 10 years (all correlation coefficients calculated based on quarterly total return data for period September 30, 1999 to September 30, 2009), commodities have exhibited a low correlation (.33) with the stock market (S&P 500). Achieving a 1.00 correlation would mean perfect correlation—that is, the movement of two different securities is perfectly correlated, and they move in tandem in either good or bad markets. Having a negative correlation or a low correlation means that the asset class is ideal to add a portfolio such as equities. Ideally one wants to construct a well-diversified portfolio of noncorrelated assets. The correlation between commodities and equities has increased over the last decade, but it is miniscule compared with other asset classes, such as foreign stocks, which have become much more highly correlated with U.S. stocks. Emerging market stocks also have a relatively high correlation. Therefore, commodities are an alternative asset class one should consider when building a diversified portfolio. Table 11.1 illustrates the correlation of commodities and other asset classes over 10 years.

One should own commodities as well as other asset classes. Wheat, for instance, has a low correlation with both equities and fixed income. Wheat has a .0770 correlation with equities and is negatively correlated with bonds (−.0296). Wheat is very much correlated to certain commodities like corn (0.5929) or soybeans (0.4214). If one desires to build a portfolio of commodities, one needs to make sure that the commodities do not have high correlations with one another. The correlations might not be apparent. In 2008, for example, gold and oil were highly correlated. Table 11.2 explores the correlation of various commodities over a 10-year period.

Diversification

If one adds just a small position of commodities (10%) to a stock and bond portfolio, returns tend to be superior to an all-equity portfolio. Commodities have a low correlation with equities and can help build a well-diversified, risk-adjusted portfolio. The graphs in Figure 11.1 illustrate growing returns based on increased diversification by adding 10%, 20%, or 30% managed futures to an equity and bond portfolio.

By themselves, managed futures are high risk, high return. However, by adding commodities to a portfolio, risk will be lowered and returns increased.

By increasing commodity exposure, risk/return is even more compelling As seen with 40% bond, 30% stock, and 30% managed future portfolio.

Nonconventional Markets

Investing in commodities also gives one the ability to be involved in nonconventional markets, such as metals, agriculture, or energy.

Bjornson and Carter suggested that commodities may act as a hedge against business cycles, as commodities and capital assets are affected differently by macroeconomic factors. Part of the reason is that stocks

Table 11.1 Correlations 10 Years: 9/30/99 to 9/30/09

	Large Cap	Small Cap	Value	Growth	EAFE	Bonds	EME	Hedge Funds	Real Estate	Eq. Market Neutral*	Commodities
Large Cap	1.00	0.94	0.92	0.94	0.92	−0.37	0.87	0.73	0.23	0.36	0.33
Small Cap		1.00	0.90	0.87	0.86	−0.39	0.83	0.67	0.20	0.35	0.25
Value			1.00	0.74	0.88	−0.22	0.76	0.63	0.29	0.42	0.35
Growth				1.00	0.83	−0.44	0.86	0.74	0.14	0.26	0.29
EAFE					1.00	−0.27	0.90	0.77	0.20	0.45	0.44
Bonds						1.00	−0.30	−0.20	−0.17	0.14	−0.12
EME							1.00	0.77	0.13	0.32	0.43
Hedge Funds								1.00	0.28	0.48	0.50
Real Estate									1.00	0.32	0.32
Eq. Market Neutral										1.00	0.49
Commodities											1.00

*Market Neutral returns include estimates found in disclosures.

All correlation coefficients calculated based on quarterly total return data for period 9/30/99 to 9/30/09.

Source: Large Cap: S&P 500 Index; Small Cap: Russell 2000; Value: Russell 1000 Value; Growth: Russell 1000 Growth; EAFE: MSCI EAFE; Bonds: Barclays Capital Aggregate; EME: MSCI Emerging Markets; Hedge Funds: SC/Tremont Multi-Strategy Index World; Real Estate: NCREIF National Property Index; Equity Market Neutral: CS/Tremont Equity Market Neutral Index; DJ UBS Commodity Index.

Table 11.2 Monthly Arithmetic Correlations: 07/96 to 06/06

	Stocks	Bonds	T-Bills	Corn	Soybeans	Wheat	Crude Oil	Silver	Gold	Copper	Hogs	Cattle	GSCI	CPI
Stocks	1.0000													
Bonds	-0.0550	1.0000												
T-Bills	0.0439	0.1102	1.0000											
Corn	0.1246	0.0033	-0.0487	1.0000										
Soybeans	0.1716	0.0728	-0.1187	0.6681	1.0000									
Wheat	0.0770	-0.0296	-0.0859	0.5923	0.4214	1.0000								
Crude oil	-0.0262	0.0214	-0.0394	-0.0123	-0.0377	0.1447	1.0000							
Silver	0.1689	-0.0781	-0.0954	0.0310	-0.0478	-0.0254	0.1154	1.0000						
Gold	-0.0346	0.1241	-0.1709	0.0173	0.0186	0.0796	0.1973	0.5694	1.0000					
Copper	0.2937	-0.1716	-0.0840	0.1117	0.0963	0.1042	0.1781	0.3463	0.3296	1.0000				
Hogs	-0.0584	0.0493	0.0193	-0.0362	0.0285	-0.0085	0.0884	-0.0215	0.0420	0.0357	1.0000			
Cattle	0.0013	-0.2024	-0.1201	0.1549	0.0466	0.2244	-0.0140	-0.1247	-0.0431	0.0344	0.3143	1.0000		
GSCI	0.0054	0.0308	-0.0768	0.1200	0.0824	0.2883	0.8969	0.1033	0.2534	0.2739	0.0964	0.0168	1.0000	
CPI	-0.0993	-0.0877	0.0315	-0.0466	0.0051	0.0169	0.1492	0.0468	0.1370	0.1160	0.0597	0.0840	0.1954	1.0000

Source: Frank Fabozzi, *The Handbook of Commodity Investing* (Hoboken, NJ: Wiley, 2008).

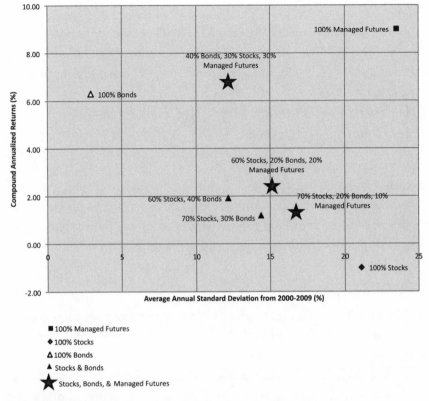

Figure 11.1 Volatility as Measured by Monthly Standard Deviation: A Hypothetical Illustration

Source: S&P 500, Barclays Capital Aggregate (Taxable) Index, Commodity Research Bureau Total Return Index.

and bonds are affected by long-term expectations of future cash flows whereas commodities are influenced primarily by short-term shocks. Therefore, we would expect some commodities and capital assets to perform much differently at different points in the business cycle. Additionally, we may expect some commodities to exhibit positive demand effects in response to economic growth.[1]

Disadvantages

As with any asset class, there are also a number of disadvantages to investing in the commodities market.

Volatility

Commodities can be volatile like equities, a "restless wave," to borrow a quote from William Whiting. However, any decline in commodities in 2008 quickly reversed itself in 2009. Commodities, in other words, came roaring back.

Long-term Performance Might Not Be Compelling if the Portfolio Is Passive

Studies show that a commodity index over very long periods produces returns that match inflation. As a result, one needs to be careful about the particular index one selects and its composition. There is no asset class anyone would want to hold forever. Portfolio adjustments (change) are needed from time to time, as indicated by Wave Theory.

Scandals

There are many individuals and companies one can hire to manage a commodities portfolio. Founded in 1969, Refco was a financial services company located in New York that was mostly known as a broker in commodities. Refco in October 2005 announced that its CEO, Phillip Bennett, had kept secret $430 million bad debts. Bennett had been secretly borrowing money from Refco in order to pay these debts off. After the announcement of the scandal, Refco's stock dropped from $28 per share to less than $1. On October 17, 2005, Refco filed for Chapter 11 to protect itself from its creditors. Bennett was sentenced to 16 years in prison for his role in a scheme to hide the commodities broker's financial troubles.

Government Risk

Commodities are a big business for countries, both in developed and emerging markets. Exports and imports are controlled by the respective governments. Besides agricultural commodities, oil is controlled by many governments. Mexico, for example, tapped its main oil field, Cantarell, for decades without investing appropriate funds needed for exploration. In fact, its state-owned Pemex contributed 40% of the national budget. In 2009, its output was about 2.5 million barrels a day; without new discoveries, its reserves are expected to run out around 2018.[2] Governments will act in their own self-interest, not a foreign investor's interest.

Taxes

Futures-based investments receive a tax treatment by the Internal Revenue Service that is unusual. Regardless of the holding period, 60% of any gains are taxed as long-term gains. The remaining 40% are taxed as short-term capital gains, which are subject to the investor's ordinary income tax rate.

High Correlation between Certain Commodities

Figure 11.2 is a Bloomberg chart that depicts wheat, corn, cereal, rice, and soybeans over a 10-year time frame.

As one can plainly see from the graph, wheat, corn, cereal, rice, and soybeans move in similar wave patterns. Owning merely these five commodities will not achieve a properly diversified commodities portfolio; an investor should own different types of commodities, such as metal or energy.[3]

Figure 11.2   10-Year Commodity Prices

Source: Bloomberg. Used with permission.

New Securities

There are many new types of securities involving commodities with little to no track record. A number of these securities can carry a high degree of risk and are sometimes difficult to understand. An investor can lose a substantial amount of money depending on the selected vehicle and when the purchase is made to access a particular commodity or group of commodities.

Performance

Table 11.3 depicts alternatives for the past 10 years. Managed futures did better than virtually all other asset classes in 2008. When the equity markets did well during 2003–2006, managed futures performed poorly. Before this time period, managed futures did well from 2000–2002 when equities did poorly. During the 1999 Internet craze (with huge returns), managed futures performed poorly.

Individual commodities function in waves. Industrial metals had huge returns during 2003–2006 but faltered in 2007–2008 (see Table 11.4). For the first half of 2009, however, they were the best-performing commodity sector with a return of +29.91%. Historically, commodities did not parallel the equity market; performance differed. Recently, the equity market and the commodities market move closely together. At one point during October 2008, the Dow had dropped 17.3% for the month as commodities were down 19.39%.[4] One of the reasons why commodities performed as badly as equities was that investors had driven up commodities prices since their wonderful performance after 2001. Commodities were essentially overvalued, and a correction was inevitable.

Commodity indexes depict waves, such as livestock, which was out of favor for 2002 and 2003 but returned to favor in 2004. In 2005–2007, it was one of the worst-performing commodity sectors until 2008, when it was the second-best performer. Commodities can also exhibit long waves, such as agriculture, which performed poorly from 1999 to 2005. Agriculture then performed well in 2006–2008.

Most commodities performed poorly in 2008. According to *Barron's*, commodities "endured one of the greatest, most violent corrections in history, especially in the second half of [2008]. The credit collapse caused demand

Table 11.3 The Wave Chart—10-Year Ranking of Asset Class Returns

	1999	2000	2001	2002	2003	2004	2005	2006	2007	2008
Better Performing	EM Equity 66.40%	US REITs 26.40%	US REITs 13.90%	Real Assets 24.70%	EM Equity 56.30%	US REITs 31.60%	EM Equity 34.50%	US REITs 35.10%	EM Equity 39.80%	Managed Futures 14.10%
	Developed Asia Equity 57.60%	US TIPS 13.20%	US Fixed Income 8.40%	Managed Futures 12.40%	Europe Equity 38.50%	EM Equity 26.00%	Private Equity 28.30%	Europe Equity 33.70%	Real Assets 31.00%	Real Assets 5.80%
	Private Equity 34.80%	US Fixed Income 11.60%	US TIPS 11.80%	US TIPS 11.60%	Developed Asia Equity 38.50%	Private Equity 24.90%	Developed Asia Equity 22.60%	EM Equity 32.60%	Private Equity 20.50%	US Fixed Income 5.20%
	Hedge Funds 31.30%	Managed Futures 7.95%	High Yield Bonds 5.80%	US Fixed Income 10.30%	US REITs 37.10%	Europe Equity 20.90%	Real Assets 17.90%	Private Equity 27.00%	Europe Equity 13.90%	US TIPS 2.40%
	US Equity 21%	Hedge Funds 5.00%	Hedge Funds 4.60%	US REITs 3.60%	US Equity 29%	Developed Asia Equity 19.00%	US REITs 12.20%	Real Assets 23.20%	US TIPS 11.60%	Hedge Funds -19.00%
	Europe Equity 15.90%	Private Equity 3.10%	Real Assets 2.10%	High Yield Bonds 2.10%	High Yield Bonds 27.90%	High Yield Bonds 12.00%	Europe Equity 9.40%	US Equity 16%	Hedge Funds 10.00%	Private Equity -22.70%
	High Yield Bonds 3.90%	High Yield Bonds -4.20%	Managed Futures 0.80%	Hedge Funds -1.50%	Private Equity 23.40%	US Equity 11%	Hedge Funds 9.30%	Hedge Funds 12.90%	Managed Futures 7.60%	High Yield Bonds -26.20%
	US TIPS 2.40%	Real Assets -6.70%	EM Equity -2.40%	EM Equity -6.00%	Hedge Funds 19.60%	Hedge Funds 9.00%	US Equity 5%	Developed Asia Equity 12.20%	US Fixed Income 7.00%	Developed Asia Equity -36.40%
	Real Assets 0.50%	Europe Equity -8.40%	Private Equity -7.70%	Private Equity -7.70%	Real Assets 19.40%	US TIPS 8.50%	US TIPS 2.80%	High Yield Bonds 12.00%	US Equity 7%	US REITs -37.76%
	US Fixed Income -0.80%	US Equity -9%	US Equity -12%	Developed Asia Equity -11.90%	US TIPS 9.4$	Real Assets 5.50%	US Fixed Income 2.40%	US Fixed Income 4.30%	Developed Asia Equity 5.30%	US Equity -38%
	Managed Futures -1.20%	Developed Asia Equity -25.80%	Europe Equity -19.90%	Europe Equity -19.90%	Managed Futures 8.70%	US Fixed Income 4.30%	High Yield Bonds 2.30%	Managed Futures 3.50%	High Yield Bonds 2.70%	Europe Equity -46.40%
Worse Performing	US REITs -4.60%	EM Equity -30.60%	Developed Asia Equity -25.40%	US Equity -25%	US Fixed Income 4.10%	Managed Futures 3.30%	Managed Futures 1.70%	US TIPS 0.40%	US REITs -15.70%	EM Equity -52.30%

Source: Author. NAREIT Index; HFRI Fund Weighted Composite Hedge Fund Index; Barclay CTA (Commodity Trading Advisors) Index; Barclay Capital TIPS Index; MSCI Emerging Markets Free Gross Index; Barclays Capital U.S. Aggregate (Taxable) Bond Index; Credit Suisse High Yield (Upper/Middle Tier) Index; MSCI Pacific (Developed Asia) Net Index; S&P 500 Index; Handy & Harman Spot Gold Price.

Table 11.4 Periodic Table of Commodity Returns, 1999–2009

1999	2000	2001	2002	2003	2004	2005	2006	2007	2008	2009*
Energy 92.39	Energy 87.54	Precious Metals 0.52	Energy 50.71	Industrial Metals 40.05	Industrial Metals 27.55	Industrial Metals 36.32	Industrial Metals 60.93	Energy 41.92	Precious Metals 0.48	Industrial Metals 29.91
GSCI Index 40.92	GSCI Index 49.74	Livestock -2.87	GSCI Index 32.07	Energy 24.57	Energy 26.09	Energy 31.19	Precious Metals 24.08	GSCI Index 32.67	Livestock -27.42	Energy 8.05
Industrial Metals 30.75	DJAIG Index 31.84	Industrial Metals -16.48	DJAIG Index 25.91	DJAIG Index 23.93	Livestock 25.49	GSCI Index 25.55	Agriculture 13.35	Agriculture 28.31	CCI-TR Index -28.6	DJAIG Index 7.79
DJAIG Index 24.35	CCI-TR Index 14.26	CCI-TR Index -17.18	Precious Metals 23.29	GSCI Index 20.72	GSCI Index 17.28	DJAIG Index 21.36	CCI-TR Index 10.75	Precious Metals 27.94	Agriculture -28.88	GSCI Index 6.55
Livestock 14.36	Livestock 8.57	DJAIG Index -19.51	CCI-TR Index 18.42	Precious Metals 19.55	CCI-TR Index 12.45	CCI-TR Index 19.75	DJAIG Index -2.07	CCI-TR Index 17.21	DJAIG Index -35.65	Precious Metals 5.7
Precious Metals 3.89	Agriculture -1.08	Agriculture -23.09	Agriculture -11.36	CCI-TR Index 11.32	DJAIG Index 9.15	Precious Metals 18.63	Livestock -6.74	DJAIG Index 16.23	GSCI Index -46.49	CCI-TR Index 2.47
CCI-TR Index 2.06	Precious Metals -1.24	Energy -40.44	Industrial Metals -0.61	Agriculture 6.59	Precious Metals 5.65	Livestock 3.46	GSCI Index -15.09	Industrial Metals -5.64	Industrial Metals -49.02	Agriculture -4.94
Agriculture -18.86	Industrial Metals -4.26	GSCI Index -31.93	Livestock -9.45	Livestock 0.03	Agriculture -20.15	Agriculture 2.35	Energy -26.79	Livestock -8.63	Energy -52.38	Livestock -11.49

*As of 6/30/09.

Source: Author.

to collapse. There was inventory liquidation in every corner of the global economy. In some cases, commodity prices declined even more than they did during the Great Depression. Crude oil fell 75% from its peak to trough."[5] Yet 2008 was nothing new. For instance, 2001 was another bad year for commodities. As further illustrated in Table 11.5, individual commodities move in waves and prices will fluctuate from year to year.

Waves

Essentially, there were four recent commodity waves: Wave I (August 1977–July 1986), Wave II (June 1986–August 1992), Wave III (August 1992–July 1999), and Wave IV (October 2001–March 2009). But waves existed well before this time (1915–1917, 1950–1957, and 1973–1974), and they will continue, like waves in the ocean. Waves continue, but you can never get the ones back that have already come and gone. The Bloomberg charts in Figures 11.3 through 11.6 depict the four most recent commodity waves.

Table 11.5 10-Year Annual Percent Change in Price for Commodities

	1998	1999	2000	2001	2002	2003	2004	2005	2006	2007	2008	2009 (1st half)
Gold	-0.28	-0.09	-5.47	2.46	24.77	19.37	5.54	17.92	23.15	30.98	5.77	5.05
Copper	-15.55	26.79	-2.03	-19.16	5.06	51.11	41.30	39.79	37.2	6.14	-56.53	76.01
Silver	-16.22	6.85	-14.50	0.43	3.46	24.27	14.86	29.20	46.40	14.65	-23.01	19.45
Lead	-16.13	4.76	-2.52	2.90	-12.27	66.06	38.67	4.68	58.33	53.25	-60.82	69.17
Tin	-4.13	18.58	-16.21	-23.98	8.81	54.35	17.88	-16.04	78.35	40.60	-33.02	30.51
Aluminum	-24.88	22.72	-8.76	-17.10	-4.64	18.73	20.14	15.02	18.12	-19.44	-40.99	0.80
Nickel	-32.34	109.1	-15.96	-17.61	21.46	133.07	-10.29	-10.12	154.45	-23.56	-55.37	31.72
Palladium	64.85	34.32	113.45	-54.14	-45.91	-18.70	-3.62	36.46	31.24	10.40	-49.29	34.09
Zinc	-16.04	35.26	-17.59	-24.83	-2.35	34.49	25.99	50.79	126.16	-47.13	-51.07	38.78
Platinum	0.61	21.17	38.42	-22.04	25.63	35.61	-5.9	12.65	17.05	34.33	-38.76	25.98
Wheat	-32.55	-29.88	-15.00	-16.78	0.82	3.94	-30.32	-8.84	20.05	52.14	-39.45	-19.13
Corn	-19.44	-4.22	13.33	-9.82	12.80	4.35	-16.77	5.37	80.88	16.72	-10.65	-12.9
Coffee	-27.52	6.92	-47.94	-29.52	30.30	7.89	59.74	3.23	17.83	7.92	-17.73	7.01
Cotton	-10.00	-15.94	22.74	-42.86	43.75	46.74	-40.36	21.04	3.69	21.04	-27.92	17.26
Cocoa	-15.40	-39.30	-9.44	72.82	54.27	-25.04	2.11	-2.78	8.71	24.47	30.96	-5.82

(Continued)

Table 11.5 10-Year Annual Percent Change in Price for Commodities *(Continued)*

	1998	1999	2000	2001	2002	2003	2004	2005	2006	2007	2008	2009 (1st half)
Sugar	−35.68	−22.14	66.67	−27.55	2.98	−25.49	59.44	62.39	−19.96	−7.91	9.15	51.14
Soybeans	−18.75	−20.37	−0.75	−17.62	38.74	53.18	−14.65	4.49	−1.60	54.35	−22.35	16.13
Heating Oil	−50.51	73.92	66.71	−36.62	41.40	21.90	39.46	25.8	−29.4	49.52	−47.20	15.76
Crude Oil	−50.12	112.39	41.99	−28.04	55.73	26.17	42.78	17.38	−20.84	40.93	−56.13	3.15
Lean Hogs	−43.42	66.92	4.27	0.40	−9.55	3.54	43.00	−14.56	−5.48	−6.20	5.18	−0.37
Live Cattle	−8.92	15.00	11.96	−9.27	12.62	−7.65	19.45	9.74	−4.02	3.97	−10.83	−0.59
Crude Oil (WTI)	−31.46	111.75	4.69	−25.97	57.26	4.23	33.61	40.48	0.02	57.25	−53.54	56.7
Unleaded Gas	−31.81	85.01	16.87	−27.13	51.02	7.27	21.44	52.48	−8.96	54.11	−57.36	79.10
Rough Rice	−16.92	−39.57	14.52	−35.80	3.00	109.97	−15.02	10.90	26.28	32.88	9.34	−18.23
Soybean Oil	−8.60	−30.33	−6.1	3.06	35.12	29.75	−23.86	5.65	36.25	65.71	−32.11	5.20
Soybean Meal	−30.24	4.86	25.86	−22.64	15.46	43.79	−30.09	18.51	1.68	66.37	−9.42	9.10
Natural Gas	−14.47	14.87	157.59	−40.73	15.79	20.2	26.26	51.08	−25.55	3.11	−15.78	−41.23
Milk	30.47	−44.46	−2.70	25.93	−17.46	21.87	35.97	−17.16	−6.13	64.14	−25.83	−34.75
Propane	−7.59	39.40	44.54	−29.63	42.11	−5.93	13.39	60.42	−5.63	59.63	−53.79	22.26

Source: Author. Bloomberg. Nat Gas from EIA.

Wave I RJ/CRB Commodity Index

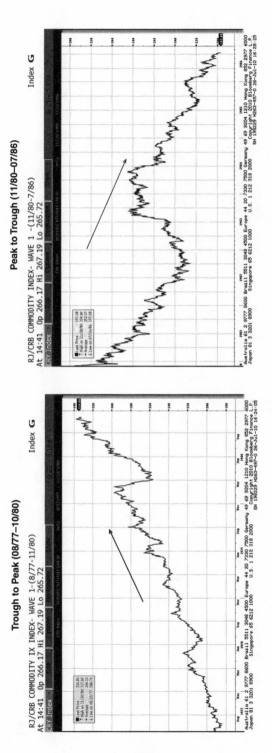

Figure 11.3 Wave I RJ/CRB Commodity Index: Trough to Peak (08/77–10/80), Peak to Trough (11/80–07/86)

Source: Bloomberg. Used with permission.

Wave II RJ/CRB Commodity Index

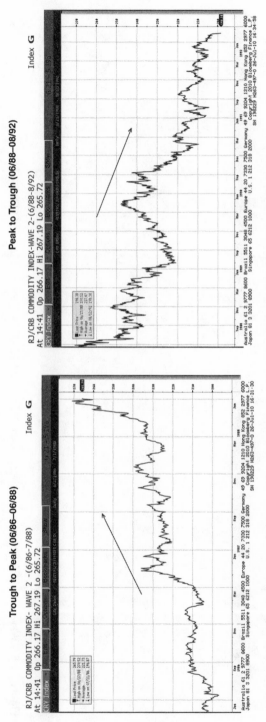

Figure 11.4 Wave II RJ/CRB Commodity Index: Trough to Peak (06/86–07/88), Peak to Trough (06/88–08/92)

Source: Bloomberg. Used with permission.

Wave III RJ/CRB Commodity Index

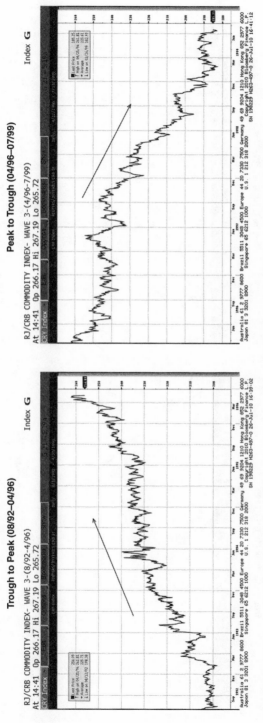

Figure 11.5 Wave III RJ/CRB Commodity Index: Trough to Peak (08/92–04/96), Peak to Trough (04/96–07/99)

Source: Bloomberg. Used with permission.

Wave IV RJ/CRB Commodity Index

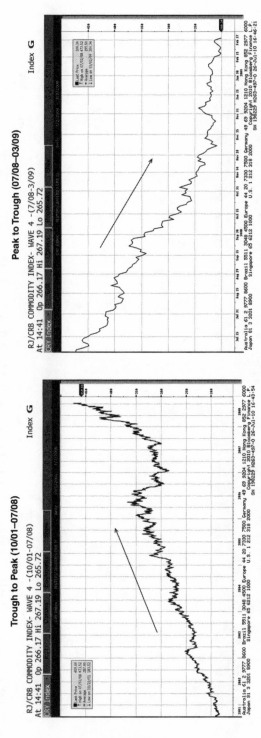

Figure 11.6 Wave IV RJ/CRB Commodity Index: Trough to Peak (10/01–07/08), Peak to Trough (07/08–03/09)

Source: Bloomberg. Used with permission.

As one can clearly see from these commodity wave charts, waves repeat themselves. There is a trough to peak followed by a peak to trough again and again. Not every cycle or pattern is predictable, nor are they perfect; waves can be distorted or erratic at certain times. Nevertheless, these waves show fairly long periods, which should be useful to an investor. For instance, Wave IV had its trough commence in 2001 and ran until 2008. Very few investments steadily climb over a 7-year stretch. Wave I showed a peak to trough that went from 1980 to 1986—again, a long period, but in reverse. In both scenarios, the waves moved for years, enabling an investor to benefit from such movement. Investors can make money in either direction. The perception of commodities is that they move up and down daily with a lot of volatility and they are "really risky." The reality is that they often exhibit long-term trends and can be immensely useful in constructing a well-diversified portfolio. All investments carry risk. The objective is to mitigate risk. Wave Theory can help an investor reduce risk when investing in commodities.

Investment Vehicles

Our focus for the rest of this chapter will be on the various investment vehicles one can use to incorporate commodities into a portfolio.

Managed Futures Funds

Although there are a few commodity-oriented mutual funds, managed futures funds have a far larger menu when it comes to commodities. *Worth* magazine noted that while other asset classes had a painful year in 2008, "managed futures—in which traders try to identify and benefit from price trends in various market sectors—boasted their best returns in nearly two decades."[6] Most investment firms or banks offer proprietary managed futures funds. These funds have either been purchased or are home grown. (See Table 11.6.)

Hedge Funds

A number of hedge funds focus or offer a fund devoted to commodities. A sampling of commodity-focused hedge funds can be found in Table 11.7.

Table 11.6   Managed Futures Funds and Fund-of-Funds

Name	Country
ACL Alternatives Fund, Ltd.	Ireland
Abingdon Futures Fund	United States
Bristol Energy Futures Funds	United States
Ceres Managed Futures LLC	United States
Emerging CTA Portfolio L.P.	United States
Orion Futures Fund L.P.	United States
Tactical Diversified Futures Fund	United States

Source: Author.

Table 11.7   Commodities-focused Hedge Funds and Hedge Fund-of-Funds

Name	Location
Abraham Trading Co.	United States
Aspect Capital/Diversified Fund	United Kingdom
BlueCrest Capital/Blue Trend	United Kingdom
BlueGold Capital Management	United States
BP Capital Management	United States
Citadel Investment Group	United States
Clive Capital	United Kingdom
Fortress/Fortress Commodities Fund	United States
Galena/Azurite Fund	United Kingdom
Galena/Energy Fund	United Kingdom
Galena/Malachite Fund	United Kingdom
Galena/Metals Fund	United Kingdom
Galena/Special Situations Fund	United Kingdom
JWH Financial and Metals Portfolio	United States
JWH Global Analytics Fund	United States
Man Investments/Man AHL Diversified Fund	United Kingdom
Ospraie/Commodity Fund	United States
Ospraie/Equity Fund	United States
Threadneedle/Commodities Crescendo Fund	United Kingdom
Vermillion Asset Management	United States
Winston Capital Management	United States

Source: Author.

In a 2009 article, *Worth* magazine summarized the benefits of hedge funds focusing on managed futures as follows:

> Managed futures traders, known as commodity trading advisors, get good returns by betting correctly on market trends, regardless of whether prices are going up or down. CTAs can go long or short on futures contracts in several different sectors—from metals, grains and energy, to equity indexes, currencies and government bonds.[7]

Individual Account

An investor can open an individual account directly with a registered futures commission merchant (FCM). Trades are done for you. The FCM will receive your funds, manage them, check your minimums, and provide trade confirmations. There is also an introducing broker one can select. An introducing broker does not handle your money or trades. Accounts are nondiscretionary (an investor's approval is required for any transaction). The benefit to individual accounts is the control that results from having to approve each trade.

Banks

Every major bank has a commodities unit. "Brad Hintz, an analyst at Stanford C. Bernstein & Co. in New York, estimates that commodity trading accounts for more than 7 percent of revenue at Goldman and Morgan Stanley."[8] Commodities make up more that 7% of both Goldman Sachs and Morgan Stanley's revenue, and served to help them survive the real estate meltdown and the credit crisis. Citigroup is another giant in commodities, and foreign banks are into commodities as well, among them Credit Suisse and Deutsche Bank. The benefit to utilizing a bank's commodities unit is that banks offer investors a myriad of choices, such as mutual funds, indexes, separately managed accounts, hedge funds, or equity-related commodities.

Indexes

"An investor who never invested in commodities before might consider walking before running," Jerry McEntee of Uhlmann Price Securities told the author. Specifically, one might select commodity indexes or exchange-traded funds/exchange-traded notes before adding individual commodities. Although commodities can be purchased individually (the actual commodity itself), indexes have become immensely popular for diversification. Over the last 30 years, the Barclay CTA has had negative returns only three times, with a compound annual return of 12.19%; the worst drop was less than 1.2%.[9] There are a number of Commodity Indexes. Two of the largest indexes are Goldman Sachs commodity index and the Dow Jones-AIG Commodity Index. One could track any of the major commodity indexes, but all have differences in performance over time because of the weightings they have in various commodities.

From the Bloomberg chart featured in Figure 11.7, one can observe how gold performance can vary among the various gold indexes. Separate from commodity indexes that focus on just one commodity like gold (single or individual commodity indexes), there are also nuances between the commodity indexes that focus on a group of commodities (general commodity indexes—broken down in Table 11.8).

GOLD INDEX PERFORMANCES   EquityG

Figure 11.7   Gold Index Performances

Source: Bloomberg. Used with permission.

Table 11.8 Commodity Indexes

	Reuter's/Jefferies CRB Index	GSCI	DJ-AIG	RICI	DBC
# of Components	19	24	19	36	6
% Energy	39	71.08	33	44	50.52
% Grains	13	4.37	21	19.94	21.1
% Industrial Metals	13	7.76	20.33	14	13.38
% Livestock	7	4.3	6.69	3	N/A
% Precious Metals	7	3.03	10.75	7.1	15
% Softs	21	9.45	8.64	11.86	N/A
% Other				0.1	

Sources: CRB, Goldman Sachs, Dow Jones, Rogers Raw Materials, Bloomberg.

Indexes are a cost-effective way to diversify broadly with commodities. Basically, there are five different commodity index funds:

1. Jefferies | TR/J CRB Global Commodity Equity Index. The Jeffries TR/J CRB Global Commodity Equity Index markets a futures contract based on Thomson Reuters–CRB Futures Price Index and provides exposure to the equity securities of a global universe of listed companies engaged in the production and distribution of commodities and commodity-related products and services in the agriculture, base/industrial metals, energy, and precious metals sectors. The CRB Index dates back to 1957 and was the first index, originally comprising 28 commodities.

2. The Goldman Sachs Commodity Index. The Goldman Sachs Commodity Index has a contract traded by the Chicago Mercantile Exchange (CME). If one examines any of the commodity indexes, such as the S&P GSCI Commodity Index (July 29, 1999–July 7, 2008), one would see resemblances in waves. Figure 11.8 shows the GSCI.

When one examines this wave, alarms should go off that the wave was excessive. No matter which commodity index an investor ultimately selected, all of them gave off warning signals. Selling commodities (or at least a portion of them) on the way up would have been prudent based on the examination of this wave chart. The *Wall Street Journal* noted in 2008 the trap that many new investors were falling into: It is often small investors who come late to the party, when prices are already lofty. and drive up prices for everything from crude oil to copper and palladium to higher-than-predicted levels.[10]

Figure 11.8 S&P GSCI Commodity Index (7/29/1999–7/7/2008)

Source: Bloomberg. Used with permission.

Figure 11.8 shows the long ascent of commodities from July 29, 1999 to July 7, 2008. It was the perfect alternatives wave to ride, with numerous opportunities along the way to generate good returns.

The next wave chart (Figure 11.9) shows where one should have sold (or reduced a position) and then bought back.

One cannot time the market perfectly, but if an investor watched his investment appreciate to the sky from July 29, 1999 to July 7, 2008, he should not have been greedy. Greed will kill you. When riding the waves up seemingly endless peaks, it is best to heed Thoreau's warning: "The waves still dash." Know when to get out. Investors had ample opportunity to take money off the table and lock in handsome profits from riding the commodities wave.

3. Deutsche Bank Liquid Commodity Index. The Deutsche Bank Commodity Service describes the PowerShares DB Commodity Index Tracking Fund, which is based on the Deutsche Bank Liquid Commodity Index, as a "rules-based index composed of futures contracts on six of the most heavily traded and important physical commodities in the world—crude oil,

S&P GSCI COMMODITY INDEX 10 YEARS (7/29/99-7/29/09)   Index **G**

Figure 11.9 S&P GSCI Commodity Index 10 Years (7/29/99–7/29/09)

Source: Bloomberg. Used with permission.

heating oil, gold, aluminum, corn and wheat."[11] The DBC Index weightings are as follows: light crude (37.86%), heating oil (17.1%), gold (13.58%), corn (9.09%), aluminum (11.27%), and wheat (11.1%).

4. Rogers International Commodity Index Fund. Jim Rogers put this index together because he did not like the other indexes. The Rogers International Commodity Index (RICI) is a composite, U.S. dollar-based, total return index designed by James B. Rogers, Jr., in the late 1990s. The index was designed to meet the need for consistent investing in a broad based international vehicle; it represents the value of a basket of commodities consumed in the global economy ranging from agricultural to the energy and metals products. The value of this basket is tracked via futures contracts on 35 different exchange-traded physical commodities, quoted in four different currencies, listed on eleven exchanges in five countries. Rogers has written several books and is considered an expert in commodities. RICI futures contracts consist of the commodities detailed in Table 11.9. For current weightings of the RIC Index go to www.rogersrawmaterials.com.

Table 11.9 The Rogers International Commodity Index

Product	Exchange	Product	Exchange
Crude Oil	NYMEX	Rice	CBOT
Brent	ICE EU	Platinum	NYMEX
Wheat	CBOT	Soybean Oil	CBOT
Corn	CBOT	Lean Hogs	CME
Aluminum	LME	Sugar	ICE US
Copper	LME	Azuki Beans	TGE
Heating Oil	NYMEX	Cocoa	ICE US
Gas Oil	ICE EU	Nickel	LME
RBOB Gasoline	NYMEX	Tin	LME
Natural Gas	NYMEX	Greasy Wool	SFE
Cotton	ICE US	Rubber	TOCOM
Soybeans	CBOT	Lumber	CME
Gold	COMEX	Barley	ICE CA
Live Cattle	CME	Canola	ICE CA
Coffee	ICE US	Orange Juice	ICE US
Zinc	LME	Oats	CBOT
Silver	COMEX	Palladium	NYMEX
Lead	LME	Soybean Meal	CBOT

Source: Rogers International Commodity Index, *The RICI Handbook* (Beeland Interests, Inc.), 2009. Used with permission.

5. Dow Jones UBS Commodity Index. Historically, the Dow Jones UBS Commodity Index (bottom line) has zigged when the S&P 500 Index (top line) zagged, and vice versa. Regardless of the commodity index, they all have a low correlation with equity indexes. The Dow Jones UBS Commodity Index, for example, has shown very little correlation with the S&P 500 Index until late 2008–2009 (Figure 11.10).

However, all the commodity indexes tracked the S&P 500 in 2008 and 2009. There are slight nuances between the commodity indexes that one should examine that explain why the appreciation has differed over the past decade, as illustrated in Figure 11.11.

Goldman has a large weighting with energy (71%) versus the DJ-AIG energy weighting (33%). Equity indexes are different from commodity indexes and they should not be viewed the same. That is, all commodity indexes carry different risk/return characteristics unlike stock indexes such as the S&P 500, Russell 3000, Dow Jones, or Wilshire 500 (which have similar risk and return ratio characteristics).

% RETURN, DOW JONES AIG INDEX VS S&P500, 1/9/91-7/31/09   Equity**G**

Figure 11.10   Percent Return, Dow Jones AIG Index versus S&P 500
Source: Bloomberg. Used with permission.

COMMODITY INDEX COMPARISON (10 YEARS) BY % APPRECIATION   Equity**G**

Figure 11.11   Commodity Index Comparison (10 Years) by % Appreciation
Source: Bloomberg. Used with permission.

Exchange-Traded Funds

Exchange-traded funds (ETFs) are publicly traded securities that represent a basket of securities that can mimic an index, such as the S&P. Quite a few companies offer ETFs for the S&P 500, such as Barclays iShares S&P 500 or Spiders (SPDRS). The ETF market has grown considerably in recent years. ETFs are similar to index funds in that they will primarily invest in the securities of companies that are included in a selected market index. An ETF will invest in either all of the securities or a representative sample of the securities included in the index. *The Economist* uses Barclays Capital as an example of the potential benefits of ETFs:

> Barclays Capital reckons $270 billion of "long only" money sits in investment vehicles, such as exchange traded funds. That is equivalent to less than 1% of the world's stock market capitalization. Only about a quarter of this is from temperamental retail investors; the rest is from institutions, such as pension funds, which are unlikely to reverse their asset-allocation decisions quickly. Furthermore, it is not typically geared-up using debt or derivatives, which means there is less of catastrophic losses.[12]

Besides equity indexes, commodity-focused ETFs have attracted billions in assets (Table 11.10). ETFs enable investors to gain exposure to certain geographic areas or sectors. There are around 40 to 50 ETFs on the market devoted to commodity-related equities.

Mutual Funds

There are not a lot of commodity mutual funds on the market. Rogers notes that there are fewer than 50 mutual funds worldwide dedicated to commodities versus 70,000 for stocks and bonds.[13] Stock funds, often called natural resources or gold and precious metals funds, can be clobbered in a stock market downturn or sell-off. Two reputable and noteworthy commodity funds that have been around awhile are:

1. Pimco Commodity Real Return Strategy Fund (PCRAX). Uses the Dow Jones-AIG Commodity Index. As of June 30, 2009, the fund had 35%

Table 11.10 The 20 Largest Equity-based Commodity ETFs

Fund Name	Symbol
Energy Select Sector SPDR	XLE
Market Vectors Gold Miners ETF	GDX
Oil Services HOLDRS	OIH
Materials Select Sector SPDR	XLV
iShares S&P North American Natural Resources	IGE
Market Vectors Agribusiness ETF	MOO
Vanguard Energy ETF	VDE
iShares S&P Global Energy Sector Index Fund	IXC
iShares S&P Global Materials Sector Index Fund	MXI
SPDR S&P Metals & Mining ETF	XME
iShares Dow Jones US Basic Materials Sector Index Fund	IYM
iShares Dow Jones US Energy Sector Index Fund	IYE
Vanguard Materials ETF	VAW
iShares Dow Jones U.S. Oil Equipment & Services	IEZ
iShares Dow Jones U.S. Oil & Gas Exploration & Production	IEO
SPDR Oil & Gas Exploration & Production ETF	XOP
First Trust ISE-Revere Natural Gas Index Fund	FCG
Market Vectors-Coal ETF	KOL
SPDR Oil & Gas Equipment & Services ETF	XES
Market Vectors Steel Index ETF	SLX

Source: Author.

energy, 23% industrial metals, 15% grains, 11% precious metals, 9% softs, 6% livestock, and 4% vegetable oil.

2. Oppenheimer Real Asset Fund (QRAAX). Uses Goldman Sachs Commodity Index. As of June 30, 2009, the fund had 13% agriculture, 72% energy, 7% industrial metals, 5% livestock, and 3% preciousmetals.

Other mutual funds that invest in commodities (or commodity-related securities) can be founding Table 11.11. The benefits to investing in mutual funds are their low minimums and liquidity.

Managed Account

A separately managed account with a minimum investment of $100,000 is another compelling investment vehicle. The manager will manage your

Table 11.11 Mutual Fund Name

Mutual Fund Name	Ticker
Aberdeen Natural Resources A	GGNAX
AIM Energy A	IENAX
BlackRock Natural Resources A	MDGRX
Columbia Energy and Natural Resources A	EENAX
Credit Suisse Commodity Return Strat A	CRSAX
Dreyfus Natural Resources A	DNLAX
Fidelity Advisor Materials A	FMFAX
Fidelity Select Materials	FSDPX
Franklin Natural Resources A	FRNRX
ING Global Resources S2	IGRTX
Ivy Energy A	IEYAX
Jennison Natural Resources A	PGNAX
Morgan Stanley Natural Resources Dev A	NREAX
PIMCO Commodity Real Ret Strat A	PCRAX

Source: Author.

account with discretionary authority (they buy and sell without your permission; you agree to give them permission to buy and sell as they see fit). Your account will be managed the same as the other investors but kept separate or segregated from other investor accounts. The benefit to investing with a managed account is the flexibility they provide with strategies and leverage.

Commodity Pool or Futures Fund

Typically, commodity pools or futures funds are limited partnerships with the purpose of trading commodity futures, requiring a minimum investment of $25,000. The commodity pool of funds is administered by a commodity pool operator, who manages the fund, and hires and supervises traders making the transactions. Similar to a mutual fund, the commodity pool is more diversified than an individual account. It also provides access to the latest and complex strategies.

Futures Options

An investor can elect to trade options on futures contracts to profit from the commodity rising in price or declining in price. If one believes a particular commodity will go up in value, they can purchase "calls." The opposite is true. On the other hand, if they think the value will decline in a certain commodity, an investor can purchase a "put." One would use options if they did not want to own the particular futures contract. The only loss one can have with buying an option is the value of that option. An option strategy gives you the right to buy or sell a futures contract. The benefit to investing in futures options is that they enable investors to obtain a right to buy or sell a particular security without spending a lot of money to own the underlying security.

Hybrids

Hybrid funds are surfacing to include commodities and other types of securities. For instance, the SunAmerica Alternative Strategies Fund provides both commodities and hedge fund exposure. According to the company, "SunAmerica has joined with Pelagos Capital Management to bring an institutional approach to investing in a mutual fund. SunAmerica's Alternative Strategies Fund provides you with access to a low-correlated strategy that contains commodity and hedge strategy exposure." Half of the fund is invested in actively managed commodities indices, and the other half is invested in hedge indices and the Pelagos Replication Strategy. The benefit is that an investor can gain exposure to both commodities and hedge funds simultaneously with low minimums. Hybrids are a new concept.

Equities

There are many companies one can elect to invest in to get exposure to a particular commodity. For example, if one were bullish on gold, one could invest in the basic materials company, Barrick Gold. Table 11.12 provides a list of the largest basic materials firms on the NYSE by market cap.

Table 11.12 Largest Basic Materials Firms (as of 5/26/2009)

Company Name	Quote	Mkt Cap ($B)
1 BHP Billiton Limited (ADR)	54.47	151.57
2 BHP Billiton plc (ADR)	46.49	129.37
3 Vale (ADR)	19.12	99.67
4 Vale (ADR)	16.32	97.27
5 Rio Tinto plc (ADR)	176.02	56.52
6 Monsanto Company	87.23	47.61
7 ArcelorMittal (ADR)	30.5	41.66
8 Potash Corp./Saskatchewan (USA)	117.2	34.62
9 Anglo American plc (ADR)	12.99	34.2
10 Barrick Gold Corporation (USA)	36.81	32.14
11 Goldcorp Inc. (USA)	37.57	27.43
12 E.I. du Pont de Nemours & Company	28.28	25.55
13 The Mosaic Company	55.91	24.85
14 POSCO (ADR)	78.93	24.5
15 Syngenta AG (ADR)	49.76	23.13
16 Sasol Limited (ADR)	35.01	22.98
17 Newmont Mining Corporation	46.63	22.82
18 Praxair, Inc.	72.5	22.29
19 Kimberly-Clark Corporation	51.92	21.51
20 Freeport-McMoRan Copper & Gold Inc.	49.7	20.46

Source: Author. Yahoo! Finance, http://finance.yahoo.com.

Exchange-Traded Notes

Barclays Bank recently devised a new debt product that functions just like an ETF called exchange-traded notes (ETNs). These products trade similar to ETFs and track the performance of underlying commodity indexes. The new ETNs are actually structured debt products. As described in *Financial Advisor*: "Barclays agrees to pay you the exact return of the underlying index (with zero tracking error), minus fees of 75 basis points."[14] Unlike other commodity funds, ETNs do not have to pay out gains each year. "The chief advantage—and it is a big one—is that Barclays believes that ETNs will never have to pay out capital gains distributions; investors will only owe taxes when they sell the notes. Barclays currently offers two broad-based ETNs, one tied to the aforementioned GSCI index and the other tied to the Dow Jones AIG Commodity Index (DJ-AIGCI)."[15] The benefit to investing ETNs is the favorable tax treatment they offer.

Commodity Fund-of-Funds

Diversification by investing in multiple commodity trading advisors lowers risk but adds to fees. An example of a commodity fund-of-funds is Abbey Capital Ltd., described by *Worth* magazine as an "Irish owned alternative investment manager with diversification across financial futures, foreign exchange and global equity markets. Abbey Capital Ltd. is registered as a Commodity Trade Advisor (CTA) and a Commodity Pool Operator (CPO) with the CFTC (USA) and is a member of the NFA (USA)."[16] Other CTA fund-of-funds include but are not limited to Dearborn Capital Management, Efficient Capital Management, Orion, and Centennial Partners. The benefit to investing in a commodity fund-of-funds is that the manager will select the advisors and provide due diligence; you do not need to decide which advisors to hire or fire. In addition, they decide when or how much of a strategy to own. The minimum investment is $100,000.

Outlook/Conclusion

As Henry David Thoreau explained, "You must live in the present, launch yourself on every wave, find your eternity in each moment." Commodities were affected by the market decline like all other asset classes. They performed reasonably well (some better than others) but could very well outperform all other asset classes in a recovery. Jim Rogers (creator of the Rogers International Commodity Index Fund) gave his position on commodities to *Fortune* magazine in March 2008:

> Virtually the only asset class I know where the fundamentals are not impaired—in fact, where they are actually improving—is commodities...if and when we come out of this [recession], commodities are going to lead the way, just as they did in the 1970s when everything was a disaster and commodities went through the roof.[17]

Part of the decline in commodities could be attributed to investors flocking to the various commodities after the last market downturn (2000–2002). The *Wall Street Journal* attributes it to the "deleveraging process gripping Wall Street," noting that "[if] the downdraft in commodities prices continues, hedge funds and other traders that made bets on raw materials with borrowed money could be forced to sell their holdings and unwind those bets."[18] Long-term (20-year or 5-year) commodities outperformed the stock market as indicated by *BusinessWeek*, detailed in Figure 11.12.

While some financial advisors have recommended commodities to clients, many are learning more about this particular alternative and

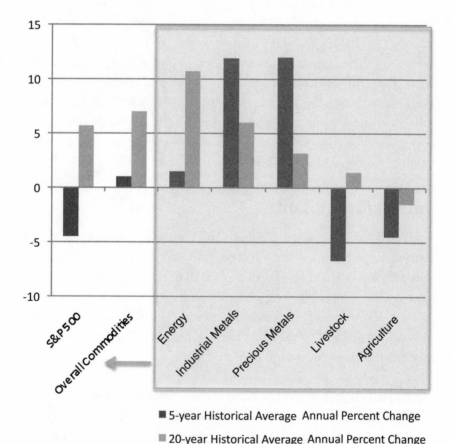

■ 5-year Historical Average Annual Percent Change

■ 20-year Historical Average Annual Percent Change

Figure 11.12 The Mixed Commodities Bag

Source: Pg. 17, Kalworski, Tara, "Commodity Prices Come Back Down To Earth," *BusinessWeek*, December 8, 2008, 17. Used with permission.

considering adding or recommending them to clients for their portfolios. In 2006, Morningstar surveyed 70,000 advisers and found that although only a little more than a quarter were "currently using 'alternative assets' in the bulk of their clients' portfolios," nearly half anticipated these assets to take on greater significance in the future.[19]

Financial advisors are learning more about commodities and see their merit. Interest in commodities will continue to grow and perhaps expand to include such things as water, diamonds, uranium, emeralds, and salt. The *Morningstar Advisor* forecasts that "more money is expected to pour into commodity indexes through exchange-traded products, mutual funds, and futures."[20] Worldwide minerals exploration spending came to a screeching halt in the late 1990s. Spending resumed and hit a high of $7 billion in 2006 after years of big profits. Production of nickel, gold, coal, iron ore, copper, and other raw materials is needed. Although the Great Recession clearly affected mining and exploration, many new projects are on the way, some even found in the ocean.[21] A number of new investment opportunities might open up for mining companies focused on discovering mineral-rich deposits on the seabed between continents.

Besides companies, ETFs and specialty funds will continue to grow. Overall, commodities will be one of the fastest-growing alternatives for investors to explore. Commodities play a role in diversification. Commodities are only in their infancy and will become much more commonplace to investors in the future.

Recommended Reading

The Chicago Board of Trade, *Commodity Trading Manual*

Ephraim Clark, *International Commodity Trading: Physical and Derivative Markets*

The Commodity Research Bureau, *The CRB Commodity Yearbook* 2008

Adam Dunsby, John Eckstein, Jess Gaspar, and Sarah Mullholland *Commodity Investing: Maximizing Returns through Fundamental Analysis*

Frank Fabozzi, *The Handbook of Commodity Investing*

W. D. Gann, *How to Make Profits in Commodities*

Hélyette Geman, *Commodities and Commodity Derivatives: Modeling and Pricing for Agriculturals, Metals and Energy*

Mary Holihan, *The Complete Guide to Investing in Commodity Trading and Futures*

George Kleinman, *The New Commodity Trading Guide: Breakthrough Strategies for Capturing Markets Profits*

George Kleinman, *Trading Commodities and Financial Futures: A Step by Step Guide to Mastering the Markets*

Emmanuelle Moors, *Structured Commodity Finance: Techniques and Applications for Successful Financing Arrangements*

Jim Rogers, *Hot Commodities: How Anyone Can Invest Profitably in the World's Best Market*

Russell Wasendorf and Thomas McCafferty, *All About Commodities: From Inside Out*

Russell Wasendorf and Pat Stahl, *Commodities Trading: the Essential Primer*

PART 4

PRECIOUS METALS (GOLD)

RIDING THE WAVE

Chapter 12

Gold Overview

I witnessed gold spike in value after the dot.com crash and 09/11 (2000–2002) as well as the real estate debacle and credit crisis during 2008–2009. Investors flock to gold in bad times. The year 2008 was one in which investors turned to gold, driving the price up almost 42% between June 2007 and June 2008.[1] U.S. citizens are not the only ones flocking to gold in bad times; investors around the world seek protection in gold. People from various Asian countries tend to buy gold jewelry because of negative past events. For instance, July 2, 1997, was the beginning of the Asian financial crisis. Investors took money out of the markets in Indonesia, Malaysia, and South Korea. *BusinessWeek* reported that in Thailand, the melting down of gold jewelry was encouraged as a means to boost the central banks' reserves.[2] Other than those two short spikes, gold did not appear very active during my 20-year observation from the late 1980s to 2008. I recall reading *Investments* in 1989 that "It would appear that the gain from adding gold to the portfolio is slight…unless you can identify an additional asset that has a high expected HPR [holding period return], the gain from further diversification will be slight."[3]

Performance, like many other alternatives, depends on which commodity one selects and when one chooses that particular commodity to invest or add to a portfolio. An investor can lose a lot of money in a very short duration with commodities if he or she buys too high. As Jim Rogers details in his book *Adventure Capitalist*:

The way of the successful investor is normally to do nothing—not until you see money lying there, somewhere over in the corner, and all that is left for you to do is go over and pick it up. That is how you invest. You wait until you see, or find, or stumble upon, or dig up by way of research something you think is a sure thing. Something without much risk. You do not buy unless it is cheap and unless you see positive change coming.[4]

There are distinct waves or cycles that one can observe with commodities not too dissimilar from patterns observed with other alternatives. such as real estate investment trusts (REITs), private equity, and hedge funds. Each alternative and every commodity is different, and together they make up a sea of investment opportunities. None of my clients over the years ever expressed a desire to own gold bars, but many purchased expensive jewelry that contained gold.

Some of my clients even bought gold coins. Unless it is your occupation, buying and selling gold coins requires a lot of knowledge. I witnessed a number of clients that overpaid or ran into trouble with coin dealers or Internet sites that they used. As with any industry, there are both honest coin dealers and dishonest (if not nefarious) ones. Older clients with memories of the 1970s (the only other time gold ran up in value since it was legal to buy) or ones familiar with the Great Depression viewed gold as a safe investment.

Ten 1933 double-eagle gold coins, thought to be among the most valuable gold coins in the world, were ordered by a judge to be returned to a Philadelphia family after they were seized by the federal government in 2004. The daughter and grandsons of the late jeweler Israel Switt originally took them to the U.S. mint in 2004 to be authenticated but they were seized by the federal government.[5] Each coin weighed one ounce, had a face value of $20, and was among 445,000 coins that were minted but never circulated.[6] In 1933 the United States went off the gold standard and all the coins except for these and another 10 were melted into gold bullion. Coins, whether they are gold or not, have a higher value when they are rare. The less made the better. There are so many pennies and nickels in circulation that they are actually worth less than their materials. It costs approximately 1.3 cents to make a penny. Condition is always important. Coins can be passed around so much that the year or image on the coin gets worn to a point that it is virtually impossible to read even with a magnifying glass. Pristine coins carry higher values.

I have noticed a pattern among wealthy entrepreneurs who took companies public and suddenly had immense wealth. Many of these individuals bought themselves or their significant others jewelry, whether it was a watch, necklace, or some other item. Jewelry accounted for 68% of the demand for gold from 2003 to 2007, detailed in Figure 12.1:

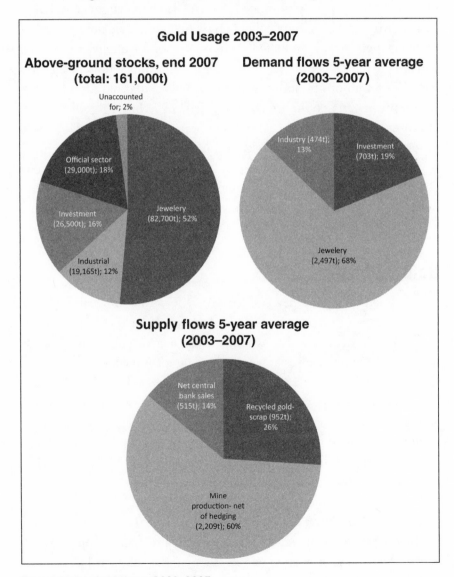

Figure 12.1 Gold Usage 2003–2007

Source: World Gold Council, "Demand and Supply,"
www.invest.gold.org/sites/en/why_gold/demand_and_supply/. Used with permission.
Data: GFMS Ltd.

I recall one Internet entrepreneur who refused to hedge or diversify his large, single-stock position during the tech bubble. In fact, the executive bought more technology stocks (failing to diversify). He spent millions of dollars buying jewelry for his wife. She loved her husband's idea to hedge by buying her expensive gold jewelry. After the tech bubble burst, his company plummeted in value. He had margin calls. Later, he got divorced. His jewelry collection (which contained gold and other precious metals) was circulated in an e-mail for anyone who wanted a bargain buying a piece of the entrepreneur's vanishing empire. Page after page listed millions of dollars worth of jewels being sold for a fraction of the price. One could argue he diversified by buying gold jewelry. However, it was done in a reckless fashion, just as his ill-fated decision to purchase more technology stocks for his already overweighted technology portfolio. Because he was desperate and in a hurry, he sold the jewelry at fire-sale prices. Desperate sellers almost never get top dollar. One never knows exactly how much they can sell something for until they actually go to sell it.

Gold Defined

In *The Rich and How They Got That Way*, Cynthia Crossen describes the prosperity of Europe in the Middle Ages, when "gold was the ultimate possession: It held its value whether shaped as a goblet, figurine or necklace."[7] Everyone loves to wear gold. The ideal medal to win for the Olympics is gold. Gold has been worn by everyone from King Tutankhamen to modern-day rappers, both notorious for wearing excessive amounts of gold and other jewels. The rapper Lil Wayne coined the term *bling* during a recording session to give a sound to blinging opulence; the word entered popular usage after the hit "Bling Bling" by the Cash Money artist B.G.[8] *Bling* is now in the Oxford English Dictionary.

There are a number of ways to define gold. Frank Fabozzi defines gold in *The Handbook of Commodity Investing*, "The precious metal gold (its elemental name, Au, comes from the Latin, Roman word *aurum*) has always fascinated people. Its metallic yellow color inspired the pharaohs to compare it with the sun. The Romans and the Incas called gold 'the metal of the gods'."[9] The CRB Commodity Yearbook defines gold this way:

Gold is a dense, bright yellow metallic element with a high luster. Gold is an inactive substance and is unaffected by air, heat, moisture, and most solvents. Gold has been coveted for centuries for its unique blend of rarity, beauty, and near indestructibility. The Egyptians mined gold before 2,000 BC. The first known, pure gold coin was made on the orders of King Croesus of Lydia in the sixth century BC. Gold is found in nature in quartz veins and secondary alluvial deposits as a free metal. Gold is produced from mines on every continent with the exception of Antarctica, where mining is forbidden. Because it is virtually indestructible, much of the gold that has ever been mined still exists above ground in one form or another. The largest producer of gold in the U.S. by far is the state of Nevada, with Alaska and California running a distant second and third. Gold is a vital industrial commodity. Pure gold is one of the most malleable and ductile of all the metals. It is a good conductor of heat and electricity. Gold melts at 1,064 degrees Celsius and boils at about 2,808 degrees Celsius. The prime industrial use of gold is in electronics. Another important sector is dental gold where it has been used for almost 3,000 years. Other applications for gold include decorative gold leaf, reflective glass, and jewelry.[10]

The Federal Reserve Bank of New York defines gold, "[O]ne of the metallic elements in earth's crust, gold is as old as the planet itself and is found and extracted on all continents. It is referred to by many as the 'king of metals' and always has been assigned a role far beyond its value as a commodity."[11]

Gold, therefore, holds value in different ways to its beholder. Some wear it, whereas others use it as an inflation hedge. Those fearful of financial markets might own gold bullion or transportable pieces in case they have to flee their homes or country. Many use gold as a status symbol. Regardless of its desired use, it is rare and will continue to be cherished by many types of people and organizations around the globe.

History of Gold

Gold has a rich history. Cynthia Crossen, in *The Rich and How They Got That Way*, notes that "Gold, the oldest precious metal known to humankind, is mentioned many times in the Old Testament. It is an almost a mystical substance with an allure that seems disproportionate to its real value."[12]

Egypt

Like everyone else, the ancient Egyptians were attracted to gold:

The most sought-after metal was gold, which the Egyptians identified as the "flesh of the gods." Found in vast deposits along the quartz-
rich plateau of the Eastern Desert from just north of Thebes to the
Fourth Cataract in Nubia, it could be extracted easily from the earth
through panning and shallow surface mines.[13]

Gold was first used in Egypt.

The first record of gold mining in Egypt dates from the Sixth
Dynasty, about 2200 BC, and the art of fashioning golden objects
had reached a high degree of perfection by 1350 BC. In that year the
boyking Tutankhamun was buried in an inner coffin of solid gold
weighing 242 pounds! This massive piece of metal was cast and then
shaped by tooling into a finely detailed portrait of the king. Buried
with one of Egypt's least important Pharaohs, this coffin indicates a
mastery of metal working unexcelled in any age, and a prodigality
with gold almost unmatched in history.[14]

Figure 12.2 is a historical view of gold since the 5000–3000 BC Egyptian
predynastic period.

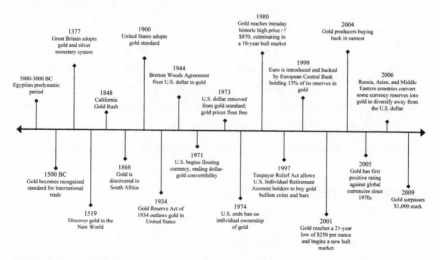

Figure 12.2   Gold: A Historical View of Precious Metal
Source: Author.

Besides its aesthetically appealing color, gold is quite malleable. Egyptian kings had many objects made out of gold. Zahi Hawass notes: "Gold is relatively easy to work: It can be manipulated cold, and does not tarnish. It was a perfect metal for intricate jewels and other objects meant to last for eternity."[15]

Iran and Iraq

"One of the oldest civilizations known to man, the Sumerians of Mesopotamia, who lived in what is modern day Iran and Iraq, first used gold as sacred, ornamental and decorative instruments in the fifth millennium BC. Around the same period, the early Egyptians—the richest gold-producing civilization of the ancient world—began the art of gold refining."[16] The Sumerians helped create the allure of gold, which still exists today. Exhibits with King Tutankhamun draw millions of visitors to view the gold objects from his tomb: ceremonial shields, a royal flail, child's chair, chests, and a ceremonial dagger and sheath are just a few of the many gold items.

Turkey and Persia

Gold coins were first produced in Turkey: "The first large-scale, private issuance of pure gold coins was under King Croesus (560–546 BC), the ruler of ancient Lydia, modern-day western Turkey. Stamped with his royal emblem of the facing heads of a lion and a bull, these first known coins eventually became the standard of exchange for worldwide trade and commerce."[17]

Greece

Gold frequently exchanges hands because of war and other conquests. "Gold has always been considered one of the spoils of war, and much of the precious metal in existence during early time passed from one conqueror to another."[18] The gold loot in Alexander the Great's conquest of Egypt alone was quite large.

Rome

Rome had the first gold currency. "Alexander the Great of Macedonia (336 BC–323 BC) subsequently established a rival coinage system that served as one of the most important factors in his conquest of Persia and the movement of gold into Europe."[19] Rome also was the first to use gold for religious purposes. "By the time the Roman Empire collapsed in the 5th century, gold had been used as both a tool of trade and as a means to accumulate wealth for many hundreds of years. For medieval Christianity, though, gold remained a mystical symbol of eternity and light, as represented in such objects as crowns, halos, and altars."[20]

Europe

Many explorers sought gold. "During the 16th century, as the New World was being explored, gold currencies became prevalent in Europe. After Christopher Columbus landed in the Americas in 1492, other expeditions set sail to uncover the gold treasures rumored to lie in these distant lands."[21]

United States

Most would believe gold was first discovered in California, but this notion is erroneous. Gold was first discovered in North Carolina in 1799, and later California in 1848. "Early in the morning of January 24, 1848, James Marshall walked to the tailrace of the dam he was constructing for a sawmill owned by John 'Captain' Sutter near Sacramento, California. Seeing a golden glint in the shallow water, Marshall reached down and picked up the piece of metal."[22]

Gold and the Government

Alternatives (all of them) are vulnerable to government intervention, even in the United States. An investor in commodities needs to be aware of not only his or her government's actions but others as well. The United States and every other country in the world has had varying policies on gold that have changed over time. Ramifications caused by one government's political moves can adversely affect a commodity that an investor owns, or even those targeting an unrelated commodity. Adverse conditions can occur with gold or any other commodity.

One example of the unintended consequences of government intervention involves tires (rubber). Sanctions were put on Chinese tire imports in 2009 by the United States. The result? China responded to the tariff on tires with unfavorable (by U.S. perspective) trading terms for both chicken and car parts.[23] An investor following the discussion that led to the tire tariff would have anticipated the obvious effect on rubber, but the effect on chicken came out of nowhere for many, and an investor in poultry would have been adversely affected. Investing in commodities can be like a lab experiment in which every action leads to another. One needs to observe government action(s) when buying or selling commodities. Most important: expect the unexpected.

The Gold Standard

In the 1870s, many countries adopted a gold standard. Robert Auerbach's *Financial Markets and Institutions* says of the gold standard:

> A country may adopt a gold standard for its money by either of the following equivalent policies:
>
> 1. The central government agrees to buy and sell an unlimited amount of gold at a fixed price.
> 2. The central government intervenes in the world market for gold by buying and selling gold in exchange for its domestic currency, in order to maintain a fixed price.[24]

The official government price of $25 per ounce of gold was in effect in the United States from 1934 until 1971. Before that, the official government price of $20.67 per ounce was in effect from 1879 until 1933 (with the exception of World War I). These prices seem hard to imagine with gold going above $1,000. On the other hand, gold reached $835 per ounce in January 1980 and dropped to $340 per ounce on March 5, 1982.

Gold Ban: Executive Order 6102

Gold was not permitted to be owned in the United States starting in the 1930s. The Presidential Executive Order 6102 on April 5, 1933, ordered the confiscation of gold coins and bullion in the United States. The purpose was to stabilize the economy by eliminating large private hoards of wealth and centralizing gold commerce.[25] Years later, on December 31, 1974, Public Law 93–373 removed the restriction.

On August 15, 1971, President Richard Nixon announced that the United States would no longer convert dollars to gold at a fixed value. The ban with owning gold in the United States was repealed by an act of Congress codified in Public Law 93–373 that went into effect December 31, 1974. As Benjamin Graham noted at the time in his book, *The Intelligent Investor,* "In the past 35 years the price of gold in the open market has advanced from $35 per ounce to $48 in early 1972—a rise of only 35%. But during all this time the holder of gold has received no income return on his capital, and instead has incurred some annual expense for storage."[26]

Bretton Woods

Bretton Woods is both a town in New Hampshire and the site at which the Bretton Woods monetary system was first conceived. As World War II drew to a close, representatives from several allied nations convened to fix the value of the U.S. dollar to gold and, subsequently, the value of other currencies to the U.S. dollar.[27]

Gold Commission

President Ronald Reagan appointed a Gold Commission in 1981 to study the possibility of returning to a gold standard; in 1982, the commission voted against suggesting a gold standard.[28]

Gold Market

Gold prices have gone up, primarily in recent years, reaching an all-time high in 2009, as illustrated by Figure 12.3 and Table 12.1. When a wave reaches such a height, buyer beware. Gold will likely plummet when the United States economy improves and the banking industry gets better.

Gold prices have changed over time.

Gold Holding

Countries—whether large or small, developed or emerging, affluent or improvised—all amass gold. The largest deposits of gold (both those of the U.S. and foreign governments) are stored at the Federal Reserve Bank of New York. The bank oversees deposits from approximately 60 nations.[29]

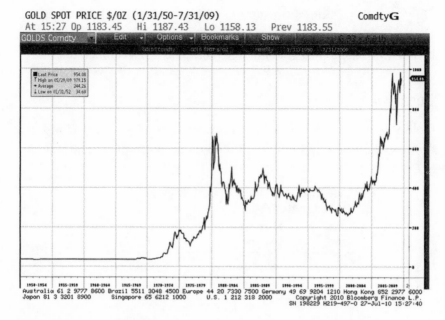

Figure 12.3 Gold Spot Price

Source: Bloomberg. Used with permission.

Table 12.1 Gold Prices 2009–1980

2009		1999	$290.25	1989	$401.00
2008	$871.96	1998	$288.70	1988	$410.15
2007	$695.39	1997	$287.05	1987	$486.50
2006	$603.46	1996	$369.00	1986	$390.90
2005	$444.74	1995	$387.00	1985	$327.00
2004	$409.72	1994	$383.25	1984	$309.00
2003	$363.38	1993	$391.75	1983	$380.00
2002	$309.73	1992	$333.00	1982	$447.00
2001	$271.04	1991	$353.15	1981	$400.00
2000	$279.11	1990	$386.20	1980	$594.90

Gold Prices 1979–1950

1979	$459.00	1969	$41.00	1959	$45.25
1978	$208.10	1968	$43.50	1958	$35.25
1977	$161.10	1967	$35.50	1957	$35.25
1976	$133.77	1966	$35.40	1956	$35.20
1975	$139.29	1965	$35.50	1955	$35.15
1974	$183.77	1964	$35.35	1954	$35.25
1973	$106.48	1963	$35.25	1953	$35.50
1972	$63.84	1962	$35.35	1952	$38.70
1971	$44.60	1961	$35.50	1951	$40.00
1970	$38.90	1960	$36.50	1950	$40.25

Source: U.S. Gold, "About Gold: World Gold Holdings," US Gold—Exploration in Nevada and Mexico, www.usgold.com/world-gold-holdings/, accessed August 1, 2009. Used with Permission.

Only a small portion of the gold kept there is U.S. gold; however, the United States has the most gold holdings of any country by far. Table 12.2 breaks down the top-25 gold holding nations as of December 2008:

Location

Gold is found almost everywhere. A maxim among prospectors was that "gold is where you find it."[30] It is found on every continent and is mined

Table 12.2 World Official Gold Holdings
(December 2008*)

Rank	Country	Tonnes
1	United States	8,133.50
2	Germany	3,412.60
3	IMF	3,217.30
4	France	2,508.80
5	Italy	2,451.80
6	Switzerland	1,040.00
7	Japan	765.2
8	Netherlands	621.4
9	China	600
10	ECB	533.6
11	Russia	495.9
12	Taiwan	422.4
13	Portugal	382.5
14	India	357.7
15	Venezuela	356.8
16	United Kingdom	310.3
17	Lebanon	286.8
18	Spain	281.6
19	Austria	280
20	Belgium	227.5
21	Algeria	173.6
22	Libya	143.8
23	Saudi Arabia	143
24	Sweden	139.5
25	Philippines	138.1

Source: www.usgold.com/world-gold-holdings

in high mountains and deserts, beneath the permanently frozen ground of the arctic and beneath the deeply weathered soil of the tropics. Cornelius Hurlburt detailed some of the geological traits common to gold strikes in his book *Minerals and Men*:

> However, there are some places that are more likely to reward the prospector than others, but these are determined by geological environment rather than by geographical location. Gold is associated with rocks of all ages and types, but it is more likely to be found in deposits related to granitic rather than to gabbroic rocks. Although there are many types of gold deposits, the most universal is gold-quartz veins found in the neighborhood of granitic rocks and probably genetically related to granite.[31]

U.S. Gold Market

Nevada leads in U.S. gold production, accounting for as much as 78% of the nation's gold in 2007, with additional sources found in Alaska, Utah, Colorado, Montana, South Dakota, California, New Mexico, Arizona, and Idaho.[32] Nevada's mines rank in output among the top four in the world, trailing only the national production of South Africa, China, and Australia. Twenty-one of the top-30 gold-producing mines situated in the United States are in Nevada.[33]

Australia Gold Market

In 1851, only two years after the gold rush to California, gold was discovered in New South Wales, Australia, and a tremendous rush followed the discovery of placer gold.[34]

South Africa Gold Market

Near the present city of Johannesburg, South Africa, gold was discovered in 1886. Almost immediately it was recognized as the world's major gold deposit. It was found in an ancient conglomerate, with the gold concentrated in narrow sheets called reefs.[35]

Gold Advantages

Worldwide, countries abandoned using gold as the benchmark against which all national currencies were measured in 1968, and the price of gold was allowed to float freely. Therefore, gold was allowed to find its own level in the world markets. The following are four key advantages to gold investments.

Diversification

Gold is an important asset class; it provides very effective diversification as a component of a balanced portfolio. Gold provides diversification through a low correlation with other asset classes. According to the World Gold Council, "[r]eturns on gold are less correlated with equity and bond indices than are returns on other commodities."[36] Figure 12.4 compares gold with the S&P 500 with a .002 R^2 correlation.

Hedge Against Inflation

Gold has also proved itself to be an effective hedge against inflation over the long run. Roy Jastram looked at more than 400 years of data in his

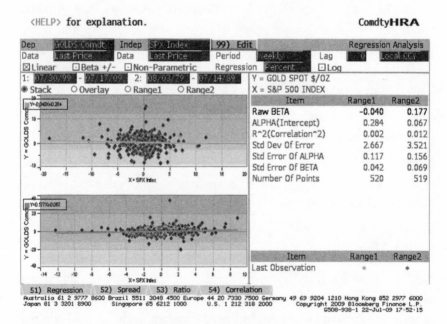

Figure 12.4 Gold versus S&P 500 Regression Analysis

Source: Bloomberg. Used with permission.

book *The Golden Constant,* comparing the price of gold with that of consumer goods, and found that regardless of inflation or deflation, "gold holds its purchasing power remarkably well over time." Gold is recognized as a potentially powerful tool in an investment portfolio. Gold can keep pace with inflation and offer a hedge against currency deflation. Gold is frequently used as a hedge against inflation. Figure 12.5 looks at the real price of gold over a nearly 60-year span.

In *Wealth Manager Magazine's* "Gold Rushes Then and Now," it is stated that:

> One common belief is that gold is a hedge against inflation. A classic study, *The Golden Constant,* by Roy Jastram examined the price of gold from 1560 to 1976—yes, 416 years—and compared it to the prices of consumer goods over the same period. Jastram found "gold holds its purchasing power remarkably well over time," including both inflationary and deflationary periods. Jastram's study looked at data from both the United Kingdom and the United States.[37]

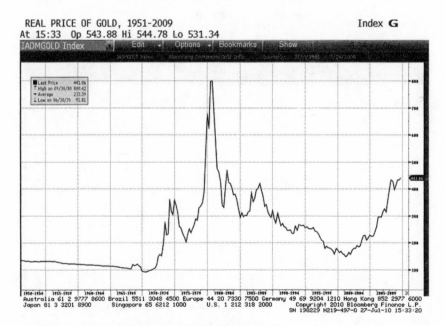

Figure 12.5   Real Price of Gold (1951–2009)

Source: Bloomberg. Used with permission.

Safe Haven

Gold also has a history as a safe haven in times of geopolitical or economic dilemmas; it generates positive returns in periods of economic stress and political upheaval. In the summer of 2006, amid concerns over inflation and with Iran's nuclear pursuits in the news, *Bloomberg Markets* noted that "[g]old surged to a 25-year high of $680 an ounce on May 8 [2006] as investors...flocked to bullion for safety."[38] Figure 12.6 shows the gold spot price from April 13, 2001 to March 14, 2008.

Take gold anywhere in the world and people value it. This is not the case with currencies. Gold is a safety blanket for investors. The Great Recession almost was a Great Depression. There were economic worries caused by a real estate collapse, which was followed by a credit crisis.[39]

Protection Against Dollar Decline

Gold is an effective hedge against a decline in the dollar. When the dollar falls in value, gold prices typically rise. The antithesis is true. When the dollar increases in value, gold normally does not do well. Traders like to buy gold in times of economic uncertainty.

Figure 12.6   Gold Spot Price

Source: Bloomberg. Used with permission.

Gold Disadvantages

Now that we have discussed the advantages to gold investment, there are also risks to consider. As with any security, gold has risk. There are a number of disadvantages to investing in gold.

Lackluster Long-term Performance

Gold might be a poor investment over extremely long periods as indicated by Jeremy Siegel's research on *Stocks for the Long Run*. Gold did not perform as well as stocks, bonds, or U.S. Treasury bills over 200 years.[40]

Siegel might be technically correct, but, as I discussed with him, I do not know anyone who has lived that long. In other words, an investor would not necessarily worry about gold over 200 years and it is a moot point. What is relevant is that gold (since 1979, when one could freely buy and sell gold) has become much more active. Looking at how gold did over 200 years is about as useful as how it did in one day. An investor in gold might examine how it performed over 1, 3, 5, 10, or 20 years or since 1979 when it was freely tradable. Those who invested in the stock market before or during the Great Recession were annihilated, whereas while gold investors were rewarded handsomely. Basically, it depends when an investor bought the gold. There are certain periods when gold appears to be a better investment than stocks and vice versa.[41]

Depending on entry point, any investment (including gold) can look good or bad, which gets back to Wave Theory. Regarding gold's long-term performance, *Forbes* magazine noted:

> Gold, the favorite of the canned-food-in-the-bomb-shelter crowd, has risen at only 4.4% a year over the past 30 years, a little above inflation. Instead of rolling over contracts four times a year you could buy a gold exchange-traded fund. The biggest, SPDR Gold Shares (ticker: GLD), runs up overhead of 0.4% a year. If it tracks the cost of living and if you hold for 30 years you'll wind up 11% poorer in real terms. Before capital gain tax.[42]

No investment should be held forever. There are times to buy and times not to buy.

Volatility

Another important characteristic of gold is its relatively low volatility. The price of gold tends to become more volatile when it is rising, whereas with equities, the reverse is often true. In the past, gold has not been known for its volatility. However, because the supply of gold has dramatically increased since 1979 along with numerous funds, exchange-traded funds, and other trading vehicles, its volatility might continue to increase in the future. Events such as the Great Recession or any future market turmoil will increase volatility for gold.

Vulnerable to Immediate and Increased Price Movement

Although gold can generally be characterized as having low volatility, negative or unpredictable events can set it off. Investors buy "hard assets" such as gold and other commodities when there are catastrophic or other events that lead to economic uncertainty. When the Great Recession teetered on becoming another Great Depression and the Dow Jones collapsed almost 7,500 points, investors ran to gold. When the price of gold raced past $900 an ounce, the StreetTracks Gold Trust, an exchange-traded fund that seeks to capture the returns of gold bullion, raked in an average of $25 million *per hour*.[43] Gold is often neglected when the stock market does well but not always; the price of gold can move with the stock market.

No Dividends and No Interest

Commodities do not generate cash nor do they pay any interest or dividends. Gold either appreciates or declines in value over time. Gold does not always move up in value. Gold soared in the 1979–1980 bear market. Had one bought then, one would have only recently gotten back to even, not including inflation.[44]

Storage

Depending on how much physical gold an investor purchases, one would need a safe, bank vault, or some other system, none of which are free.

However, there are more companies focusing on storage, including FideliTrade Inc. FideliTrade Inc. stores gold, silver, platinum, and palladium, marking the unique identifiers of each stored bar so that it can keep track of both its owner and its location within their complex.

Bad Timing

If you buy gold at the wrong time, you can lose a lot of money, especially during periods of high anxiety. Gold frequently moves the opposite of the dollar. "When the buck falls, gold rises, and vice versa."[45]

Limited Supply

Gold is a shiny, durable commodity that is limited in supply. World gold output in 1980 was estimated to be 42.5 million ounces by the Gold Institute, a trade association representing more than 200 companies that mine or refine gold.[46] South Africa, the Soviet Union, and the United States were the largest gold producers. The U.S. government had approximately 265 million ounces of gold in 1980, which, valued at $350 per ounce, would be worth $92,750 million.[47]

Gold Performance

According to *Pensions and Investments*, gold was the best-performing asset class over the last 5 and 10 years (illustrated in Table 12.3):

Table 12.3   Gold Standard

Gold has been the top-performing asset class over the past 10 years, but over 30 years it has barely outpaced inflation. It does not correlate highly with other asset classes.

RETURNS

Class	1-year return	5-year return	10-year return	15-year return	30-year return
Gold (spot)	0.13%	18.63%	13.43%	6.00%	4.10%
Stocks	−26.54%	−1.79%	−1.79%	6.96%	10.61%
Bonds	6.05%	5.01%	5.97%	6.58%	8.48%
Commodities	−59.69%	−3.45%	6.31%	4.07%	6.83%
Hedge Funds	−13.71%	4.95%	7.02%	9.74%	

(*Continued*)

Table 12.3 Gold Standard *(Continued)*

AVERAGE MONTHLY CORRELATIONS JUNE 1999–JUNE 2009

	Gold	Stocks	Bonds	Commodities	Hedge Funds
Gold	1				
Stocks	−0.03	1			
Bonds	0.12	0.04	1		
Commodities	0.19	0.05	0.05	1	
Hedge Funds*	0.14	0.53	0.08	0.21	1

*Hedge fund correlation data December 2003–June 2009.

Originally compiled and designed by Aaron M. Cunningham and Gregg A. Ruburg

Indexes: Russell 3000; Barclays Aggregate; S&P GSCI Total Returns; and Credit Suisse/Tremont Hedge Fund

Source: Aaron M. Cunningham and Greg Ruberg, "Gold Standard," *Pensions & Investments* (July 27, 2009). Used with permission.

However, over very long periods, gold might not be a great investment. JP Morgan showed that gold returned 3.9% over 20 years (Figure 12.7) Table 12.4 is a rolling year returns and risk chart for 1, 3, 5, 10, and 15 years (ending March 2009). Table 12.4 compares real assets (Handy & Harman Spot Gold Index) to other asset classes over 1-, 3-, 5-, 10-, and 15-year periods. Any time an investor considers an investment in gold, commodities in general, or any other alternative, they should examine returns and standard deviation. The more knowledge an investor has, the better.

Standard deviation was 27.28 for gold from April 2008 to March 2009, compared with the stock market (S&P 500 Index), which had a standard deviation of 25.90. Over a rolling 15-year period (April 1994–March 2009), gold had a standard deviation of 14.85 versus the S&P 500, which had 15.50. Gold slightly outperformed the S&P 500 with a 6.10% return over 15 years versus the S&P 500 with 5.90%. Short term, gold also looked better with a one-year return of .23% versus −38.09% for the S&P 500. However, gold did not perform as well as equities over 30 years. Risk and return should always be examined. Investors typically chase good returns after they have been made by others.

When investors see standard deviation and returns over longer periods, they are often surprised. For instance, hedge funds have a standard deviation of 7.31 over a 15-year period (April 1994–March 2009) compared with gold, with a 14.85 standard deviation and stocks 15.50. Hedge funds

Bear Market Cycles versus Subsequent Bull Runs						
Market Peak	Market Low	Bear Return	Length of Decline	Bull Run	Bull Run Length	Yrs to Reach Prev. Peak
05/29/46	05/19/47	-28.6%	12	257.6%	122	3.1 yrs
07/15/57	10/22/57	-20.7%	3	86.4%	50	0.9 yrs
12/12/61	06/26/62	-28.0%	6	79.8%	44	1.2 yrs
02/09/66	10/07/66	-22.2%	8	48.0%	26	0.6 yrs
11/29/68	05/26/70	-36.1%	18	74.2%	31	1.8 yrs
01/05/73	10/03/74	-48.4%	21	125.6%	74	5.8 yrs
11/28/80	08/12/82	-27.1%	20	228.8%	60	0.2 yrs
08/25/87	12/04/87	-33.5%	3	582.1%	148	1.6 yrs
03/24/00	10/09/02	-49.1%	31	101.5%	60*	4.6 yrs
Average		-32.60%	14 mo's	176.0%	68 mo's	2.2 yrs

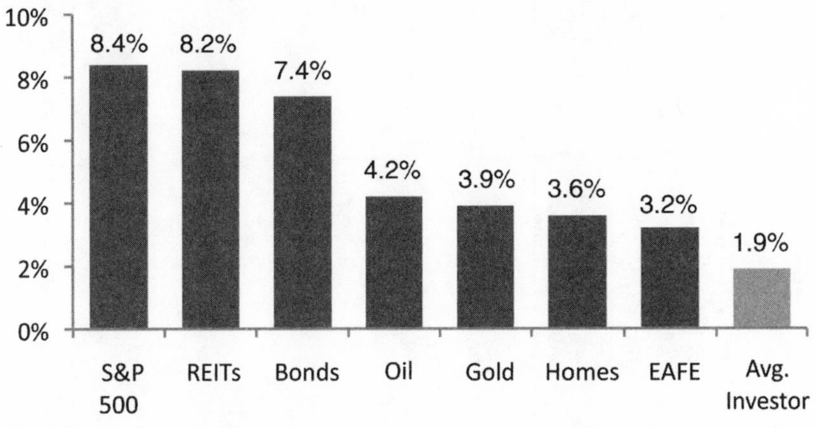

Figure 12.7   Long-term Returns and Bear Market Cycles

Source: JP Morgan Asset Management, Long-term Return and Bear Market Cycles (chart), *Market Insight Series Guide to the Markets* (March 31, 2009). Used with permission.

(HFRI Fund Weighted Composite Index) returned 9.19% versus 6.10% for gold and 5.90% for equities over the same 15-year period.

Gold and other asset classes can change over time by expanding our observation window with risk and return from April 1994 to March 2009. Gold appeared to be a better investment than equities over 1-, 3-, 5-, 10- and 15-year periods. Before this time period U.S. equities outperformed gold. Alternatives move in waves, and it is extremely important to know where exactly you are investing. Knowledge is power.

Table 12.4 Rolling Year Returns and Risk

1 Year, 3 Years, 5 Years, 10 Years, and 15 Years (ending March 2009)

Asset Class	Index	Rolling 1 Year (Apr 08 –Mar 09) CAGR%	Standard Deviation	Rolling 3 Years (Apr 06 –Mar 09) CAGR%	Standard Deviation	Rolling 5 Years (Apr 04 –Mar 09) CAGR%	Standard Deviation	Rolling 10 Years (Apr 99 –Mar 09) CAGR%	Standard Deviation	Rolling 15 Years (Apr 94 –Mar 09) CAGR%	Standard Deviation
Equity											
U.S. Equity	S&P 500	−38.09	25.9	−13.07	17.67	−4.77	14.69	−3	15.8	5.9	15.5
Non-U.S. Equity											
Europe	MSCI Europe Index	−49.9	29.86	14.28	22.15	−1.77	22.15	−0.98	18.43	5.26	16.94
Fixed Income											
U.S. Treasury Note	U.S. Treasury 10–Year Note	10.51	13.37	10.19	8.52	5.88	7.95	6.16	7.78	6.79	7.41
Alternative Investments											
Real Assets	Handy & Harman Spot Gold Index	0.23	27.28	16.87	21.02	18.36	18.83	12.35	16.73	6.1	14.85
Hedge Funds	HFRI Fund Weighted Composite Index	−15.69	9.84	−1.58	7.75	3.03	6.89	6.99	7.32	9.19	7.31
Managed Futures	Barclays CTA Index	5.45	5.75	7.51	6.34	4.70	6.31	5.67	7.39	6.59	7.81

Source: Author. Hedge Fund Research, Barclays Trading Group, MSCI Europe Index, S&P 500 Index, U.S. Treasury Index. Used with permission.

Chapter 13

Gold Waves and Investments

I n Herman Melville's *Moby Dick*, the author explained that "[t]he sea was as a crucible of molten gold, that bubblingly leaps with light and heat."[1] One can plainly see waves with the commodity gold. The gold wave chart (July 17, 2008–July 17, 2009) in Figure 13.1 is a good example of Wave Theory. This graph exemplifies the existence of minicycles in the spot price of gold on a monthly basis over one year. Gold has its peaks and troughs in both short and long periods.

Figure 13.1 Gold Wave Chart

Source: Bloomberg. Used with permission.

Thus, individual commodities might be traded on a short-term basis rather than with a buy-and-hold strategy. Hypothetically, one could be buying gold at the top of each curved cycle, which (in many cases) matches gold's lowest spot price. The converse is also true; the bottom or end of the curved cycle matches a peak in the gold spot price. One could short gold at this juncture. In this example, an investor in gold would make money nine out of ten times following these cycles. The vertical lines show where the buy and sell points are to consider. Events can affect gold prices, as seen in the gold chart found in Figure 13.2, such as Lehman Brothers' bankruptcy, Bernie Madoff stealing clients money in a massive ponzi scheme, Fed commentary, and AIG teetering on collapse because of credit default swaps. Other supply-and-demand variables that can affect gold include demand from India and China, inflation fears, and production problems.

Although other waves exist, the charts in Figures 13.3 through 13.7 depict five gold waves and clearly show each from trough to peak and peak to trough. The waves are as follows: Gold Wave I (January 30, 1970–August 27, 1976), Gold Wave II (August 27, 1976–July 2, 1982), Gold Wave III (July 2, 1982–March 1, 1985), Gold Wave IV (March 1,

Figure 13.2

Source: Bloomberg. Used with permission.

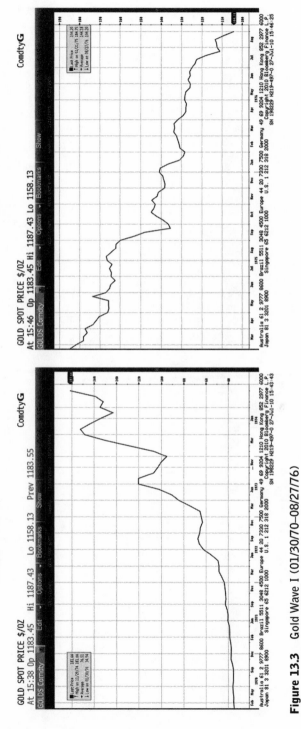

Figure 13.3 Gold Wave I (01/30/70–08/27/76)

Source: Bloomberg. Used with permission.

Gold Wave II (08/27/76–07/02/82)

Trough to Peak   **Peak to Trough**

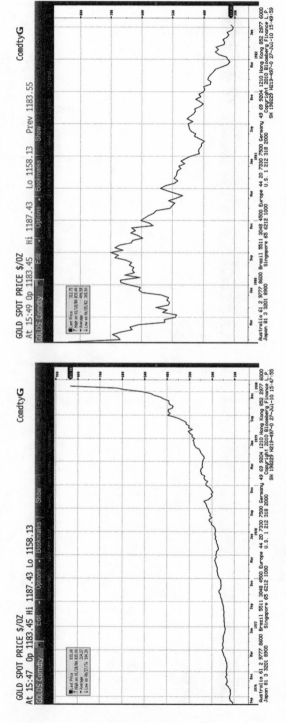

Figure 13.4   Gold Wave II (08/27/76–07/02/82)

Source: Bloomberg. Used with permission.

Gold Wave III (07/02/82–03/01/85)

Trough to Peak

Peak to Trough

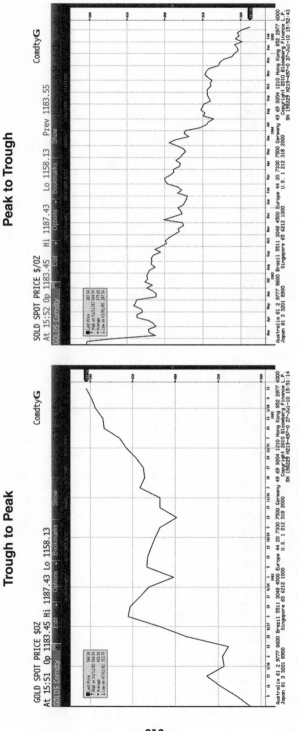

Figure 13.5 Gold Wave III (07/02/82–03/01/85)

Source: Bloomberg. Used with permission.

Gold Wave IV (03/01/85–03/12/93)

Trough to Peak   **Peak to Trough**

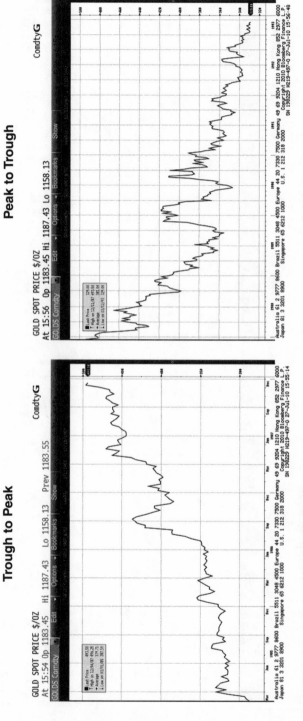

Figure 13.6   Gold Wave IV (03/01/85–03/12/93)

Source: Bloomberg. Used with permission.

Gold Wave V (03/12/93–04/20/01)

Trough to Peak

Peak to Trough

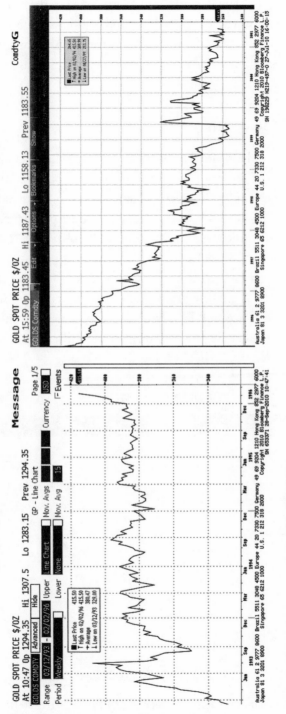

Figure 13.7 Gold Wave V (03/12/93–04/20/01)

Source: Bloomberg. Used with permission.

1985–March 12, 1993), and Gold Wave V (March 12, 1993–April 20, 2001). Certain waves are quite long in duration, such as Gold Wave V. Shorter waves exist as well, like Gold Wave III. Although very different, the following sets of waves exemplify the patterns, trends, or cycles found with gold.

Gold/Silver Ratio

The price of gold is divided by the price of silver. The ratio shows the number of ounces of silver needed to equal an ounce of gold. Historically, the average has been in the 30s. Depending on the ratio, an investor could short one and go long the other. The gold/silver trade is popular among traders. Figure 13.8 provides a gold-silver ratio over 10 years (September 30, 1999–September 18, 2009).

The return varies depending on the price of both gold and silver. Investors use this strategy to make a profit when there are extremes in the market. Exchange-traded funds (ETFs) or options can be used for this strategy. For example, an investor can buy puts on gold and calls on silver when the ratio is high, and vice versa when it is low.

Figure 13.8 Gold-Silver Ratio 10-Year (09/30/1999–09/18/2009)

Source: Bloomberg. Used with permission.

Gold is similar in nature to silver:

> The reason for the frequent presence of appreciable silver in gold is that the atomic structure of silver and gold is the same and the size of the atoms nearly identical. Thus, during the process of crystallization, some silver atoms can take the place of gold atoms without disrupting the structure. In fact, silver and gold atoms can substitute for each other in any proportion, so that it is possible to find natural alloys of silver and gold in which the amounts of the two metals are approximately equal.[2]

Gold and silver sometimes go hand in hand, whether one is wearing jewelry or making investments. According to Ramiro Salas Bravo and Meinrad Maria Grewenig, "In ancient America, gold was the symbol of the sun, and silver that of the moon. Gold represented the male element and silver the female."[3] Gold, to the Incas, was "the sweat of the sun" and silver "the tears of the moon."[4] Incidentally, tidal currents (which create waves) are affected by the sun and different phases of the moon. Silver has similar waves as gold; silver is somewhat correlated with gold even more so than platinum or palladium. The wave relationship between the precious metals is illustrated in Figure 13.9.

Figure 13.9 Gold, Silver, Platinum, and Palladiun Spot Price 10-Year

Source: Bloomberg. Used with permission.

It is important to understand the relationship between commodities and how they relate to one another when investing. Sometimes commodities (though very different) can act similarly and exhibit mirror waves. For example, gold occasionally mirrors oil, as evidenced by Figure 13.10.

Certain commodities have waves that resemble others that are entirely unrelated and not obvious, such as this example with gold (metal) and oil (energy). When one invests in a single commodity or builds a portfolio, it is important to note or realize correlations between asset classes. One might incorrectly view oil (an energy commodity) as having nothing to do with metal generally or gold specifically. However, this thinking is erroneous. As one can see from the oil/gold comparison, the two commodities can be highly correlated at times. Gold, for the most part, has behaved very differently from the equity market. The S&P 500, as illustrated in Figure 13.11, has had very different returns for gold.

Figures 13.12 and 13.13 show the importance of looking short term as well as long term when investing in gold. What an investor will see

Figure 13.10   Gold versus WTI Crude Spot Price (2/89–9/08)

Source: Bloomberg. Used with permission.

GOLD VS S&P BY PERCENT RETURNS　　　　　　　　　　　　　　Equity**G**

Figure 13.11　Gold versus S&P 500 by Percent Returns

Source: Bloomberg. Used with permission.

after looking at both figures is that gold has clearly had a nice run for the better part of a decade. To apply Wave Theory, imagine first looking at a graph similar to Figure 13.12, where the far right represents the most current data. You might think that you were standing on a peak and that the best time to invest would be after the price dipped down to its fall 2007 levels. Of course, doing your due diligence, you'd take a step back and look at Figure 13.13, which gives you data for the previous decade. Viewing different periods is prudent. With the big picture in front of you, seeing the steady rise in price of gold over 10 years, an investor would acknowledge that gold has had a nice run for the better part of a decade, but you might now be hesitant to seek out a long-term gold investment. Generally, it is never a good idea to rush into an alternative or any other asset class without doing one's homework. If you are unclear about buying low or too high, you can always dollar-cost average or invest less than what you originally had in mind to be conservative or safeguard against loss.

Figure 13.12   Gold Spot Price Index 2 Years (07/30/2007–07/28/2009)

Source: Bloomberg. Used with permission.

Figure 13.13   Gold Spot Price Index 10 Years (07/30/1999–07/24/2009)

Source: Bloomberg. Used with permission.

Gold Investment Vehicles

Below one will find multiple options for investing in gold.

Gold Bars

Many of the gold bars weigh 400 troy ounces (12 troy ounces to a pound). Normally, these bars are stamped with insignia, such as with the Soviet Union, which, along with South Africa, mines much of the world's gold.[5]

Gold Coins

There are many gold coins on the market:

- **Gold American Buffalos.** Through the Presidential Coin Act of 2005, the gold American Buffalo was first minted in 2006. More than 300,000 of the coins were produced and sold that year, representing the United States's first large-scale circulation of a .9999 (or four-nines) fine gold coin in the mint's history.[6]
- **Gold American Eagles.** The first gold coins produced in America were $10 gold Eagle coins originally minted by the U.S. Mint starting in 1795. The gold American Eagle is the first modern bullion coin to be authorized by the U.S. Congress. It is backed by the U.S. Mint for its weight, content, and purity.[7]
- **Gold South African Krugerrands.** The South African Krugerrand is the original 1 troy ounce gold bullion coin made by a government and valued on the content of its gold rather than the face value of the coin, which was originally minted in 1967 in an effort to help market South African gold to the international market.[8] The Krugerrand is one of the primary gold bullion coins in the world.

Exchange-Traded Funds

There is a plethora of gold ETFs that an investor can select. Table 13.1 provides a number of the more popular gold exchange-traded products.

Table 13.1   Gold Exchange-Traded Funds

streetTRACKS GoldShares	GLD
iShares COMEX Gold Trust	IAU
PowerShares DB Precious Metals Fund	DBP
SPRDs S&P Metals & Mining ETF	XME
Market Vectors Gold Miners ETF	GDX
DB Gold Double Long ETN	DGP
DB Gold Double Short ETN	DZZ
DB Gold Short ETN	DGZ

Source: Trang Ho, SPDR Gold Trust, "Asset Managers: Buy Gold, Commodities," *Investor's Business Daily* (September 26, 2008). Used with permission.

ETFs that hold physical gold bullion tend to perform the best. The following gold ETF (GLD) tracks gold closely and has a high correlation as shown in Figure 13.14.

Two of the most popular gold ETF investments are GLD and GDX. Investors bought a net $9.7 billion worth of gold in 2008 through ETFs,

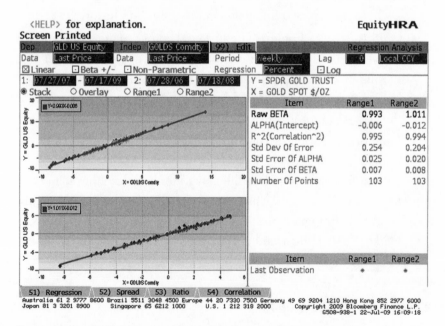

Figure 13.14   Gold ETF (SPDR Gold Trust) versus Gold Spot Price

Source: Bloomberg. Used with permission.

according to the World Gold Council.[9] They are both popular with retail investors, and institutions prefer them as well. In fact, 15 of the largest hedge funds invested billions in gold as indicated in the chart from the August 27, 2009, issue of *Pensions & Investments*, reprinted in Figure 13.15.

Individual investors want to be on the same side as institutional money, otherwise known as the "smart money." An investor need not be on the same side of the fence or own everything institutions own (mimic them), but one also does not want to wager bets against large institutional investors. It's like swimming against the tide; it will not work. If institutions are selling, one should not be fortuitous. Going against the tide is dangerous and foolish. Pay attention to the "smart money." Observe the institutional waves of buying or selling. Newspapers such as *Investor's Business Daily* list what mutual funds are buying and selling. Be careful not to follow or be late to the party. If institutions have been investing heavily in oil for three years and you decide oil might make sense at $140.00, it might be too late. Institutions have better information and often large groups working for them as opposed to a retail investor with far fewer resources.

If an investor believes gold is prudent to buy and they are attracted to ETFs, technical analysis can help them make buy/sell decisions. Although this book is by no means another "how to read a commodity chart book"

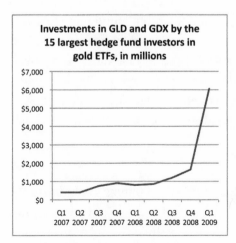

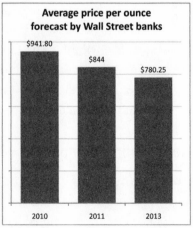

Figure 13.15   24K or Fool's Gold?

Source: Aaron M. Cunningham and Gregg A. Runburg, 24K or Fools Gold? (chart), *Pensions & Investments* (July 27, 2009). Used with permission.

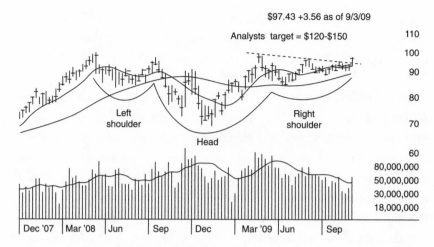

Figure 13.16   SPDR Gold Trust (GLD)

Source: Trang Ho, "Gold Nears '08 Peak on Weaker Dollar," *Investor's Business Daily* (September 3, 2009). Used with permission.

(there are a ton of them), Figure 13.16 provides a unique technical chart called an inverse head and shoulders, which can indicate a reversal of a current downtrend. In other words, gold might increase in price.

The SPDR gold trust from *Investor's Business Daily* indicates an inverse head and shoulders. However, one can also encounter a head-and-shoulders pattern. A head-and-shoulders pattern refers to a pattern that is visually similar to a human head with two shoulders but found in price charts of financially traded assets, such as stocks or bonds. The chart pattern is known for its reliability. The Chicago Board of Trade has characterized the head-and-shoulders formation as "one of the most reliable patterns indicating a major reversal in the market."[10] There are numerous chart patterns used in technical analysis; head and shoulders is only one of them.

Gold-Mining Companies

If one buys a gold stock, it is more than likely it is a mining stock. There are other indirect ways of investing in gold, such as investing in jewelry companies like Fuqi International. However, it is a stretch. Similar to oil exploration companies, miners are a way to gain exposure to gold. However, selecting a gold-mining company to invest in is difficult because each property has its unique risks. The location of the mine, quality of ore, and local taxes can be difficult to access by an investor.[11] It is very hard for an investor to understand the economies of mining, but not impossible.

As the price of a commodity escalates, buyers may favor other commodities. For instance, if gold becomes too high priced, buyers might turn to another commodity like silver. Further, if gold gets too high in price (as with anything), replacements will be sought. There is no gold substitute today. However, it could theoretically be manufactured—similar to diamonds. Until recently, diamonds could never be manufactured, but today, there are high-quality diamonds made through crystal synthesis research.

Substitutes can hurt miners. For example, if gold is too highly priced, dentists will use materials other than gold to fill teeth, which explains why gold fillings are almost nonexistent today. Another issue for miners is cost. Fuel prices, labor complications, politics, equipment issues, access (land versus sea), and other variables can affect cost.

Table 13.2 lists some gold-mining companies. Investing in gold miners is not the same as investing in gold. The problems that mining companies encounter (e.g., high production costs, lower output, operational issue) have very little to do with the price of gold. In a 2009 report on Goldcorp, the *Wall Street Journal* noted that the company "experienced delays at its biggest mine last year due to operational problems, slowdowns especially painful as the price of gold climbed."[12]

Yet gold can adversely affect the mining companies, as an unexpected price dip in 2008 (shown in Figure 13.12) took "the mining companies along with them on the roller coaster."[13] During this particular stretch, any gain in gold-mining companies quickly dissipated, as, at the time, Anglo-Gold shares were down 35%, Barrick 24%, and Newmont Mining 15%.[14]

Gold-mining companies are popular among investors and are found in many mutual funds and indexes. Investors tend to prefer larger gold-mining companies over smaller ones. Many acquisitions occurred when gold-mining companies such as Barrick spent $10.4 billion to acquire Placer Dome. When gold is doing well, mining companies tend to do well, and it is easy for them to raise money as well as acquire other companies. As *On Wall Street* noted in 2008: "The historical correlation between mining stocks and the broad equity market is low, but returns will vary depending upon company-specific factors, including management ability, capital, structure and operational costs."[15]

Table 13.2   Gold-Mining Companies and Producers 2008–2009

Name	Country	Ticker (NYSE)	Market Cap ($)	Focus
Alamos Gold	Canada	AGI – TSE	1.01B	Gold
Aurizon Mines	Canada	AZK	690.89M	Gold
Barrick Gold	Canada	ABX	32.25B	Gold, copper
Eldorado Gold	Canada	EGO	4.06B	Gold
Goldcorp	Canada	GG	28.76B	Gold
Harmony Gold	South Africa	HMY	4.59B	Gold
IAMGOLD	Canada	IAG	5.08B	Gold
Lihir Gold	Papua New Guinea	LIHR – NASDAQ	6.54B	Gold
Newmont Mining	United States	NEM	21.17B	Gold
Yamana Gold	Canada	AUY	7.63B	Gold

Gold Mutual Funds

If an investor is not comfortable selecting individual equities, he or she can select a mutual fund, such as Nuveen Tradewinds Value Opportunities or ING Value Choice. Both funds are run by David Iben of Tradewinds Global Investors. The top-four holdings of both funds are gold-mining stocks: Lihir Gold Limited, Newmont Mining, Barrick Gold, and Kinross Gold.[16] Gold funds can be divided into three different types of funds (precious metals, natural resources, and gold), detailed in Tables 13.3 through 13.5.

Analyzing a gold mutual fund requires careful due diligence, just like investing in any other fund. A prudent investor will examine variables such as manager tenure, expense ratio, performance, market cap, number of holdings, standard deviation, sector weightings, top holdings, assets, and investment style.

Gold Retailers

Certain investors select domestic jewelry retailers and wholesalers as another way to invest in gold. Retailers such as Tiffany and Co. fell in 2009 when gold went up. Foreign jewelers, however, deal with a different clientele than the United States. Most notably, in Muslim, Hindu, and Asian

Table 13.3 Precious Metals Funds

Name	Morning Star Rating	Tot Ret YTD (current)	Tot Ret 12 Mo (current)	Tot Ret 3-Yr Annlzd (current)	Tot Ret 5-Yr Annlzd (current)	Manager Name
1 AIM Gold Prec Met	****	9.56%	−22.57%	−0.76%	13.02%	Andrew Lees
2 AmCent Global Gold	**	2.54%	−23.23%	−6.36%	9.46%	William Martin
3 DWS Gold&PrecMet	**	2.54%	−31.54%	−4.73%	7.30%	Euan Leckie
4 Evergreen Prec Metals	****	2.45%	−22.16%	0.83%	15.19%	Michael P. Bradshaw
5 Fidelity Adv Gold	*****	1.34%	−19.44%	N/A	N/A	S. Joseph Wickwire
6 First Eagle Gold	*****	4.42%	−12.38%	2.62%	13.36%	Jean-Marie Eveillard
7 Franklin Gold&Prec Met	***	9.77%	−27%	−0.70%	14.77%	Steve Land
8 GAMCO Gold	***	5.69%	−27.88%	−2.18%	12.59%	Caesar Bryan
9 ING Glb Natural Res	**	−0.81%	−45.41%	−9.85%	6.48%	David R. Powers
10 Midas	*	14.62%	−52.29%	−14.93%	5.99%	Thomas B. Winmill
11 OCM Gold	***	5.77%	−19.50%	−1.08%	11.92%	Greg Orrell
12 Oppenheimer Gold&Spec	***	12.40%	−33.56%	−2.21%	14.60%	Shanquan Li
13 ProFunds PrMtl Ult Sec	*	−4.11%	−55.90%	−22.11%	−0.95%	Hratch Najarian
14 RiverSource Prc Met&Min	***	2.89%	−24.26%	−3.42%	8.79%	Clay L. Hoes
15 Rydex Precious Metals	**	3.88%	−35.66%	−8.94%	N/A	Michael Byrum
16 Tocqueville Gold	****	14.23%	−24.25%	−4.43%	10.73%	John C. Hathaway
17 US Global Inv Gold	***	1.66%	−27.15%	−4.63%	14.03%	Frank E. Holmes
18 USAA Precous Metals&Min	****	8.60%	−21.10%	3.62%	17.21%	Mark W. Johnson
19 Van Eck Intl Gold	***	5.93%	−24.95%	0.36%	16.11%	Joseph M. Foster

Source: Morningstar Version 5.6 with data as of 4/27/2009. Used with permission.

Table 13.4 Natural Resources Funds

Name	Morning Star Rating	Tot Ret YTD (current)	Tot Ret 12 Mo (current)	Tot Ret 3-Yr Annlzd (current)	Tot Ret 5-Yr Annlzd (current)	Manager Name
1 Aberdeen Nat Res	****	6.75%	−47.71%	−6.55%	N/A	Jason Kotik
2 AIM Energy	****	5.47%	−47.06%	−5.47%	11.43%	Andrew Lees
3 Allianz RCM Global Res	**	5.61%	−54.14%	−10.58%	N/A	Paul Strand
4 Allianz RCM Glb Water	**	−4.50%	−37.46%	N/A	N/A	Andreas Fruschki
5 BlackRock Engy&Res Inv	***	9.41%	−57.01%	−16.14%	6.75%	Daniel J. Rice III
6 BlackRock Natural Res	****	8.54%	−48.92%	−8.11%	9.91%	Robert M. Shearer
7 Columbia Engy&Nat Res	****	3.34%	−49.60%	N/A	N/A	Michael E. Hoover
8 CS Commodity Return Strategy	****	−6.32%	−47.82%	−11.92%	N/A	Christopher Burton
9 Dreyfus Nat Res	***	5.45%	−53.02%	−10.05%	7%	Robin Wehbe
10 Fidelity Adv Energy	***	7.13%	−53.86%	−11.46%	6.98%	John Dowd
11 Fidelity Adv Materials	**	16.98%	−41.92%	N/A	N/A	Tobias Welo
12 Fidelity Sel Energy	***	7.18%	−53.83%	−11.22%	8.18%	John Dowd
13 Franklin Nat Res	***	14.18%	−48.74%	−8.05%	7.58%	Fred Fromm
14 ICON Energy	*****	−7.08%	−38.72%	−7.05%	10.25%	Derek Rollingson
15 ING Global Res	***	−0.78%	−45%	N/A	N/A	David R. Powers
16 Ivy Energy	N/A	4.08%	−47.39%	−7.86%	N/A	David Ginther
17 JennDry Jenn Nat Resour	****	15.54%	−49.76%	−7.13%	12.15%	David A. Kiefer
18 JHancock2 Glbl Timber	N/A	−11.90%	N/A	N/A	N/A	Norman Ali
19 Morgan Stan Natrl Res	***	−2.91%	−50.81%	−10.43%	7.02%	Neil Chakraborty
20 Neuberger Berman Clim	N/A	−0.75%	N/A	N/A	N/A	Ronald Silvestri

Source: Morningstar Version 5.6 with data as of 4/27/2009. Used with permission.

Table 13.5 Gold Funds

Name	Morning Star Rating	Tot Ret YTD (current)	Tot Ret 12 Mo (current)	Tot Ret 3-Yr Annlzd (current)	Tot Ret 5-Yr Annlzd (current)	Manager Name
1 AIM Gold Prec Met	****	9.56%	−24.57%	−0.76%	13.02%	Andrew Lees
2 AmCent Global Gold	**	2.54%	−23.23%	−6.36%	9.46%	William Martin
3 DWS Gold&Prec Met	**	2.54%	−31.54%	−4.73%	7.30%	Euan Leckie
4 Evergreen PrecMet	****	2.45%	−22.16%	0.83%	15.19%	Michael P. Bradshaw
5 Fidelity Adv Gold	*****	1.34%	−19.44%	N/A	N/A	S. Joseph Wickwire
6 First Eagle Gold	******	4.42%	−12.38%	2.62%	13.36%	Jean-Marie Eveillard
7 Franklin Gold&Prec Met	***	9.77%	−27.00%	−0.70%	14.77%	Steve Land
8 GAMCO Gold	***	5.69%	−27.88%	−2.18%	12.59%	Caesar Bryan
9 ING Glb Natural Res	**	−0.81%	−45.41%	−9.85%	6.48	David R. Powers
10 Oppenheimer Gold & Spec	***	12.40%	−33.56%	−2.21%	14.60%	Shanquan Li
11 RiverSource Prc Met&Min	***	2.89%	−24.26%	−3.42%	8.79%	Clay L. Hoes
12 Rydex Precious Metals	**	3.88%	−35.66%	−8.94%	N/A	Michael Byrum
13 Van Eck Intl Inv Gold	***	5.93%	−24.95%	0.36%	16.11%	Joseph M. Foster

Source: Morningstar Version 5.6 with data as of 4/27/2009. Used with permission.

cultures, gold may serve as the only financial asset for women.[17] Gold is primarily purchased in the United States as jewelry, not so much as a financial asset. Even when higher prices lead U.S. consumers to seek out substitutes, vast jewelry demand in China and India will continue to drive gold's demand.

Investor's Business Daily captured this perspective in a discussion of China's views on gold with Roth capital analyst Elizabeth Pierce. Pierce noted that "Shoppers in China see gold jewelry as a hedge against inflation and a form of household wealth. For Fuqi (pronounced fu-chi), that trait has limited the kind of impact on demand dogging U.S. jewelry stores."[18]

Asia will most likely drive the demand for gold for the foreseeable future. When gold is popular, exploration increases like it did in the early 1990s. It peaked in 1997 and plummeted to $1.9 billion in 2002.

Conclusion: Gold Outlook

Ultimately, gold is a viable alternative investment that will be around forever, especially considering that much of the gold that has been mined from the earth still exists in some shape or form above ground. The best time to buy gold appears to be when the stock market is doing well and gold is low in price. Gold tends to be relatively inexpensive in bull equity markets. The contrapositive is true in bear markets; gold or silver appreciates in value. Demand for gold increases in bad times and in fact rose by 64% between 2007 and 2008 as the Great Recession came to bear.[19] When the equity market is robust, gold tends to perform poorly. If one is patient and has a long-term view, purchases of gold in an equity bull market might be prudent.

The ideal time to invest is when the stock market is overvalued or when a crisis first breaks out. Typically, this is the time to dust off the surfboard. One could also dollar-cost average a purchase of gold over a long period because gold has flat-lined for long periods in the past. The tumultuous market in the fourth quarter of 2008 sent many commodities down, including gold. As the *Wall Street Journal* reported, gold and silver "were down substantially by 4.1% and 5.3%, respectively. Platinum and palladium were down 8.6% and 11.5%, respectively. Copper, the bellwether industrial metal, fell another 5.6%."[20]

Based on the U.S. economy in 2009, gold appears to be invincible. In May 2009, *Bloomberg Markets* reported the following: "In a deep slump with deflation, paper currencies will be debased, boosting demand for gold. In a rebound, the money that governments have spent to escape the crisis will fuel inflation, which may also spark demand for gold."[21] Gold appears to be a win/win solution, but it will correct as it has in the past. Loading up on any commodity at its all-time high is dangerous.

Recommended Reading and Web Sites

Books

Callie Brown, *The Complete Guide to Investing in Gold and Precious Metals*

Cliff Droke, *How to Trade and Invest in Gold Stocks*

John Katz, *The Goldwatcher: Demystifying Gold Investing*

Nathan Lewis, *Gold: The Once and Future Money*

Shayne McGuire, *Buy Gold Now: How a Real Estate Bust, Our Bulging National Debt, and the Languishing Dollar Will Push Gold to Record Highs*

Howard Ruff, *Ruff's Little Book of Big Fortunes in Gold and Silver*

Peter Schiff and John Downes, *Crash Proof: How to Profit From the Coming Economic Collapse*

Jonathan Spall, *Investing in Gold: The Essential Safe Haven Investment for Every Portfolio*

Craig Smith, *Rediscovering Gold in the 21st Century*

James Turk, *The Collapse of the Dollar and How to Profit from It: Make a Fortune by Investing in Gold and Other Hard Assets*

Web Sites

www.24hgold.com
www.apmex.com/
www.bostonbullion.com/
www.blanchardonline.com/

www.bullion.org.za
www.certifiedmint.com
www.cmi-gold-silver.com
www.eaglewing.com
www.forex.com/index.html
www.galmarley.com
www.gfms.co.uk
www.gold.com
www.goldbarsworldwide.com
www.goldcoins.com
www.goldinfo.net
www.goldprice.org
www.goldseek.com
www.goldsheetlinks.com
www.gold-eagle.com
www.invest.gold.org/sites/en/why_gold
www.kitco.com
www.miningnerds.com
www.monex.com
www.onlygold.com
www.royalmint.com
www.taxfreegold.co.uk
www.thebulliondesk.com
www.usagold.com
www.usgs.com
www.usmint.gov
www.xignite.com

PART 5

HEDGE FUNDS

RIDING THE WAVE

Chapter 14

Hedge Fund Overview

Commencing in the mid–1990s, I helped my clients hire various hedge fund managers and was an integral part of introducing the very first hedge fund-of-funds. Bankers Trust (which acquired Alex. Brown) created the first hedge fund-of-funds called Topiary. I liked the concept and helped place a sizeable amount of this fund with individuals and institutions. As a result, I became familiar with hedge funds.

There is a very long list of both positive and negative attributes of hedge funds. Back in the mid–1990s, hedge funds were not very well known. Among the many tricky things about investing in hedge funds are understanding the different types of managers, when you should invest, and when you should not. As Edward Gibbon explained, "The winds and the waves are always on the side of the ablest navigators."[1]

Many strategies or styles of hedge funds exist that are far different from indexes, mutual funds, separately managed accounts, or exchange-traded funds. For instance, one could select a midcap growth manager for any of these vehicles. Hedge funds, on the other hand, can be broken down into different segments or styles, such as global macro, event driven, equity hedge, or relative value. These segments or subsectors should be observed when investing in single hedge funds because they tend to move in and out of favor. Hedge funds have waves just like other alternative investments.

Although they have grown in popularity over the last couple of decades, hedge funds remain somewhat of an enigma to affluent investors and institutions. A survey conducted by the Spectrem Group of 514 families with more than a half-million dollars in investable assets each found that only 18% understood hedge funds.[2] The general perception of the affluent or high-net-worth individual is that hedge funds are still risky vehicles. The same survey found that when presented with the hedge funds, commodities, precious metals, private equity, and real estate investment trusts, 39% of those polled believed hedge funds to be the riskiest investment.[3] Institutional investors have been more accepting of hedge funds but struggle with finding and hiring the best ones.

News stories tend to focus solely on negative news with hedge funds, such as with Cerberus Capital Management, a hedge fund that had its first negative return in 2008 out of the firm's 17-year history. The *Wall Street Journal* reported on the company: "Investors in hedge funds run by Cerberus Capital Management LP, whose audacious multibillion-dollar bet on the U.S. auto industry went bust, are bolting for the door, clinching one of the highest-profile falls from grace of the investment world."[4]

As a result of the bad year and the negative publicity for Cerberus, investors ran for the exit. But even the best money managers or mutual fund managers can have a bad year. Similarly, the best surfers can fall off a surfboard (or, as they say, wipe out). Cerberus could very well pull through. As Plato said in the *Republic*, "Yes, that was a mighty wave which you have escaped. Yes, I said, but a greater is coming: you will not think much of it when you see the next one."[5] All investors are looking for opportunity now, and hedge funds are a viable option. Although negative sentiment toward hedge funds during 2008 and the first half of 2009 would lead most to believe that the hedge fund market will collapse, hedge funds will recover and most likely reach new highs with asset inflows.

Hedge funds will continue to grow in the United States as well as the rest of the world. Hedge fund assets most likely will reach $2 trillion again with expectations for greater growth in the future. Foreign hedge funds, which are in their infancy, will likely experience massive growth, particularly in Asia, whose hedge-fund industry topped $70+ million in recent years. China and India will probably experience the most growth with hedge funds. Almost 24% of Asia-focused hedge funds are found there—up 5% from 2008 levels.[6]

Defining Hedge Funds

Hedge funds are privately operated investment vehicles structured either as limited partnerships for U.S. investors, offshore investment companies, or unit trusts for non-U.S. investors. They have gained in popularity, but hedge funds still perplex investors. According to Vinh Q. Tran, the author of *Evaluating Hedge Fund Performance*, "Hedge funds are complicated trading strategies with high turnover and often use complex derivatives structured by financial engineers and math wizards. They also employ leverage to enhance returns, which at the same time exposes them to greater risks."[7]

While there are many definitions of hedge funds, they are simply unregulated investment vehicles with a variety of money management styles run by talented and creative individuals who can think outside the box. Hedge fund managers attempt to generate returns greater than the market over time. Unlike mutual funds and money managers with strict objectives, hedge funds are flexible and have the ability to select from a vast array of securities and strategies that the hedge fund managers desire in order to achieve those returns. Despite the fact that some hedge funds have been more successful than others, a primary goal amongst all hedge funds is to "hedge" or guard against market declines.

Because the hedge fund space is so large and complex, there are many different definitions. Compelling returns frequently drive investors to hedge funds regardless of risk, which can lead to trouble. According to Andrew W. Lo, the Harris and Harris Group Professor at MIT, "Unregulated and opaque investment partnerships that engage in a variety of active investment strategies, hedge funds have generally yielded double-digit returns historically but not without commensurate risks, and such risks are currently not widely appreciated or well understood."[8] As with any investment, risk should be considered and contemplated before investing.

Hedge funds may operate one or more funds in multiple jurisdictions. For United States–based investors who pay tax, hedge funds are often structured as limited partnerships. The hedge fund manager is the general partner, and the investors are the limited partners. The general partner makes the investment decisions. Non-U.S. investors and U.S. entities that do not pay tax (such as pension funds) do not receive the same benefits from limited partnerships.

The goal of hedge funds is positive absolute returns regardless of market conditions—that is, hedge funds should earn a positive rate of return regardless of how well or not the stock market is performing. A "hedge" implies protecting or hedging an investment whether the market is rising or falling. Hedging involves shorting (selling) or buying puts (options) to help save principle. Hedging might involve buying one security and selling another to lower risk. A perfect hedge offers a riskless portfolio. At the center of every hedge fund's portfolio is the Capital Asset Pricing Model (CAPM). The CAPM was developed by Stanford professor William Sharpe, who believed that there are two different types of risk (market risk and unsystematic risk or unique risk). The model is based on the proposition that any stock's required rate of return is equal to the risk-free rate of return plus its risk premium where risk reflects diversification.[9]

Market risk affects all stocks. Market risk is the part of a security's risk that cannot be eradicated. Market risk stems from factors that systematically affect all firms, such as war, inflation, recession, and high interest rates.[10] Beta measures how sensitive a security is to market movements or systematic risk. Franklin Allen, Richard A. Brealey, and Stewart C. Meyers note that "Stocks with betas greater than 1.0 tend to amplify the overall movements of the market. Stocks with betas between 1 and 1.0 tend to move in the same direction as the market but not as far."[11] Alpha, on the other hand, is the rate or return on a security in excess of what would be predicted by an equilibrium model like CAPM. With hedge funds, alpha refers to the investment returns generated by a manager's skill or value added as opposed to the movement of the market. A high alpha manager is one that tends to outperform the market over the peer group.

Lowering market risk by creating a portfolio with a low beta is an important feature for a hedge fund. By investing in stocks that have both positive and negative betas, hedge funds can effectively bring market risk down to or close to zero.[12] This can be done by investing in two different companies that react differently to the market and are thus negatively correlated.[13] An example is a fund that invests in both an oil company and an airline company. Should gas prices rise, the airline will be negatively affected and the oil company will be positively affected. Risk with an individual security is different from the risk associated with a portfolio of securities. Hedge funds can buy virtually anything as an investment, but few invest everything into just one security or single company. Some hedge funds bet heavily on sectors like Amaranth with natural gas or take large positions in a company, but very few (if any) bet everything on just one company. Portfolio risk needs to be carefully examined with hedge funds. CAPM helps with the process.

Hedge funds deploy a variety of tools. For instance, a tool frequently used by hedge funds is market neutral long/short equity trading. In this practice, hedge funds short a stock they believe is about to fall and buy the stock that is about to rise. These long/short combinations hedge against each other because both stocks are affected by market changes in opposite ways.[14]

A hedge fund is an investment fund that because of structuring falls outside the regulations of the Securities and Exchange Commission (SEC) that apply to the other financial institutions. In a staff report to the SEC regarding hedge funds, the following was noted:

> The term has no precise legal or universally accepted definition and generally identifies an entity that holds a pool of securities and perhaps other assets that does not register its securities offerings under the Securities Act and which is not registered as an investment company under the Investment Company Act.[15]

Private equity firms use a similar structure. This allows them to take higher-risk positions and use more complex investment strategies that a mutual fund may not be able to. One key component of the hedge fund is leverage. Leverage is the use of debt to increase the expected return. Leverage creates a high-risk scenario but at the same time magnifies returns. Leverage typically works better in more stable markets with less volatility. Mark Anson, president and executive director of investment services at Nuveen Investments Inc., Chicago, precisely summed up hedge funds' use of leverage in a 2008 essay, stating:

> [H]edge fund managers often employ a significant amount of leverage to maximize the amount of the financial premium they can collect. In less volatile markets, this strategy works well. In volatile markets, however, the use of leverage only exacerbates the losses of the hedge fund manager.[16]

Besides hedge funds and mutual funds, there is another vehicle gaining popularity called a hedge fund-of-funds, which is a vehicle that combines multiple hedge funds. Hedge funds are offered as unregistered securities available to a very limited pool of investors whereas a hedge fund-of-funds can provide a less restrictive and more diversified way to invest in a number of hedge funds. A hedge fund-of-funds permits a greater number of investors and allows lower minimums. A number of hedge fund-of-funds are registered. Allowed the right to register with the SEC under Investment Company Act of 1940, these hedge fund-of-funds can be advertised and sold to the public. Minimum investments can be $25,000, but investors cannot withdraw their shares on demand. A hedge fund-of-funds also offers a greater diversity of investment sectors, styles, and strategies than offered in single hedge funds. As can be expected because there are many investments, hedge funds-of-funds typically have higher fees than mutual funds.

Leverage, short selling, lack of transparency, and regulation are all reasons to consider hedge funds risky. Hedge funds differ from mutual funds in that individual hedge funds are not regulated by the SEC and their investors must be accredited.[17] According to the Securities Act of 1933 and the Securities Exchange Act of 1934, hedge funds issue "private offerings" and are not required to provide any sort of report or pricing to regulatory bodies.[18] Abiding by one of two sections of the Investment Company Act of 1940 requiring an investment group to have fewer than 100 investors(a 3c1 fund) or restrict investment to qualified purchasers (a 3c7 fund), hedge funds are able to avoid substantial monitoring and limitations. A qualified purchaser is an individual with more than $5 million in investment assets. A 3c7 fund is permitted an infinite number of investors, requiring SEC registration when membership reaches 500, whereas a 3c1 fund can sell to an accredited investor. Accredited investors include individuals with a minimum annual income of $200,000 ($300,000 with spouse) or $1 million in net worth and most institutions with $5 million in assets. Both types of hedge funds are sold privately with no public advertisement allowed under the Securities Act of 1933, and both also are allowed to charge performance and incentive fees.[19] Similarly, hedge fund managers, who usually have a large personal investment in the hedge fund, are not required to register, according to the Investment Advisers Act of 1940, as long as they have fewer than 14 clients, with separate hedge funds each counting as only one client under commission rules.[20]

Mutual funds are one of the most tightly regulated investment options in the United States. They are investment companies that must register with and are subjected to thorough oversight by the SEC.[21] According to the SEC, "Mutual funds are subject to SEC registration and regulation,

Table 14.1   Hedge Funds versus Mutual Funds

	Hedge Funds	Mutual Funds
Performance Evaluation	Absolute Return	Specified Benchmark
Minimum Investment	High Minimum	
	(Typically $1M and above)	$1,000
Transparency	No	Yes
Daily Liquidity	No	Yes
Performance Tracking		
(daily, weekly)	No	Yes
Regulated	No	Yes
Broad Diversification	No	No
Cost Effectiveness	No	Yes
Management Fees and	2/20 Rule: 2% management	Management Fees (typically
Sales Charges*	fee, and 20% of net profit	1–1.5%), front or back-end
		loads (sales charge range
		from 0–5%), and 12(b)–1 fees
Flexibility	Yes	No
Expanded Investment		
Universe	Yes	No
Increased Risk-adjusted		
Portfolio Performance	Yes	No

Source: Author.

and are subject to numerous requirements imposed for the protection of investors. Mutual funds are regulated primarily under the Investment Company Act of 1940 and also subject to the Securities Act of 1933 and the Securities Exchanges Act of 1934."[22] Unlike hedge funds, mutual funds do not have a minimum investment requirement, often accepting new accounts with investments of $1,000 or sometimes less.[23] Table 14.1 depicts the differences between hedge funds and mutual funds.

Hedge Fund Strategies

Hedge funds are very different from equity and fixed income mutual funds. Mixing long and short securities reduces a fund's exposure to the market. The goal of market-neutral hedge funds is to have no market exposure, which can be achieved by having equal amounts in long and short positions. Many funds accomplish this by combing through individual sectors, longing the stocks they believe will outperform the market, and shorting the stocks they believe will underperform. Essentially, there are six core hedge fund strategies with 35 subcategories, as illustrated in Figure 14.1.

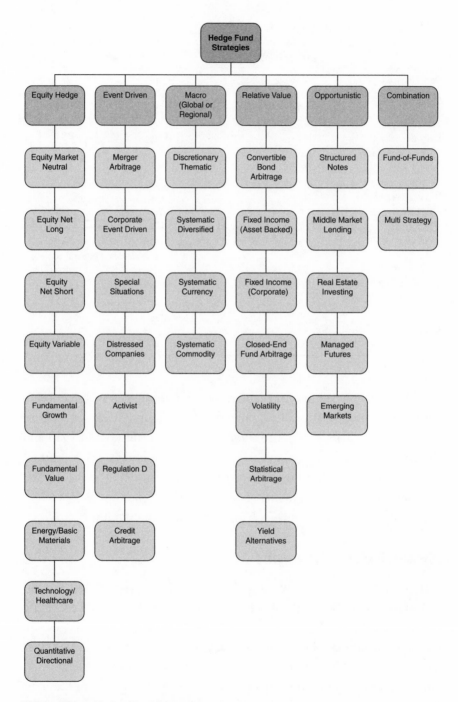

Figure 14.1 Hedge Fund Strategies

Source: Author.

Equity Hedge Strategies

Equity hedge strategies represent a variety of strategies that feature equities with both long (buying) and short (selling) positions using derivatives, short sales, and indexes. Depending on which way the equity market is headed, managers make adjustments.

> Managers generally increase net long exposure in bull markets and decrease net long exposure, or may even be net short in bear markets. Generally, the short exposure is intended to generate an ongoing positive return in addition to acting as a hedge against a general stock market decline. Stock index put options or exchange-traded funds are also often used as a hedge against market risk.[24]

Equity hedges vary widely in the level of diversification, net exposure, holding period, leverage, market capitalization, and valuation.

Equity Market Neutral. A strategy whereby capital is invested both long and short to "neutralize" market risk. Overvalued securities are sold and undervalued securities are bought. According to Joseph G. Nicholas, Founder and Chairman of HFR Group, L.L.C., "Equity market-neutral strategies strive to generate consistent returns in both up and down economies by selecting equity positions with a net portfolio exposure of zero."[25] A number of long equity positions are held, as well as an equal—or close to equal—dollar amount of offsetting short positions, which results in a net exposure of zero. Equity market neutral involves equities as the name implies but other hedge funds might deploy a "market neutral" strategy by using securities other than equities.

> "Market-neutral" investing refers to a group of investment strategies that seek to neutralize certain market risks by taking offsetting long and short positions in instruments with actual or theoretical relationships. These approaches seek to limit exposure to systemic changes in price caused by shifts in macro-economic variables or market sentiment.[26]

Market neutral is sometimes referred to as a long/short strategy. Returns are derived from the amount by which long positions outperform short positions, or the long/short spread.

Equity Net Long. A strategy that results in a fund having more long positions than shorts. The fund will often use leveraged positions to maximize returns. Managers are bullish and believe that the underlying securities will go up or appreciate in value.

Equity Net Short. A strategy whereby the fund maintains consistent short exposure and expects to outperform traditional equity managers in declining equity markets. Overvalued companies are selected to short and buy back at a lower price to lock in a profit. An equity net short strategy is the contrapositive of equity net long. Managers that short tend to perform well in down markets but poorly in up markets. Sudden reversals in the market can harm performance with this strategy.

Equity Variable. A strategy in which investment managers maintain both long and short positions in equity and equity derivative securities. Fundamental and/or quantitative analysis is used to determine how much of a long or short position to take.

Fundamental Growth. A strategy that seeks to identify companies with probabilities for earnings growth and capital appreciation exceeding those of the general equity market. Growth potential is the main focus. For instance, technology companies with high PE (price to earnings) ratios might be part of this hedge fund.

Fundamental Value. A strategy that identifies the securities of companies that a manager believes to be undervalued when compared with relevant benchmarks. Fundamental value is the antithesis of fundamental growth. Managers assess the company's market cap, historical earnings, and future earnings prospects. The valuation is then based on those factors that differ from the value of other investments. Fundamental value strategies "employ investment processes designed to identify attractive opportunities in securities of companies that trade at valuation metrics by which the manager determines them to be inexpensive and undervalued when compared with relevant benchmarks."[27]

Energy/Basic Materials. Largely commodities-based funds, these funds actively trade physical energy as well as derivatives. The principals are often experts in a specific industry area and leverage their expertise to attract investors such as master limited partnerships (MLPs). An MLP is a publically traded limited partnership that engages in natural resources, including the extraction and transportation of petroleum and natural gas.

Technology/Health Care. Funds of this type "maintain a level of expertise that exceeds that of a market generalist in identifying opportunities in companies engaged in all development, production and application of technology, biotechnology and as related to production of pharmaceuticals and health care industry."[28] For example, a group of doctors or experts in a medical field such as oncology might focus on a fund to invest in new promising companies devoted to finding cures for cancer. Often these funds are called focus funds because they concentrate on one area. The majority of investors will not have such expertise or information available to them to make such specialized investments themselves.

Quantitative Directional. Fund managers of this type tend not to be sector or segment specialists. These funds "employ sophisticated quantitative analysis of price and other technical and fundamental data to ascertain relationships among securities and to select securities for purchase and sale."[29]

Event Driven

When event-driven strategies are pursued, they are not affected by the direction of the markets in which they operate but have defined events as their trigger points. As author Vinh Tran notes in his book *Evaluating Hedge Fund Performance*, "The event driven strategy seeks to capture profits from price movements of securities of companies experiencing significant corporate events."[30]

Event-driven hedge funds are another example of using a strategy in which there is highly complex information that most likely traders or other experts (like bankruptcy lawyers) have the ability to analyze and make correct assumptions. Stuart McCrary sums up the approach in his book, *How to Create and Manage a Hedge Fund*, stating that the event-driven strategies "rely on fundamental research to appraise the deals quickly. Often, the team of analysts is given considerable input into the portfolio decision making. In some funds, the traders/portfolio managers take on the responsibility of doing the analysis."[31] A lot of work goes into attempting to foresee a possible outcome. For example, one might ask "is a particular biotech company likely to get FDA approval or not?"

Merger Arbitrage. Merger arbitrage or risk arbitrage is a strategy that involves going long (buying or owning shares of a target company) in a takeover and selling short the stock of the acquiring company. Typically, the acquired stock rises and the acquiring company stock falls; the fund profits on the spread. Securities are traded on companies involved in announced corporate takeovers or mergers and acquisitions. Merger arbitrage is sometimes referred to as risk arbitrage because there is a risk that the transaction or deal might not go through.

Corporate Event Driven. Strategies involving some form of corporate restructuring such as a merger, acquisition, or bankruptcy. The strategy is driven by the deal, not by the market.

Special Situations. Funds of this type focus on opportunities that arise uniquely or infrequently. These situations include mergers and acquisitions, bankruptcies, share buy-backs, special dividends, division spin-offs, and any other significant market event. Spin-offs occur when a large company spins out a division or takes it public. Spin-offs tend to be lucrative. A hedge fund might buy shares of the initial public offering or the entire division with the goal of taking it public. By their very nature, these events are nonrecurring and provide significant uncertainty.

Distressed Companies. The strategy of investing in securities of companies that are in trouble or "distressed." Typically, these companies are on the verge of going bankrupt. Hedge funds bet the company will turn around and the securities will eventually appreciate. Strategies of this type employ a process focused on corporate fixed-income instruments, primarily with corporate credit instruments of companies trading at significant discounts.[32] That is, hedge funds buy bonds involved with a bankruptcy of a particular company and hope to sell them later at a higher price. In some cases, creditors might not be permitted or have the patience to wait for a restructuring, so the hedge fund can buy at a deep discount. Another way of creating value is to become involved with the bankruptcy process and developing an edge. One needs to be quite good at negotiating with judges and investors as well as being creative.

Activist. Managers using this strategy buy large equity stakes to "obtain representation on the company's board of directors in an effort to impact the firm's policies or strategic direction and in some cases may advocate activities such as division or asset sales, partial or complete corporate divestiture, dividend or share buybacks, and changes in management."[33] These investment strategies revolve around corporate transactions. Managers often identify a weakness with the company and push for change. Often public battles over board seats are depicted by the news media as being fueled by Gordon Gekko types (from the movie *Wall Street*); however, quite a few activist hedge funds have brought positive change to companies that were poorly run. These hedge fund managers are helpful in making sure shareholders' interests are put first and not have company money being spent on $7,000 shower curtains as was done with Tyco.

Regulation D. A strategy that focuses on companies that are private and illiquid. The securities are issued by companies in need of growth capital. There is a waiting period for the private share offering to be registered by the SEC. The rewards can be handsome for those with patience. Further, private equity often rewards investors for the lack of liquidity with the investment.

Credit Arbitrage. Funds that follow this strategy "isolate attractive opportunities in corporate fixed income securities."[34] Using convertible securities, the manager goes long (buys the bond) while selling short the stock. They also use interest rate derivatives or swaps to hedge against interest rate hikes that would lower the bond price.

Macro

Strategies in this category are based on future movements in underlying instruments as opposed to a security merely increasing in value. Themes are important, as well as overall market risk. Interest rates, recessions, shortages in commodities, and other macro issues are explored around the world. As an example, a macro hedge fund might go long the dollar and short the euro. Global macro or macro funds can invest anywhere.

Macro hedge funds can invest in a wide array of securities, such as currencies, commodities, or derivatives. According to Hedge Fund Research Inc.:

Macro (total) investment managers [use] a broad range of strategies in which the investment process is predicated on movements in underlying economic variables and the impact these have on equity, fixed income, hard currency and commodity markets. Managers employ a variety of techniques, discretionary analysis, combinations of top down and bottom up, quantitative and fundamental approaches and long and short term holding periods.[35]

Out of all the hedge fund strategies, global macro has the most flexibility in that the managers can invest in basically anything anywhere in the world. The strategy is normally top-down when investment selection is made after examining macroeconomic variables such as gross domestic product or demographics.

Discretionary Thematic. Discretionary thematic strategies are "primarily reliant on the evaluation of market data, relationships, and influences, as interpreted by an individual or group of individuals who make decisions on portfolio positions; strategies employ an investment process most heavily influenced by top down analysis of macroeconomic variables."[36] The hedge fund manager will select investment based on his or her outlooks in a variety of markets, such as with commodities, currencies, and fixed income (interest rates). If the manager feels that emerging markets are more attractive than the United States or other developed countries, he might build a strategy around this theme. For example, the manager might buy calls or go long with an emerging market index while shorting selected developed countries.

Systematic Diversified. Strategy using technical models or algorithms to identify market opportunities. This strategy tends to do well with environments that have identifiable trends, i.e., a bull or bear market.

Systematic Currency. This strategy involves mathematical and technical models. Funds in this group invest in currencies strategically and in fixed-income markets only incidentally or as part of an arbitrage strategy.

Systematic Commodity. Commodity arbitrage consists of relative-value trades conducted between closely related commodity instruments, including physical commodities, futures, and options on commodities and securities whose movements are fundamentally tied to a commodity price. Funds of this type use mathematical models rather than fundamental analysis.

Relative-Value Strategies

Relative-value strategies identify and profit from differences between multiple securities. According to Filippo Stefanini, author of *Investment Strategies of Hedge Funds,* "Hedge fund arbitrages in practice are directional positions on spreads: if the spread widens or narrows as anticipated, the manager makes a profit; otherwise he suffers a loss."[37]

Convertible Bond Arbitrage. This strategy is based on a valuation discrepancy for convertible bonds or preferred stock. Managers go long or buy convertible securities (bonds or preferreds) that can be exchanged for a finite number of shares of another security (common shares) at a predetermined price while shorting the underlying equities.

Fixed Income (Asset Backed). This strategy is predicated on the spread between securities when a fixed income instrument is backed by obligations such as loans, mortgages, and credit cards.[38] For example, GNMA (Ginnie Mae) bonds are mortgage-backed securities that are backed by the full faith and credit of the U.S. government.

Fixed Income (Corporate). An investment process to find attractive opportunities between a variety of fixed-income instruments, typically realizing an attractive spread between multiple corporate bonds or between a corporate and risk-free government bond.[39] Depending on interest rates and the market, bond prices can drop whereby yields increase and vice versa. One bond in the same industry such as the beverage industry might trade at a premium while another one will trade at a discount for no apparent reason. Coca-Cola, for instance might trade at a huge premium to PepsiCo bonds or vice versa. A hedge fund manager might short Coca-Cola and buy PepsiCo bonds. There are numerous ways a hedge fund manager can make money with corporate bonds.

Closed-End Arbitrage. Closed-end funds raise money through initial public offerings. These funds differentiate themselves from open-end mutual funds, in which investors purchase shares in the fund directly from the fund itself. The intrinsic value of the underlying securities can be worth more than the value at which the shares trade, creating an opportunity. Closed-end funds have a fixed number of shares, whereas a mutual fund does not. Shares trade solely on a supply-and-demand balance, which might not be indicative of the true value of the securities. A closed-end arbitrage hedge fund can take advantage of this relationship.

Volatility. A strategy that trades volatility as an asset class. It employs a variety of strategic methods. As Hedge Fund Research, Inc., explains it, "[d]irectional volatility strategies maintain exposure to the direction of implied volatility of a particular asset or, more generally, to the trend of implied volatility in broader asset classes. Arbitrage strategies employ an investment process designed to isolate opportunities between the prices of multiple options."[40]

Statistical Arbitrage. This quantitative strategy closely resembles equity market neutral strategies except that it foregoes fundamental analysis in favor of quantitative factor models. In *Guide to Hedge Funds*, Philip Coggan remarks that "[t]hose involved in statistical arbitrage (stat arb, for short) are the real rocket scientists of the industry, using highly sophisticated models to try to find statistical relationships between various securities."[41]

Yield Alternatives. Funds using this strategy realize a spread between related yield-oriented securities including equity, real estate investment trusts (REITs), preferred stock, listed partnerships, and other corporate obligations. They typically quantify the relationship between instruments and identify positions in which the risk-adjusted spread represents an attractive opportunity.

Opportunistic

Opportunistic strategies are tactics whereby managers identify unique investments or special situations in areas that traditionally are not well understood or that offer significant upside.

Middle Market Lending. Managers invest their fund to finance the growing needs of midsized companies. They opportunistically seek spreads in the growing middle market.

Real Estate Investing. Funds in the real estate sector invest in securities of REITs and other real estate companies. Some funds may also invest directly in real estate property.

Managed Future. Funds of this type offer means to increase exposure to commodities. Managed futures funds are registered as commodity pool operators or commodity trading advisors. These funds invest in physical commodities, futures, and futures options. They are essentially funds that invest in the futures markets. The managed futures strategy is directional. Managers use trend-following strategies in futures.

Emerging Markets. Funds invest in securities of companies or the sovereign debt of developing countries. Investments are usually made long. Given that many foreign markets do not allow short selling, managers are limited in the hedging actions they can make.

Combination Strategies

These strategies use a variety of approaches. They do not specialize but adapt based on market movements and the discretion of the principals.

Fund-of-Funds. These managers invest their capital in other hedge funds. They practice tactical asset allocation: reallocating capital across hedge fund strategies as each strategy offers greater or smaller returns.

Multistrategy. Multistrategy pertains to a manager that includes other strategies with their main strategy. For example, Och-Ziff expanded from merger arbitrage to become a multistrategy manager; they invest in event-driven sectors and convertible arbitrage. As a hedge fund grows, it can diversify into other strategies and not just handle one strategy. Another form of multistrategy fund is similar to a hedge fund-of-funds but all the hedge funds or strategies are owned and managed by one group. As Coggan summarizes, "The idea behind multi-strategy funds is that they switch money on the clients' behalf. An asset allocator sits at the centre of the structure, deciding which strategies and which managers are likely to produce the best future returns. Because all the strategies are part of one group, the allocator does not have to worry about notice periods."[42] Unlike a hedge fund-of-funds, which invests in outside managers, the multistrategy has its own strategies. The similarity is that the manager shifts money among the various styles.

History of Hedge Funds

According to *Investing in Hedge Funds*, the term *hedge fund* was first used by *Fortune* journalist Carl Loomis. In 1966 Loomis wrote an article titled "The Jones Nobody Keeps Up With" referencing the strategy created in

1949 by a former *Fortune* columnist named Alfred Winslow Jones.[43] Jones's portfolio consisted of two types of holdings: stocks that rose faster than the markets during a bull market and fell more sluggishly than the market when a bear came along, and stocks with the exact opposite traits.[44] Taking a long position on the good stocks and shorting the poor stocks, he minimized risk and guaranteed profit no matter what direction the market was moving. He developed the long-short market model that is still at the essence of hedge funds.[45]

The original goal of hedge funds was to reduce risk by limiting exposure to the market. Most mutual funds take only long positions and thus have 100% exposure to the market. Hedge funds, on the other hand, can take short positions. A short position is when a hedge fund sells a stock without owning it, hoping the position drops in value and is able to be purchased in the future at a lower price. Proceeds from the sale can be used to invest in long positions. A funds net position is the difference between its long position and short position. Market neutral funds have the same amount long and short.

Hedge funds began to move away from the hedging strategy in the 1970s as more funds increased their exposure to the market. Today, hedge funds are limited partnerships or limited liability corporations made up of qualified purchasers (individuals with $5 million or more in investable assets). Because of their requirements, hedge funds are exempt from filing as a registered investment company under the 1940 Investment Company Act. Officials have presented guidelines concerning hedge funds but no rules.

Throughout the 1960s, hedge funds moved from risk-adverse vehicles to speculative funds with increased market exposure. The bear markets of the late 1960s and early 1970s caused major losses at many hedge funds and led in a sharp decrease in the number of funds. The decrease, however, was not permanent. History tends to repeat itself in finance. Hedge funds exploded in growth until 2008, when they had a high correlation to the stock market; as a result, investors withdrew once again.

One of the most noted names in the hedge fund industry, George Soros, got his start in 1969 when he formed the Quantum Fund with only $6 million in capital. Soros was successful during the 1970s despite the market downturn; he bought when others were fearful. As the late surfer Buzzy Trent used to say, "Waves are not measured in feet and inches, they are measured in increments of fear." Soros became infamous in the 1990s for his activity in currencies, including shorting the English pound in 1992. The Quantum Fund's flagship endowment fund plummeted in 2000 but would later recover. In a press conference in 2000, Soros said "I am anxious to reduce my market exposure and be more conservative. We will accept lower returns because we will cut the risk profile."[46] The October 6, 2008, issue of *Forbes* listed Soros as one of the Forbes 400 with a net worth of $11 billion.[47]

Julian Robertson's Tiger Management also helped to attract investors to the world of hedge funds. Robertson opened the fund in 1987 with $8 million in capital. In its first 6 years, the Tiger Fund recorded annual returns of +43%. The Tiger Fund reached its peak in 1998 before falling in the technology bubble and closing in 2000. The equity market was negative for 2 years after this from 2001 to 2002. Instead of battling the markets, Robertson built a golf course in New Zealand. Robertson is a member of the Forbes 400 and a billionaire.

Hedge funds did not experience much growth during the 1970s and 1980s. Starting in the 1990s, hedge fund growth exploded. In 1990, there were only 530 hedge funds with $38.9 billion in capital, but by 2000, there were 3,335 funds with $490.6 billion in capital. This change represents a 20% annualized increase in the number of funds and 29% annualized increase in capital.

Because of the risk with single hedge funds, the hedge fund-of-funds industry blossomed. *Bloomberg Markets* notes that "The first funds of hedge funds were established in 1969 by Geneva-based La Compagnie Financière Edmond de Rothschild Group and by the Belgo-Dutch bank Fortis."[48] A hedge fund-of-funds is a fund-of-funds that invests in a portfolio of different hedge funds to provide broad exposure to the hedge fund industry and to diversify the risk associated with a single investment fund. A hedge fund-of-fund selects hedge fund managers and constructs portfolios based on those funds in it, thus allowing ordinary investors into a highly acclaimed fund or many hedge funds at once.

Hedge Fund Debacle Time Line

The frequency of hedge fund calamities has increased over time:

- **1998:** Along with **Long Term Capital Management's** infamous $4.6 billion downfall, the hedge fund used a complex series of transactions to evade taxes, prompting the Internal Revenue Service to seek $75 million in back taxes.

- **1999:** Hedge fund manager **Martin Frankel** mysteriously vanished from his Greenwich, Connecticut, mansion with documents smoldering in a fireplace. He was indicted and later convicted for insurance fraud, racketeering, and money laundering.

- **2000:** **Mark Yagalla**, a 23-year-old hedge fund manager "prodigy," capitalized on early success by using his investors' money to purchase lavish luxuries, such as sports cars, mansions, jewelry, and vacations.

- **2005:** **Bayou Management LLC.** Founder Sam Israel and partner Dan Marino fabricated returns and collected huge fees on the $450 million hedge fund they ran. Bayou filed for Chapter 11.

- **2005:** The SEC sued **Wood River Capital Management's** founder John Whittier. The *New York Times* on October 14, 2005, claimed Whittier "did not disclose to investors that he had at one point as much as 98 percent of one of his funds invested in a speculative stock with no recent history of profitability."[49]

- **2006:** Kirk Wright's **International Management Associates** claimed $185 million in assets but investigators find less than $150,000 invested. He is responsible for scamming football players, doctors, and retirees out of more than $100 million.

- **2006:** $6 billion of **Amaranth Advisors'** $9 billion fund evaporated with a bad bet on natural gas commodities.

- **2007:** **Second Curve Capital** declined 30% as of March 31, 2007, because of huge bets on lenders that grant loans to people with shaky credit histories.

- 2007: **Sowood Capital Management LP**, run by Jeff Larson, a former Harvard University endowment manager, lost $1.6 billion, or about 60% of its value, and returned the rest to investors
- 2007: **Goldman Sach's Global Alpha Fund** fell to $6 billion from $10 billion, partly as a result of bad bets on the yen and the Australian dollar. Investors bated out of the fund.
- 2008: **Citigroup**, one of the largest U.S. banks, was forced to face investors who lost nearly $2 billion through the bank's failing hedge funds. Moreover, Citigroup was forced to shut down both their Falcon Strategies Fund and Old Lane Partners Fund.
- 2008: One of the most devastating hedge fund collapses in the Great Recession was at **Bear Stearns**. Two of Bear's hedge funds blew up after investing in risky collateralized debt obligations, costing investors $1.6 billion. The funds' failures played a vital role in the collapse of Bear Stearns.
- 2008: **Daniel Zwirn's** company was investigated by the SEC for suspicious activities including charging his private Gulfstream jet to investors and moving money between onshore and offshore accounts.
- 2008: **Dillon Read Capital Management**, a hedge fund started by UBS in 2005, was closed because of heavy losses. Dillon Read's failure was a key factor that led UBS "to lose $38 billion betting on American mortgage-backed assets, battering its core capital and share price,"[50] as written in the April 26, 2008, edition of the *Economist*.
- 2008: **Bernard L. Madoff** ran one of the largest ponzi schemes in history. The $50 billion scheme affected both institutional and high-net-worth investors.

Chapter 15

The Hedge Fund Market

Today, the U.S. East Coast is the leader in hedge funds, with New York City and Connecticut having the highest concentration. London is the second-largest holder with about half the hedge funds on the East Coast. The majority of hedge funds are in the United States, but they are situated globally. The locations of the top-50 hedge funds in 2008 are detailed in Figure 15.1.

In 1990, there were approximately 610 hedge funds (including hedge fund-of-funds) as opposed to the peak of Q1 2008, when there were 10,233 hedge funds. Year after year, there were annual increases in the number of hedge funds, from 1990 to 2008. According to the U.S. Securities and

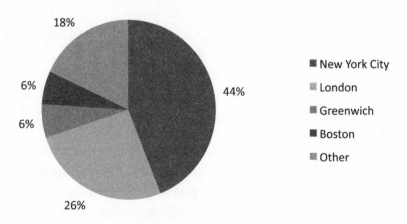

Figure 15.1   Locations of Top-50 Hedge Funds

Source: Hedge Fund Research Inc. Used with permission.

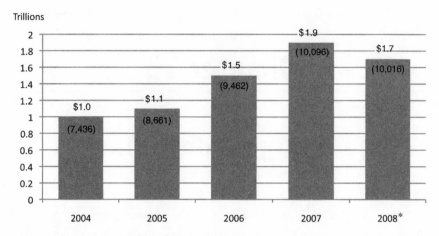

Figure 15.2   Hedge Fund Assets in Trillions and Number of Funds

Source: *Bloomberg Markets.* Hedge Fund Research. Used with permission

*As of Sept. 30. All other figures are as of Dec. 31.

Exchange Commission (SEC), "Hedge funds, while representing a relatively small portion of the US financial markets, have grown significantly in size and influence in recent years."[1] The growth of the hedge fund market was fairly consistent until 2008; the number of hedge funds declined during the third quarter of 2008. The drop in hedge funds during Q3 of 2008 was precipitous. Figure 15.2 illustrates the rise and fall of hedge fund quantity at the time of the Great Recession.

As the market further crashed, the number of hedge funds dropped to 9,762 funds. Mutual funds dropped in numbers as well, but not as much as hedge funds, as illustrated in Figure 15.3.

Mutual funds, unlike hedge funds, went through a major correction from 2000 to 2002 that resulted in merged mutual funds or closed mutual funds. Assets initially increased as well, from $38.91 billion in 1990 to a pinnacle of $1.93 trillion in Q2 2008. The decrease in assets started in Q3 2008 with $1.72 trillion and quickly reached $1.564 by October 2008. According to *Bloomberg Markets*, "[a]t least 118 funds of funds closed in the four months from the end of June to the end of October, while the number of hedge funds fell by 693 in the first nine months of the year, a record pace."[2] Hedge funds are one of the fastest-growing areas of money management, but they have far less in assets when compared with mutual funds.

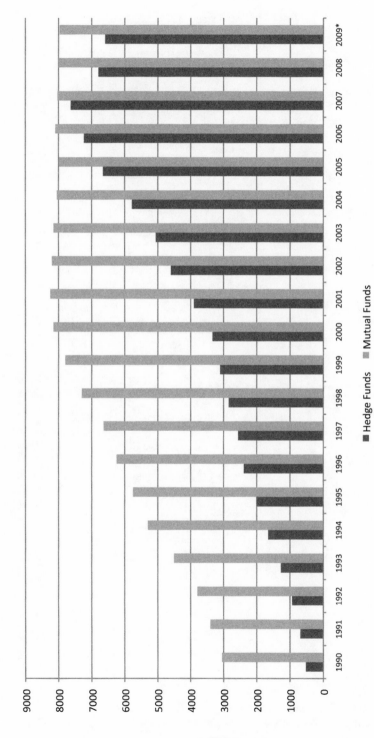

Figure 15.3 Number of Mutual Funds versus Number of Hedge Funds (1990–2008)

■ Hedge Funds ■ Mutual Funds

Source: Author.

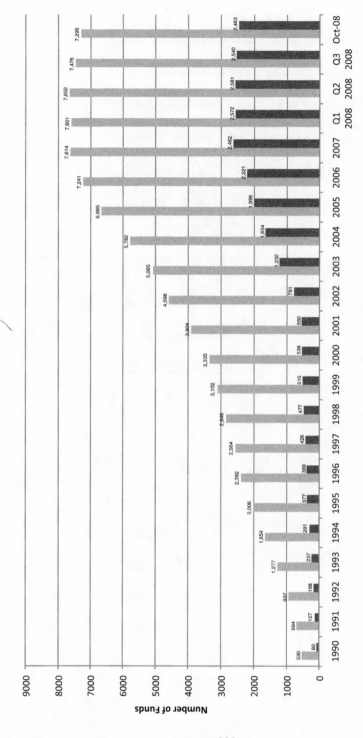

Figure 15.4 Estimated Number of Funds: Hedge Funds versus Fund-of-Funds, 1990–October 2008

Source: HFR, "HFR Global Hedge Fund Industry Report: Special Edition," October 2008.

Hedge funds dropped not just domestically in 2008, but offshore as well. According to Hedge Fund Research, Inc., there were approximately $9.56 billion in onshore funds in 1990 versus $29.35 billion in offshore funds. During Q1 2008, there were approximately $619 billion in onshore funds versus $1.23 trillion in offshore funds. Q2 2008 showed a decline of funds to $590 billion domestically, but an increase to $1.34 trillion for offshore funds. Q3 2008 showed a drop domestically to $529 billion and a drop for offshore funds to $1.19 trillion. Similarly, October 2008 was another decline when onshore hedge funds hit $479 billion and offshore funds dropped to $1.08 trillion. Hedge fund losses in 2008 were far worse than previous years, with the average fund losing 19%.[3]

Hedge funds showed a drop in value, but they were not alone. Mutual funds lost assets in 2008 as well, as illustrated in Figure 15.5. The U.S. mutual fund market showed a massive decline in value and redemptions as "investors yanked a record $72.3 billion from stock funds in October, the fifth straight month of outflow."[4] Mutual funds declined abroad as well. More precisely, "for the 12 months ended Oct. 31, emerging markets, international and global funds swung to a combined $33.1 billion outflow versus $130 billion inflow a year earlier. Aggressive growth funds saw $57.9 billion outflow this year. Stock fund assets fell to $3.9 trillion from $6.4 trillion a year ago."[5]

The mutual fund industry is much larger than the hedge fund universe and similar in asset size to the separately managed accounts market, as depicted by Figure 15.6.

As hedge funds became more popular, the returns from the traditional hedging strategies might become less lucrative. A plethora of new strategies arose that were designed to profit from market inefficiencies and price discrepancies. For example, many hedge funds began to speculate on currencies. In September 1992, George Soros and several other funds began to short the British pound, which threw the European exchange rate system into turmoil. In 1997, Soros took another position in currencies, against the Thai baht. Several Asian countries had their currencies plummet in what was known as the Asian Currency Crisis. A few of the new strategies worked well, whereas others were unmitigated disasters.

The biggest shock to the hedge fund world occurred in 1998 with the collapse of Long-Term Capital Management (LTCM). LTCM was

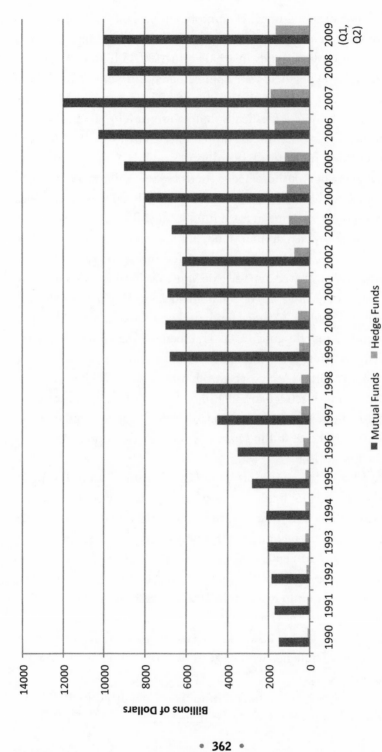

Figure 15.5 Total Net Assets of Mutual and Hedge Funds (1990–2009)

Source: Author.

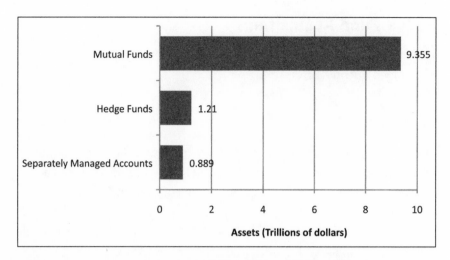

Figure 15.6   Assets: Mutual Funds, Hedge Funds, and Seprately Managed Accounts

Source: Investment Company Institute, 2008 Assets (graph), Investment Company Institute, in "Ownership of Mutual Funds, Shareholder Sentiment and Use of the Internet" (2008).

founded by John Meriwether and had a well-known board of directors, including Myron Scholes and Robert Merton. LTCM focused primarily on government bonds but also traded in many types of derivatives.[6] LTCM also was highly leveraged. The use of leverage increases risk. Leverage or borrowing might work on the way up (the market is doing well and in your favor), but it can quickly turn and magnify losses. In 1998, LTCM had around $5 billion in capital when Russia defaulted in its national debt, causing liquidity problems and increased spreads in the government debt markets. This was a problem for LTCM's model. The fund imploded and the Federal Reserve System helped bail out LTCM .

Over time, hedge funds have taken on different roles. Some hedge funds have even acted more like leveraged buyout funds than your typical hedge fund. According to *BusinessWeek*, "Hedge funds accounted for at least 50 private equity deals in 2006" and "in many ways, hedge funds' move into private equity is a natural progression, especially for the larger funds."[7] Hedge funds like to grow and manage more assets. Also, hedge funds started to expand into new areas for diversification purposes and offer investors more of a menu.

Hedge Fund Acquisitions

The following are hedge funds that have acquired companies much like a leveraged buyout (LBO) fund:

AdultVest

AdultVest Inc. announced the acquisition of iPorn.com. The acquisition expanded the firm's online marketplace, and helped provide capital to invest in the adult entertainment industry. AdultVest, is a company which launched the Bacchus Investment Fund and the Priapus Investment Fund to seek open-minded investors along with the billions of dollars spent on the adult entertainment industry in North America every year.[8] Sex sells, as they say.

Bay Harbour Management

Bay Harbour Management made an offer in August 2008 to take over the bankrupt retailer Steve & Barry's. In hopes to avoid liquidation, Steve & Barry's has filed a "stalking-horse" purchase agreement with Bay Harbour that will allow the hedge fund to acquire a majority of the chain's assets for $168 million.[9]

Citadel Investment Group

Ion Media Networks Inc., a communication company based in south Florida, was acquired in May 2007 by Citadel. The deal was valued at $173 million, and Citadel pledged to invest an additional $100 million toward the future development of Ion Media Networks.[10]

Davidson Kempner Capital Management LLC

Davidson Kempner Capital Management LLC gained control over the board of the Chicago Sun Times Media Group. At the time, DKCM planned to replace all but one of the directors after the previous administration burned through upward of $20 million a quarter and had the group on the verge of bankruptcy.[11]

D. E. Shaw

The D. E. Shaw Group agreed to acquire casualty insurer the James River Group. The price is 92% above the James River Group's $18 a share initial public offering (IPO).[12]

ELS

In March 2003, Eddie Lambert's ELS purchased the bankrupt giant K-mart. K-mart reemerged as a viable company and its stock soared. On November 17, 2004, it was announced that K-mart and fellow retailer Sears would merge under the umbrella of ESL and form the Sears Holding Company.[13] This was the largest merger between two retail companies.

Farallon Capital Management

Early in 2007, a consortium consisting of the Simon Property Group and the hedge fund Farallon Capital Management acquired the real estate investment trust Mills Corp.[14] Until this time, hedge funds were not well known for buying real estate investment trust companies.

Fortress Investment Group LLC

In May 2007, the Fortress Investment Group bought Florida East Coast Industries Inc. for $3.5 billion.[15] The company owns 351 miles of track between Jacksonville and Miami, along with thousands of acres of Florida real estate.

Man Group

In March 2008, the Man Group, based out of London, purchased a 50% stake in Ore Hill Partners LLC, an American provider of investment management services. Shortly afterward, Ore Hill partners bought a 50% stake in Pemba Credit, a company involved in managing European credit portfolios.[16]

Och-Ziff Capital Management

Och-Ziff expanded its global reach. In December 2006, Och-Ziff Capital Management acquired 25% of Nitesh Estates for $55 to $60 million, which was Och-Ziff's first investment in the emerging Indian market.

RAB Capital

In November 2004, RAB bought a 20% stake in the Tokyo-based Prestige Capital Management to access the Japanese asset management business.[17]

Soros Fund Management

In January 2009, Soros Fund Management joined a group of six hedge funds to purchase IndyMac Bank for $13.9 billion. With the acquisition, the group of hedge funds took over IndyMac's bank deposits and investments and its $160 billion loan servicing business from the Federal Deposit Insurance Corporation (FDIC).[18] Hedge funds until this time were not known for buying banks, which shows how hedge funds are nimble and can take advantage of a discrepancy in the market place; banks were undervalued at the time.

Triarc Partners

In December 2008, Triarc Partners announced that they would purchase more shares of fast-food operator Wendy's/Arby's Group which would increase their stake in the company.

Auger Capital

In January 2009, German insurer Wurttembergische und Badische Versicherung sold off its marine insurer and reinsurer subsidiary, Deutsche Versicherungs Ruck A.G., to Auger Capital.

SAC Capital Partners

SAC Capital Partners teamed up with the LBO firm Kohlberg Kravis Roberts & Co. on a $3.1 billion deal for the higher-learning outfit Laureate Education Inc. in late January 2007.[19]

Publicly Traded Hedge Funds

Hedge funds have grown very large and powerful. A few have even gone public, such as Och-Ziff. Both Europe and the United States have certain rules regarding IPOs. In Europe, "Stock exchanges are vying to attract public listings from alternative investment funds, including private-equity and hedge funds. Hitherto these were accessible mostly to very rich individuals and institutions. Now anyone can take a punt."[20] Figure 15.7 shows the market capitalization of alternative investment funds.

Listings in London have been primarily those of fund-management firms. The Man Group, for example, went public in 1994. Britain allows single strategy for "overseas, single-strategy funds on the London Stock Exchange (LSE). Until now, investors had been restricted to the LSE's junior Alternative Investment Market, because of rules on the main market against listing companies that sold short or did not have diversified investments."[21] The United States, however, does not allow individual funds to go public; only the initial public offerings of fund-management firms are permissible. Figure 15.8 shows the decline of Fortress after its IPO.

Fortress was considered a hot IPO at the time but investors lost faith probably because it was known as just a hedge fund (which is not the case), and its IPO shares plummeted. As *Bloomberg Markets* noted in spring 2009, "Shares of Fortress have lost most of their value, falling 95 percent to $1.56

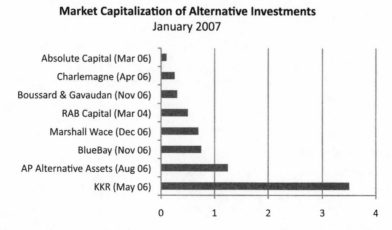

Market Capitalization of Alternative Investments
January 2007

Figure 15.7 Hedging Their Bets

Source: "Lifting the Lid," *The Economist* (January 27, 2007). Used with permission.

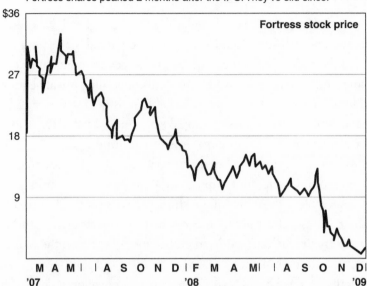

Figure 15.8 Downhill Racer

Source: Anthony Effinger, Downhill Racer (chart), *Bloomberg Markets* (March 2009). Used with permission.

as of Jan. 12 from $31 on Feb. 9, 2007, their first trading day. Fortress is more than just a hedge fund in that it is a very well-diversified company. It should be interesting to see whether investors will understand and appreciate the model. A number of companies that offer hedge funds are publicly traded (Table 15.1).

Table 15.1 World's Largest Public Hedge Fund Firms

Fund	Ticker	Assets Under Management, in Billions
J P Morgan Chase	JPM	$41
Och-Ziff Capital Mgmt. Group	OZM	31
Barclays Global Investors	BCS	27
Goldman Sachs	GS	27
GLG Partners	GLG	24
Fortress Investment Group	FIG	18

Source: Author.

Investors need to be careful about investing in publicly traded hedge funds as a way of getting access to the hedge fund market. Buying shares of a hedge fund IPO is not the same as investing in a hedge fund. When one examines what Fortress owns, one learns that Fortress manages a lot of different funds and companies, not just a single hedge fund, as detailed in Table 15.2.

Fortress owns various other equity funds, four or more different types of hedge funds, and a variety of real estate funds. Fortress is a good example to show how investing in a publicly traded hedge fund company is not the same as owning a single hedge fund. An investor should strive to understand both types of investments because each carries its own risks and rewards.

Some investors take solace in making investments through large companies or publicly traded companies. Bloomberg categorizes JPMorgan Chase as the world's largest hedge fund firm. JPMorgan acquired 55% of Highbridge Capital Management for more than $1.3 billion. The fund then grew rapidly to $36.4 billion by mid–2007. Highbridge, which was

Table 15.2   A Tangled Web

Fortress's Edens manages a diverse group of funds and companies.
Assets Under Management in Billions

Private Equity Funds
Intrawest (resorts)
RailAmerican (railroads)
Mapeley (U.K. property management)
GateHouse Media (newspapers)
Brookdale Senior Living (assisted living centers)

Liquid Hedge Funds
Drawbride Special Opportunity Funds
Fortress Partners Funds

Castles
Aircastles (aircraft leasing)
Newcastles Investment (U.S. real estate debt)
Eurocaslte Investment (European real estate)
Seacastle (shipping containers)

Source: Fortress Investment Group. Anthony Effinger, "High-Wire Act at Fortress," Bloomberg Markets (March 2009). Used with permission.

founded by Glenn Dubin and Henry Swieca in 2004, is a hedge fund firm that is involved in a plethora of different investment activities. Just like mutual fund families, in which there are a number of funds with different styles under one roof, the hedge fund industry is doing the same thing. For instance, Highbridge Capital Management offers the following funds:

- Highbridge Multi-Strategy
- Highbridge Statistical Opportunities
- Highbridge Fixed Income Opportunity
- Highbridge Event Driven/Relative Value
- Highbridge Long/Short Equity
- Highbridge Asia Opportunities
- Louis Dreyfus Highbridge Energy

Because hedge fund styles go in and out of favor over time, large hedge funds and/or hedge fund firms, like Highbridge, diversify to attract more assets. Performance will vary at any given point in time. Thus, Highbridge might have some funds doing well over a certain period; whereas others might not be doing so well, as illustrated in Figure 15.9.

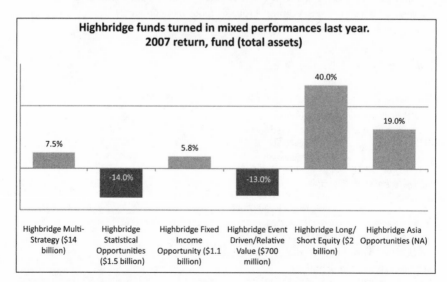

Figure 15.9   High and Low

Source: *Bloomberg Markets*, April 2008. Used with permission.

A few years from now, the numbers could very well be reversed. High-bridge Long/Short Equity, in other words, might not do as well as Event Driven/Relative Value. Interestingly enough, hedge fund styles change over time, not too dissimilar from mutual funds. For instance, small-cap, mid-cap, and large-cap funds have good years and bad years. Value and growth mutual funds tend to alternate over time as far as performance is concerned.

Highbridge is also involved in a bond fund, a European mutual fund, com-modities, real estate, and private equity. In fact, according to the *Bloomberg Markets* article "High-Wire Act at Highbridge," the firm's "range of investments is the most diverse. Everybody in the industry is talking about convergence between hedge funds and long-only mutual funds and private equity. . . Highbridge and JPMorgan are the only ones who've done it to this extent." Highbridge has had several successes. Its most popular fund, Highbridge Sta-tistical Opportunities, uses "computers to identify mispriced securities and other instruments and automatically pile in to the cheap ones and short the pricey ones. . . . The Highbridge Multistrategy fund returned +14.7 percent annualized through December since its September 1992 start. That compares with +10.7 percent for the Standard & Poor's 500 Index."[22] Nevertheless, other large funds have not matched its performance.

Most investment firms and a handful of large banks can provide due diligence. Odds are they would have uncovered wrongdoing when exam-ining Madoff; many of the banks are also prime brokers, which gives them additional information or knowledge about hedge funds.

Noteworthy Hedge Funds

What follows are profiles of hedge funds that are known for positive per-formance, including brief histories, discussions of their methodologies, and measurements of their success.

Ken Griffin—Citadel Investment Group LLC

Ken Griffin started Citadel Investment Group in 1990 based out of Chicago. One of the largest and successful hedge funds of all time, Citadel deploys serious capital across a wide spectrum of asset classes, from natural gas to stock, bonds, and currencies. According to *Bloomberg Markets*, "Citadel has recorded a 26 percent annualized rate of return; 1994 was the sole money-losing year for its flagship Citadel Wellington LLC fund. A $100,000 investment at the firm's inception is now valued at about $2.6 million, making Citadel one of the world's best-performing hedge funds."[23] With billions in reported assets under management, Citadel accounts for substantial daily trading volume on the various international exchanges. Citadel was the first hedge fund to issue bonds in 2006.[24]

John Horseman—Horseman Capital Management LP

Horseman Capital Management was cofounded by John Horseman, Christopher Harrison, and Mark Driver in 2001 based in London. The Horseman Global Fund, a long/short equity hedge fund, earned impressive returns of +32% in 2008 and has earned on average more than +15% per year since it was started.[25]

Chris Levett—Clive Capital LLP

Chris Levett gained recognition when his $1.3 billion hedge fund excelled in the first quarter of 2008. Clive Capital, a commodities fund, gained +17.6% with the rise of energy and metals. By December 2008, his fund was worth $3 billion and had returned +44% that year. Levett decided to cap Clive Capital at $3.5 billion.[26]

Eric Mindich—Eton Park Capital Management

Eton Park Capital Management was founded by Eric Mindich, former Goldman Sachs partner, in 2004. His fund is known as having one of the biggest launches ever with approximately $3 billion. In raising initial capital, Mindich had strict criterion. According to the *Wall Street Journal*, "Investors would have to allocate at least $5 million to the fund, pay stiff management fees and be subject to huge penalties if they withdrew their funds before 4 and a half years."[27]

John Paulson—Paulson & Co.

Four of the 20 most profitable hedge funds of the first 9 months of 2008 were Paulson's funds. This success is widely the result of Paulson's foresight, which led the fund to bet against rising real estate. Foreseeing the housing market collapse ultimately generated $3 billion in profits for the firm in 2007. "In mid-November 2007, Paulson said] that more than 50 percent of the assets he managed were in cash and that the money he had invested was equally weighted between short and long positions."[28] By September 2008, Paulson Co. earned $1.05 billion, an outstanding performance compared with all other hedge funds. Paulson's Advantage Plus had an annual return of +24.6% by September 30, 2008.

Craig Effron—Scoggin Capital Management

Craig Effron is the chief executive officer and founding partner of Scoggin Capital Management, a hedge fund that was established in 1988. Scoggin primarily invests in event-driven situations such as bankruptcies, mergers and spin-offs. Craig Effron's "$3.25 billion hedge fund, Scoggin Capital Management LP, buys and sells the stocks and bonds primarily of companies that are merging, spinning off units or going through difficulttimes. From November 1988, when he started the fund, to Aug. 1 [2007], he produced an average annual return of +18.2% after fees."[29]

Jim Simons—Renaissance Technologies

Renaissance Technologies, which manages $30 billion, "only hires scientists to develop its trading strategies, all of which are executed entirely by computers."[30] Renaissance Technologies' Medallion Fund had the highest return for a hedge fund in 2008, a return of +58% in a year, which proved the downfall of a large number of firms.[31]

Jeffrey Vinik—Vinik Asset Management

A hedge fund started by Jeffrey Vinik, former manager of Fidelity's Magellan Fund, has provided sizable returns since its inception in 1996, where "Vinik Asset Management says it chalked up a return of +645% before fees and +440% after fees—compared with the +106% after fees gains for the average hedge fund for the same period."[32] Vinik's investment strategy was relatively straightforward. He used GARP (Growth At A Reasonable Price). After an impressive performance over a span of a few years, however, Vinik opted to liquidate his $4.2 billion dollar fund in order to spend more time with his family. According to *Investor's Business Daily*,

Vinik added, "We will be managing a small portfolio consisting of family assets. We will be able to take more time off. With outside investors, you're obligated to invest to the best of your abilities and all the time. Now we can devote time and energy to our families."[33]

Brevan Howard Asset Management LLP

Brevan Howard Asset Management LLP is an investment manager authorized and regulated by the Financial Services Authority in the United Kingdom. One of Europe's largest hedge funds, this global macro hedge fund was founded in 2002 by former members of the Credit Suisse First Boston Developed Market Rates trading team. One of the founders, Alan Howard, was previously the former head of interest rate derivative trading at CSFB. The fund had assets of $20.8 billion as of December 31, 2009.

Jamie Dinan—York Capital Management LP

Founder and CEO Jamie Dinan founded York Capital in 1991. As with many hedge funds, the goal of the fund was to "provide consistent, superior risk-adjusted investment returns relatively independent of the overall market."[34] Dinan is known for identifying overlooked value in companies. Since its inception, York's flagship fund has produced an annualized return of +17.2% through October 2006.[35]

Problematic Hedge Funds

The hedge funds detailed below have been unsuccessful for their investors and in many cases plagued by scandal.

Long-Term Capital Management and JWM Partners LLC

LTCM was a model-based hedge fund founded in 1994 by John Meriwether. LTCM performed well in its early stages, using high-risk trading strategies such as leverage, pairs trading, and various types of arbitrage. Among LTCM's board of directors were Nobel laureates Myron Scholes and Robert Merton.

Initially, the fund had good performance and attracted many new investors. However, when the Russian government defaulted on $40 billion of debt in August 1998, the LTCM model failed. LTCM's equity dropped from $2.3 billion to $600 million in the first three weeks of September 1998, and when LTCM incurred more leverage in an attempt to stay afloat, they continued to encounter losses across totaling losses of $4.6 billion.[36] The Federal Reserve Bank of New York summoned a consortium of Wall Street firms to rescue LTCM. Oddly, Meriwether launched a new fund, JWM Partners, which employed similar strategies but with less leverage.

Apparently, 10 years after the LTCM debacle, John Meriwether found himself encountering a similar situation with his new hedge fund, JWM Partners. Meriwether has lost more than one fourth of his investors' money—more than $300 million—and Meriwether attempted to persuade clients not to withdraw their funds and deplete JWM's capital base.[37] If someone loses all of your money, they might do it again and again. Sometimes it is better to run, not walk, away.

Creative Partners Fund LP

Martin Frankel started Creative Partners Fund LP after forming an investor base through other investment firms Winthrop Capital and the Frankel Fund. Despite being banned from securities trading for life by the U.S. Securities and Exchange Commission, Frankel developed a ponzi scheme in which he purchased problematic insurance companies and used their money reserves. Eventually his activities caught the eye of the Mississippi Insurance Commissioner in 1999, and Frankel was indicted for fraud worth $208 million later that year.

Before that, however, Frankel gained notoriety when he "vanished from his home in early May, shortly before police found it abandoned and with documents smoldering in a fireplace. On May 4, he flew to Rome on a chartered jet from White Plains, N.Y., apparently accompanied by two of the numerous young women who coddled him. He apparently received a $454,000 wire transfer in Rome and a cache of diamonds before he left."[38]

Once he was caught, Frankel was extradited from Germany back to the United States. He pleaded guilty to 24 of 36 federal charges, among them insurance fraud, racketeering, and money laundering and is currently serving a 16-year sentence. The moral of the story is: where there is smoke, there is usually fire.

Bayou Hedge Fund Group

Bayou, the $450 million hedge fund in Connecticut that filed under Chapter 11 in May 2006 after hiding losses for years with phony profits, was founded in 1996 by Samuel Israel III.[39] Israel's lack of talent as a manager was reflected immediately as the small Bayou fund struggled: "Even as the U.S. stock market ignited, sending the S&P 500 soaring 20 percent in 1996 and then 31 percent in 1997, Bayou lost money."[40] While fraudulently reporting good returns to investors, Israel made money for himself through commissions by churning and executing vast amounts of trades with his affiliated Bayou Securities firm. In an effort to keep hiding losses, Israel set up a fake accounting firm named Richmond-Fairfield Associates. Bayou hemorrhaged. False suicide notes followed shortly after, but Israel turned up after a widespread manhunt and is now serving time. A prudent investor will examine closely the firm auditing the statements. It might also seem obvious, but many investors fail to learn something about to whom they are entrusting their money; always learn about the manager.

International Management Associates LLC

Kirk Wright, who founded the Marietta, Georgia–based IMA, faced 24 federal charges of mail and securities fraud after more than $150 million went missing from his fund while he was telling clients that "he could bring them annual returns in the region of 27 percent by short selling stocks."[41] Wright stole from professional football players, doctors, and retirees. When all was said and done, he claimed almost $185 million in assets, but investigators could locate less than $150,000. He was sent to prison and later committed suicide in his cell. Word of mouth with no due diligence is a silly way to invest and often leads to devastating results.

Amaranth Advisors LLC

Amaranth was initially a multistrategy hedge fund started by Nicholas Maounis in Greenwich, Connecticut. As trading opportunities coinciding with Amaranth's original strategy became difficult to find, it shifted much of its capital base to energy trading in 2004–2005. Brian Hunter, who had made millions bullishly betting on natural gas spreads, proved his worth when his "natural gas bets made $1 billion in the wake of Hurricanes Katrina and Rita."[42] Unfortunately, an abrupt market reversal in 2006 exposed Amaranth's lack of diversification and amounted to colossal losses—$6 billion of its $9 billion in assets.[43] A number of large banks put client money into Amaranth and lost it. Previously, Amaranth had a good reputation and few would expect a fund to allow a trader to take such aggressive bets with so much of the fund's assets. Big bets can lead to big losses for investors. Hedge funds can be wreckless and irresponsible with client money as can any other money manager. Further, the demise of Amaranth shows that investors and advisors must monitor on an ongoing basis any hedge fund and not rely solely on others.

Sowood Capital Management LP

Sowood Capital Management was a Boston-based firm that was founded by Jeff Larson in 2004. Larson hoped his track record at Harvard's endowment would bode well for his new fund. This was not the case, and Sowood "lost $1.6 billion, or about 60 percent of its value."[44] As a result of Sowood's problems, Chicago-based Citadel Investment Group bought a number of Sowood's positions, similar to what they had done with Amaranth Advisors LLC earlier in the year. Hedge fund cannibalism is not uncommon.

Vikram Pandit Citigroup Inc.

Surprisingly, Mr. Pandit's failed attempt to run a hedge fund for Citigroup, Inc., was followed by him being chosen as Citigroup's CEO. Pandit's management company, Old Lane Partners, was bought by Citigroup for more than $800 million only to be shut down and sold off after less than a year of management turnover and unsatisfactory fund returns.[45] Pandit's ability to run Citigroup was equally if not more calamitous than his time at Old Lane Partners. As early as May 2008, concerns were expressed about Pandit's ability to lead Citigroup. The *Wall Street Journal* article "Citigroup's Pandit Faces Test as Pressure on Bank Grows" states, "Citigroup's financial condition has continued worsening under his watch. Since he took over in December, the New York Company has posted total losses of nearly $15 billion for the past two quarters."[46]

Despite a massive life support system by the U.S. Government, Citigroup recorded a new low when it was forced to sell profitable divisions. The bank lost almost all its value, with shares at one time falling as low as $0.97, dropping the then-market value down from $277 billion in 2006 to $6 billion two years later—despite $45 billion in stimulus funds.[47] Former federal officials dubbed Citigroup the "Death Star," comparing the bank's threat to the financial system with the planet-destroying superweapon in the *Star Wars* movies and others regard the banking giant as "unmanageable."[48]

Bernard L. Madoff Investment Securities

Bernard Madoff founded BMIS in 1960 primarily as a market maker—a middleman between share buyers and sellers. However, he expanded and grew the business into other areas. By implementing a strategy in which he "trade[d] in and out of large-cap stocks and b[ought] options on those shares to help smooth the ups and downs," he promised investors consistent and substantial returns.[49]

Unless it is a CD or bond, few investments (let alone a hedge fund) have steady returns. These steady returns, despite tumultuous markets, raised red flags and eventually led to his arrest on December 11, 2008. According to an SEC press release, "The Madoff firm had more than $17 billion in assets under management as of the beginning of 2008. It appears that virtually all assets of the advisory business are missing."[50] The largest fraud in history is wide ranging and will affect both private and institutional investors. Many investors were enamored and felt safe by the famous investors Madoff attracted but one should never trust hype. Bernard Madoff was sentenced to 150 years in federal prison, giving little solace to the investors who were wiped out and lives that he destroyed. One should always perform their own due diligence or hire a competent advisor to help them. Herd mentality is a bad way to invest.

Wood River Capital Management

In 2005, the SEC filed a suit against Wood River Capital Management and its manager, John H. Whittier, for not disclosing that "as much as 98 percent of one of his funds [was] invested in a speculative stock with no recent history of profitability. There is nothing more risky than a single stock position. Unhedged, single stock positions are extremely risky and should never dominate a portfolio of investments. Investors in Wood River lost approximately $88 million. Whittier was indicted on a fraud charge. As stated previously, prudent investors will pay close attention to the firm responsible for auditing a fund.

Pequot Capital, Management Inc.

Even large, reputable hedge funds can encounter problems. In 2001, Pequot Capital Management Inc. managed $15 billion, making it one of the largest hedge funds in the world. However, investors shunned it, because of an investigation into insider trading. While denying any wrongdoing, the CEO, Arthur Samberg, shut down Pequot in May 2009 despite one of the best track records in the hedge fund industry.

Atticus

In a letter to investors, Atticus founder Tim Barakett stated that he would give back $3 billion to investors and close two large funds he managed. Early in 2008, Atticus had around $20 billion under management. However, Barakett invested in a handful of stocks such as the Deutsche Borse AG that ran into problems as the financial markets plummeted. Besides the market downturn, leverage hurt the funds that Barakett managed. Leverage (especially excessive leverage) can kill a hedge fund.

Chapter 16

Hedge Fund Advantages and Disadvantages

In the previous chapters, we detailed the history of hedge funds and looked at some of the elements that have made them both successful and problematic. As we have done throughout this book, we will now explore some of the advantages and disadvantages of hedge fund investments, further preparing you to make your own prudent decisions.

Advantages of Single Hedge Funds

As with any asset class, hedge funds have their advantages and disadvantages. Here are nine advantages to a single hedge fund investment.

Talent

Generally, there are three types of active money management (as opposed to indexes or passive investing): mutual funds, money managers, and hedge funds. Hedge funds tend to be run by the crème de la crème of money managers; they are the best money can buy. The reason the best and the brightest flock toward managing hedge funds as opposed to mutual funds and/or money managers (separately managed accounts) is simple and can be described using one word: money. The financial rewards are huge for talented hedge fund managers.

Table 16.1   Wall Street's Highest Earners

James Simons	Renaissance Technologies	$2,800,000,000.00
John Paulson	Paulson & Co.	$1,900,000,000.00
John Arnold	Centaurus Energy	$1,000,000,000.00
George Soros	Soros Fund Management	$ 800,000,000.00
Ray Dalio	Bridgewater Associates	$ 470,000,000.00
Henry Laufer	Renaissance Technologies	$ 390,000,000.00
Bruce Kovier	Caxton Associates	$ 370,000,000.00
Alan Howard	Brevan Howard Asset Mgmt.	$ 330,000,000.00
James Chanos	Kynikos Associates	$ 300,000,000.00
David Harding	Winton Capital	$ 290,000,000.00

Source: "The 400 Richest People in America," *Forbes* (October 6, 2008). Used with permission.

On October 6, 2008, *Forbes* listed "The 400 Richest People in America." The list included a total of 90 "market masters."[1] Therein, it was revealed that 25 of the "Market Masters" had earned their fortunes solely from running hedge funds. If you are skilled, you will want higher compensation, which is evidenced by the "2 and 20" compensation offered by many hedge funds. Hedge funds typically charge a 2% managed fee and collect 20% of the upside. Table 16.1 highlights a few of the highest earners.

There are many examples of managers who left high-profile positions to run hedge funds. The former manager of Magellan, Jeffrey Vinik, left Fidelity to start Vinik Asset Management. Besides Vinik, the former head of Harvard's management company, Jack R. Meyer, left to start Convexity Capital Management LP in Boston. But not every hedge fund manager has the pedigree of either Vinik or Meyer. For instance, Bloomberg recently identified a number of the world's best-performing hedge funds (listed in Table 16.2).

Investment Flexibility

Hedge fund managers can deploy a variety of tools, unlike most mutual fund and money managers. Hedge fund managers can utilize short selling, derivatives, options, swaps, leverage, managed futures, and various

Table 16.2 World's Best-Performing Hedge Funds

	Fund	Firm	Strategy	
1	Medallion	Renaissance Technologies	Quantitative	58.0%
2	Paulson Advantage Plus	Paulson & Co.	Event Driven	24.6
3	Clive	Clive Capital	Commodities	19.4
4	Comac Global Macro	Comac International	Macro	19.2
5	Clarium	Calrium Capital Management	Macro	18.9
6	Paulson Credit Opportunities	Paulson & Co.	Credit	18.6
7	Horseman European Select	Horseman Capital Mgmt.	Long/Short	18.0
8	Horseman Global	Horseman Capital Mgmt.	Long/Short	17.4
9	Paulson Credit Opportunities II	Paulson & Co.	Credit	15.8
10	BlueTrend	BlueCrest Capital Mgmt.	Managed Futures	15.7
11	Paulson Advantage	Paulson & Co.	Event Driven	15.0
12	Brevan Howard	Brevan Howard Asset Mgmt.	Macro	14.1
13	Brevan Howard Asia	Brevan Howard Asset Mgmt.	Macro	13.8
14	Altis Global Futures Portfolio	Atlis Partners	Managed Futures	11.9
15	Artradis Barracuda	Artradis Fund Mgmt.	Multistrategy	11.9
16	Graham Global-K4 Portfolio	Graham Capital Mgmt.	Macro	11.8
17	Quantitative Global Program	Quantitative Investment Mgmt.	Managed Futures	11.5
18	Winton Futures	Winton Capital Mgmt.	Managed Futures	8.8
19	Capula Global Relative Value	Capula Investment	Fixed-Income Arbitrage	7.8
20	Man AHL Diversified	Man Fund Mgmt.	Managed Futures	7.7

Source: Bloomberg, World's Best-Performing Hedge Funds (chart), *Bloomberg Markets* (January 2009), 35. Used with permission.

hedging technologies. Further, they can invest in illiquid securities such as art, venture capital, or real estate. The sky is the limit for hedge fund investors. The benefit of being nimble is that hedge funds can adjust quickly to rapidly changing environments. For instance, if interest rates look like they will be increased a series of times, the outlook for bonds will be grim. An astute hedge fund manager might short bonds. If news indicates that the equity market will be negative, the hedge fund manager might short an index like the Dow Jones, S&P 500, or NASDAQ. Perhaps negative news surfaces, similar to the dot.com crash. Instead of watching one's equity mutual fund get annihilated (which occurred in 2000, 2001, 2002), a hedge fund manager might just short a technology index just to safeguard a portfolio.

Few Restrictions

Hedge funds do not have to follow the rules imposed on mutual funds and money managers. Hedge funds can invest as much or as little in any sector or individual security they desire. There are no geographic boundaries nor constraints on style that hedge funds can pick. For example, Van Kampen Comstock A is a large value manager. The focus of this Van Kampen fund is to invest solely in large capital value equities. A hedge fund, however, can invest in many different styles such as large-cap, mid-cap, or small-cap equities. Hedge funds can select either growth, value, or a combination of both types of equity. They can also combine these selections with domestic or foreign equities. Similarly, hedge funds can invest in different types of fixed income (e.g., high yield, corporate, U.S. Treasury, domestic, or foreign). In short, hedge funds are extremely flexible and can invest in any of these securities as well as any combination with different amounts or weightings. They can change the investment mix any time they want. Hedge funds are nimble and can make quick changes. If large-cap value equities go out of favor, Van Kampen Comstock might increase its cash position as a defensive move. A mutual fund, such as Van Kampen Comstock, is composed of individual equities. As of December 31, 2008, Van Kampen Comstock had $5.83 billion in 79 holdings. Its asset allocation was as follows: 2.34% cash, 93.17% U.S. stocks, 4.49% non-U.S. stocks, 0% bonds, and 0% other. On July 31, 2001, Van Kampen Comstock had $3.4 billion in 102 holdings. At that time, its asset allocation was 5.80% cash, 87.30% U.S. stocks, 7% non-U.S. stocks, with no investments in bonds or other securities. Table 16.3 compares Van Kampen Comstock's holdings over time.

In short, there was little change except an increase in equities and fewer holdings. Selling huge amounts of stocks for any large mutual fund would take time and might adversely affect the trading of individual company stocks it buys or sells. American Growth Fund is $52.3 billion. Similar to Van Kampen, American Growth Fund is investing primarily in equities. On July 31, 2001, American Growth Fund had 75.70% invested in U.S. stocks and 69.52% in U.S. stocks on December 31, 2008. That is, factors such as trading volume, market conditions, or support of the stock will affect large buys or sells. A hedge fund, on the other hand, might short a

Table 16.3   Van Kampen Comstock A

Release Date	7/31/2001	12/31/2008
Rating	* * * * *	* *
Net assets	$3,389.1 M	$5,828.2 M
Equity style	Large value	Large value
Comp. % of Assets, as of	3/31/2001	9/30/2008
Cash	5.80%	2.34%
U.S. stocks	87.30%	93.17%
Non-U.S. stocks	7.00%	4.49%
Bonds	0.00%	0.00%
Other	0.00%	0.00%
Regional exp % as of	3/31/2001	9/30/2008
Americas	89.80%	95.30%
Greater Europe	4.80%	4.50%
Greater Asia	0.20%	0.20%
Total Number of holdings	102	79

Source: Morningstar. Used with permission.

large-cap value index such as the Russell 1000 value index. Likewise, American Growth Fund does not short or utilize leverage. There are no private, illiquid securities in its portfolio.

Low Correlation with Traditional Equities and Bonds

Individuals and institutions can further diversify with hedge funds. Historically, only large institutions accessed the hedge fund world. CalPERS invests in private equity and hedge fund investment structures with the objective of diversifying its investment portfolio, managing risk, and adding value to the total fund.[2] Presently, individuals can access many of the same managers. A key benefit of further diversifying with hedge funds is their low correlation with other asset classes. "One of the most compelling reasons for investing in hedge funds is that their returns seem relatively uncorrelated with market indexes such as the S&P 500, and modern portfolio theory has convinced even the most hardened skeptic of the benefits of diversification."[3] Table 16.4 features a 10-year correlation of quarterly returns from September 30, 1999 through September 30, 2009.

Table 16.4 Correlation: 10-Year Quarterly Returns (9/30/99–9/30/09)

	Large Cap	Small Cap	Value	Growth	EAFE	Bonds	EME	Hedge Funds	Real Estate	Eq Market Neutral*	Commodities
Large Cap	1.00	0.94	0.92	0.94	0.92	−0.37	0.87	0.73	0.23	0.36	0.33
Small Cap		1.00	0.90	0.87	0.86	−0.39	0.83	0.67	0.20	0.35	0.25
Value			1.00	0.74	0.88	−0.22	0.76	0.63	0.29	0.42	0.35
Growth				1.00	0.83	−0.44	0.86	0.74	0.14	0.26	0.29
EAFE					1.00	−0.27	0.90	0.77	0.20	0.45	0.44
Bonds						1.00	−0.30	−0.20	−0.17	0.14	−0.12
EME							1.00	0.77	0.13	0.32	0.43
Hedge Funds								1.00	0.28	0.48	0.50
Real Estate									1.00	0.32	0.32
Eq Market Neutral										1.00	0.49
Commodities											1.00

Source: Standard & Poor's, Russell, Barclays Capital Inc., MSCI Inc., Credit Suisse/Tremont, NCREIF, DJ UBS, JPMorgan Asset Management

Indexes used – Large Cap: S&P 500 Index; Small Cap: Russell 2000; Value: Russell 1000 Value; Growth: Russell 1000 Growth; EAFE: MSCI EAFE; Bonds: Barclays Capital Aggregate; EME: MSCI Emerging Markets; Hedge Funds: SC/Tremont Multi-Strategy Index World; Real Estate: NCREIF National Property Index; Equity Market Neutral: CS/Tremont Equity Market Neutral Index; DJ UBS Commodity Index.

*Market Neutral returns include estimates found in disclosures.

All correlation coefficients calculated based on quarterly total return data for period 9/30/99 to 9/30/09.

The above data was originally presented in JPMorgan's Guide to the Markets, 1Q 2010, as of December 31, 2009.

Hedge funds have a low correlation with a number of assets. However, in the past few years the correlation rose between hedge funds and equities, especially the Russell 2000 Growth, MSCI Europe, and the MSCI Emerging Markets Index. Hedge funds still have a low correlation with the following: U.S. Treasury 10-Year Note, Barclays Aggregate Bond, Barclays 7-Year Municipal, Barclays 1–3 Year Aggregate, JPM Global ex-U.S. Bond Index, Handy & Harman Spot Gold Price Index, and the Barclay CTA Index.

When adding hedge funds to a portfolio, it is important to note how the assets correlate with one another. If the assets are too similar, there will not be proper diversification. Correlations can also change over time; they are not set in stone. As more hedge funds came into existence and invested in large-cap equities, their correlation increased with equities. Over time, commodities, real estate investment trusts, and global bonds typically have a lower correlation with hedge funds. Hypothetically, if an investor owned only hedge funds, he or she might benefit from adding other asset classes as opposed to adding only international stock, which would merely increase risk and lower returns. Investors need to be careful how they build a portfolio and the types of assets they select.

Absolute Return

Hedge funds seek positive returns regardless of market conditions. When *Bloomberg Markets* wrote about "The Richest Hedge Funds," they observed this resiliency, reporting that "[f]rom 1990 through 2007, the HFR Fund Weighted Composite Index registered just a single down year, 2002, when the industry lost 1.45 percent. And in that year the S&P lost 22.1 percent."[4] The article goes on to cite a +14.2% annual return for hedge funds from 1990 to 2007. Although not every year is positive (as exemplified in 2008), hedge funds have typically outperformed mutual funds in poor equity markets, highlighted in Table 16.5.

Just like with mutual funds, hedge funds can have good managers as well as bad. *Pensions & Investments* ranked the performance of single-strategy hedge funds as well as hedge fund-of-funds through October 31, 2008 (Table 16.6).

Table 16.5 Hedge Funds versus the S&P 500 and Mutual Funds in Falling Equity Markets

	S&P 500	VAN U.S. Hedge Fund Index	Morningstar Average Equity Mutual Index
1Q90	−3.00%	2.20%	−2.80%
3Q90	−13.70%	−3.70%	−15.40%
2Q91	−0.20%	2.30%	−0.90%
1Q92	−2.50%	5.00%	−0.70%
1Q94	−3.80%	−0.80%	−3.20%
4Q94	−0.02%	−1.20%	−2.60%
3Q98	−9.90%	−6.10%	−15.00%
3Q99	−6.20%	2.10%	−3.20%
2Q00	−2.70%	0.30%	−3.60%
3Q00	−1.00%	3.00%	0.60%
4Q00	−7.80%	−2.40%	−7.80%
1Q01	−11.90%	−1.10%	−12.70%
3Q01	−14.70%	−3.80%	−17.20%
2Q02	−13.40%	−1.40%	−10.70%
3Q02	−17.30%	−3.60%	−16.60%
1Q05	−2.59%	0.10%	−2.20%
Total	−113.01%	−10.30%	−115.70%

Source: Hedge Fund Association, Hedge Funds Outperform Mutual Funds in Falling Equity Markets (chart), http://thehfa.org/advantages.cfm. Used with permission.

One can clearly see the wide range of performance. For example, the Mulvaney Global Markets Fund produced a +85.47% return, whereas RAB Northwest Warrant Fund had a –8.10% return. Hedge fund-of-funds also had a wide range of returns, although not as extreme as the single-strategy hedge fund. One might also note that certain strategies become more favorable, such as in this example, in which HF Global Trend was the strategy that did the best, whereas most of the worst performers happened to be HF Emerging Market Equity. These strategies shift where they are favorable over certain periods and then unfavorable. Like other alternatives, hedge funds move in waves (Table 16.7).

Table 16.6 Hedge Fund Winners and Losers (Single Strategy and Hedge Fund-of-Funds)

Top performing hedge funds, by type, ranked by year-to-date performance through Oct. 31.

Single strategy top 10	Manager	Return	Morningstar category
Mulvaney Global Markets Fund Ltd.	Mulvaney Capital Mgmt, Ltd.	85.47%	HF Global Trend
JWH Global Analytics	John W. Henry & Co. Inc.	72.46%	HF Global Trend
Dighton Aggressive SP (SFT2X)	Dighton Services SA	63.30%	HF Global Trend
Arcas Fund II LP (Arcas Interests)	Derivative Consulting Group LLC	58.26%	HF Global Trend
Drury Diversified TF Program	Drury Capital Inc.	56.88%	HF Global Trend
Roy G. Niederhoffer Neg. Correlation	Roy G. Niederhoffer Capital Mgmt.	56.62%	HF Global Non-Trend
Rising China Fund	Pinpoint Investment Advisor Ltd.	55.98%	HF Global Trend
Superfund C EUR SICAV	Superfund Capital Mgmt.	54.32%	HF Global Trend
Vegasoul Fund – Class A	Vegasoul Capital Mgmt.	51.27%	HF Global Trend
Tulip Trend Fund Ltd. Class A EUR	Progressive Capital Partners Ltd.	47.82%	HF Global Trend

Single strategy bottom 10	Manager	Return	Morningstar category
RAB Northwest Warrant Fund Ltd. EUR	RAB Capital PLC	−88.10%	HF Emerging Market Equity
New Russian Generation Ltd.	Prosperity Capital Mgmt. Ltd.	−83.83%	HF Emerging Market Equity
Troika Russia Fund-US	TDAM (Cyprus) Ltd.	−83.13%	HF Emerging Market Equity
Vitava Sicav	Vitava Fund Sicav PLC	−78.30%	HF U.S. Equity
Hedgeforeningen Sydinvest afd. VirklÂn Acc.	Hedgeforeningen Sydinvest	−75.00%	HF Global Debt
PVB (CH) Russian Prosperity USD Inc.	PvB Pernet von Ballmoos AG	−73.18%	HF Emerging Market Equity
Renaissance Russia Small Cap Fund	Renaissance Capital Invest. Mgmt.	−72.32%	HF Emerging Market Equity
LIM China Index Ltd. H	LIM Advisors Ltd.	−71.90%	HF Emerging Market Equity
Russian Prosperity Fund (EUR)	Prosperity Capital Mgmt. Ltd.	−68.09%	HF Emerging Market Equity
LG Asian Natural Res. Fund Acc.	Lloyd George Mgmt.	−68.06%	HF Developed Asia Equity

(Continued)

Table 16.6 *(Continued)*

Fund-of-funds top 10	Manager	Return	Morningstar category
Roy G. Niederhoffer Div. Offshore Ltd. A	Roy G. Niederhoffer Capital Mgmt.	54.94%	HF Fund of Funds – Non-directional
TrendSquare Ltd. A	UBP Asset Mgmt. Bermuda Ltd.	16.45%	HF Fund of Funds – Multistrategy
HI Volksbank Global Trend	HANSAINVEST, Hanseatische Inv. GmbH	15.92%	HF Fund of Funds – Derivatives
Tremont Trading – Ireland A1	Tremont Capital Mgmt.	15.27%	HF Fund of Funds – Derivatives
Centennial Global Macro Fund Ltd.	Centennial Partners LLC	14.35%	HF Fund of Funds – Derivatives
HI Varengold B Acc.	HANSAINVEST, Hanseatische Inv. GmbH	14.15%	HF Fund of Funds – Derivatives
Lighthouse Managed Futures Composite SPC	Lighthouse Partners LLC	12.30%	HF Fund of Funds – Derivatives
GMO Multi Strategy	GMO LLC	11.85%	HF Fund of Funds – Debt
Pinnacle Natural Resources LP	Pinnacle Asset Mgmt. LP	11.10%	HF Fund of Funds – Non-directional
Tremont Trading Fund LLC	Tremont Capital Mgmt.	10.71%	HF Fund of Funds – Derivatives

Fund-of-funds bottom 10	Manager	Return	Morningstar category
FMG Russia A Eur Acc.	FMG Fund Managers Ltd.	−74.58%	HF Fund of Funds – Equity
OPM Alfa Offensiv Plus Inc.	Optimized Port Mgmt. Stockholm AB	−52.16%	HF Fund of Funds – Multistrategy
StoneWater Cap. Asia (Ex-Japan) LLC	StoneWater Capital LLC	−50.40%	HF Fund of Funds – Equity
3A Windrider EUR	Alternative Asset Advisors SA	−50.38%	HF Fund of Funds – Multistrategy
RAB Diversifed Commodities Fd. Ltd. A	Rab Capital PLC	−50.12%	HF Fund of Funds – Derivatives
Gottex Market Neutral Fund Class AA	Gottex Fund Mgmt.	−47.81%	HF Fund of Funds – Multistrategy
Generali Hedg Fds. Event Driven B EUR Acc.	BSI SA	−47.70%	HF Fund of Funds – Event
Generali Hedge Fds. Multi Arbit G EUR Acc.	BSI SA	−46.75%	HF Fund of Funds – Non-directional
Grandway Multi-Strategy Fund Ltd. Class A	Grandway Asset Mgmt. Inc.	−45.68%	HF Fund of Funds – Multistrategy
Select Gottex Enh. Mkt. Neut. AUD	Select Asset Mgmt. Ltd.	−44.53%	HF Fund of Funds – Multistrategy

Source: "Hedge Funds Winners and Losers," *Pensions and Investments* (December 22, 2008). Used with permission.

Table 16.7 Alternative Investment Returns

Hedge Funds (as of 9/30/09)	1 Year	3 Year	5 Year	10 Year
CSFB/Tremont HF Index	3.2%	3.5%	6.3%	7.9%
Multi-Strategy	−5.0%	1.5%	4.9%	7.0%
Distressed	−8.0%	0.6%	5.9%	8.6%
Convertible Arbitrage	1.0%	0.6%	2.0%	6.9%
Equity Market Neutral*	4.6%	5.9%	6.8%	8.1%
Risk Arbitrage	3.1%	5.8%	5.9%	6.0%
Fixed Income Arbitrage	−11.0%	−3.4%	−0.4%	3.3%
Global Macro	−3.5%	7.3%	8.9%	12.5%

Source: Cambridge Associates LLC, NCREIF, CS/Tremont, JPMorgan Asset Management.

Returns for all periods are as of 9/30/09 with the exception of Private Equity returns, which are as of 6/30/09.

All returns are annualized for periods greater than 1 year.

*Market Neutral returns include estimates found in disclosures.

The above data was originally presented in JPMorgan's *Guide to the Markets,* 1Q|2010, as of December 31, 2009.

Diversification

As previously described in Chapter 14, hedge funds offer six different strategies (equity hedge, event driven, macro, relative value, opportunistic, and combination) with at least 38 different objectives. Hypothetically, one might diversify a stock and bond portfolio with individual hedge funds that specialize in volatility, merger arbitrage, managed futures, or quantitative directional styles. One could also add a hedge fund-of-funds along with a few individual hedge funds, which I call a core-satellite approach. The core or center is a hedge fund-of-funds that is surrounded by smaller investments in individual or single hedge funds. Hedge funds offer thousands of different choices. As of October 2008 (after an epic decline in the market), there were 9,762 hedge funds and plenty of hedge fund-of-funds to select (illustrated in Figure 16.1).

Risk Reduction

If used properly, hedge funds can lower the risk level in a portfolio. Hedge funds themselves are a lot like waves in that they can be easygoing or they can hurt you. As Cicero explained in *The Republic*, "But that maniac, as those fellows call him, without being compelled by any necessity, chose to be buffeted by these stormy waves right into extreme old age, instead of enjoying the delightfully tranquil and easy life they extol."[5] Table 16.8 presents rolling

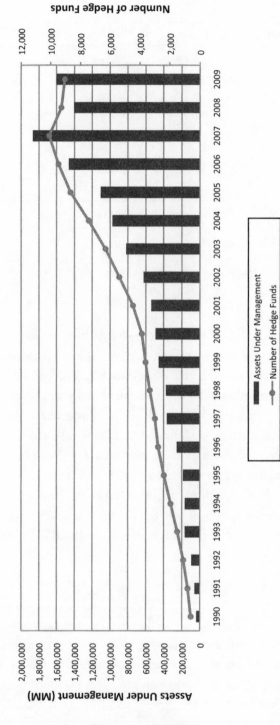

Figure 16.1 Hedge Fund Industry 1990–Q2 2008: Assets Under Management and Number of Hedge Funds

Source: HFR Global Hedge Fund Industry Report—Second Quarter 2008. Used with permission.

Table 16.8 Rolling Year Returns and Risk: Equity, Non-U.S. Equity, Fixed Income, and Alternative Investments

Rolling Year Returns and Risk

1 Year, 3 Years, 5 years, 10 Years, and 15 Years (ending October 2008)

Asset Class	Index	Rolling 1 Year (Nov. 07 – Oct. 08) CAGR%	Standard Deviation	Rolling 3 Years (Nov. 05 – Oct. 08) CAGR%	Standard Deviation	Rolling 5 Years (Nov. 03 – Oct. 08) CAGR%	Standard Deviation	Rolling 10 Years (Nov. 98 – Oct.08) CAGR%	Standard Deviation	Rolling 15 Years (Nov. 93 – Oct. 08) CAGR%	Standard Deviation
Equity											
U.S. Equity	S&P 500	−36.09	20.34	−5.22	14.95	0.25	12.67	0.39	15.15	6.93	14.86
Non-U.S. Equity											
Europe	MSCI Europ Index	−48.01	26.04	−4.29	20.24	4.44	20.24	1.53	17.59	6.77	16.41
Fixed Income											
U.S. Treasury Note	U.S. Treasury 10-Year Note	7.75	6.71	5.47	5.29	4.54	5.8	4.58	6.93	5.39	6.93
Alternative Investments											
Real Assets	Handy & Harman Spot Gold Index	−9.90	26.30	16.08	20.28	13.27	17.92	9.24	16.09	4.49	14.40
Hedge Funds	HFRI Fund Weighted Composite Index	−16.89	8.91	2.79	7.51	5.18	6.46	8.52	7.24	9.79	7.22
Managed Futures	Barclays CTA Index	12.58	7.13	8.06	6.42	5.90	6.49	5.57	7.44	6.47	7.88

Source: Author.

year returns and risk for 1, 3, 5, 10, and 15 years (ending October 2008). The table compares the risk and return characterstics of U.S. equity, non-U.S. equity, fixed income, and alternative investments (real assets, hedge funds, and managed futures).

Many investors dismiss hedge funds because they are too "risky." Yet the risk or standard deviation of hedge funds is less than equities and many bonds as shown in Table 16.8. In periods of market declines, hedge funds have exhibited lower volatility because they are positioned to take protective actions, whereas long-only managers do not have or avail themselves of the same flexibility.[6] For instance, over a rolling 10-year period (November 1998–October 2008), the standard deviation for the S&P 500 index was 15.15, MSCI Europe 17.59, and U.S. Treasury notes 6.93 (as seen in Table 16.8). The standard deviation for hedge funds over the same time frame was 7.24. Over 1-, 3-, 5-, 10-, and 15-year periods, hedge funds had about half the risk of the S&P 500 Index. One might jump to the erroneous conclusion that the returns of hedge funds might not be compelling. However, the compound annual growth rate (CAGR) over a 10-year period (November 1998–October 2008) was .39 for the S&P 500, 1.53 for MSCI Europe, 4.58 for U.S. Treasury notes, and 8.52 for the HFRI Fund Weighted Composite Index. When the market turmoil heightened over the 1-year period (November 2007–October 2008), the S&P 500 had a standard deviation of 20.34 and a CAGR of –36.09%. The MSCI Europe had a 26.04 standard deviation and a CAGR of –48.01%. U.S. Treasury notes had a standard deviation of 6.71 and a CAGR of 7.75%. Although not as good as U.S. Treasuries in the short term, hedge funds performed much better than equities with a standard deviation of 8.91 and a CAGR of –16.89%. The risk was much lower (less than half) of the S&P 500 and MSCI Europe with far better returns.

Opportunistic

Hedge funds are very nimble and can adapt quickly to take advantage of changing environments. The managers can move into and out of various markets or securities with alacrity. Many develop a leading edge, which is not easy to replicate.

Risk-Adjusted Returns

Over the past decade, hedge funds were consistently middle-of-the-road performers; they did not have the highest returns, nor did they exhibit the lowest returns. As one can see in Table 16.9, over the past decade, hedge funds as a whole were neither the highest return generators nor the lowest performers. Over 1, 3, 5, and 10-year periods, hedge funds had admirable performance. The HFR Hedge Fund Composite Index consists of not just one hedge fund style but many styles. As we will explore later, individual hedge funds carry far greater risk (depending on the manager) than a hedge fund-of-funds, hedge fund indexes, or replication strategies.

Advantages of Hedge Fund-of-Funds

Similar to individual hedge funds, hedge fund-of-funds also have their advantages.

Ongoing Monitoring

By hiring a manager to oversee a portfolio of hedge funds or hedge fund-of-funds, one will presumably receive ongoing monitoring. The manager will monitor the performance of each hedge fund manager, making changes when necessary. Further, the manager might increase, decrease, or eradicate certain styles depending on market conditions. For instance, a manager overseeing a hedge fund-of-funds might increase a weighting of a portfolio toward global macro if market conditions look attractive. Hiring a hedge fund-of-funds manager removes the headache of attempting to select the area or sector for hedge funds as well as deciding what weighting and when one should be making changes. One bank even offers a hedge fund-of-funds with numerous styles that can be broken into relative value, directional, or event-driven hedge fund investing. Each of these categories are then broken down into 18 specific hedge fund styles or subsectors for diversification. Astute investors in single hedge funds (as well as hedge fund-of-funds) should be cognizant of trends in the market. A manager might also replace a hedge fund for poor performance, irregularities, or excessive risk.

Table 16.9 Hedge Fund Performance Compared to Equities and Bonds (2000–2009)

2000	2001	2002	2003	2004	2005	2006	2007	2008	2009
DJ US REIT 31.04%	Russell 2000 Value 14.02%	BarCap Aggregate Bond 10.25%	Russell 2000 Growth 48.54%	DJ US REIT 33.16%	DJ US REIT 13.82%	DJ US REIT 35.97%	Russell 2000 Growth 7.05%	BarCap Aggregate Bond 5.24%	Russell Mid Cap Growth TR USD 46.29%
Russell 2000 Value 22.83%	DJ US REIT 12.35%	DJ US REIT 3.58%	Russell 2000 Value 46.03%	Russell Mid Cap Value 23.71%	MSCI EAFE 13.54%	MSCI EAFE 26.34%	Russell 1000 Growth 11.81%	HFRI Fund Weighted Index −19.03%	Russell 1000 Growth TR USD 37.21%
Russell Mid Cap Value 19.18%	BarCap Aggregate Bond 8.44%	HFRI Fund Weighted Index −1.45%	Russell Mid Cap Growth 42.71%	Russell 2000 Value 22.25%	Russell Mid Cap Value 12.65%	Russell 2000 Value 23.48%	Russell Mid Cap Growth 11.43%	Russell 2000 Value −28.92%	Russell 2000 Growth TR USD 34.47%
BarCap Aggregate Bond 11.63%	HFRI Fund Weighted Index 4.62%	Russell Mid Cap Value −9.64%	MSCI EAFE 38.59%	MSCI EAFE 20.25%	Russell Mid Cap Growth 12.10%	Russell 1000 Value 22.25%	MSCI EAFE 11.17%	Russell 1000 Value −36.85%	Russell Mid Cap Value TR USD 34.21%
Russell 1000 Value 7.01%	Russell Mid Cap Value 2.33%	Russell 2000 Value −11.43%	Russell Mid Cap Value 38.07%	Russell 1000 Value 16.49%	HFRI Fund Weighted Index 9.30%	Russell Mid Cap Value 20.22%	HFRI Fund Weighted Index 9.96%	S&P 500 −37.00%	MSCI EAFE NR USD 31.78%
HFRI Fund Weighted Index 4.98%	Russell 1000 Value −5.59%	Russell 1000 Value −15.52%	DJ US REIT 36.18%	Russell Mid Cap Growth 15.48%	Russell 1000 Value 7.05%	S&P 500 15.79%	BarCap Aggregate Bond 6.97%	Russell 1000 Growth −38.44%	DJ US Select REIT TR USD 28.46%
S&P 500 −9.10%	Russell 2000 Growth −9.23%	MSCI EAFE −15.94%	Russell 1000 Value 30.03%	Russell 2000 Growth 14.31%	Russell 1000 Growth 5.26%	Russell 2000 Growth 13.35%	S&P 500 5.49%	Russell Mid Cap Value −38.44%	S&P 500 TR 26.46%
Russell Mid Cap Growth −11.75%	S&P 500 −11.89%	S&P 500 −22.10%	Russell 1000 Growth 29.75%	S&P 500 10.88%	S&P 500 4.91%	HFRI Fund Weighted Index 12.89%	Russell 1000 Value −0.17%	Russell 2000 Growth −38.54%	Russell 2000 Value TR USD 20.58%
MSCI EAFE −14.17%	Russell Mid Cap Growth −20.15%	Russell Mid Cap Growth −27.41%	S&P 500 28.68%	HFRI Fund Weighted Index 9.03%	Russell 2000 Value 4.71%	Russell Mid Cap Growth 10.66%	Russell Mid Cap Value −1.42%	DJ US REIT −39.20%	HFRI Fund Weighted Index 19.98%
Russell 1000 Growth −22.42%	Russell 1000 Growth −22.42%	Russell 1000 Growth −27.88%	HFRI Fund Weighted Index 19.55%	Russell 1000 Growth 6.30%	Russell 2000 Growth 4.15%	Russell 1000 Growth 9.07%	Russell 2000 Value −9.78%	MSCI EAFE −43.38%	Russell 1000 Value TR USD 19.69%
Russell 2000 Growth −22.43%	MSCI EAFE −21.44%	Russell 2000 Growth −30.26%	BarCap Aggregate Bond 4.10%	BarCap Aggregate Bond 4.34%	BarCap Aggregate Bond 2.34%	BarCap Aggregate Bond 4.33%	DJ US REIT −17.56%	Russell Mid Cap Growth −44.32%	BarCap US Agg Bond TR USD 5.93%

Source: Author.

Diversification

Hedge fund-of-funds have broad diversification across different spectrums of hedge fund investing. Rather than just one style of hedge fund, an investor can easily diversify with a hedge fund-of-funds because most invest in 20 to 30 different hedge funds. Hedge fund-of-funds generally invest in a variety of hedge fund strategies to build a well-diversified portfolio.

As discussed in Chapter 14, the six main styles for hedge funds are equity hedge, event driven, macro, relative value, opportunistic, and combination. Among these styles there are at least 38 subcategories or types of hedge funds. Each of these styles has a strategy such as arbitrage. Arbitrage strategies tend to use more leverage while profiting from mispriced securities, which are closely related or highly correlated. Hedge funds that use event-driven strategies attempt to profit from a specific corporate event like a merger.

Hedge fund-of-funds structures tend to vary in terms of manager concentration and style. Many combinations are possible from conservative to more aggressive structures. Most funds try to balance opportunistic managers with defensive managers (e.g., 60% opportunistic, 40% defensive), and often attempts are made to assess correlations between managers to find those that have low correlations.[7]

Professional Manager Search

Many large investment firms or banks offer hedge fund-of-funds. Because they have knowledge and expertise that the typical investor does not have, it might behoove the investor to select a hedge fund-of-funds through an investment firm (R.W. Baird, Raymond James, or Jeffries) or bank (JPMorgan, Goldman Sachs, Credit Suisse, or BNY).

Lower Volatility

By investing in a hedge fund-of-funds, one is gaining broad diversification among many asset classes and managers. Some funds might even have 50 to 60 managers. Such broad diversification among so many assets classes on a global basis will lower volatility. When the equity markets were off 40% or more in 2008, the hedge fund-of-funds as a whole were down 20%, approximately half the equity market.

Access

A hedge fund-of-funds gives new investors access to hedge funds that might be otherwise closed to them or require large minimums. Hedge fund-of-funds have been around a fair amount of time. Because some of these older hedge fund-of-funds invested in single hedge funds years ago that now might be closed to new investors, they might be grandfathered or allowed to put more into a fund. Thus, an investor might be able to access compelling hedge fund managers that are closed to new investors via the hedge fund of funds. A number of hedge funds also have large minimums, up to and exceeding $25 million. An investment of $25 million is a lot for any investor, no matter how wealthy. Again, if the hedge fund-of-funds is invested with a particular hedge fund that has high minimums, an investor would not have to meet those minimums because he or she is invested in the hedge fund-of-funds, which met the minimum requirement and has money with the high-minimum hedge fund. Hypothetically, if an investor invests $100,000 into a hedge fund-of-funds that has 30 different funds, they would have a mere $3,333 invested with the high-minimum hedge fund that usually requires $25 million.

Rebalancing

Unless one is spending quite a bit of time analyzing trends in the hedge fund market, it is extremely difficult to judge which style to select. With good management, a hedge fund-of-funds will regularly rebalance investments to not only have proper diversification but also shift weightings to different styles when necessary.

Low Correlation with Traditional Assets

A hedge fund-of-funds can select any number of hedge funds with any style. The menu is almost limitless. Individual managers frequently short securities or use derivatives that make them have a low correlation with traditional asset classes. Combining a number of hedge funds to form a hedge fund-of-funds also has a low correlation with traditional assets such as equities.

Opportunistic

Individual or single hedge funds can offer terrific new opportunities not easily achieved by regular means of investing through mutual funds or indexes. A talented hedge fund manager in the health-care space, for example, might employ doctors, analysts, and/or engineers who can offer opinions on whether a new medical device company situated in China has merit. Depending on the investor's asset allocation, one could add hedge funds to take advantage of special situations that are difficult to access or understand.

Disadvantages of Single Hedge Funds

In the pages to follow, we will discuss a number of disadvantages for single hedge funds.

Transparency

Hedge funds tend to be secretive. Because they are unregulated, hedge funds are not required to disclose holdings or strategies like a mutual fund. Many hedge fund managers attempt to justify a lack of transparency because it would be tantamount to giving away the secret sauce. A 2009 *Pensions & Investments* article characterizes the mentality of hedge fund managers who play it close to the vest:

> Top-tier investors regard the details of their portfolios as their competitive edge and therefore as highly proprietary. While managers generally will share information about their portfolio's overall exposure, most will not provide full position-level transparency even to an investor that promises confidentiality. An investor who insists on receiving position-level transparency will likely miss out on the opportunity to invest with some of the world's best hedge fund managers. This is a significant trade-off.[8]

An investor should be cautious about a hedge fund that refuses to disclose anything about what they are doing or buying. Bernie Madoff refused to explain his investment philosophy. Regardless of whether it will actually hurt performance, there is a simple way to see what hedge funds are buying or selling. In other words, the exception is that any hedge fund with more than $100 million of equities must disclose positions to the SEC within 45 days of each quarter's close. These filings are called 13F and might help reveal a hedge fund's strategy or headed direction. Figure 16.2 reviews the 13F filing for Maverick Capital Ltd.

From this information, an investor can see what sectors the hedge fund prefers and their weightings. In addition, one can learn the names of the companies the hedge fund is holding as well as the market value and the percentage of the overall portfolio.

Leverage

Hedge funds can borrow money to make more investments for the fund. Leverage increases risk of loss and might also increase volatility. When markets turn south, assets will decline in value, and the fund might get margin calls where more collateral must be posted. Leverage hurt funds in the market decline of 2008–2009 and forced many to sell.

Illiquid

Hedge funds can invest in anything. They can purchase art, venture capital, wine, or other illiquid assets. Hedge funds can have long lockups (ranging from one quarter to several years). Dismayed by managers that locked up, gated, froze, or otherwise restricted redemptions in 2008, institutional investors are actively investigating moves into hedge investment vehicles that guarantee liquidity and investor control over the investment.[9] Similarly, there is no regulated secondary market for hedge funds.

Speculative Investments

Hedge funds can carry a high degree of risk. Due to the types of investments that hedge funds can make, volatility can increase, as well as the possibility of a loss. Table 16.10 highlights some key hedge fund losses.

Example of a 13-F Filing–Maverick Capital LTD

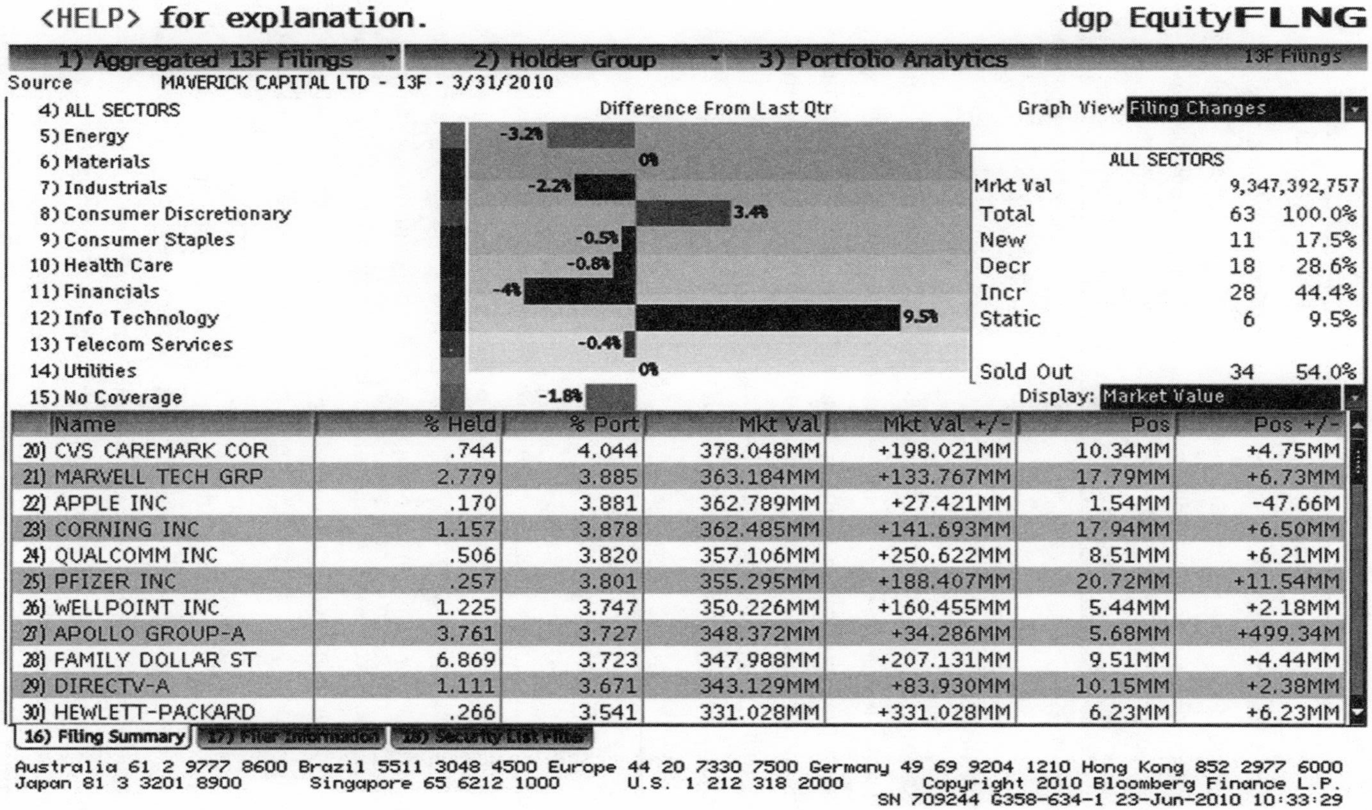
<HELP> for explanation. dgp EquityFLNG

1) Aggregated 13F Filings 2) Holder Group 3) Portfolio Analytics 13F Filings

Source MAVERICK CAPITAL LTD - 13F - 3/31/2010

Difference From Last Qtr — Graph View Filing Changes

Sector	Difference From Last Qtr
4) ALL SECTORS	
5) Energy	-3.2%
6) Materials	0%
7) Industrials	-2.2%
8) Consumer Discretionary	3.4%
9) Consumer Staples	-0.5%
10) Health Care	-0.8%
11) Financials	-4%
12) Info Technology	9.5%
13) Telecom Services	-0.4%
14) Utilities	0%
15) No Coverage	-1.8%

ALL SECTORS		
Mrkt Val		9,347,392,757
Total	63	100.0%
New	11	17.5%
Decr	18	28.6%
Incr	28	44.4%
Static	6	9.5%
Sold Out	34	54.0%

Display: Market Value

Name	% Held	% Port	Mkt Val	Mkt Val +/-	Pos	Pos +/-
20) CVS CAREMARK COR	.744	4.044	378.048MM	+198.021MM	10.34MM	+4.75MM
21) MARVELL TECH GRP	2.779	3.885	363.184MM	+133.767MM	17.79MM	+6.73MM
22) APPLE INC	.170	3.881	362.789MM	+27.421MM	1.54MM	-47.66M
23) CORNING INC	1.157	3.878	362.485MM	+141.693MM	17.94MM	+6.50MM
24) QUALCOMM INC	.506	3.820	357.106MM	+250.622MM	8.51MM	+6.21MM
25) PFIZER INC	.257	3.801	355.295MM	+188.407MM	20.72MM	+11.54MM
26) WELLPOINT INC	1.225	3.747	350.226MM	+160.455MM	5.44MM	+2.18MM
27) APOLLO GROUP-A	3.761	3.727	348.372MM	+34.286MM	5.68MM	+499.34M
28) FAMILY DOLLAR ST	6.869	3.723	347.988MM	+207.131MM	9.51MM	+4.44MM
29) DIRECTV-A	1.111	3.671	343.129MM	+83.930MM	10.15MM	+2.38MM
30) HEWLETT-PACKARD	.266	3.541	331.028MM	+331.028MM	6.23MM	+6.23MM

16) Filing Summary 17) Filer Information 18) Security List Filter

Australia 61 2 9777 8600 Brazil 5511 3048 4500 Europe 44 20 7330 7500 Germany 49 69 9204 1210 Hong Kong 852 2977 6000
Japan 81 3 3201 8900 Singapore 65 6212 1000 U.S. 1 212 318 2000 Copyright 2010 Bloomberg Finance L.P.
SN 709244 G358-634-1 23-Jun-2010 10:33:29

Figure 16.2 13-F Filing for Maverick Capital Ltd (3/31/2010)

Source: Bloomberg. Used with permission.

Table 16.10 Hedge Fund Blowups

Firm	Loss	Year	Reason
Amaranth Advisors	$6.6 Billion	2006	Natural Gas
Long-Term Capital	$4.0 Billion	1998	Bonds
Bear Stearns	$1.6 Billion	2007	Subprime Loans
Sowood Capital	$1.5 Billion	2007	Subprime Loans
Vairocana	$700 Million	1994	Bonds

Source: Katherine Burton, "Hedge Fund Blowups," *Bloomberg Markets* (October 2007). Used with permission.

Unregulated

Hedge funds do not have to report performance, holdings, or valuation like mutual funds. In June 2006, a short-lived rule giving the SEC some regulatory power over hedge funds (requiring registration and allowing for random audits) was nixed by a federal court. The court judged the rule to be "arbitrary" and returned regulation to its previous levels, in which only the request and granting of a formal request could allow the SEC to review a fund's books.

Fees and Expenses

Hedge fund managers usually receive two types of fees. The first is a management fee, generally 2% of the firm's net asset value. The second fee is the performance fee, which is usually 20% of gross returns and is an incentive for managers to perform well. A hedge fund can charge 2% and 20%. However, some funds charge as much as 5% and 50%. Some argue that the manager incentive fee might encourage greater risk taking. If the fund does well, they win. If not, they can close the fund and start another.

Investors should make sure there is a high-water mark, in which managers do not receive compensation the year after a loss until that loss has been recouped. A high-water mark is usually implemented on these fees, though, so the manager should keep the investor's best interest in mind and not seek overtly risky trades. There is also a hurdle rate, which is sometimes used to prevent the manager from collecting a performance fee until the fund's performance exceeds a certain rate. Not all investors are charged the same. A hedge fund manager can also use "side letters." Side letters are basically secret letters to a handful of investors who receive special privileges, such as liquidity, information on investments, or lower fees.

Fees are a concern with institutional investors. The *Journal of Indexes* summed up the balance required of fee structures by citing a 2007 survey of institutional hedge fund investors and reporting that high fees disproportionately offsetting investment gains were viewed the greatest threat to hedge fund investing. While hedge funds can still deliver powerful returns and valuable portfolio characteristics, increasingly investors are paying alpha fees for beta or market returns.[10]

Tax Considerations

High turnover and a lack of tax efficiency can increase taxes, which might be more suitable for an institution like an endowment but not for an individual that is in a high tax bracket. Hedge funds typically generate a K–1 statements, which can delay payment of taxes.

Lockup

A lockup is a period of time that a hedge fund requires investors to keep money in a fund. A 1-year lockup is common, with quarterly withdrawals after the investor meets the holding period. Because hedge funds can own esoteric securities, thinly traded equities, or even private stock, some hedge funds need longer lockups than others. Lockups can vary from one to two quarters all the way to 5 years, depending on the hedge fund. Hedge funds have the ability to ban withdrawals and often do so when investors want to pull their money out most: in times of economic downturn. Seventy-five hedge funds blocked their investors from pulling out money at the end of 2008, among them Citadel Investment Management, Whitebox Advisors, and GLG Partners.[11] The industry term for refusing to allow an investor to remove money is *gating*.

Single Manager Risk

In 2006, Amaranth Advisors, which managed $9 billion in assets and whose collapse made headlines around the world, was only one of 83

Table 16.11 Large Hedge Funds that closed in 2008

Fund	Manager(s), Firm	Assets in Billions
1 Old Lane Partners	Guru Ramakrishnan	
	Citigroup	$4.5
2 Global Opportunities, Absolute Return, Low Volatility	Anthony Faillace, Steve Luttrell	
	Drake Management	4.0
3 Ospraie	Dwight Anderson	
	Ospraie Management	2.8
4 Tribeca Global Investments Group	Andrew Wang, Jeffery Chmielewski	
	Citigroup	2.0
5 ABS	Ron Beller, Geoff Grant	
	Peloton Partners	1.8
6 Highland Crusader, Highland Credit Strategies	James Dondero, Patrick Daugherty	
	Citigroup	1.5
7 Multi Strategy Flagship	Michael Humphries, Keith DeCalarruci, MartinTonnby;	
	MKM Longboat Capital Advisors	1.5
8 Sunova Capital	Matthew Byrnes, Felice Gelman	
	Sunova Capital	1.3
9 Multistrategy Credit	Mark Fishman	
	Sailfish Capital Partners	1.0
10 Millenium Global Emerging Credit	Michael Balboa	
	Millennium Global Investments	0.8

Source: Teitelbaum, Richard. "The Richest Hedge Funds: John Paulson Strikes Again," *Bloomberg Markets*, January 2009. Used with permission.

funds that ceased operation during 2006.[12] As seen in Table 16.11, a number of large hedge funds closed in 2008.

Valuation

Hedge funds can put money into separate accounts known as side pockets to invest in assets that are not easily valued, such as real estate or private equity. These side pockets are not factored into performance calculations, giving regulators cause for concern.[13] Susan Ferris Wyderko, the acting director of the SEC's Investment Management Division, remarked that one of the factors in many cases against hedge funds has been the "valuation of fund assets in order to hide losses or to artificially boost performance."[14] Side pockets can be 5% to 15% of a fund's overall assets so an investor should attempt to know how much of the fund is devoted to the side pocket as well as the type of investments being made. Thus, side pockets are legitimate but can easily become problematic.

Style Rotation

Because of their many styles or subsectors, hedge funds (collectively), tend to perform differently in various market conditions. The aggregate does not show huge waves or periods of very good performance versus ones with bad performance as the case might be with real estate, commodities, or private equity. However, individual hedge fund styles or subsectors tend to be more volatile. For example, HFRI Emerging Markets performed poorly in 1998 with a −32.96% return. In 1999, on the other hand, HFRI Emerging Markets did the best out of all hedge fund categories, with a +55.86%. The year 2000, however, did poorly, with an HFRI Emerging Markets return of −10.71%. In 2001, HFRI Emerging Markets did better, with a +10.36% return. Likewise, other areas or styles of hedge fund investing did well one year and then did not do well during others. For instance, HFRI RV: Convertible Arbitrage did very well from 2000 to 2002. In 2003–2005, HFRI RV: Convertible Arbitrage did not do well and, in fact, was one of the worst sectors or styles to own.

Excessive Government Regulations

Restrictions or increased regulation by any government for hedge funds usually will increase costs for investors. As a government imposes higher fees, the costs usually get passed onto investors. Further, many hedge funds will go out of business which means less choice or selection an investor can make. Fewer funds means fewer options. If a government hits hedge funds and the managers of these funds with higher taxes, the result is that a number of funds might move to a more favorable tax jurisdiction. The best and brightest money managers in the world are hedge fund managers who are rewarded for generating high returns and making clients a lot of money. If the incentive is taken away, the talent will walk. Excessive regulation can mean that the rules imposed on an unregulated industry, such as hedge funds, becomes so restrictive that there will be no difference from that of a mutual fund. Returns might ultimately get diluted as a result of increased regulation.

Disadvantages of Hedge Fund of Funds

In addition to the advantages discussed above, there are several disadvantages or negative factors specific to hedge fund-of-funds that potential investors should know about.

Illiquid

A hedge fund-of-funds typically invests in 30 to 70 different hedge funds, which all have different redemption schedules or exit policies. The shortest time period to take out money is 3 months while some impose a year or longer waiting period.

Tax Risk Potential

Hedge fund-of-funds can have short-term trades like individual funds. In addition, they can have complicated tax structures. Similar to single hedge funds, they also have K–1s and can have delayed reporting resulting in extensions for paying taxes. Hedge fund-of-funds are not tax efficient.

Transparency

Hedge fund-of-funds are not required to provide valuation information and let investors know which hedge funds they own. Hedge fund-of-funds are both private and unregulated. Problems can occur when an investor has no idea what he or she is buying.

Layering of Fees

A hedge fund-of-funds has an extra layer of fees that one may or may not feel comfortable paying. In addition to the typical 2% management fee and 20% performance fee for individual hedge funds, there will be a fee charged by the manager who selects, monitors, and rebalances the individual or single hedge funds inside hedge fund-of-funds. Fees vary depending on the

Table 16.12   Fees for Hedge Fund-of-Funds

- Management fees are usually between 1–3% of overall fund assets
- Performance fees range from 20–50% of the profits
- A fixed management fee (typically ranging between 1–2% of assets)
- Administrative expenses, which are typically 25 bp (basis points or $\frac{1}{4}$ of 1%)
- Shareholder servicing fees, which range between 25 bp and 50 bp
- Placement fees, which vary depending on the vehicle selected, but can be around 3–4% for $100–$500k but less when $1 million or more is invested (placement fees are paid by investors in addition to and separate from the fund fees.)

Source: Author.

types of funds that the manager can access and the monitoring they will provide. Sometimes good advice is worth paying for. Table 16.12 provides a guide to fees commonly found with a hedge fund-of-funds:

Lockups

Unlike mutual funds, stock indexes, bonds, exchange-traded funds, and other liquid securities, hedge funds carry lockups for a variety of reasons. Andrew Lo's *Hedge Funds: An Analytic Perspective* discusses the lockup in greater detail and differentiates the hedge fund-of-funds from the standard hedge fund lockup:

> For certain event-driven strategies involving very illiquid securities for private equity, a lockup of a year or more may be needed to give the fund time to set up investments. For many hedge funds, a lengthy lockup period is not necessary for any investment purpose. Nevertheless, some still demand a lockup period in order to discourage so-called hot money and short-term investors. For this reason, a reasonable lockup period, say six months, may work to the benefit of both investors and managers. . . . It is noteworthy that funds of funds tend to require longer lockup periods of up to one year in order to satisfy the varying lockup periods required by their underlying hedge funds.[15]

Hedge fund-of-funds, which have money invested with many different hedge funds, might take a long time to redeem or have money taken out because every hedge fund has its own lockup.

Chapter 17

Hedge Fund Performance

Over the last decade, hedge funds have evolved to the point that there are distinct styles that move in waves, as shown in Table 17.1. The HFRI Indices Annual Investment Returns (1998–2009) chart is one of the most helpful charts in existence for an investor who wants to use Wave Theory for hedge funds. Data are more meaningful in the hedge fund world than in the past. Hypothetically, if an investor is interested in emerging growth hedge funds, he or she can see certain patterns, trends, or cycles using the HFRI index. Emerging markets was the worst performing hedge fund style in 1998, when the group had a −32.96% return. The following year, it was the best performer, but then moved to last place the next year (2000) with a −10.71% return. Emerging markets improved again in 2001–2002 but was either the best or second-best performer of hedge fund styles in 2003–2007. In 2008, the category was the second-worst style with a return of −36.60%. Convertible arbitrage did well from 2000 to 2002 but poorly or middle of the road from 2003 to 2008. Equity hedge did well in 1998 and 1999 but not so well in 2001–2002. Distressed had the second-best performance in 2006 with a return of +15.94% but was the worst performer in 2007 with a +5.08% return.

Waves exist with hedge funds, but they are especially distinct with market corrections and rallies. For example, convertible arbitrage was the third-worst performer in the downturn for hedge fund investing. In 2007, convertible arbitrage had a 5.33% return and −33.71% return for 2008. At the same time, macro did much better in the financial storm. Macro did well for 2 years in a row until conditions improved and they became one of the worst performers for hedge funds in 2009. In other words, macro performed

Table 17.1 HFRI Indices Annual Investment Returns (1998–2008)

1998	1999	2000	2001	2002	2003	2004	2005	2006	2007	2008	2009
S&P 500 28.59%	HFRI Emerging Markets 55.86%	HFRI ED: Merger Arb 18.02%	HFRI RV: ConvertArb 13.37%	Barclays Gov't/Credit 12.10%	HFRI Emerging Markets 39.36%	HFRI ED: Distressed 18.89%	HFRI Emerging Markets 21.04%	HFRI Emerging Markets 24.26%	HFRI Emerging Markets 24.92%	Barclays Gov't/Credit 6.09%	HFRI RV: ConvertArb 60.18%
HFRI Equity Hedge 22.83%	HFRI Equity Hedge 44.22%	HFRI EH: Eq Mrkt Ntrl 14.56%	HFRI ED: Distressed 13.28%	HFRI RV: ConvertArb 9.05%	HFRI ED: Distressed 29.56%	HFRI Emerging Markets 18.42%	HFRI Equity Hedge 10.60%	HFRI ED: Distressed 15.94%	HFRI: Macro 11.11%	HFRI: Macro 4.83%	HFRI Emerging Markets 40.46%
Barclays Gov't/Credit 12.00%	HFRI Fund Wghtd Comp 31.29%	HFRI RV: ConvertArb 14.50%	HFRI Event-Driven 12.18%	HFRI: Macro 7.44%	S&P 500 28.67%	HFRI Event-Driven 15.01%	HFRI Fund Wghtd Comp 9.30%	S&P 500 15.78%	HFRI Equity Hedge 10.48%	HFRI ED: Merger Arb -5.36%	HFRI ED: Distressed 29.24%
HFRI EH: Eq Mrkt Ntrl 8.30%	HFRI FOF Composite 26.47%	HFRI Relative Value 13.41%	HFRI Emerging Markets 10.36%	HFRI Relative Value 5.44%	HFRI Event-Driven 25.33%	S&P 500 10.86%	HFRI ED: Distressed 8.27%	HFRI Event-Driven 15.33%	HFRI FOF Composite 10.25%	HFRI EH: Eq Mrkt Ntrl -5.93%	S&P 500 26.47%
HFRI RV: ConvertArb 7.77%	HFRI Event-Driven 24.33%	Barclays Gov't/Credit 13.27%	Barclays Gov't/Credit 9.40%	HFRI ED: Distressed 5.28%	HFRI: Macro 21.42%	HFRI Fund Wghtd Comp 9.03%	HFRI FOF Composite 7.49%	HFRI ED: Merger Arb 14.24%	HFRI Fund Wghtd Comp 9.96%	HFRI Relative Value -18.04%	HFRI Relative Value 25.97%
HFRI ED: Merger Arb 7.23%	S&P 500 21.03%	HFRI Equity Hedge 9.09%	HFRI Relative Value 8.92%	HFRI Emerging Markets 3.70%	HFRI Equity Hedge 20.54%	HFRI Equity Hedge 7.68%	HFRI Event-Driven 7.29%	HFRI Fund Wghtd Comp 12.89%	HFRI Relative Value 8.94%	HFRI Fund Wghtd Comp -19.02%	HFRI Event-Driven 25.89%
HFRI: Macro 6.19%	HFRI: Macro 17.62%	HFRI Event-Driven 6.74%	HFRI: Macro 6.87%	HFRI FOF Composite 1.02%	HFRI Fund Wghtd Comp 19.55%	HFRI FOF Composite 6.86%	HFRI: Macro 6.79%	HFRI Relative Value 12.37%	Barclays Gov't/Credit 7.75%	HFRI FOF Composite -21.36%	HFRI Equity Hedge 24.96%
HFRI Relative Value 2.81%	HFRI ED: Distressed 16.94%	HFRI Fund Wghtd Comp 4.98%	HFRI EH: Eq Mrkt Ntrl 6.71%	HFRI EH: Eq Mrkt Ntrl 0.98%	HFRI FOF Composite 11.61%	HFRI Relative Value 5.58%	HFRI ED: Merger Arb 6.25%	HFRI RV: ConvertArb 12.17%	HFRI ED: Merger Arb 7.05%	HFRI Event-Driven -21.82%	HFRI Fund Wghtd Comp 20.12%
HFRI Fund Wghtd Comp 2.62%	HFRI Relative Value 14.73%	HFRI FOF Composite 4.07%	HFRI Fund Wghtd Comp 4.62%	HFRI ED: Merger Arb -0.87%	HFRI RV: ConvertArb 9.93%	HFRI: Macro 4.63%	HFRI EH: Eq Mrkt Ntrl 6.22%	HFRI Equity Hedge 11.71%	HFRI Event-Driven 6.61%	HFRI ED: Distressed -25.20%	HFRI ED: Merger Arb 11.59%
HFRI Event-Driven 1.70%	HFRI RV: ConvertArb 14.41%	HFRI ED: Distressed 2.78%	HFRI FOF Composite 2.80%	HFRI Fund Wghtd Comp -1.45%	HFRI Relative Value 9.72%	Barclays Gov't/Credit 4.54%	HFRI Relative Value 6.02%	HFRI FOF Composite 10.39%	S&P 500 5.49%	HFRI Equity Hedge -26.65%	HFRI FOF Composite 11.55%
HFRI ED: Distressed -4.23%	HFRI ED: Merger Arb 14.34%	HFRI: Macro 1.97%	HFRI ED: Merger Arb 2.76%	HFRI Event-Driven -4.30%	HFRI ED: Merger Arb 7.47%	HFRI EH: Eq Mrkt Ntrl 4.15%	S&P 500 4.91%	HFRI: Macro 8.15%	HFRI RV: ConvertArb 5.33%	HFRI RV: ConvertArb -33.71%	Barclays Gov't/Credit 5%
HFRI FOF Composite -5.11%	HFRI EH: Eq Mrkt Ntrl 7.09%	S&P 500 -9.09%	HFRI Equity Hedge 0.40%	HFRI Equity Hedge -4.71%	Barclays Gov't/Credit 5.07%	HFRI ED: Merger Arb 4.08%	Barclays Gov't/Credit 2.55%	HFRI EH: Eq Mrkt Ntrl 7.32%	HFRI EH: Eq Mrkt Ntrl 5.29%	HFRI Emerging Markets -36.99%	HFRI: Macro 4.19%
HFRI Emerging Markets -32.96%	Barclays Gov't/Credit -2.40%	HFRI Emerging Markets -10.71%	S&P 500 -11.85%	S&P 500 -22.09%	HFRI EH: Eq Mrkt Ntrl 2.44%	HFRI RV: ConvertArb 1.18%	HFRI RV: ConvertArb -1.86%	Barclays Gov't/Credit 4.07%	HFRI ED: Distressed 5.08%	S&P 500 -37.26%	HFRI EH: Eq Mrkt Ntrl 1.73%

Source: Hedge Fund Research Inc., *Year End Report 2008*. Used with permission.

well during the market collapse with a +11.11% return in 2007 and +4.83% return in 2008. Macro was the second best performer in both of these years for hedge funds.

Macro did well in a horrible market, which attracted a lot of assets and interest by investors. There were reasons behind this performance. First, macro funds typically do not use a lot of leverage like the other hedge fund styles. Hedge funds with a lot of leverage tended to perform badly in the market downturn. Second, macro funds are highly liquid as opposed to a number of the other hedge fund styles, such as distressed, which cannot be sold in a hurry. Investors flocked to macro hedge funds in 2009 after 2 years of terrific performance. However, they missed the wave. As 2009 rebounded with the equity market, macro did a flip flop. Macro had 4.19% return which was the second-worst hedge fund style of the year and far below equity managers and other asset classes. Did all the macro hedge fund managers fall asleep or suddenly perform very badly for some unknown reason during 2009? No. The market frequently changes and equities and other classes changed.

Anyone investing in alternatives must pay attention to the market and what is going on around them before investing. One service that I use for market intelligence is called The Hennessee Group LLC (www. Hennesseegroup.com), which is a consultant and advisor to direct investors in hedge funds. They have very good research on hedge funds as well as the market, in my view. Similarly, Morningstar has good research for investors. For example, the Morningstar Alternative Investment Center offers articles, presentations, and reports (www.alterantiveinvestments.com). The macro style for hedge fund investing underperformed when the market improved. A change in market conditions will affect any style of hedge fund investing as far as performance is concerned.

As more data become available, it is evident that waves exist with individual hedge fund styles. For instance, macro tends to outperform the S&P 500 as well as other styles of hedge funds in bad markets. In 2008, arguably one of the worst markets for equities, hedge funds, and virtually all asset classes, macro did the best. The HFRI Macro Index had a +5.18% return, whereas the S&P 500 had a −36.99% return. During the same time period, other hedge fund styles all performed worse than the HFRI macro: merger arb (−4.62%), market neutral (−6.20%), relative value (−16.77%), fund weighted comp (−18.36%), fund-of-funds composite (−20.68%), event driven (−21.26%), distressed (−24.94%), equity hedge (−26.16%), convert arb (−34.67%), and emerging markets (−36.80%). A cynic might ask, "So what?" or suggest "It might be per chance."

If one applies Wave Theory, they would know that macro performed the second best in 2007 and 2008 out of all hedge funds and even did better than the S&P 500. The year before, however, macro did not do as well and was third to last. Hypothetically, an investor might be encouraged to put all his or her money into a macro fund for 2009. A lot of investors invested heavily in macro during 2009. News releases were positive about macro for 3 years (2007–2009).

It would be easy to decide that macro was bullet proof. Yet Wave Theory indicates that it might not be prudent to invest all your money in macro because there are identifiable trends, cycles, and problems showing various hedge fund styles moving in and out of favor. Hypothetically, an investor might ignore Wave Theory and put a large amount of money into a macro fund. The year 2009 started out looking like the end of the world and then turned positive in the summer. How would the investor have done in the macro fund (assuming it had average performance) by July 31, 2009? Not well. In fact, macro performed the worst out of all hedge fund strategies and was the only style to have a below-average year. Figure 17.1 shows the estimated change in hedge fund assets per main strategy (net asset flow versus performance, full year 2009) compared with macro funds. Only the macro hedge funds were underperforming compared to the other hedge fund styles as well as the total hedge fund market and hedge fund-of-funds.

Previously, the equity market performed well in 1998 when the S&P 500 was at +28.59%. Macro did not perform as well. Macro had a return of +6.19%. What happened during the tech bubble when the S&P 500 was either the worst or one of the worst performers (−9.09% in 2000, −11.85% in 2001, −22.09% in 2002)? Macro outperformed the S&P 500 in 2000, 2001, and 2002, as well as many other hedge fund styles. Hedge funds (the composite as well as individual styles) move in waves. One should be cognizant of these waves before investing. Sometimes the worst performers quickly turn into the best performers and vice versa as depicted Figure 17.2.

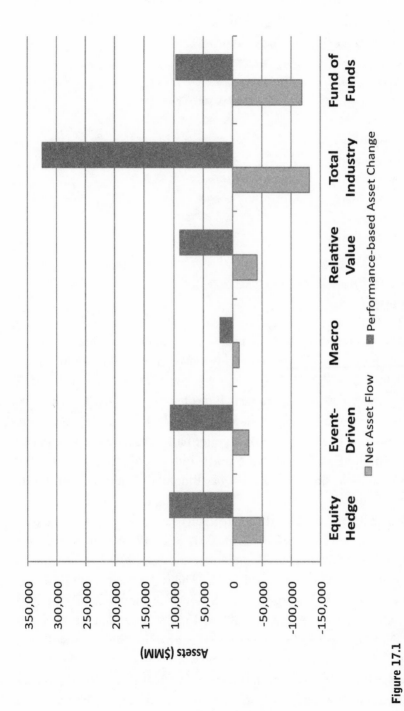

Figure 17.1

Source: HFR, "Estimated Change in Assets per Main Strategy: Net Asset Flow versus Performance-based Full Year 2009," Global Hedge Fund Industry Report Year End 2009.

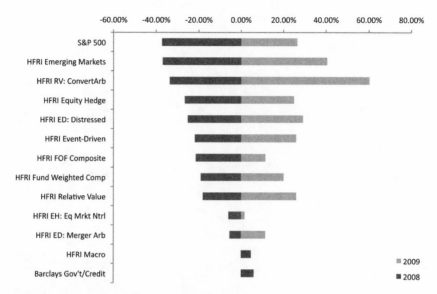

Figure 17.2   Hedge Fund Styles 2008–2009
Source: Author.

Additional trends, patterns, or cycles are clear amongst the various types of hedge funds. For example, emerging markets used to have a much lower correlation with the S&P 500. In 1998, the S&P 500 had a +28.59% return, whereas Emerging Markets Index had −32.96% return. In 2000, the beginning of the market collapse, the S&P 500 (−9.09%) and emerging markets (−10.71%) had similar performances again. When the market recovered, the HFRI Emerging Markets Index performed far better than the S&P 500, as shown in the 10-year Bloomberg chart comparing the index with the S&P 500 and the VIX Index (Figure 17.3).

From 2003 to 2007, the HFRI Emerging Markets Index performed quite well: +39.36% in 2003, +18.42% in 2004, +21.04% in 2005, +24.26% in 2006, and +24.92% in 2007. As any surfer knows, wind helps create waves, or as Henry David Thoreau explained, "The water itself is rippled by the wind."[1] By way of comparison, the S&P 500 returned +28.87% in 2003, +10.86% in 2004, +4.91% in 2005, +15.78% in 2006, and +5.49% in 2007. Not surprisingly, emerging markets crashed in 2008 and volatility hit a high. Emerging markets was the second worst performer with hedge funds in 2008, with a −36.99% return. But emerging markets was the second best performer in 2009 with a +40.46% return when the equity market rallied.

<HELP> for explanation.   EquityG

Figure 17.3   HFRI Emerging Markets Index versus S&P 500 Index and VIX Index
Source: Bloomberg. Used with permission.

It should be interesting to see if history will repeat itself by the end of 2010 and the years after. Will the HFRI emerging markets outperform again? It is impossible to tell the future, but the waves with hedge funds are much more apparent today. The HFRI Emerging Markets Index and the S&P 500 were the two worst performers together in 2008. One might note that the exact same thing happened during the last market collapse in 2000.

Tables 17.2 and 17.3 provide some historical background for the largest and top-performing hedge funds from 2004 to 2006. In 2008, the best-performing hedge fund, Mulvaney Global Markets Fund Ltd., outperformed the worst-performing hedge fund by 173.57%. While Mulvaney earned +85.47% that year, RAB Northwest Warrant Fund Ltd. Europe earned –88.10%.[2] Finding and investing in the right hedge fund, therefore, is critical to earning the returns that attract many to the industry. Many investors make the mistake of putting their money with the largest fund, believing it is more likely to succeed not only because of what is believed to be a decreased risk of bankruptcy but because of their greater ability to diversify. Nevertheless, choosing a hedge fund based merely on size might not be prudent.

Table 17.2 Largest Hedge Funds Ranked by Total Assets Under Management

	Nov. 15, 2004[1]		Nov. 30, 2005[2]		Dec. 11, 2006[3]	
	Fund	Assets	Fund	Assets	Fund	Assets
1	Highbridge Capital	$6.144 B	Orbis Global Equity	$6.345 B	Renaissance Inst'l Equities	$13.523 B
2	Fairfield Sentry	$5.000 B	Highbridge Capital	$5.700 B	Orbis Global Equity	$9.164 B
3	Orbis Global Equity	$4.225 B	Bridgewater Pure Alpha 1	$5.308 B	Highbridge Capital	$7.963 B
4	Vega Relative Value	$3.717 B	Fairfield Sentry	$5.180 B	Bridgewater Pure Alpha I	$5.700 B
5	Cerberus International	$3.700 B	Orbis Optimal (US)	$4.017 B	Renaissance Inst'l Equities B	$5.374 B
6	Orbis Optimul (U.S.)	$3.441 B	Winton Diversified Futures	$4.010 B	Fairfield Sentry	$4.800 B
7	Vega Global	$3.376 B	Cerberus International	$4.000 B	Amber Master	$4.700 B
8	Shepherd Investments Intl.	$3.213 B	Shepherd Investments Int'l A	$3.937 B	Cerberus International	$4.400 B
9	King Street Capital	$3.191 B	King Street Capital	$3.609 B	Orbis Optimal	$4.234 B
10	WG Trading Co.	$2.753 B	Ashmore Emerging Markets Liquid Inve	$3.350 B	Orbis Optimal	$4.234 B

Source: Author.

Table 17.3 Top-Performing Hedge Funds Ranked by Annual Returns

	Sept 30, 2004[1]			Sept 30, 2005[2]			Sept 30, 2006[3]	
	Fund	Returns		Fund	Return		Fund	Assets
1	J-K Navigator	111.02%	1	Ukraine Value Opp.	233.10%	1	Vision Opp. Capital Partners	211.33%
2	Firebird Global	93.82%	2	Gazinvest	202.80%	2	Phalanx Japan AustralAsia	193.59%
3	Tradewinds Russia Partners I	80.12%	3	Prosperity Quest	159.30%	3	Trophy Fund	166.95%
4	JMBO Fund	77.74%	4	East Capital Bering Russia	138.50%	4	Gazinvest Fund	148.33%
5	Westcliff Energy Partners	74.71%	5	Foyll E Europe & Russia	116.50%	5	Forza Partners	123.75%
6	RAB Special Situations A	71.08%	6	Select Contrarian Value	104.20%	6	Rosseau	97.76%
7	AccessTurkey	69.53%	7	BP Capital Energy	102.70%	7	AES Capital Partners	96.95%
8	Gazinvest Fund	67.60%	8	DeltaOne Energy	99.50%	8	Regent Fund NZD	91.25%
9	Tradewinds Debt Strataegies	67.33%	9	Kotak Indian Mid-cap	92.10%	9	PXP Vietnam Fund	88.63%
10	Dynamis Energy	59.30%	10	Russian Prosperity	91.90%	10	Tradewinds Russia Partners I	75.45%

Source: Author.

Comparing the largest 10 hedge funds in 2004, 2005, and 2006 (Table 17.2), with the best-performing hedge funds in those years (Table 17.3) shows no correlation between a fund's size and its returns. None of the largest hedge funds were able to rank as one of the 10 best-performing funds. By way of comparison, large money managers or mutual fund managers own thousands of different securities. AllianceBernstein, for example, has $203 billion in equity assets and 5,636 securities. Fidelity Management and Research has $427 billion in equity assets but 4,570 different securities. In other words, they have more than twice the amount of assets but less securities. Each money manager holds a different view on how many equities one should own as well as hedge funds. Fidelity has more than twice the assets of Alliance-Bernstein. Large money managers can own thousands of securities.

The number of securities dramatically increases (like mutual funds) as hedge fund assets escalate. The majority of the time, it is more difficult to manage unwieldy multibillion dollar funds as compared with smaller, more nimble funds.

However, the most profitable hedge funds of 2008 discovered that both Winton Futures and Fairfield Sentry had seen large profits (see Tables 17.2 and 17.3). Winton Futures, which ranked sixth-largest hedge fund of 2005 with more than $4 billion dollars in assets, earned $146 million dollars in 2008. Fairfield Sentry, which ranked as one of the ten largest hedge funds in 2004, 2005, and 2006, ranked 14th most-profitable hedge fund in 2008 with profits of $82.7 million.[3]

While a similar comparison for hedge fund-of-funds presents the same results, the increased ability of hedge fund-of-funds to diversify would imply that they would be able to decrease risk and thereby the variation between best- and worst-performing fund (Table 17.4). Although it is true that the spread between top and bottom hedge fund-of-funds is smaller than that of hedge funds, it is still substantial at 129.52%. Compared with the best-performing hedge fund-of-funds, which had a return of +54.94%, the worst lost an astounding −74.58%.[4]

Waves

Hedge funds move in waves; certain styles are in favor and then out of favor. Compared with other alternatives over the past decade, hedge funds

Table 17.4 Examples of Hedge Fund-of-Funds

Fund	Sponsor	Min. Inv.	2004 Return	2005 Return	2006 Return
BACAP Alt Multi-Strat Fund	BofA Inv. Advisors	$50,000	9.88%	2.59%	6.38%
BNY/Ivy Multi-Strat Hedge Fund	BNY Inv. Advisors	$100,000	8.38%	5.10%	13.51%
Columbia Mgmt Multi-Strat H.Fund	BofA Inv. Advisors	$50,000	11.27%	4.22%	9.34%
Credit Suisse Alt Cap L/S Equity Fund	CS Alt. Capital	$50,000			17.05%
Credit Suisse Alt Cap I Multi-Strat Fund	CS Alt. Capital	$50,000			13.47%
Excelsior Abs Return Fund of Funds	US Trust HF Mgmt	$100,000	4.85%	4.31%	8.04%
Hatteras Multi-Strategy Fund I	Hatteras Inv Partners	$100,000			10.46%
JPMorgan Multi-Strategy Fund	JPM Alt Asset Mgmt	$50,000		4.56%	8.54%
Man-Glenwood Lexington	Glenwood Cap Inv	$25,000	5.31%	0.46%	13.48%
Morgan Stanley AIP Abs Return Fund	Morgan Stanley	$100,000			9.38%
PNC Absolute Return Fund	Mercantile Cap Advisors	$75,000	9.13%	5.27%	7.14%
PNC Alt. Strategies Fund	Mercantile Cap Advisors	$75,000	10.54%	5.39%	9.99%
PNC Long-Short Manager Fund	Mercantile Cap Advisors	$75,000	13.35%	3.91%	17.24%
NT Alpha Strategies Fund	Northern Trust Glob Adv	$10,000		2.78%	6.77%
Robeco Sage Multi-Strategy Fund	Robeco Alternatives	$100,000		1.47%	9.11%
SEI Opportunity Fund	SEI Investments	$25,000		5.06%	8.47%
Torrey International Strategy Partners	Torrey Associates	$100,000	15.64%	1.64%	21.02%
Torrey U.S. Strategy Partners	Torrey Associates	$100,000	20.73%	8.35%	14.85%
UBP Selectinvest 1.25	Union Bancaire Privee	$500,000	8.08%	8.34%	16.21%
STANDARD & POOR'S 500			35.12%	6.69%	11.72%

Source: Author.

as a whole tend to be middle of the road in performance. In other words, an index or large group of hedge funds tends not to go to extremes with very high or exceptionally low returns, as do many other asset classes. Real estate investment trusts, on the other hand, were ranked the top-performing asset class four out of the last 10 years as well as two of the ten-worst performers. Emerging market equities also tend to be volatile. During the last decade (1999–2008), hedge funds as a whole were neither a top nor bottom performer (Table 17.5). Taken separately, various hedge fund sectors behave differently. Hedge funds, in large numbers, act similar to a diversified group of nonalternative asset classes. Hedge funds have so many different styles today that one could achieve similar diversification as one holding foreign equities, domestic equities (large, mid, and small cap), cash, and fixed income. Twenty-plus years ago, Jack Coates replaced the Weyerhaeuser pension fund (consisting of stocks, bonds, and cash) with a 100% allocation to alternatives. In August 2000, *Pensions & Investments* selected his fund as the number one-performing pension manager in the United States over a 10-year period (for the period ended December 31, 1999). Mr. Coates understood the benefits of alternatives far earlier than most investors, who, at the time, knew very little about alternatives; it was more than 20 years ago when alternatives were not too well known like they are today. Mr. Coates knows how to surf alternative waves.

Table 17.5 The Wave Chart: 10-year Ranking of Asset Class Returns

Better Performing ⟶ Worse Performing (left axis)

1999	2000	2001	2002	2003	2004	2005	2006	2007	2008
EM Equity 66.40%	US REITs 26.40%	US REITs 13.90%	Real Assets 24.70%	EM Equity 56.30%	US REITs 31.60%	EM Equity 34.50%	US REITs 35.10%	EM Equity 39.80%	Managed Futures 14.10%
Developed Asia Equity 57.60%	US TIPS 13.20%	US Fixed Income 8.40%	Managed Futures 12.40%	Europe Equity 38.50%	EM Equity 26.00%	Private Equity 28.30%	Europe Equity 33.70%	Real Assets 31.00%	Real Assets 5.80%
Private Equity 34.80%	US Fixed Income 11.60%	US TIPS 11.80%	US TIPS 11.60%	Developed Asia Equity 38.50%	Private Equity 24.90%	Developed Asia Equity 22.60%	EM Equity 32.60%	Private Equity 20.50%	US Fixed Income 5.20%
Hedge Funds 31.30%	Managed Futures 7.95%	High Yield Bonds 5.80%	US Fixed Income 10.30%	US REITs 37.10%	Europe Equity 20.90%	Real Assets 17.90%	Private Equity 27.00%	Europe Equity 13.90%	US TIPS 2.40%
US Equity 21%	Hedge Funds 5.00%	Hedge Funds 4.60%	US REITs 3.60%	US Equity 29%	Developed Asia Equity 19.00%	US REITs 12.20%	Real Assets 23.20%	US TIPS 11.60%	Hedge Funds -19.00%
Europe Equity 15.90%	Private Equity 3.10%	Real Assets 2.10%	High Yield Bonds 2.10%	High Yield Bonds 27.90%	High Yield Bonds 12.00%	Europe Equity 9.40%	US Equity 16%	Hedge Funds 10.00%	Private Equity -22.70%
High Yield Bonds 3.90%	High Yield Bonds -4.20%	Managed Futures 0.80%	Hedge Funds -1.50%	Private Equity 23.40%	US Equity 11%	Hedge Funds 9.30%	Hedge Funds 12.90%	Managed Futures 7.60%	High Yield Bonds -26.20%
US TIPS 2.40%	Real Assets -6.70%	EM Equity -2.40%	EM Equity -6.00%	Hedge Funds 19.60%	Hedge Funds 9.00%	US Equity 5%	Developed Asia Equity 12.20%	US Fixed Income 7.00%	Developed Asia Equity -36.40%
Real Assets 0.50%	Europe Equity -8.40%	Private Equity -7.70%	Private Equity -7.70%	Real Assets 19.40%	US TIPS 8.50%	US TIPS 2.80%	High Yield Bonds 12.00%	US Equity 7%	US REITs -37.70%
US Fixed Income -0.80%	US Equity -9%	US Equity -12%	Developed Asia Equity -11.90%	US TIPS 9.4$	Real Assets 5.50%	US Fixed Income 2.40%	US Fixed Income 4.30%	Developed Asia Equity 5.30%	US Equity -38%
Managed Futures -1.20%	Developed Asia Equity -25.80%	Europe Equity -19.90%	Europe Equity -19.90%	Managed Futures 8.70%	US Fixed Income 4.30%	High Yield Bonds 2.30%	Managed Futures 3.50%	High Yield Bonds 2.70%	Europe Equity -46.40%
US REITs -4.60%	EM Equity -30.60%	Developed Asia Equity -25.40%	US Equity -25%	US Fixed Income 4.10%	Managed Futures 3.30%	Managed Futures 1.70%	US TIPS 0.40%	US REITs -15.70%	EM Equity -52.30%

Sources: Author. Cambridge Associates LLC; Russell Investments; Hedge Fund Research; Barclay Trading Group; U.S. Department of Agriculture; MSCI Barra; NAREIT Index; Cambridge Associates U.S. Private Equity Index; HFRI Fund Weighted Composite Hedge Fund Index; Barclay CTA (Commodity Trading Advisors) Index; Barclay Capital TIPS Index MSCI Emerging Markets Free Gross Index; Barclays Capital U.S. Aggregate (Taxable) Bond Index Credit Suisse High Yield Index; MSCI Pacific (Developed Asia) Net Index; S&P 500 Index; Handy & Harman Spot Gold Price.

Chapter 18

Hedge Fund
Investment Vehicles

Before making an investment in hedge funds, proper due diligence should be taken regardless of the type of vehicle selected. In other words, fraud can exist with hedge funds but also with hedge fund-of-funds, which are generally thought to be safer. Particular care should be exercised in due diligence of hedge funds because of the complex investment strategies they employ, the fact that hedge fund organizations are frequently new and not well established, their use of leverage and the associated risks, the possibilities of concentrated exposure to market and counterparty risks, and the generally more lightly regulated nature of these organizations.[1] Fraud is a major concern. A thorough review, however, can identify whether a fund manager is fabricating returns or generating excessive commissions. Due diligence is extremely important.

It takes a lot of time and practice hiring suitable hedge funds or hedge fund-of-funds. Attempting to find the best managers (whether they are hedge funds, separately managed accounts, or mutual funds) is no easy task. Some investors get intimidated asking a hedge fund manager questions. Surfers have an expression that one is "clucked" or afraid of waves. Do not be afraid. All investors are entitled to ask questions, providing they are reasonable. If one would rather hire an expert to perform due diligence, make sure they have done due diligence meetings before and have experience. Table 18.1 is a list of due diligence meetings that I had during the first quarter of 2009.

Table 18.1   Due Diligence Meetings

Aberdeen	First Trust	Mass Mutual	Pioneer
Allegiant	Ishares	Miller Howard	Prudential
Allianz	Legg Mason	Morgan Stanley	Revenue Shares
Fidelity	Lincoln	Nationwide	Robeco
First Eagle	Lord Abbett	Pacific Life	Van Eck Global

Source: Author.

If an investor does not wish to spend countless hours on hedge fund due diligence, it might be prudent to hire an advisor who specializes in alternative investments such as hedge funds.

After an interview with a hedge fund manager, a lengthy questionnaire is typically sent to the manager called the due diligence questionnaire (DDQ). For anyone with common sense, it should have risen a red flag when Bernard Madoff refused to divulge any information on his fund. If a hedge fund refuses to give basic information, it is not a good sign. One might experience what surfers refer to as the "washing machine," which means getting spun around and around underwater by a wave, such as happened with Madoff. Evasive hedge funds should be avoided.

Besides the questions asked in the DDQ, it is also important to do a background check on the hedge fund manager. Information on managers can be found in public databases such as Google, Bing, Yahoo, and LexisNexis. The basic advice from the U.S. Securities and Exchange Commission (SEC) on hedge fund due diligence is as follows:[2]

1. Read a fund's prospectus or offering memorandum and related materials.
2. Understand how a fund's assets are valued.
3. Ask questions about fees.
4. Understand any limitations on your right to redeem your shares.
5. Research the backgrounds of hedge fund managers.
6. Don't be afraid to ask questions.

Basically, any type of due diligence is better than no due diligence. Those who do no due diligence might be "worked," as surfers say. To get worked is to wipe out and be thrown around while simultaneously being held under water. Most respectable and responsible wealth managers develop their own questions to ask as part of the value they bring to clients. Over the years, I developed my own set of questions to ask managers as part of due diligence done on behalf of clients (see sidebar).

Alternative Investment Manager Due Diligence

Questions to ask:

1. Who runs your organization?
   - CEO name
   - Address of company or parent company
   - Phone number
   - E-mail address
   - Web site
   - History
   - Number of employees
   - Assets under management (AUM)
2. Is your organization public or private?
3. What is your investment strategy?
   - What kind of securities can your fund buy?
   - What area do you make investments (geographic location)?
   - Does your strategy include derivatives and what kind?
   - Do you use a benchmark? If so, which benchmark do you use?
   - What is your fund's objective?
   - How would you describe your style?
   - Do you use leverage?
4. Who runs your fund(s)?
   - Name(s) of portfolio managers
   - Educational background
   - Manager tenure

- Phone numbers
- Work experience

5. What is your organization's view on the economy?

6. Who are your biggest competitors?

7. What has been the performance of your fund as well as any other fund you offer?

8. What is your top-performing fund and how long has it been around?

9. What are the assets for each of your funds?

10. What are your fees?
    - Management fees
    - Sales charges
    - Incentive fees
    - Early redemption fees
    - Other fees
    - Do any of your investors receive preferential treatment?

11. What is your sell strategy?

12. What are the terms for your fund?
    - Lockup
    - Leverage
    - Hurdle rate
    - High-water mark
    - Coinvestment opportunities
    - Side letters

13. What kind of compliance or risk control do you have?

14. Operations
    - Who is your prime broker?
    - Which banks do you use for trades?
    - Who handles your legal work?
    - Who does your accounting work?

15. Administration

- Do you have a compliance officer?
- Do you carry liability insurance?
- How many offices do you have and where are they situated?
- What are your policies on employees purchasing securities for their own accounts?

Information to request:

1. Form ADV
2. Contact information
3. Organizational chart
4. Recent client statement and update (if available)
5. Institutional client list
6. Marketing materials
7. Fund's offering and subscription documents

If an investor elects not to use an advisor or consultant, he or she should be careful not to overdo it or be obsessed with hundreds of questions. It is one thing to ask useful questions; it is another to be burdensome or obnoxious. I recall a client spending months requesting so much information and asking so many questions that the hedge fund thought the inquisitive client might be working for a competitor. A happy medium of questions exists: one does not want to ask too many or too few questions. If a manager seems evasive and refuses to answer any reasonable questions, my advice is to run, do not walk. Run.

When evaluating hedge funds or hedge fund-of-funds, comparisons are useful, such as the Zephyr charts in Figures 18.1 and 18.2. Figure 18.1 compares the risk/return of hedge funds to indexes such as the S&P 500, while Figure 18.2 compares hedge funds with their peer group. The importance of such charts is to be aware of how your hedge fund is doing compared with other hedge funds. When selecting a hedge fund, one needs a basis for comparison. Among other things, Zephyr Associates provides performance comparisons to a fund's peer group as well as various indexes.

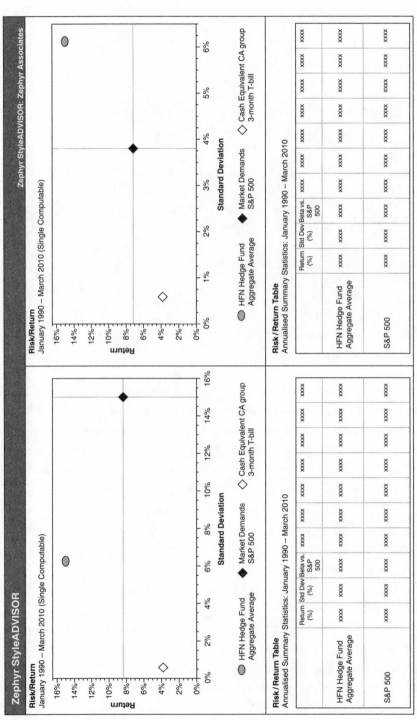

Figure 18.1 Manager Risk/Return

Source: Zephyr Associates Inc., www.styleadvisor.com/products/styleadvisor/hedge_funds.html (accessed August 1, 2008). Used with permission.

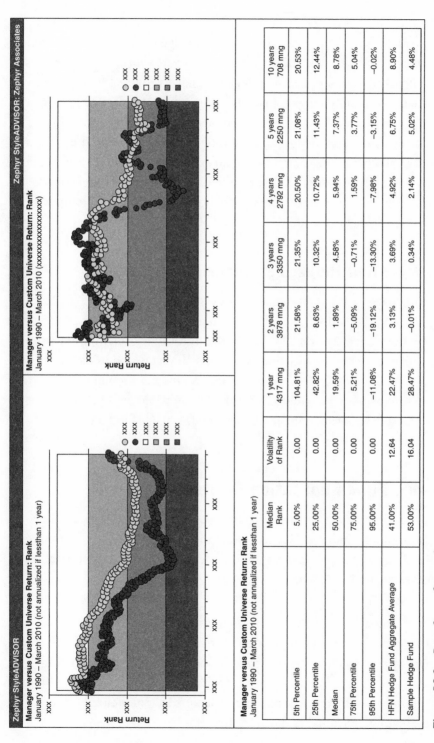

Figure 18.2 Peer Group Comparison

Source: Zephyr Associates Inc., www.styleadvisor.com/products/styleadvisor/hedge_funds.html (accessed August 1, 2008). Used with permission.

Other services besides Zephyr exist on the market. However, Zephyr is easy to use and extremely helpful. If one hires a hedge fund manager to invest in emerging markets, how did the manager compare with other hedge funds in general and other emerging markets managers (mutual funds, money managers, or other emerging markets hedge funds)? Table 18.2 features a list of the top-performing large hedge funds.

Besides individual hedge funds and hedge fund-of-funds, there are a number of indexes one can select to gain exposure to this asset class. Some companies offer investment opportunities, whereas others merely serve as a benchmark for an investor to compare how the asset class performs with a traditional asset class, such as the S&P 500.

Hedge Fund Indexes/Replication Strategies

Unlike many of the major equity indexes (Dow Jones, S&P 500, NAS-DAQ, or MSCI EAFE), there is no standard hedge fund index. Further, the performance reported by one hedge fund index might differ from another one. For example, if one examines a 10-year period using the HFR Weighted Composite Hedge Fund Index and the CS/Tremont HF Composite Index to see how hedge funds fared compared with the S&P 500, one can see significant differences between the hedge fund indexes, highlighted in Table 18.3.

Hedge Fund Replication Strategies

There are companies that mix various indexes to form their own synthetic or "replication" indexes. Hedge fund replication strategies aim to mimic returns of hedge funds, permitting easy access, liquidity, low correlation to other assets classes, and lower fees:

The synthetic replication of hedge fund indexes addresses some of the common overarching issues in the hedge fund space, including idiosyncratic manager risk, high fees, and the difficulty of separating true alpha from beta (and paying appropriately for both types of returns). But there are a number of factors to watch closely when evaluating individual replication strategies.[3]

Table 18.2 The World's Top Performing Large Hedge Funds

Fund, Manager(s)	Firm	Strategy	09 Return (%)	08 Return (%)
1 Appaloosa Investment, *David Tepper*	Appaloosa Mgmt, US	Global Credit	117.3	−26.7%
2 Redwood Capital Master, *Jonathan Kolatch*	Redwood Capital Mgmt., US	Distressed	69.1	−33.0
3 Glenview Institutional Partners, *Larry Robbins*	Glenview Capital Management, US	Long/Short	67.1	−49.0
4 PARS IV, *Changhong Zhu*	Pacific Investment Mgmt., US	Global Credit	61.0	−17.0
5 Tennenbaum Opportunities V, *TCP Investment Committee*	Tennenbaum Capital Partners, US	Credit	58.5	−51.2
6 Kensington Global Strategies, *Kenneth Griffin*	Citadel Investment Group, US	Multistrategy	57.0	−55.0
7 BlueGold Global, *Pierre Andurand, Dennis Crema*	BlueGold Capital Mgmt., UK	Commodities	54.6	209.4
8 Waterstone Market Neutral Master, *Shawn Bergerson*	Waterstone Capital Mgmt., US	Convertible arbitrage	50.3	12.0
9 Canyon Value Realization, *Mitchell Julis, Joshua Friedman*	Canyon Partners, US	Credit	49.6	−29.0
10 Discovery Global Opportunity, *Robert Citrone*	Discovery Capital Mgmt., US	Long/Short	47.9	−31.0
11 Bay Resource Partners, *Thomas Claugus*	GMT Capital Offshore Mgmt., US	Long/Short	44.7	−22.4
12 Tosca, *Martin Hughes*	Toscafund Asset Mgmt., UK	Long/Short	44.2	−65.0
13 Harbinger Capital Partners, *Phillip Falcone*	Harbinger Capital Partners, US	Multistrategy	42.0	−27.0
14 BlueCrest Capital International, *Michael Platt*	Bluecrest Capital Mgmt., US	Multistrategy	41.3	6.2
15 Lansdowne Global Financials, *William de Winton*	Lansdowne Partners, UK	Long/Short	41.0	−13.0
16 Medallion, *Jim Simons*	Renaissance Technologies, US	Quantitative	38.0	80.0
17 Brigade Leveraged Capital Structures, *Don Morgan*	Brigade Capital Mgmt., UK	Long/Short	37.6	−17.1
18 Brummer & Partners Nektar, *Kerim Kaskal, Kent Janer*	Nektar Asset Mgmt. Sweden	Fixed-Income arbitrage	37.2	−6.1
19 SR Global G-Emerging Markets, *Richard Chenevix-Trench*	Sloane Robinson Inv. Mgmt., UK	Emerging Market	36.5	−29.9
20 Stratus Double Leverage, *Marc Potters*	Capital Fund Mgmt. Intl., France	Multistrategy	36.1	16.3

Source: Richard Teitelbaum, "Bullish at the Brink," *Bloomberg Markets* (February 2010), 37. Used with permission.

Certain risks should be examined with any company offering strategies that involve short selling, derivatives, leverage, tracking error, and fees. Table 18.4 lists a number of relatively new hedge fund replication strategies that attempt to give investors the beta component of hedge fund universe similar to the HFRI Index.

Table 18.3 Hedge Fund Indices versus S&P 500

Year	Standard & Poor's 500 Index	HFR Fund Weighted Composite Hedge Fund Index	CS/Tremont HF Composite Index
1999	21.00%	31.30%	23.40%
2000	−9.10%	5.00%	4.80%
2001	−11.90%	4.60%	4.40%
2002	−22.10%	−1.50%	3.00%
2003	28.70%	19.60%	15.50%
2004	10.90%	9.00%	9.60%
2005	4.90%	9.30%	7.60%
2006	15.80%	12.90%	13.90%
2007	5.50%	10.00%	12.60%
2008	−37.00%	−18.30%	−19.10%

Source: Author.

Table 18.4 Hedge Fund Replication Strategies

Company	Security Name	Description	Ticker
IndexIQ	IQ Hedge Multi-Strategy Tracker ETF	Corresponds to price and yield performance of the IQ Hedge Multi-Strategy Index	QAI
Goldman Sachs	Goldman Sachs Absolute Return Tracker A	Seeks to achieve investment results that approximate the performance of the GS-ART index	GARTX
IndexIQ	IQ Hedge Macro Tracker ETF	Corresponds generally to the price and yield performance of the IQ Hedge Macro Index	MCRO
Natixis	Natixis ASG Global Altnernatives A	Seeks to capital appreciation consistent with the return and risk characteristics of a diversified portfolio of hedge funds	GAFAX

Company	Security Name	Description	Ticker
Highbridge	Highbridge Statistical Mkt Neutral-A	Seeks to provide long-term returns in all market environments from a broadly diversified portfolio of stocks while neutralizing the general risks associated with stock market investing	HSKAX
Rydex	Rydex Multi-Hedge Strategies A	Pursues multiple investment styles or mandates that correspond to investment strategies widely employed by hedge funds	RYMQX
ING	ING Alternative Beta Fund	Seeks to deliver investment results that approximate the return and risk characteristics of the broad universe of hedge funds	IABAX

Source: Author.

Hedge Fund Indices

The following pages profile select hedge fund indices and provide historical data on each of them.

Barclays Hedge Fund Indices

Barclays has created 18 proprietary hedge fund indices, detailed in Table 18.5.

Hennessee Hedge Fund Indices

The Hennessee Hedge Fund Advisory Group has been around since 1987. The company assists clients with direct hedge fund investing. Clients of Hennessee Group LLC have direct investments in 100 hedge funds. The Hennessee Hedge Fund Indices are calculated from performance data reported to the Hennessee Hedge Fund Advisory Group by a diversified group of hedge funds. The Hennessee Hedge Fund Index is an equally weighted average of the funds in the Hennessee Hedge Fund Indices. The funds in the Hennessee Hedge Fund Index are believed to be statistically representative of the larger Hennessee Universe, currently consisting of over 3,500 hedge funds and are net of fees and unaudited. They use four main indices: Hennessee Hedge Fund Index, Long/Short Equity Index, Arbitrage/Event Driven Index and Global/Macro.

The 10-year annual performance for the Hennessee Hedge Fund Index and the three major substrategies is shown in Table 18.6.

Table 18.5 Barclays Hedge Fund Indices

	April ROR	Number of Funds Reporting	YTD through April
INDEX			
Barclays Hedge Fund Index	1.31%	2,097	4.58%
Hedge Fund Industry Money Under Management			
SUB INDICES			
Convertible Arbitrage Index	2.10%	29	5.10%
Distressed Securities Index	2.73%	50	9.44%
Emerging Markets Index	1.36%	340	5.30%
Equity Long Bias Index	1.84%	257	5.53%
Equity Long/Short Index	1.08%	415	3.42%
Equity Market Neutral Index	0.21%	82	0.96%
Equity Short Bias Index	−5.28%	7	−10.64%
European Equities Index	0.11%	108	2.40%
Event Driven Index	1.51%	82	5.93%
Fixed Income Arbitrage Index	1.53%	30	5.31%
Fund of Funds Index	0.92%	1,057	2.37%
Global Macro Index	0.53%	123	1.50%
Healthcare & Biotechnology Index	−0.15%	23	5.52%
Merger Arbitrage Index	0.30%	16	2.29%
Multi Strategy Index	1.10%	66	4.52%
Pacific Rim Equities Index	1.62%	56	5.06%

Source: Barclays, *Barclays Hedge Fund Indices* (December 31, 2008). Used with permission.

Table 18.6 Annual Performance Return for Hennessee Hedge Fund Indices

	Hennessee Hedge Fund Index	Hennessee Long/Short Equity Index	Hennessee Arbitrage/Event Driven Index	Hennessee Global/Macro Index
2009	25.21%	21.69%	31.51%	24.40%
2008	−19.84%	−18.64%	−20.59%	−20.57%
2007	11.22%	11.79%	7.36%	14.89%
2006	11.40%	11.09%	12.29%	10.53%

	Hennessee Hedge Fund Index	Hennessee Long/Short Equity Index	Hennessee Arbitrage/Event Driven Index	Hennessee Global/Macro Index
2005	7.85%	6.78%	5.22%	14.23%
2004	8.24%	7.78%	8.49%	8.70%
2003	18.80%	19.45%	13.85%	27.56%
2002	−2.88%	−6.46%	2.15%	−1.44%
2001	4.36%	2.89%	8.98%	1.52%
2000	8.16%	10.21%	9.49%	1.34%

Source: Hennessee Group LLC. Used with permission.

HFRX Indices

Hedge Fund Research, Inc., is the leading provider of data and analysis of the hedge fund industry. They provide a wealth of information on the hedge fund industry with two primary groups of indices and many sub-categories. According to their Web site (https://www.hedgefundresearch.com/ index.php?fuse=indices):

> The HFRI Monthly Indices ("HFRI") are a series of benchmarks designed to reflect hedge fund industry performance by constructing equally weighted composites of constituent funds, as reported by the hedge fund managers listed within HFR Database. The HFRI range in breadth from the industry-level view of the HFRI Fund Weighted Composite Index, which encompasses over 2000 funds, to the increasingly specific-level of the sub-strategy classifications.
>
> The HFRX Indices ("HFRX") are a series of benchmarks of hedge fund industry performance which are engineered to achieve representative performance of a larger universe of hedge fund strategies. Hedge Fund Research, Inc. ("HFR, Inc.") employs the HFRX Methodology, a proprietary and highly *quantitative* process by which hedge funds are selected as constituents for the HFRX Indices. This methodology includes robust classification, cluster analysis, correlation analysis, advanced optimization and Monte Carlo simulations.

Table 18.7 is a screenshot from the HFRX Web site that display the indices and returns.

Table 18.7 HFRX™ Global and Strategy Indices

| HFRX Index | Daily – 12/30/2008 | | | | Nov-08 | 2007 | 2006 | 2005 | 2004 | 2003 |
	DTD	MTD	YTD	Value	ROR	TOTAL	TOTAL	TOTAL	TOTAL	TOTAL
HFRX Global Hedge Fund Index	0.0668	−1.0221	−23.0974	1022.57	−3.04	4.23	9.26	2.72	2.69	13.39
HFRX Equal Weighted Strategies Index	0.1449	−1.1436	−21.4688	1003.59	−2.73	3.97	8.83	1.28	2.72	11.32
HFRX Absolute Return Index	−0.0454	−1.1839	−12.0301	1033.22	−1.78	6.68	7.43	−0.03	3.20	11.95
HFRX Market Directional Index	0.0152	−3.1396	−29.7522	889.96	−5.15	5.28	10.45	4.20	4.85	25.22
HFRX Convertible Arbitrage Index	0.0539	−5.2521	−58.1530	438.46	−10.50	−0.95	9.57	−5.69	−0.14	8.85
HFRX Distressed Securities Index	−0.1562	−5.1608	−27.6220	1047.76	−6.15	3.99	9.56	1.21	8.95	20.90
HFRX Equity Hedge Index	−0.1733	−2.0449	−25.7209	999.62	−2.49	3.21	9.23	4.19	2.18	14.47
HFRX Equity Market Neutral Index	−0.1012	−1.6644	−0.6887	1047.88	0.69	3.11	4.76	0.21	0.32	−2.38
HFRX Event Driven Index	0.4633	−1.0604	−22.3294	1152.97	−2.74	4.88	10.32	2.81	6.93	18.47
HFRX Macro Index	−0.1311	3.7979	6.1658	1374.65	1.48	3.19	5.61	6.67	−0.32	14.61
HFRX Merger Arbitrage Index	0.7493	1.8855	3.3632	1330.72	1.57	4.85	10.73	3.72	2.80	4.26
HFRX Relative Value Arbitrage Index	0.4063	−2.6932	−37.5573	789.06	−7.91	5.80	10.65	−0.97	1.98	9.15

Source: "HFRX Indices—Index Descriptions," Hedge Fund Research, Inc., http://www.hedgefundresearch.com/index.php?fuse=hfrx_strats&1267599608 (accessed August 1, 2008). Used with permission.

Credit Suisse/Tremont Hedge Fund Index

Credit Suisse is a large, reputable bank in Switzerland that is known for its prowess with alternative investments including hedge funds. The Credit Suisse/Tremont Hedge Fund Index is asset weighted. Also, it uses the Credit Suisse/Tremont database, which tracks more than 5,000 funds. Both open and closed funds located in the United States and offshore are included, but it does not include fund-of-funds. It is the first asset-weighted hedge fund index in the industry, and unlike equal weighting, it provides a more accurate description of an investment within the asset class.[4] The funds are separated into 10 main subcategories. Credit Suisse/Tremont evaluates the percentage of assets invested in each individual subcategory and chooses the funds for the index based on those percentages "matching the shape of the index to the shape of the universe."[5] Figure 18.3 displays the weights for each subindex.

Greenwich Global Hedge Fund Index

Greenwich Alternative Investments (GAI) offers GAI Global HF Index, GAI Investable HF Index, and the GAIN HF Replicator Index. This index has been published since 1995 and is considered one of the oldest.

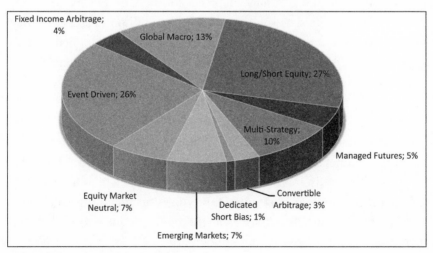

Figure 18.3 All Hedge Index Weights

Source: "AllHedge Indexes," Credit Suisse,
www.hedgeindex.com/hedgeindex/en/weights.aspx?ChartType=PieChart&cy=USD&indexname=SECT
(accessed August 1, 2008).

It reflects a broad hedge fund universe. The index is calculated from hedge funds that report to the GAI database, which includes approximately 7,000 funds and 1,550 defunct funds.[6]

Table 18.8 is directly from the GAI Web site. It indicates the total returns for March and April 2010, and the weights for 2010 are given.

MSCI Investable Hedge Fund Indices

Designed to mirror the overall structure and composition of a distinct hedge fund opportunity set, the strategies within these indices are weighted by accounting for their weights in the hedge fund universe.[7] MSCI provides approximately 190 indices with more than 3,000 hedge funds. MSCI also offers equal-weighted indices versus asset-weighted indices. Table 18.9 shows the indices' recent performances according to each individual strategy.

Alternative Funds

Alternative mutual funds that are liquid, regulated, easy to track, and have low minimums will attract new investors. Even in bad markets, these types of alternative mutual funds tend to attract assets. According to Morningstar, as of August 2009, alternative mutual funds had $41.3 billion in assets, and investors invested more money each year for the past 5 years, including 2008, when shareholders sold more than $100 billion of shares of their stock funds.[8] The wide array of investment options in 2010 for hedge funds gives investors the option to select between illiquid, hard-to-track, high-minimum, unregulated hedge funds or alternative mutual funds (a hedge fund–type of mutual fund or replication strategy) that are liquid, easy to track, have low minimums, and are regulated. Although options exist for investors to select between these, it might be a bad idea to force hedge funds to become as regulated as mutual funds. The concept of a hedge fund, in other words, might be diluted to the point to which there will be no difference from that of a mutual fund. Investors might ultimately lose.

A January 2010 article in the *Economist* reinforced the notion that alternative mutual funds are growing in popularity:

Hedge-fund managers have offered mutual funds before. The first wave came back in 2005, according to Nadia Papagiannis of

Table 18.8 Greenwich Alternative Investments (GAI)

| | 8/28/10 | | | | | | | | |
| | Total Return | | | | | 3-Yr Annualized | | 5-Yr Annualized | |
	Apr-14	Mar-14	YTD	3 Month	1 Year	CAR	STD	CAR	STD
Greenwich Strategy Group Indices									
Greenwich Global Hedge Fund Index	1.10%	2.70%	3.70%	4.50%	19.40%	3.40%	8.10%	7.20%	6.80%
Market Neutral Group	1.20%	1.70%	4.30%	3.50%	19.10%	3.60%	6.20%	6.50%	5.10%
Equity Market Neutral	0.30%	0.60%	1.40%	1.40%	4.90%	1.50%	3.70%	4.30%	3.20%
Event-Driven	2.00%	2.60%	6.60%	5.50%	29.10%	4.50%	8.10%	8.10%	6.60%
Distressed Securities	2.70%	3.00%	8.30%	5.90%	33.00%	1.60%	9.10%	6.70%	7.40%
Merger Arbitrage	0.10%	1.10%	2.60%	2.10%	8.80%	3.40%	4.40%	6.60%	3.90%
Diversified Event-Driven	2.60%	2.90%	7.30%	6.90%	32.90%	6.90%	9.00%	9.40%	7.30%
Arbitrage	1.30%	1.50%	4.40%	3.30%	21.00%	4.60%	7.20%	6.70%	5.70%
Convertible Arbitrage	3.00%	2.70%	6.60%	6.20%	37.60%	0.20%	16.70%	4.30%	13.00%
Other Arbitrage	1.00%	−0.40%	1.30%	1.00%	11.60%	4.70%	5.20%	7.30%	4.20%
Fixed Income Arbitrage	0.50%	1.50%	4.50%	2.70%	23.20%	5.50%	7.00%	6.60%	5.50%
Long-Short Equity Group	1.10%	3.60%	4.40%	5.70%	23.20%	2.10%	10.50%	7.40%	8.90%
Growth	1.00%	4.80%	5.00%	7.00%	28.00%	1.40%	13.40%	7.00%	11.30%
Opportunistic	0.90%	2.70%	5.30%	4.20%	19.70%	4.50%	8.90%	9.70%	8.00%
Short-Biased	−0.60%	−3.40%	−3.70%	−4.90%	−14.20%	5.80%	12.50%	0.70%	11.30%
Value	1.40%	3.50%	5.00%	5.90%	24.70%	10.90%	12.10%	20.10%	14.10%
Directional Trading Group	0.90%	2.30%	1.80%	3.90%	5.90%	7.60%	6.20%	8.00%	5.90%
Futures	1.00%	2.70%	1.50%	4.50%	3.60%	9.40%	8.40%	8.90%	8.10%
Macro	0.70%	1.50%	2.40%	2.80%	10.00%	5.30%	5.60%	6.80%	4.80%
Specialty Strategies Group	1.20%	1.90%	3.80%	3.30%	26.90%	3.70%	11.70%	8.80%	9.70%
Long-Short Credit	1.50%	2.10%	5.30%	4.00%	23.70%	4.60%	6.40%	6.30%	5.00%
Multi-Strategy	0.90%	1.80%	2.90%	2.90%	16.30%	4.00%	7.10%	8.10%	6.20%

Source: "About Us," Greenwich Alternative Investments, www.greenwichai.com/index.php?option5com_content&view5article&id531&Itemid59((accessed August 1, 2008). Used with permission.

Table 18.9 MSCI Hedge Invest Indices (as of December 30, 2008)

Index Name	Official Weekly Index Level (USD)	Daily Indicative Index Level (USD)	Daily	WTD	MTD	Since YTD	Inception
MSCI Hedge Invest Index	9367.92	9367.92	0.00%	0.09%	−1.74%	−25.59%	−6.32%
Convertible Arbitrage	6832.85	6832.85	−0.78%	0.00%	1.13%	−37.69%	−31.67%
Discretionary Trading	10156.51	10156.51	−0.35%	0.00%	−0.03%	−12.47%	1.57%
Equity Non−Directional	10803.42	10803.42	0.28%	0.00%	−2.61%	−14.13%	8.03%
Event Driven	11057.45	11057.45	−0.20%	0.00%	1.33%	−15.55%	10.57%
Fixed Income	6578.61	6578.61	0.03%	0.00%	−4.91%	−39.74%	−34.21%
Long Bias	9273.05	9273.05	−0.01%	0.00%	−2.24%	−36.27%	−7.27%
Systematic Trading	12446.10	12446.10	−0.06%	0.00%	1.41%	1.36%	24.46%
Variable Bias	11156.06	11156.06	−0.05%	0.00%	−0.28%	−17.52%	11.56%

Source: "Hedge Fund Indices," MSCI, www.mscibarra.com/resources/pdfs/HFI_faq.pdf (accessed January 15, 2009).

Morningstar, a research firm, when infatuation with hedge funds was near its peak. Managers offered mutual funds as a way to include individuals without the cash to invest in hedge funds themselves. Investors now seem hungry for products that shield them from market swings, as alternative strategies should, but that lack hedge funds' most infuriating traits. Mutual funds have neither lockups nor fees of one-fifth of profits. Complaints about a lack of transparency are countered by mutual funds' reporting requirements. Fears of illiquidity and leverage are calmed by mutual funds' rules on both. American alternative mutual funds were wildly popular in 2009. New flows from January to November reached $11.2 billion, nearly quadruple those for all of 2008.[9]

Besides mutual fund companies, hedge funds themselves are now offering alternative mutual funds so investors can make a decision as to which is most appropriate for them. One example, reported by the the *Wall Street Journal*, is AQR Capital Management LLC, which is described as being "among the first big hedge funds for mom-and-pop investors." AQR raised "more than $1 billion in assets in less than a year," positioning themselves as "a potential challenge to the struggling mutual fund industry."[10]

Morningstar classifies four different types of mutual funds that use hedge fund strategy: currency, long-short, precious metals, and bear market. Excluding redundancies and different share classes, Morningstar listed 75 long-short funds, 9 currency funds, 42 precious metal funds, and 46 bear market funds as of January 30, 2009. Mutual funds that use hedge fund strategies are even appearing in national magazines and newspapers alongside regular mutual funds. Alternative mutual funds are basically mutual funds with hedge fund characteristics. For example, Aberdeen Equity Long-Short Fund seeks "long-term capital appreciation," as do many regular mutual funds. However, the strategy involves "complex securities transactions, such as short-selling, leverage, and investing in derivatives, which may cause the Fund to have greater risk and volatility."[11] Unlike hedge funds, alternative mutual funds have very low minimums and—in some cases, are only a $2,000 minimum investment. Table 18.10 lists the best-performing long/short funds in 2006 and 2008.

Table 18.10 Best-Performing-Long/Short Funds

	2006				2008		
Fund	1-year Return	3-year Return	5-year return	Fund	1-year Return	3-year Return	5-year return
Analytic Global Long/Short	13.40%	10.30%	9.60%	GMO Alpha Only III	12.30%	7.80%	6.00%
Calamos Market Neutral A	8.40%	3.70%	5.50%	JPMorgan Market Neutral I	0.80%	5.70%	3.30%
Diamond Hill Long-Short A	16.90%	18.40%	12.80%	Merger	0.80%	3.20%	2.80%
Gateway	10.10%	7.20%	5.50%	Arbitrage I	0.60%	4.10%	2.60%
Hussman Strategic Growth	3.50%	4.80%	9.70%	JPMorgan Multi-Cap Market	-0.30%	1.50%	2.50%
James Market Neutral	-0.40%	5.30%	4.10%	Virtus Market Neutral A	-2.90%	-3.80%	-1.40%
Laudus Rosenberg Global Long/Short	3.20%	3.90%	5.70%	Caldwell & Orkin Market Opportunity	-3.20%	10.50%	6.00%
Laudus Rosenberg U.S. Large/Mid Long/Short	6.80%	7.00%	5.60%	James Market Neutral	-4.90%	-0.40%	3.10%
Merger	11.00%	4.70%	3.80%	Vanguard Market Neutral I	-6.40%	2.50%	4.80%
Templeton Global Long Short A	14.40%	7.30%	6.20%	Hussman Strategic Growth	-7.60%	-0.90%	1.60%

Source: Author.

Morningstar, as of December 31, 2008, had 87 long-short funds in its database. Unlike hedge funds, these funds offer daily liquidity and do not have lockups. Quite a few banks have introduced alternative mutual funds with hedge fund strategies. For example, Deutsche Bank Group offers the DWS Disciplined Market Neutral Fund. According to Deutsche Bank, a market-neutral strategy offers the following benefits: "low correlation to traditional asset classes to aid portfolio diversification, potential for higher returns with low volatility, and potential to improve risk/return characteristics when added to a portfolio."[12]

But buyers of mutual funds that attempt to emulate hedge funds need to be cognizant of the risks. For instance, many of the 130/30 mutual funds that invest mainly in U.S. stocks fell more than the S&P 500 in 2008.[13] A 130/30 strategy means an investor is long 130% and short 30% to have 100% exposure to the market. Similar to hedge funds, 130/30 mutual funds can utilize leverage. Leverage works in good markets, but downturns can quickly magnify steep losses.

The *Wall Street Journal* feature on January 24–25, 2009, asked and answered the question: "How do 130/30 funds work? For every $100 invested, the fund will borrow stocks valued at $30 to sell 'short' and invest this cash raised in the market, thus making the gross investment equal to $130."[14]

Separately Managed Accounts

Technically, a separately managed account is not a hedge fund. As author Joseph Nicholas explained it, "it is a method for accessing the investment talents of hedge fund managers. Rather than investing in an existing fund, an investor can place assets in a separate account and hire a hedge fund manager as an investment advisor to trade on a discretionary basis."[15]

Depending on the hedge fund company or manager, separately managed accounts may or may not be available. Not all hedge funds offer separately managed accounts. Multiple separate accounts are difficult to manage. As a result, the hedge funds that offer those accounts typically have very high minimums starting at $3 to $5 million.

The Hybrid Hedge

While it is not a security nor readily available, there is a new method of investing in a vehicle similar to a hedge fund which I have nicknamed the hybrid hedge. The hybrid hedge combines many of the positive attributes of both of the mutual fund industry and the hedge fund industry. A hybrid hedge can be viewed as an investment platform that provides the performance of a hedge fund with the transparency of a mutual fund. Hypothetically, an investor could own the same equities that hedge funds buy with such a vehicle as the hybrid hedge. Hedge funds buy and sell a lot of equities. Investors can purchase these same names. Hedge funds have purchased a lot of large-cap growth stocks during the Great Recession. As of 6/30/09, hedge funds owned names that any investor could purchase, such as Apple, Pfizer, Walgreen Company, Hewlett-Packard, Microsoft, Wal-Mart, or Monsanto. Hedge funds' biggest negatives are a lack of transparency, daily liquidity, performance tracking, high price tag, and lack of regulation. The hybrid hedge fund combines the best of both hedge funds and mutual funds, as laid out in Table 18.11.

Conclusion

My sentiment toward hedge funds has changed very little over the last 15 to 20 years. Hedge funds are a viable asset class and a means of diversifying, but investors must really do their homework. It is not easy to identify the

Table 18.11

	Hedge Funds	Hybrid Hedge Funds	Mutual Funds
Transparency	No	Yes	Yes
Daily Liquidity	No	Yes	Yes
Performance Tracking (daily, weekly)	No	Yes	Yes
Regulated	No	Yes	Yes
Broad Diversification	No	Yes	No
Cost Effectiveness	No	Yes	No
Flexibility	Yes	Yes	No
Expanded investment universe	Yes	Yes	No
Increased risk adjusted portfolio performance	Yes	Yes	No

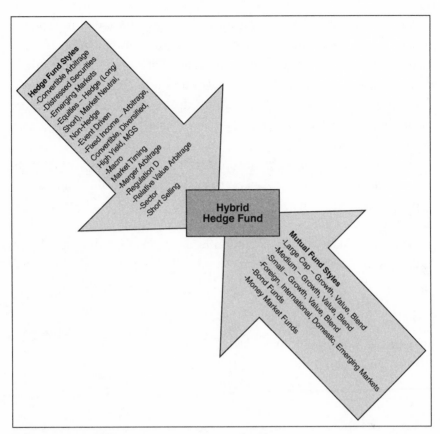

Figure 18.4 Hybrid Hedge Funds
Source: Author.

next "rock star" hedge fund manager, let alone select a hedge fund-of-funds one can implicitly trust. The hedge fund space has improved over the years but is not perfect. Because the industry is unregulated, it attracts scamsters like Bernie Madoff who prey on innocent investors. Madoff's deceptive ways not only bamboozled many high-net-worth individuals but also institutional investors and hedge fund-of-funds.

Hedge funds performed quite well during the equity downturn in 2000, 2001, and 2002, different from the lackluster results in 2008. If one believed all the negative news, investors might be inclined to sell their hedge funds. The general sentiment toward hedge funds (because of Bernie Madoff's large-scale ponzi scheme and other negative news) was extremely negative early in 2009, but hedge funds did well the first quarter of 2009. While the S&P 500 experienced a 12% decline, hedge funds recorded gains of 52 basis points during the same tumultuous period.[16] Hedge funds experienced a number of unusual complications during 2008. The most devastating event was the credit market shutting down. Because of the credit crisis, banks ended up hurting many hedge funds. Banks cut back lending to hedge funds during the latter part of 2008. A number of hedge funds even had difficulty withdrawing their funds from banks as they collpased.

The investment firm Lehman Brothers also caused hedge funds problems because it was a prime broker (in the business of lending money and securities to hedge funds). *Bloomberg Markets* described the linkage between the two, noting "[w]hen some funds learned that money they had parked at Lehman was now frozen in legal proceedings, they decided to pull cash and assets from Morgan Stanley."[17] There was a concern that other investment firms might follow Lehman. Figure 18.5 demonstrates the functions of a prime broker.

Large banks (Citigroup, JPMorgan, and others) and, at the same time, investment firms (Goldman Sachs, Morgan Stanley, Lehman, Bear Stearns, and others) all served as prime brokers for hedge funds. If you are a hedge fund and you lose your prime broker, you have problems. It is

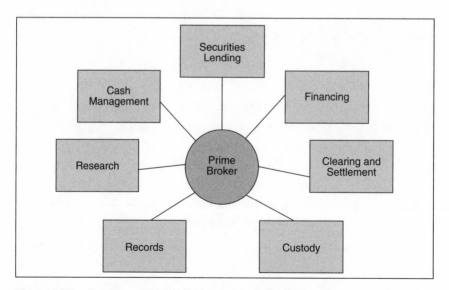

Figure 18.5 Functions of a Prime Broker for Hedge Funds

Source: Author.

similar to being a surfer and losing your surfboard. Hedge funds dealt with a variety of firms such as Lehman Brothers, which collapsed.

There was also a government-imposed ban on shorting, which adversely affected hedge funds. Hedge funds can short securities and frequently do so, as their name implies. Restricting this ability is tantamount to hand-cuffing someone and asking them to swim after you push them off a boat into the ocean. Restrictions on short selling render obsolete one of the most important defensive tools in many hedge fund arsenals.[18] There is nothing inherently wrong with shorting but there should be more guidelines; shorting should be allowed but regulated. There is risk to shorting that is different from going long or owning a security.

One can also have a naked short in which a security (that you do not own) is sold. A naked short is riskier than just shorting (selling) a stock that you own. According to JPMorgan, "When a stock is owned outright any losses are limited to its purchase price. When a stock is shorted, potential losses theoretically have no limit, since it must eventually be returned to the lender at whatever price it is currently trading for."[19]

Unfortunately, malicious people or groups spread rumors and sold short financial companies, including Morgan Stanley, to profit. The short sellers in these circumstances were not hedge funds. Unfairly, Morgan Stanley's stock plummeted and hit $6.71 a share on October 10, 2008. Sitting on the edge of my chair in dire suspense, fielding calls from panic stricken investors, wondering if Morgan Stanley would go under, I grinded my teeth so hard I cracked a tooth and ultimately needed a root canal. On the way to the dentist, my mother called and asked if Morgan Stanley was in trouble. The concern or fear, at the time, was that Morgan Stanley would end up like Lehman.

All of these negative factors in the market helped hedge funds have a dismal return when the U.S. government banned short selling. The short selling ban covered approximately 1000 different companies. The relevance is not why or should a government ban short selling; rather, government involvement is a possibility that every investor needs to be cognizant of when investing in alternatives. Investors should weigh all risks when buying alternatives. Some are known; others are unforseen.

It is true that hedge funds declined in number and lost assets. Hedge funds use leverage, and they deleveraged during this time. Removing leveraged assets will show a drop in value. Investors pulling money out also reduces assets. Hedge fund managers are well compensated, but the stress is unbearable for most individuals despite, the potential to make a lot of money. As a result, a number of hedge fund managers, such as Jeff Vinik, retired early. Stress can kill you. The year 2008 caused some 2,000 hedge funds to shut down.

Despite all these calamities, hedge funds did relatively well. Hedge funds lost money, and so did numerous other investment vehicles. Indexes or mutual funds also dropped in value. Even with an average loss of −18.30% (HFR Index), hedge funds did far better than domestic equities (S&P 500 −37.0%) or foreign equities (−43.4% MSCI EAFE Net Index) for 2008. Given the curve balls that hedge funds were thrown in 2008, one could easily argue they did their job and did it well.

The hedge fund world remains difficult to navigate. However, for those fortuitous enough, the risk:reward ratio is compelling. Even if one is an experienced investor with hedge funds, there is always room to learn more. Many institutions and savvy investors have been burned with hedge funds. Like experienced surfers who are adept enough to navigate a barrel (where the wave is hollow when breaking), it takes practice. Fortunately, there are plenty of new investment vehicles that do not require tens of millions to invest but rather have minimums as low as $2,000.

As I forecasted at an alternatives event, "Sizing Up a Hedge," on September 19, 2006, at The Merion Cricket Club in Haverford, Pennsylvania, "Hedge funds will become more mutual fund–like over time" and "Mutual funds will become more hedge fund like over time." Early pioneer Deutsche Bank introduced the DWS Disciplined Market Neutral Fund. They were also among the first to offer a mutual fund version of a hedge fund-of-funds, the DWS Alternative Asset Allocation Plus Fund. Besides alternative mutual funds, hedge fund replication indexes will also be appealing to investors. Similar to mutual funds with hedge fund strategies, the indexes have similar features, such as liquidity or performance tracking.

Presently, one of the biggest threats to hedge funds and investing in these funds is excessive government regulation. Similar to other alternatives, government involvement is needed only in moderation. A number of tentative proposals are being explored that might adversely affect the hedge fund industry and could ultimately harm investors. The Registration Act of 2009 essentially recommends forcing any and all managers with more than $30 million in assets to register with the SEC. At first glance, the overhaul of the hedge fund industry by the government might seem like a good idea to the average investor. However, it might be bad for investors. If there is some hedge fund regulation, it might be beneficial for all parties involved. However, too much will most likely be bad for investors, and one should be cognizant of how increased regulations might affect hedge funds as a whole as well as individual styles of hedge fund investing. Excessive government regulation will most likely result in hedge funds setting up operations abroad. Another likely scenario is that many of the most successful funds, in which the managers are already very wealthy, will close their doors or just manage their own money going forward—that is, the most successful hedge fund managers do not need new investors.

The government is also exploring imposing taxes on carried interest from its current rate of 15% to the 35% tax level applied to ordinary income.[20] At first blush, this might seem like a good idea, but what happens when the hedge funds pack up and move overseas to countries like Switzerland, as they did under similar circumstances in the U.K.? One of London's most successful hedge funds, Blue Crest, announced a new office in Geneva. While this opening of a new office might have been a coincidence, it should be interesting to see if a trend develops and hedge funds leave London. Increased taxes will most likely result in either hedge funds closing or leaving the United States for a more conducive environment. There is no doubt there have been a handful of unethical, nefarious, iniquitous, self-absorbed, maniac hedge fund managers who tainted an otherwise respectable industry. But financial reform should not be excessive.

Investors need to be aware of all risk factors (such as government change or regulation) when investing in hedge funds or any other alternative investment. Regardless of one's political beliefs, government regulation can affect alternative investments, especially hedge funds. And what red flag might an investor in hedge funds look for in order to tell if change by a government (anywhere) is forthcoming? The wonderful thing about hedge funds is that they can make money in virtually any environment. A good hedge fund manager will adapt for the times. Appaloosa amply demonstrated this fact as well as many other hedge funds that bought bank shares at the absolute bottom of the market. The remarkable thing is that these hedge funds found a way to make money even when their own industry (finance) looked as though it was going into an abyss. Ironically, the same hedge funds that are in the limelight with the U.S. government are the same group that actually saved the United States from a financial collapse. Hedge funds and leveraged buyout firms bought shares of troubled banks themselves, distressed assets of banks, or U.S. government securities. One of the best-performing hedge funds of 2009, Appaloosa Management LP, went long on various bank, insurance, and other securities that the U.S. government was trying to revive. Appaloosa bought various securities in Bank of America, Citigroup, Fifth Third Bancorp, Sun Trust Bank, AIG, and others, which also led to a gain of $1 billion for the hedge funds' investors.[21] Appaloosa's David Tepper correctly called that banks would not be nationalized. Without Tepper and other hedge funds' assistance, the United States might have entered into another Depression. Large banks would have toppled over like a game of dominos if it were not for hedge funds. Hedge funds were the heroes, not the villains in this regard. If financial reform goes through, hedge fund investors need to examine whether or not that will be good for the particular hedge fund they own. How will the landscape change? How will their hedge fund be affected?

Trends to Occur with Hedge Funds

Financial Darwinism

Because of the way hedge funds are compensated (typically a "2% + 20%" rule), two things are likely to happen. First, the number of players on the hedge fund playing field will decrease. Financial Darwinism has a way of weeding out the good from the bad. Sixty percent or so of all hedge funds have less than $100 million in assets. These smaller players or funds will have no incentive fee until they make up losses. The result of many of these firms not being able to make money is that they will close. Any hedge fund that cannot make money will close regardless of size. For example, Cantillon Capital Management closed in 2009. Because of the method hedge funds use to charge investors, back-to-back negative years can be harmful to them. Besides compensation issues, excessive government regulation in the hedge fund space might have unforeseen consequences and could possibly destroy many of the smaller hedge funds; increased legal and accounting expenses will be extremely costly and burdensome for smaller hedge funds. The biannual AR New Funds Survey published in the February issue of AR magazine reported that assets raised by hedge fund start-ups in 2009 fell 36 % to $15 billion from the previous year.[22] Smaller hedge funds will most likely either sell to larger ones, move off-shore, struggle or go out of business. Years ago, the Sarbanes-Oxley Act was harmful to the venture capital world and investors. The proposed financial reform plan would most likely hurt hedge funds (as well as other private equity managers). The threat of too much government regulation with hedge funds might have an effect similar to Sarbanes-Oxley and the venture capital world: it might cause more harm than good. The investor (especially individuals) will probably be hurt the most.

Reasonable Fees

Another possible trend, one might see a trend of more reasonable fees with hedge funds. There probably will not be too many hedge funds charging egregious 5% annual fees andtaking 50% of the upside. Institutional investors would be foolish not to attempt to lower the excessively high fees that certain hedge funds demanded in the past with a take-it-or-leave-it mentality. Hedge funds, especially those with high fees and poor per-formance, might not be able to demand such onerous terms like not allow-ing investors to leave. According to the *Wall Street Journal*, "CalPERS, the California public pension fund that is one of the biggest investors in hedge funds, is demanding better terms from funds, including lower prices and 'clawbacks' of fees if performance weakens."[23]

Reduced Lockups

Hedge fund lockups used to go out many years but over time they have gradually been reduced. That trend is likely to continue although it serves a purpose and lockups will remain in existence. Hedge funds need time sometimes to deploy a strategy and do not want cash moving in and out of their fund on a short-term basis like a mutual fund.

No Gating

Preventing withdrawals or "gating" is somewhat frowned upon in the hedge fund industry. It is similar to a surfer being "caught inside" (when a surfer is too far in and the waves are breaking further out); you want out, but you are thwarted. Surprisingly, a number of well-respected hedge funds hindered clients from withdrawing monies. For example, the Citadel Investment Group, one of the largest hedge funds in the world at the time, faced incredible loss in the second half of 2008 when its value dropped by $10 billion. According to the *New York Times*, Citadel was down 55%, whereas the average fund was down 18% in 2008, and Kenneth C. Griffin, the founder of Citadel, took it personally.[24] These losses will affect Citadel for years due to an agreement with their investors that states that "managers are supposed to recoup all losses before skimming fees from their profits again."[25] Because of the big drop in assets, the fund suspended withdrawals by investors. The drastic action that the hedge fund took might have been necessary for its survival. In the future, having better terms with investors will be fruitful. Hedge funds, whether they are large like Citadel or small, cannot charge top dollar with poor performance and then prevent investors from taking money out on a timely basis. Thwarting withdrawals only makes matters worse.

Opportunistic

Hedge funds will continue to be opportunistic. Few asset classes will be able to take advantage of the severe dislocations investors have seen with various asset classes as astute hedge fund managers can select. For instance, Universa Investments LP's Mark Spitznagel made a lot of money betting on volatility. He collaborates with Nassin Nicholas Taleb, author of *The Black Swan*. His new fund, Universa, will bet on the rate of inflation rising in the future.[26] The years after 2009 and 2010 will most likely be an attractive time for hedge funds because they do not have as much capital competing for the investments as they did before September 2008. Hedge funds are designed to take advantage of market dislocations. Significant profit opportunities have been created—many in the areas most affected by the harsh conditions in September 2008, when significant discounts and relationships between similar asset classes are so out of kilter that savvy traders should be able to profit.[27] Few asset classes do well in volatile markets, as evidenced during the later part of 2008. Volatility tends to be cyclical.

Average hedge-fund gain/loss

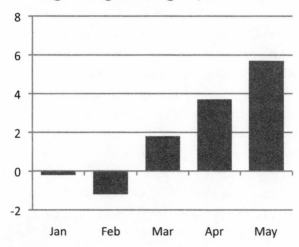

Figure 18.6 Hedge Fund Performance (2009)

Source: Jenny Strasburg, "Cantillion Pulls Plug on Ailing Hedge Funds," *Wall Street Journal* (June 18, 2009). Used with permission.

Increased Market Share

Because of the unusual events that transpired the fourth quarter of 2008 and early 2009, hedge funds initially did not perform as well as they typically do in a down market. Hedge funds, however, outperformed mutual funds and other equity managers. Hedge funds will likely take market share from mutual funds and separately managed accounts. HFRI reported positive returns in 2009 starting in March (Figure 18.6).

Asia

Hedge funds will likely have stellar growth in China and India. Foreign banks will likely create hedge funds and various vehicles for investors such as the hedge fund-of-funds or the hybrid hedge. The hedge fund industry in Asia is similar to the United States 10 years ago; Asia is in its infancy with regards to hedge funds. Various events are gaining attention such as the Eurekahedge Asian Hedge Fund Awards 2010 which was an huge success with over 300 hedge fund industry players from across the region recognizing the top achievers for 2009 and 1Q 2010.

New Options

Lastly, new choices for investors to invest in hedge funds will develop. The U.S. government might not need to overregulate hedge funds because changes are occurring anyway. The market collapse affected all industries; hedge funds were no different. A number of banks have developed programs that enable advisors or wealth managers to create portfolios specifically designed for his or her individual or insitutional clients. These platforms are not the same as a hedge fund but can be a suitable replacement if an investor desire liqudity, transparancy, lower fees, more oversight, and no lock ups. Although it is not perfect, I see it as the beginning of a new area that I call the *Hybrid Hedge*. See Figure 18.5, which shows the best attributes of both hedge funds and mutual funds. Hedge fund-of- funds will most likely remain a viable option. Prudent investors will focus on entities that perform proper due diligence. Similar to individual hedge funds, fees being charged for hedge fund-of-funds will likely be be lower in the future, and many will close down—especially those that invested heavily in Bernie Madoff. Performance will be increasingly important going forward with both individual funds as well as with hedge fund-of-funds. Alternative mutual funds will most likely continue growing and gaining investor interest. Repllication strategies and other new areas will surely transpire, helping grow the hedge fund industry.

Other hedge fund vehicles might become more popular going forward such as hedge fund replication strategies. The Goldman Sachs White Paper, "Hedge Fund Yet Replication and the Goldman Sachs Absolute Return Tracker Index," reviews a replication called factor replication. Yet, replication strategies are complex. In addition, there are different types of replication strategies being created:

> One of the most widely used hedge fund replication methods is factor replication. The goal of factor replication is to identify a basket of component factors ("risk factors") which explain the returns of an independent index (in this case, hedge fund returns). Factor replication typically relies on extensive multi-factor regressions that are run to determine the most relevant risk factor basket. The outcome is a combination of risk factors with the most significant explanatory power when used in combination with one another.

Constraints can be added (for example, maximum allocation to a single factor, bias for the most liquid underlying factors, etc.). The resulting risk factor basket should generate returns that are similar to the independent index, inclusive of the error term.[28]

Regardless of means, smart money will continue to flow into hedge funds. In April 2009, *Pensions & Investments* cited a research report that "[h]edge fund assets are expected to surge 160% to $2.6 trillion by the end of 2013, fueled by $800 billion of net inflows, mostly from North American institutional investors."[29] Although retail investors might be spooked by the news of Bernie Madoff, many institutions are not. Institutions are moving money to hedge funds. The *Pensions & Investments* article also estimates that "[b]y 2013, 46% of all hedge fund investors worldwide will be institutions including public, corporate, and union pension funds, endowments, foundations, and sovereign wealth funds."[30] Figure 18.7 features a chart of net hedge fund flows from John C. Casey and his firm, Casey Quick. Casey Quick provides excellent research.

Hedge funds are and will remain a viable alternative asset class. They offer attractive risk/reward characteristics to investors. Globally, the smart

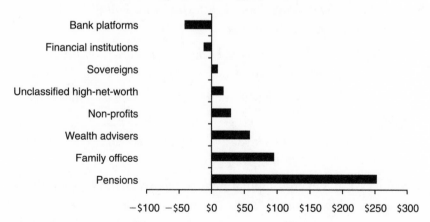

Projected cumulative net hedge fund flows, in billions, by investor type, 2009-2013

Figure 18.7 Who's Investing?

Source: Author. Bank of New York Mellon, Casey Quirk. Used with permission.

money will be heading toward hedge funds. For example, one of the U.K.'s biggest pension plans decided to invest hundreds of millions of pounds in alternative assets, potentially including hedge funds for the first time.[31] Boeing Co., Chicago, plans to search early next year for direct hedge funds to invest almost $1.7 billion.[32] As stated in the August 7, 2009, *Wall Street Journal* article, "Hedge Funds Rally as Cash Flows Back In," "Hedge-fund investors have started writing checks again, slowing a prolonged outflow of money from the industry. But they are being selective." Similarly, Fidelity Institutional Wealth Services indicated, "RIAs [registered investment advisors] put a significant amount of additional money into custodian's alternatives products platform last year...assets on their alternative products platform grew 50 percent in 2009....As for next year, in a study of 200 RIAs, more than half of respondents said they plan to increase their allocation to alternatives, including hedge funds in 2010."[33] The HFR Fund Weighted Composite Index ended 2009 up +20.12%, one of the best-performing years over the past decade. As the markets recover, institutions as well as individual investors are seeing the benefits of owning hedge funds.

Recommended Reading and Web Sites

Books on How to Evaluate Hedge Funds

Mark Boucher, *The Hedge Fund Edge Maximum Profit/Minimum Risk Global Trend Trading Strategies*

Katherine Burton, *Hedge Hunters: Hedge Fund Masters on the Rewards, the Risk, and the Reckoning*

Beverly Chandler, *Investing with the Hedge Fund Giants: Profit Whether Markets Rise or Fall*

Phillip Coggan, *Guide to Hedge Funds: What They Are, What They Do, Their Risks, Their Advantages*

Alexander M. Ineichen, *Absolute Returns the Risk and Opportunities of Hedge Fund Investing*

Robert A. Jaeger, *All About Hedge Funds: The Easy Way to Get Started*

Andy Kessler, *Running Money: Hedge Fund Honchos, Monster Markets and My Hunt for the Big Score*

Andrew Lo, *Hedge Funds: An Analytic Perspective (Advances in Financial Engineering)*

Stuart McCrary, *How to Create and Manage a Hedge Fund: A Professional's Guide*

Joseph G. Nicolas, *Investing in Hedge Funds, Revised and Updated Edition*

James P. Owen, *The Prudent Investor's Guide to Hedge Funds: Profiting from Uncertainty and Volatility*

Filippo Stefanini, *Investment Strategies of Hedge Funds*

Daniel A. Strachman, *The Fundamentals of Hedge Fund Management: How to Successfully Launch and Operate a Hedge Fund*

Peter Temple, *Hedge Funds: Courtesans of Capitalism*

Vinh Tran and Thomas Schneeweis, *Evaluating Hedge Fund Performance*

Magazines on How to Evaluate Hedge Funds

Alpha Magazine compiles various ranking about hedge funds, including rankings of top hedge fund managers, investors, and fund-of-funds.
Bloomberg Magazine features in-depth articles on hedge funds and their strategies.
The Dow Jones Hedge Fund Trades focuses on the trades made by hedge funds and publishes a ranking of the best ten annual trades.

Hedge Fund Research Online

Listed below are various resources that contain up-to-date information on hedge funds:
Bloomberg: www.bloomberg.com
CISDM: cisdm.som.umass.edu/index.asp
Eureka Hedge: www.eurekahedge.com
Hedge Fund.Net: www.hedgefund.net
Hedge Fund Research: www.hedgefundresearch.com/
Lipper Inc.: www.lipperweb.com/
Morningstar: www.morningstar.com/homepage/default.aspx
Seeking Alpha: Hedge Funds: seekingalpha.com/tag/hedge-funds

Notes

Introduction

1. Susan Watters, "The Discreet Style of the Gentleman Bankers Inside Alex. Brown," M November 1987, 87.
2. "The IPO Professionals," *Upside*, April 1994, 66.
3. Rebecca McReynolds, "Think Like an Institution," *On Wall Street*, 2007, 11.
4. Jeffrey Daniels, "Alex. Brown Shows Wall St. How It's Done," *Investor's Daily*, April 12, 1990. Volume 7, No. 4.
5. David F. Swensen, *Unconventional Success: A Fundamental Approach to Personal Investment*, New York: Free Press, 2005, 146.
6. Jason Zweig, "The Other Reason for Warren Buffett's Success," *Wall Street Journal*, November 1, 2008, B1.
7. Ibid.
8. James Picerno, "A Necessary Evil," *Financial Advisor Magazine*, May 2009, 74.
9. Tara Kalwarski, "Hedge Your Bets Like the Big Boys," *BusinessWeek*, December 28, 2009, 82.
10. Ibid.
11. Peter A. McKay and Tom Lauricella, "Yes, Dow's Record Was Year Ago Today," *Wall Street Journal*, October 8, 2008, C1.
12. Michael Tsang and Alexis Xydias, "Cheapest Stocks since 1995 Show Cash Exceeds Market." *Bloomberg Markets*, www.bloomberg.com/apps/news?pid= 20601110&sid=ahiVT6 vmGNEA, accessed December 8, 2008.
13. Daniel Dafoe, *Robinson Crusoe*, New York: Signet Classic, 1961, 83.
14. James Picerno, "Stress Test," *Wealth Manager*, October 31, 2008, 13.
15. Paul Katzeff, "Stock Funds Disgorge Record $56 Billion," *Investor's Business Daily*, October 31, 2008, A7.
16. Brendan Moynihan, "Remodeling Wall Street," *Bloomberg Markets*, November 2008, 62.
17. Peter Temple, *Hedge Funds: Courtesans of Capitalism*, New York: Wiley, 2001, 162–163.
18. Brendan Moynihan, "Remodeling Wall Street," *Bloomberg Markets*, November 2008, 62.
19. Ibid.
20. "Clearing the Fog," *Economist*, April 22, 2008, 90.
21. Steve Forbes, "Fear Will Subside," *Forbes*, October 27, 2008, 21.
22. Diana Farrell, "New Thinking for a New Financial Order," *Harvard Business Review*, September 2008, 26–27.
23. Leslie Scism and Daisy Maxey, "No Place to Hide," *Wall Street Journal*, November 3, 2008, R1.

24. Arleen Jacobius and Christine Williamson, "Alternatives: The Capacity Problem," *Pensions & Investments*, April 4, 2009, 15.

25. Peter L. Bernstein, *Against the Gods: The Remarkable Story of Risk*, New York: Wiley, 1998, 221.

26. James Picerno, "The Risk Within," *Wealth Manager Magazine*, December 1, 2008, 20.

27. Jennifer Levitz, "When Stocks Tank, Some Investors Stampede to Alpacas and Turn to Drink," *Wall Street Journal*, October 3, 2008, A1.

28. David F. Swensen, *Unconventional Success: A Fundamental Approach to Personal Investment*, New York: Free Press, 2005, 91.

29. Ben Warwick, "Hedging or Speculating," *Wealth Manager*, August 31, 2008, 46.

30. Rydex SGI, "Alternative Investments," *Essentials of Alternatives: Modern Investment Tools Simplified*, 2009, 1.

31. Nassim Nicholas Taleb, *The Black Swan: The Impact of the Highly Improbable*, New York: Random House, 2007, xvii-xviii.

32. Peter L. Bernstein, *Against the Gods: The Remarkable Story of Risk*, New York: Wiley, 1998, 251.

33. Nancy R. Mandell, "Time to Hop on the Alternatives Bandwagon," *Wealth Manager*, October 2008.

34. U.S. Trust, "Findings Reveal Thoughts and Concerns of New Subset—Those with $25 Million in Total Assets," (26th U.S. Trust Survey of Affluent Americans) with New Focus on Higher Net Worth, April 4, 2007, 20.

35. Hannah Shaw Grove, "To Each His Own," *Private Wealth Management*, August–September 2007, 20.

36. "Mr. Ziff Lands in Middle of Shrub Scandal," *Wall Street Journal*, November 10, 2008, C1.

37. Rydex SGI, "Alternative Investments," *Essentials of Alternatives: Modern Investment Tools Simplified*, 2009, 1.

38. Stephen S. Roach, "Enough Scapegoating: The Panic of '08," *International Herald Tribune*, October 1, 2008, 6.

39. Peter L. Bernstein, *Against the Gods: The Remarkable Story of Risk*, New York: Wiley, 1998, 252–253.

40. Joeseph Weber, "The House of Pritzker," *BusinessWeek*, March 17, 2003, 64.

41. Matthew Miller and Peter Necvcomb, "At Your Service," *Forbes*, October 10, 2005, 214.

42. Robert F. Whitelaw and Sujeet Banerjee, "Hedge Funds for the Rest of Us," *Journal of Indexes*, July/August 2007, 12.

43. Ibid.

44. Kathy Chu, "Wealthy Families Still Favor Alternative Investment Vehicles," *Wall Street Journal*, May 24, 2005, D2.

45. Rydex SGI, *Alternatives 2.0: What is the Prudent Investor to do?* 2009, 4.

46. "Alternative Managers Make Up 40% of All Hires in 2007," *Pensions & Investments*, March 17, 2008, 24.

47. Carterm Adrienne, "The Pickings are Good for Vultures," *BusinessWeek*, July 27, 2009, 55.

48. Ron Leuty, "Hyperion Raises $60M Despite Scarce VC Funding," *San Francisco Business Times*, July 7, 2009-July 9, 2009, 5.

49. "CalPERS committee OKs Hikes in Private Equity, Fixed Income," *Pensions & Investments*, June 29, 2009, 27.

50. Thao Hua, "SWFs Expected to Hike Equities, Alternatives," *Pensions & Investments*, July 13, 2009, 1.
51. Christine Williamson, "Looking for the Silver Lining," *Pensions & Investments*, June 1, 2009, 3, 23.
52. Barry A. Burr, "Wisconsin May Pioneer Leveraged Approach," *Pensions & Investments*, January 11, 2010, 1, 27.
53. J. Alex. Tarquinio, "Exotic Bets to Hedge a Portfolio," *New York Times*, October 29, 2009, 4.
54. Rebecca McReynolds, "Think Like an Institution," *On Wall Street*, 2007, 14.

Chapter 1

1. Franklin Allen, Richard A. Brealey, and Stewart C. Myers, *Principles of Corporate Finance*, 4th ed., New York: McGraw-Hill/Irwin, 2006, 846.
2. Robert F.,Bruner, *Applied Mergers and Acquisitions*, New York: Wiley, 2004, 74.
3. Ibid.
4. Robert F. Bruner, *Applied Mergers and Acquisitions*, New York: Wiley, 2004, 84.
5. Hilary Kramer, *Ahead of the Curve: Nine Simple Ways to Create Wealth by Spotting Stock Trends*, New York: Free Press, 2007, 92.
6. David Knox Barker, *The K Wave: Profiting from the Cyclical Booms and Busts in the Global Economy*, Milwaukee, WI: Irwin Professional Publishing, 1995, 173.
7. Herman Melville, *Moby Dick*, New York: W.W. Norton and Company, 1967, 399.
8. Francois-Xavier Chevallier, *Greenspan's Taming of the Wave*, New York: St. Martin's Press, 2000, 149.
9. Cool math.com, "Online Graphing Calculator—Graph It!" and Cool math.com, "An amusement park of math and more! Math lessons, math games, math practice, math fun!," www.coolmath.com/graphit/?, accessed July 1, 2009.
10. Ingmar Lehmann and Alfred S. Posamentier, *Fabulous Fibonacci Numbers*, Buffalo, NY: Prometheus Books, 2007, 179.
11. BBC, "BBC—Science & Nature—Horizon—Freak Wave," BBC home page, www.bbc.co.uk/science/horizon/2002/freakwaves.html, accessed August 1, 2009.
12. Elliott Wave International, "Elliott Wave International—Info. Elliott Wave International: Expert Market Forecasting using the Elliott Wave Principle." www.elliottwave.com/info/, accessed July 22, 2009.
13. Robert D. Edwards, and John Magee Jr., *Technical Analysis of Stock Trends*, Paris: Stock Trend Service, 1948.
14. BlackRock, Asset Class Returns: 20 Year Snapshot, Chart. www.colorado.metlife.com/files/23151/20Yr_Asset%20Class_Returns.pdf.
15. Alan Greenspan, "Remarks by Chairman Alan Greenspan," speech presented at the Annual Dinner and Francis Boyer Lecture of the American Enterprise Institute for Public Policy Research, Washington, DC, December 5, 1996.
16. Scott DeCarlo, "The World's Leading Companies," *Forbes*, April 18, 2005, 164–230.
17. Fidelity Investments, "The Perils of Herding to Cash," *Fidelity Investor's Publications*, March 13, 2009.
18. George Kleinman, *Trading Commodities and Financial Future: A Step by Step Guide to Mastering the Markets*, 4th ed., Albany, NY: FT Press, 2008, 84.

19. Ibid.
20. Sri Sathya Sai Baba Divine Teachings, "Thoughts for the Day," www.saibaba.ws/teachings/thoughtsfortheday.htm. accessed July 12, 2010.

Chapter 2

1. HobbyStop: The Modern Stay Sports Encyclopedia, "Surfing: Learning to Perform Popular Surfing Maneuvers," www.hobbystop.net/Surfing/Learning_To_Perform_Popular_Surfing_Maneuvers.html, accessed July 12, 2010.
2. "An Interview With Kelly Slater!," *Intensity Magazine*, www.bodybuilding.com/fun/inmag56.htm, accessed July 14, 2010.
3. Robert Dinwiddie, *Ocean: The World's Last Wilderness Revealed*, New York: Dorling Kindersley Publishing, 2008, 76.
4. "The Incredible Shrinking Funds," *Economist*, October 25, 2008, 83.
5. Diana Farrell, "New Thinking for a New Financial Order," *Harvard Business Review*, September 2008, 27.
6. William Shakespeare, *Julius Caesar*, Act 1, Scene 3, New York: Digireads.com, 2005, 17.
7. Robert Dinwiddie, *Ocean: The World's Last Wilderness Revealed*, New York: Dorling Kindersley Publishing, 2008, 76.
8. William J. Broad, "Rogue Giants At Sea," *New York Times*, July 11, 2006, F1.
9. M. A. Donelan and A. K. Magnusson, "The Role of Meteorological Focusing in Generating Rogue Wave Conditions," Ph.D. diss., University of Miami and Norwegian Meteorological Institute, 1991.
10. seafriends.org, "Waves and Wind," www.seafriends.org.nz/oceano/waves.htm#wind. Accessed March 1, 2010.
11. Barron's, "Market Data Center," online.barrons.com/mdc/public/page/9_3000.html?mod=bol_mdc_topnav_9_3002.
12. Ibid.
13. Bill Bradley, Margaret Thomas Buchholz, and Larry Savadore, *Great Storms of the Jersey Shore*, Harvey Cedars, NJ: Down the Shore Publishing, 1997, 13.
14. Data from Standard & Poor's Index Services, S&P 500 monthly returns.
15. Bradley, Buchholz, and Savadore, *Great Storms of the Jersey Shore*, 112.
16. Leslie Scism and Daisy Maxey, "No Place to Hide," *Wall Street Journal*, November 3, 2008, R1.
17. Trang Ho, "No Corner of the Earth Spared in October's Worldwide Sell-Off," *Investor's Business Daily*, November 5, 2008, A6.
18. Leslie Scism and Daisy Maxey, "No Place to Hide," *Wall Street Journal*, November 3, 2008, R1.
19. Jaqueline Urgo, "Surf's Up, and So Is Danger, and Bill Approaches," *Philadelphia Inquirer* (Jersey edition), August 22, 2009, A1.
20. Kenneth Silber, "When Florida Sizzled," researchmag.com, August 1, 2009, www.researchmag.com/Issues/2009/August–1–2009/Pages/When-Florida-Sizzled.aspx, accessed August 1, 2009.
21. seafriends.org, "Waves and Wind," www.seafriends.org.nz/oceano/waves.htm#wind, accessed March 1, 2010.
22. Ibid.

23. Ibid.
24. Capital Management Partners, Inc., "Commodity Futures Facts," www.capmgt.com/com_futures.html, accessed July 14, 2010.

Chapter 3

1. Internet Geography, "Waves," www.geography.learnontheinternet.co.uk/topics/waves.html#wave, accessed March 1, 2010.
2. seafriends.org, "Waves and Wind," www.seafriends.org.nz/oceano/waves.htm#wind, accessed March 1, 2010.
3. Robert Dinwiddie, *Ocean: The World's Last Wilderness Revealed*, New York: Dorling Kindersley Publishing, 2008, 76.
4. David Harper, "Hedge Funds: Higher Returns or Just High Fees?," www.investopedia.com/articles/03/121003.asp, accessed July 14, 2010.
5. APM Funds, "Managed Futures: Benefits of Managed Futures in a Balanced Portfolio," www.apmfunds.com/managed_futures_basic.aspx, accessed July 14, 2010.
6. Wikipedia, "Venture Capital," en.wikipedia.org/wiki/Venture_capital, accessed July 14, 2010.
7. Professional Wealth Management, "Taking Advantage of the Opportunity to Add Commodities to Your Portfolio," www.pwmnet.com/news/fullstory.php/aid/1453/Taking_advantage_of_the_opportunity_to_add_commodities_to_your_portfolio.html, accessed April 1, 2006.
8. Stock Market News, "Making Money in Troubled Times with Gold—Seeking Alpha," seekingalpha.com/article/115682-making-money-in-troubled-times-with-gold, accessed January 19, 2010.
9. Drew Kampion, "What Make a Surfer Great?" *Surfer Magazine*, August 2009.
10. GetAlts.com, "Information about Investing in Alternatives," www.getalts.com/what/history.shtml, accessed July 14, 2010.
11. *Business Week*, July 28, 2008.
12. Kevin Kneafsey, "The Four Demons," lecture, Barclays Global Investors from Barclays, New York, January 1, 2007.
13. Chrirstine Williamson, "Solid Growth Pushes Assets Above $50 Billion," *Pensions & Investments*, January 22, 2007, 60.
14. Rebecca McReynolds, "Alternative Investments Are One Key to Outperforming the Market," *On Wall Street Magazine*, August 2007, 14.
15. Tyler Savery, "Survey Finds Widespread Use of Alternative Investments among Institutions and Financial Advisors; Growth Expected to Continue," www.istockanalyst.com/article/viewiStockNews/articleid/2786501, accessed November 10, 2008.
16. Marcia Vickers, "The Money Game: In A League of Their Own," *Fortune*, October 3, 2005, 60.
17. Andrew Barry, "Crash Course," *Barron's*, November 10, 2008, 34.
18. Raul Guisado, *The Art of Surfing: A Training Manual for the Developing and Competitive Surfer*, Santa Fe, NM: Falcon, 2002, 70–71.
19. Alan R. Elliott, "Time Distance Erase Distribution Days," *Investor's Business Daily*, June 3, 2009, B1.

20. Alan R. Elliott, "Use Tables to Identify Sector Rotation," *Investor's Business Daily*, September 4, 2009, B7.
21. Alan R. Elliott, "New Data Sectors' Recent Trends," *Investor's Business Daily*, May 13, 2009, B1.
22. Howard Kurtz, *The Fortune Tellers: Inside Wall Street's Game of Money, Media and Manipulation*, New York: Free Press, 2001.
23. *Time Magazine*, December 9, 1974.
24. *Time Magazine*, December 3, 1984.
25. *Time Magazine*, January 13, 1992.
26. National Hurricane Center, "Hurricane Basics," www.nhc.noaa.gov/HAW2/english/basics.shtml.
27. Rebecca McReynolds, "Think Like an Institution," *On Wall Street Magazine*, August 2007, 10–16.
28. Robert Dinwiddie, *Ocean: The World's Last Wilderness Revealed*, New York: Dorling Kindersley Publishing, 2008, 76.
29. Andrew Barry, "Crash Course," *Barron's*, November 10, 2008, 34.
30. Ibid.
31. Geraldine Fabrikant, "Return of 8% for Harvard Endowment," *New York Times*, September 13, 2008, C3.
32. Andrew Barry, "Crash Course," *Barron's*, November 10, 2008, 34.
33. Shefali Anand, "The Alternatives Route Was Tough Going in 2008," *Wall Street Journal*, March 1, 2009, R7.
34. Craig Karmin, "College Try: Chicago's Stock Sale," *Wall Street Journal*, August 25, 2009, C1.

Chapter 4

1. Franklin Allen, Richard A. Brealey, and Stewart C Myers, *Principles of Corporate Finance*, 4th ed., New York: McGraw-Hill/Irwin, 2006, 355.
2. David F. Swensen, *Unconventional Success: A Fundamental Approach to Personal Investment*, New York: Free Press, 2005, 139.
3. Alex. Brown, *Private Equity: A Game of Strategy and Kill, Not Chance*, company report, August 1997.
4. James Joyce, *A Portrait of the Artist as a Young Man*, 1916, reprint, New York: Dover Publications, 1994, 268.
5. Randall E. Stross, *eBoys: The First Inside Account of Venture Capitalists at Work*, New York: Ballantine Books, 2000, 181–183.
6. John Battelle, *The Search: How Google and Its Rivals Rewrote the Rules of Business and Transformed Our Culture*, New York: Portfolio, 2005, 86.
7. Ibid., 89.
8. Mike Wright and Ken Robbie, *Management Buy-Outs and Venture Capital: Into the Next Millennium*, London: Edward Elgar Publishing, 1999, 1.
9. U.S. Securities and Exchange Commission, "Rule 505," www.sec.gov/info/smallbus/qasbsec.htm, accessed January 31, 2010.
10. Robert D. Auerbach, *Financial Markets and Institutions*, Boston: Prentice Hall College Division, 1983, 556.

11. "Piling On," *Economist*, May 30, 2009, 13.
12. Spencer E. Ante, "Fertile Ground for Startups," *BusinessWeek*, November 23, 2009, 46–49.
13. "Piling On," *Economist*, May 30, 2009, 13.
14. Brian Deagon, "Most Entrepreneurs Tap Friends, Family, Not Venture Funding," *Investor's Business Daily*, January 21, 2005, A4.
15. Ibid.
16. Ibid.
17. Robert E. Wright, *The First Wall Street: Chestnut Street, Philadelphia, and the Birth of American Finance*, Chicago: University of Chicago Press, 2005, 4.
18. Vincent Mao, "He Made McDonald's Sizzle," *Investor's Business Daily*, October 9, 2009, A3.
19. Edward E. Williams, Albert Napier, and T&NO Corp., "Entrepreneurial Process," www.entrepreneurialprocess.com/history.htm, accessed August 1, 2009.
20. Karl H. Vesper, *New Venture Strategies*, rev. ed., Englewood Cliffs, NJ: Prentice Hall, 1990, 2.
21. Christopher Farrell, "The Boom in IPOs," *BusinessWeek*, December 18, 1995, 64–72.
22. Spencer E. Ante, "These Angels Go Where Others Fear to Tread," *BusinessWeek*, June 1, 2009, 44–48.
23. Guy Fraser-Sampson, *Private Equity as an Asset Class*, New York: Wiley, 2007, 5.
24. Robert E. Wright, *First Wall Street: Chestnut Street, Philadelphia, and the Birth of American Finance*, Chicago: University of Chicago Press, 2005, 3–4.
25. "Piling On," *Economist*, May 30, 2009, 13.
26. William D. Bygrave and Jeffry A. Timmons, *Venture Capital at the Crossroads*, New York: Harvard Business School Press, 1992, 1.
27. Zippo Manufacturing Company, "Zippo Corporate Information," www.zippo.com/corporateInfo/index.aspx?bhcp=1, accessed August 1, 2009.
28. Jed Graham, "He Truly Was a Crafty Cheese Maker and Marketer," *Investor's Business Daily*, February 13, 2007, A3.
29. Scott Stoddard, "He Made Rubber Fit to Roll," *Investor's Business Daily*, May 29, 2009, A3.
30. Eli Lilly and Company, "About Us," lilly.com/about/, accessed March 3, 2009.
31. Smith & Wesson, "History: Smith & Wesson," www.smith-wesson.com/webapp/wcs/stores/servlet/CustomContentDisplay?langId=1&storeId=10001&catalogId=10001&content=11504§ionId=10002y, accessed August 1, 2009.
32. Ibid.
33. Justin Hibbard, "Mission Possible," *Red Herring*, December 10, 2001, 56.
34. Lizette Wilson, "Venture Capital Firms Join CIA to Fight Terror," *San Francisco Business Times*, October 19, 2001.
35. Biran Bergstein, "CIA Makes a Tech Investment," *Philadelphia Inquirer*, January 17, 2002, F3.
36. Ann Grimes, "War Fuels Rush to Invest in Security Ventures," *Wall Street Journal*, March 24, 2003, C1.

Chapter 5

1. Charles R. Morris, *The Tycoons: How Andrew Carnegie, John D. Rockefeller, Jay Gould, and J. P. Morgan Invented the American Supereconomy*, New York: Owl Books, 2006, 38–39.
2. Lee Tom Perry, "The Capital Connection: How Relationships between Founders and Venture Capitalists Affect Innovation in New Ventures," *The Academy of Management Executive*, August 1988, 205–212.
3. Ron Chernow, *Titan: The Life of John D. Rockefeller, Sr.*, New York: Vintage, 2004, 104.
4. James C. Bachman IV, James M. Kocis, Austin M. Long, and Craig J. Nickels, *Inside Private Equity: The Professional Investor's Handbook*, New York: Wiley, 2009, 4.
5. Benjamin Franklin, *Benjamin Franklin: Autobiography*, reprint, New York: Holt, Rinehart, and Winston, Inc., 1948, 165.
6. Paul Israel, "Thomas Edison: American Inventor," Lucidcafé Interactive Café and Information Resource, www.lucidcafe.com/library/96feb/edison.html, accessed August 1, 2009.
7. David Cannadine, *Mellon: An American Life*, New York: Random House, 2006, 113.
8. Ibid., 601.
9. Ibid., 141.
10. Ibid., 98.
11. Ibid., 254.
12. Ibid.
13. Paul Gompers and Josh Lerners, *The Venture Capital Cycle*, 2nd ed, London: The MIT Press, 2004, 33.
14. Udayan Gupta, *Done Deals: Venture Capitalists Tell Their Stories*, New York: Harvard Business School Press, 2000, 107.
15. Venrock, "The Venrock Story," www.venrock.com/index.cfm?fuseaction= content.contentDetail&id=8747, accessed April 2, 2010.
16. J. Bonasia, "Henry Bessemer's Iron Will," *Investor's Business Daily*, February 18, 2009, A3.
17. Charles R. Morris, *The Tycoons: How Andrew Carnegie, John D. Rockefeller, Jay Gould, and J. P. Morgan Invented the American Supereconomy*, New York: Owl Books, 2006, 91.
18. David Nasaw, *Andrew Carnegie*, Boston: Penguin, 2007, 76.
19. Spencer E. Ante, "Creative Capital," *BusinessWeek*, April 14, 2008, 48.
20. Ibid.
21. Trevor Jensen, "Edgar F. 'Ned' Heizer Jr., 1929–2009: 'Giant' in the Venture Capital Industry," *Chicago Tribune*, December 11, 2009, 41.
22. "John Hay Whitney Dies at 77; Publisher Led in Many Fields," *New York Times*, February 9, 1982, B16.
23. Udayan Gupta, ed., *Done Deals: Venture Capitalists Tell Their Stories*, New York: Harvard Business School Press, 2000, 95.
24. Chris Mahoney, "PE Pioneer Hope to Drive Industry Back to Its Roots," *Boston Business Journal*, October 9, 2009, boston.bizjournals.com/boston/stories/2009/10/12/focus3.html, accessed October 9, 2009.
25. Ibid.
26. Reinhardt Krause, "A Gem Among Venture Capitalists," *Investor's Business Daily*, April 22, 2009, A3.

27. William D. Bygrave and Jeffry A. Timmons, *Venture Capital at the Crossroads*, New York: Harvard Business School Press, 1992, 2.
28. Udayan Gupta, ed. *Done Deals: Venture Capitalists Tell Their Stories*, 101.
29. Reinhardt Krause, "He Ventured Forth, Cashed In," *Investor's Business Daily*, October 15, 2009, A3.
30. Erika Brown, "Growing Up Green: The Young Stars of Venture Capital Aim to Do in Alternative Energy What Their Bosses Once Did in Computing," *Forbes*, February 11, 2008, www.forbes.com/fdc/welcome_mjx.shtml, accessed February 11, 2008.
31. Sky Dayton, "When Capital Corrupts," *Forbes*, March 25, 2002, 19.
32. Erika Brown, "Growing Up Green: The Young Stars of Venture Capital Aim to Do in Alternative Energy What Their Bosses Once Did in Computing," *Forbes*, February 11, 2008, 70–74.
33. Ibid.
34. Kambiz Foroohar, "Rocket Man," *Bloomberg Markets*, June 2008.
35. Bo Peabody, *Lucky or Smart?: Secrets to an Entrepreneurial Life*. New York: Random House, 2004, xi.
36. Deepak Gopinath, "Macro Man," *Bloomberg Markets*, January 2007.
37. Deepak Gopinath, "The Many Lives of Peter Thiel," *Bloomberg Markets*, January 2007.
38. Mike Wright and Ken Robbie, *Management Buy-Outs and Venture Capital: Into the Next Millennium*, London: Edward Elgar Publishing, 1999, 1.
39. William D. Bygrave and Jeffry A. Timmons, *Venture Capital at the Crossroads*, New York: Harvard Business School Press, 1992, 38.
40. Carl Schramm and Harold Bradley, "How Venture Capital Lost Its Way," *BusinessWeek*, November 30, 2009, 80.
41. Scott Denne, "Exit Deferred: PE-backed Firms Eschew Public Offerings," *Boston Business Journal*, October 14, 2005, boston.bizjournals.com/boston/stories/2005/10/17/focus3.html?page=2, accessed October 14, 2005.
42. William D. Bygrave and Jeffry A. Timmons, *Venture Capital at the Crossroads*, 25.
43. Stephen P. Farrell, "Corporate Governance: An Overview of Public Company Requirements," www.morganlewis.com/index.cfm/publicationID/7d455dfd–1d0d–41a0–9d46–5878a6b7732d/fuseaction/publication.detail, accessed August 1, 2009.
44. Murray Beach, *Regulation in All the Wrong Places*, working paper.
45. Doug Halonen, "Systemic Risk? Not Us, Say Private Equity Firms," *Pensions & Investments*, April 6, 2009, 26.
46. Delbert Smith, interview with author.
47. Mike Wright and Ken Robbie, *Management Buy-Outs and Venture Capital: Into the Next Millennium*, 50.
48. Brian Womack, "'Green' VC Funding Sets New Record," *Investor's Business Daily*, July 8, 2008, A4.
49. George M. Taber, "A Modest Comeback for IPOs," *NJ Biz*, January 1, 2004.
50. Mike Wright and Ken Robbie, *Management Buy-Outs and Venture Capital: Into the Next Millennium*, 27.
51. Quoted in Udayan Gupta, *Done Deals: Venture Capitalists Tell Their Stories*, New York: Harvard Business School Press, 2000, 320.
52. Mike Wright and Ken Robbie, *Management Buy-Outs and Venture Capital: Into the Next Millennium*.

53. William D. Bygrave and Jeffry A. Timmons, *Venture Capital at the Crossroads*, 38.
54. Ernst&Young, "3Q'09 Venture Insights, 2009," www.ey.com/Publication/vwLUAssets/ 3Q_2009_Venture_Insights/$File/3Q%202009%20Venture%20Insights.pdf, accessed October 20, 2010.
55. Raymond Hennessey, "IPO Market Mounts a Strong Comeback," *Wall Street Journal*, January 3, 2005, R10.
56. Scott Denne, "Exit Deferred: PE-backed Firms Eschew Public Offerings," *Boston Business Journal*, October 14, 2005, boston.bizjournals.com/boston/stories/2005/10/17/ focus3.html?page=2, accessed October 14, 2005.
57. Richard A. Silfen, interview with author.
58. Pui-Wing Tam, "Cash-Rich Venture Capital Isn't Carefree," *Wall Street Journal*, January 2, 2007, R18.

Chapter 6

1. Private Edge Group, State Street Corporation. Alternative Investment Management Program—Quarterly Review. California Public Employees' Retirement System. www.calpers.ca.gov/eip-docs/about/press/news/invest-corp/quart-perf-report/qrtly-perform-review.pdf, accessed August 1, 2009.
2. Galen Moore, "VC Turnover on the Uptick as Investing Remains Cool," *Boston Business Journal*, July 7–July 16, 2009. http://boston.bizjournals.com/boston/stories/ 2009/07/13/story4.html.
3. Lindsay Riddell, "Venture Firms Are Learning to Play by New Rules," *San Francisco Business Times*, November 17, 2009, www.informationweek.com/blog/ main/archives/2009/04/introducing_inf_2.html, accessed April 20, 2009.
4. Russ Garland and Brian Gormley, "Grooming the Next IPOs," *Barron's*, January 9, 2006, 22.
5. Brian Deagon, "Venture Investment Near 13-Year Lows, Even After Q2 Uptick," *Investor's Business Daily*, July 21, 2009, A5.
6. Bo Peabody, *Lucky or Smart: Secrets to an Entrepreneurial Life*, New York: Random House, 2004, xi.
7. Paul Gompers and Josh Lerner, *The Venture Capital Cycle*, 2nd ed., London: The MIT Press, 2004, 42.
8. Steve Goodman, interview with author.
9. Michael J. Heller, interview with author.
10. Foley & Lardner LLP, "Foley & Lardner Survey Reveals Signs of Optimism, Lingering Challenges among Emerging Technology Executives and Investors," www.foley.com/news/news_detail.aspx?newsid=4044, accessed August 1, 2009.
11. Martha Woodall, "eBay to Acquire Half.com; Price Tops $312 Million," *Philadelphia Inquirer*, June 14, 2000, D1.
12. Heidi Mason and Tim Rohner, *The Venture Imperative*, Boston: Harvard Business Press, 2002, 20–21.
13. Christopher Farrell, "The Boom in IPOs," *BusinessWeek*, December 18, 1995, www.businessweek.com/1995/51/b34551.htm, accessed July 14, 2010.
14. Gloria Lau, "Kid (Aged 72) in a Candy Store," *Forbes*, July 27, 1998, 58–59.
15. Carlos Martinez, "Biotech Billionare Says Market Not Ready for IPO," *Los Angeles Business Journal*, April 8, 2002.

16. Stephanie Clifford, "Two Online Health Site Operators to Announce a Merger," *New York Times*, October 3, 2008, C2.

17. Claire Cain Miller, "A Father of Netscape Begins a Silicon Valley Venture Firm," *New York Times*, July 6, 2009, B6.

18. Brian Deagon, "New Venture Fund Has Money to Spend Beyond Skype Splash," *Investor's Business Daily*, September 8, 2009, A6.

19. Ron Leuty, "Diagnostic Test Maker Sees Positive Signs from Insurers," *San Francisco Business Times*, October 9–October 15, 2009, sanfrancisco.bizjournals.com/sanfrancisco/stories/2009/10/12/smallb2.html, accessed October 15, 2009.

20. Ibid.

21. Pui-Wing Tam, "Cash-Rich Venture Capital Isn't Carefree," *Wall Street Journal*, January 2, 2007, R18.

22. Pui-Wing Tam, "Venture Funds Sweetening the Terms," *Wall Street Journal*, November 23, 2009, C1.

23. Harry Cendrowski, James P. Martin, Louis W. Petro, and Adam A. Wadecki, *Private Equity: History, Governance, and Operations*, New York: Wiley, 2008, 78.

24. Stephen Baker and Adam Aston, "The Business of Nanotech," *BusinessWeek*, February 14, 2005, 65.

25. J. Bonasia and Doug Tsuruoka, "Sweeping Changes Coming with Smart Dust," *Investor's Business Daily*, December 8, 2008, A5.

26. Ibid.

27. Brian Deagon, "VC Investments Slid 8% in 2008 Despite 42% Jump for Cleantech," *Investor's Business Daily*, January 26, 2009, A5.

28. Brian Womack, "'Green' VC Funding Sets New Record," *Investor's Business Daily*, July 8, 2008, A4.

29. Aaron Ricadela, "Who Will Be the Green VC Giant?" *BusinessWeek*, October 2, 2009, 54.

30. "Top VC Funded Cleantech Firms in the Greater Bay Area," chart, *Book of Lists*, San Francisco: San Francisco Business Journal, 2009.

31. Elizabeth Millard, "Alternative Energy Offers Plenty of Opportunities," *Minneapolis St. Paul Business Journal*, August 24, 2009.

32. Steve E. F. Brown, "Green and Clean VC Investment Booms," *San Francisco Business Times*, October 2–October 9, 2009.

33. Brian Deagon, "Venture Capitalists to Entrepreneurs: Hard Times Continue," *Investor's Business Daily*, June 10, 2009, A4.

34. Centers for Disease Control and Prevention, "Heart Disease and Stroke Prevention: Addressing the Nation's Leading Killers: At A Glance—2009," www.cdc.gov/nccdphp/publications/AAG/pdf/dhdsp.pdf, accessed March 10, 2010.

35. Jared A. Favole, "Patient Group Seeks Increase in Heart-Research Funding," *Wall Street Journal*, March 17, 2009, D6.

36. Heather Chambers, "Medical Firm Targeting $3B Market for Plaque Detection," *San Diego Business Journal*, October 8, 2007.

37. Resverlogix Corp., "Resverlogix Corp.—Home," www.resverlogix.com/, accessed April 2, 2010.

38. Brian Deagan, "Venture Firms Eye Private Equity, with IPO Market Still in the Dumps; U.S. Venture Association Expects 8% Increase in VC Investments in 2007," *Investor's Business Daily*, December 19, 2006, A4.

39. Doug Tsurouka, "ChiNext Exchange Opens Door to Capital for Small Local Firms," *Investor's Business Daily*, November 9, 2009, A1.

40. Doug Tsurouka, "ChiNext Exchange Opens Door to Capital for Small Local Firms," *Investors Business Daily*, November 9, 2009, A1, A6.

41. Babson, "Executive Summary and Key Findings of the GEM 2008 U.S. Report," *What Entrepreneurs Are Up To: Global Entrepreneurship Monitor—2008 National Entrepreneurial Assessment for the United States of America*, 2009, www3.babson.edu/ESHIP/research-publications/upload/GEM_2008_US_Executive_Report.pdf, 7.

42. Alex. Brown, *Private Equity: A Game of Strategy and Kill, Not Chance*, company report, August 1997, 64.

43. Christopher Farrell, "The Boom in IPOs," *BusinessWeek*, December 18, 1995, www.businessweek.com/1995/51/b34551.htm, accessed July 14, 2010.

44. Ernst & Young, "Winning through Excellence and Innovation in a Downturn," *From Survival to Growth: Global Venture Capital Insights and Trends Report 2009*, 2009, 4.

45. Justin J. Camp, *Venture Capital Due Diligence: A Guide to Making Smart Investment Choices and Increasing Your Portfolio Returns*, New York: Wiley, 2002, 201.

46. Jack Gage, "Heads Up Don't Peek," *Forbes*, November 17, 2009, 32.

47. Lee R. Petillon, "Alternatives to Conventional IPOs," *Business Law Update*, Winter 2008, 3.

48. Committee on Capital Markets Regulation, *Committee on Capital Markets Regulation Completes Survey Regarding the Use by Foreign Issuers of the Private Rule 144A Equity Markets*, Disclosure Statement, February 13, 2009, 1.

49. Reinhardt Krause, "Private Share Market May Supplant IPOs," *Investor's Business Daily*, November 10, 2009, A5.

50. Sjostrom, William K., "The Birth of Rule 144A Equity Offerings," *UCLA Law Review*, Vol. 56, p. 409, 2008.

51. Randall Smith, "Goldman Takes 'Private' Equity to a New Level," *Wall Street Journal*, May 24, 2007, C1.

52. Portal Alliance, "Portal Alliance Platform FAQs," www.portalalliancemarket.com/PA_FAQ.pdf, accessed August 1, 2009.

53. Ibid.

54. Reinhardt Krause, "Private Share Market May Supplant IPOs," *Investor's Business Daily*, November 10, 2009, A5.

55. Reinhardt Krause, "Weak IPO Market Has VCs Hoping for Private Trading," *Investor's Business Daily*, November 10, 2009, A5.

56. Murray Beach, *Regulation in All the Wrong Places*. Working paper.

57. "Tweeting All the Way to the Bank," *Economist*, July 25, 2009, 61–62.

58. Andrew Gluck, "Making Sense of Twitters and Tweets," *Financial Advisory Magazine*, May 2009, www.fa-mag.com/component/content/article/1-features/4095-making-sense-of-twitters-and-tweets.html, accessed May 2009.

59. "Avid Radiopharmaceuticals: Vision into Debilitating Neuro Disease," *Insight: The Science Center Magazine*, Winter 2009, www.sciencecenter.org/resident-companies/success-stories, accessed January 2010.

60. John George, "Life Sciences," *Philadelphia Business Journal*, June 27, 2008.

61. Jonathan Fahey, "Take My Juice," *Forbes*, September 7, 2009, 29.

Chapter 7

1. John Cassidy, *dot.com: How America Lost Its Mind and Money in the Internet Era*, New York: Harper Perennial, 2002, 6.
2. David Darst, "Investment Strategy and Asset Allocation Commentary," *Morgan Stanley Global Wealth Management Asset Allocation*, September 29, 2008, 10.
3. Pui-Wing Tam, "Venture Funds Sweetening the Terms," *Wall Street Journal*, November 23, 2009, C1.
4. Liam Denning, "Public Markets Lock Down Private Equity," *Wall Street Journal*, April 13, 2009, C1.
5. Pui-Wing Tam, "Venture Funds Sweetening the Terms," *Wall Street Journal*, November 23, 2009, C1.
6. Ibid.
7. Peter Key, "Investors' Suit Alleges They Were Defrauded by S.R. One," *Philadelphia Business Journal*, April 1,2005, philadelphia.bizjournals.com/philadelphia/stories/2005/04/04/story6.html, accessed April 1, 2005.
8. Quoted in Scott Standard, "He Made Rubber Fit to Roll," *Investor's Business Daily*, May 29, 2009, A3.
9. Stephen Muniz, "Preferred Stock Provisions May Not Provide Protection," *Boston Business Journal*, February 18, 2005, boston.bizjournals.com/boston/stories/2005/02/21/focus7.html, accessed February 18, 2005.
10. Karl H. Vesper, *New Venture Strategies*, revised ed., 2nd ed., Alexandria, VA.: Prentice Hall, 1989, 9.
11. "Who Says the Startup Is Dead?" *Business 2.0*, April 2002, http://money.cnn.com/magazines/business2/articles/mag/0,1640,38667,FF.html, accessed April 2, 2002.
12. U.S. Securities and Exchange Commission, "Rule 144: Selling Restricted and Control Securities," www.sec.gov/investor/pubs/rule144.htm.
13. Ibid.
14. Ibid.
15. David M. Darst, *The Little Book That Saves Your Assets: What the Rich Do to Stay Wealthy in Up and Down Markets*, Hoboken, NJ: Wiley, 2008, 119.
16. Bo Peabody, *Lucky or Smart?: Secrets to an Entrepreneurial Life*, New York: Random House, 2004, 5.
17. Gary S. Becker, Steven J. Davis, and Kevin M. Murphy, "Uncertainty and the Slow Recovery," *Wall Street Journal*, January 4, 2010, A17.
18. Leslie A. Jeng and Philippe C. Wells, "The Determinants of Venture Capital Funding: Evidence Across Countries," *Journal of Corporate Finance*, May 1998, 241–242.

Chapter 8

1. Arleen Jacobius, "Crisis of Confidence in Venture Capital," *Pensions & Investments*, July 27, 2009, 3, 34.
2. Pui-Wing Tam, "Venture Funds Sweetening the Terms," *Wall Street Journal*, November 23, 2009, C1.
3. The Washington State Investment Board, Quarterly Report, September 30, 2009, Investment Reports, September 30, 2009, 3.
4. Capital Dynamics, Washington State Investment Board Portfolio Overview by Strategy (review), June 30, 2009.

5. State Street Corportation, CalPERS AIM Quarterly Review (report), June 30, 2009, 2.
6. Guy Fraser-Sampson, *Private Equity as an Asset Class*, New York: Wiley, 2007, xiv.
7. Guy Fraser-Sampson, *Private Equity as an Asset Class*, 25.
8. James C. Bachman IV, James M. Kocis, Austin M. Long III, and Craig J. Nickels, *Inside Private Equity: The Professional Investor's Handbook*, New York: Wiley, 2009, 103.
9. Eugene F. Brigham and Joel F. Houston, *Fundamentals of Financial Management*, concise 5th ed., Mason, OH: Thompson-South Western, 2007, 351.
10. James C. Bachman IV, James M. Kocis, Austin M. Long III, and Craig J. Nickels, *Inside Private Equity: The Professional Investor's Handbook*, New York: Wiley, 2009, 91.
11. Eugene F. Brigham and Joel F. Houston, *Fundamentals of Financial Management*, concise 5th ed., Mason, Ohio: Thompson-South Western, 2007, 359.
12. Ibid.
13. Guy Fraser-Sampson, *Private Equity as an Asset Class*, New York: Wiley, 2007, 43.
14. William D. Bygrave and Jeffry A. Timmons, *Venture Capital at the Crossroads*, New York: Harvard Business School Press, 1992, 20.
15. William P. Loftus, interview with author.
16. William D. Bygrave and Jeffry A. Timmons, *Venture Capital at the Crossroads*, New York: Harvard Business School Press, 1992, 158.
17. Mike Wright and Ken Robbie, *Management Buy-Outs and Venture Capital: Into the Next Millennium*, London: Edward Elgar Publishing, 1999, 38.
18. Ibid., 41.
19. Ibid., 46.
20. Andrew P. Madden, "The New VCs," *Red Herring*, November, 1999.
21. Russ Garland and Brian Gormley, "Gromming the Next IPOs," *Barron's*, January 9, 2006, 22.
22. Andy Stone, Shlomo Reifman, and Scott DeCarlo, "New Issues, Fresh Hopes," *Forbes*, July 4, 2005, 86.
23. Brian Deagon, "Their Decks Cleared after Bubble Venture Investing Sails Forward," *Investor's Business Daily*, January 5, 2005, A4.
24. Ann Grimes, "How Venture Capital Got Its Groove Back," *Wall Street Journal*, January 3, 2005, R16.
25. Brian Deagon, "Their Decks Cleared after Bubble, Venture Investing Sailing Forward," *Investor's Business Daily*, January 5, 2005, A4.
26. Pui-Wing Tam, "Cash-Rich Venture Capital Isn't Carefree," *Wall Street Journal*, Year-End Review of Markets and Finance 2006, January 2, 2007, R18.

Chapter 9

1. Lizette Wilson, "Venture Investments Rise over First Quarter," *San Francisco Business Times*, July 25–31, 2003.
2. Rebecca Buckman, "Venture to Nowhere," *Forbes*, January 12, 2009, 66–71.
3. William D. Bygrave and Jeffry A. Timmons, *Venture Capital at the Crossroads*, New York: Harvard Business School Press, 1992, 13.
4. Kasey Wehrum, "Angel Investing 2009," *Inc.*, January–February 2009, 83–89.
5. "More Important Than Ever Today," *Boston Business Journal*, April 17, 2009, www.bizjournals.com/boston/stories/2009/04/20/focus6.html, accessed April 17, 2009.

6. Ann Grimes, "Venture Funds' Best Kept Secrets," *Wall Street Journal*, May 27, 2004, C1.
7. Arleen Jacobius, "Fund of Funds Investors Get Shut Out by Sequoia," *Pensions & Investments*, June 26, 2006, 2, 39.
8. Jack Biddle, Virginia Bonker, Guy Bradley, Jan Buettner, Jonathan Goldstein, Suzanne King, Mark Lotke, Michael Moritz, Heidi Roizen, and Nuri Wissa, "Suzanne King: New Enterprise Associates," in *Inside the Minds: Venture Capitalists—Inside the High Stakes and Fast Moving World of Venture Capital*, eBrandedBooks.com, 2000, 96.
9. Ibid., 99.
10. Susan Smith Hendrickson, "On the Hunt for VC? Get All Your Ducks in a Row . . ." *Boston Business Journal*, April, 13, 2007.
11. Ben Warwick, "Buying When There's Blood in the Streets: The Logic Behind Private Equity Is More Compelling Than One Might Think," *Wealth Manager*, November 2008.
12. Kieran Beer, "Dean of Investing," *Bloomberg Markets*, January 2006.
13. Marcia Vickers, "The Money Game," *Fortune*, October 3, 2005, money.cnn.com/magazines/fortune/fortune_archive/2005/10/03/8356742/index.htm, accessed October 3, 2005.
14. David F. Swensen, *Unconventional Success: A Fundamental Approach to Personal Investment*, New York: Free Press, 2005, 11.
15. Rebecca McReynolds, "Think Like an Institution," *On Wall Street*, August 2007.
16. Susan Snyder, "Despite Economy, Penn's Endowment Stays Even," *Philadelphia Inquirer*, November 7, 2009, B2.
17. Craig Karmin, "Harvard Endowment Regroups," *Wall Street Journal*, August 24, 2009, C1.
18. Susan Snyder, "Penn's Endowment Outperforms Its Ivy League Peers," *Philadelphia Inquirer*, November 6, 2009.
19. Victor Reklaitis, "They Sparked a Hot Tea Firm," *Investor's Business Daily*, August 6, 2009, www.investors.com/NewsAndAnalysis/Article.aspx?id=502559, accessed August 6, 2009.
20. Ibid.
21. Lawrence Aragon, "VC Whispers: Putting Cash into Stash," *Red Herring*, September 15, 2001, www.redherring.com/Home/1028, accessed October 7, 2001.
22. Rebecca Buckman, "As High-Tech IPO's Dwindle, Start-Ups Look to Private Money for More Backing," *Wall Street Journal*, July 1, 2008.
23. Amanda Fung, "New York Venture Capital Funding Up in 2008—Crain's New York Business," Crain's New York Business, www.crainsnewyork.com/article/20090124/FREE/901239955, accessed January 24, 2009.
24. Lark Park, "Where the Seed Money Is," *Industry Standard*, February 26, 2001.
25. Patrick Hoge, "Khosla Near Closing $1B in Funds," *San Francisco Business Times*, July 24–30, 2009, www.bizjournals.com/sanjose/stories/2009/07/20/daily36.html, accessed July 21, 2009.
26. Spencer Ante, "These Angels Go Where Others Fear to Tread," *BusinessWeek*, June 1, 2009, bx.businessweek.com/venture-capital/reference//, accessed June 1, 2009.
27. Barry B. Burr, "Pay Czar's Influence could be Widespread," *Pensions & Investments*, November 2, 2009, 4, 36.
28. Arleen Jacobius, "Crisis of Confidence in Venture Capital," *Pensions & Investments*, July 27, 2009, 3, 34.

29. Christine Williamson, "Texas Teachers Sticking with Agenda," *Pensions & Investments*, July 27, 2009, 2, 33.
30. Drew Carter, "Fund Profile South Korea," *Pensions & Investments*, July 13, 2009, 12.
31. Lindsay Riddell, "VC's Seek Sarbanes Shift to Ease Flow of New IPOs," *San Francisco Business Times*, June 19–25, 2009.
32. Noel Francisco, interview with author.
33. Marilyn Alva, "Kaiser of Industry and of Health," *Investor's Business Daily*, November 25, 2009, A4.
34. Ibid.
35. "More Important Than Ever Today," *Boston Business Journal*, April 17, 2009, www.bizjournals.com/boston/stories/2009/04/20/focus6.html, accessed April 17, 2009.
36. "About ACA," Angel Capital Association, www.angelcapitalassociation.org/dir_about/overview.aspx?referer=www.clickfind.com.au, accessed December 23, 2009.
37. Vanessa Wong, "Brigham Young's Entrepreneur Factory," *BusinessWeek*, December 7, 2009, 54.
38. Heidi Mason and Tim Rohner, *The Venture Imperative*, Boston: Harvard Business Press, 2002, 9.
39. Mark Calvey, "IPOs Are Extinct Species in VC's Prehistoric Landscape," *San Francisco Business Journal*, January 9–15, 2009, sanfrancisco.bizjournals.com/sanfrancisco/stories/2009/01/12/newscolumn2.html, accessed January 9, 2009.
40. Arleen Jacobius, "Investments, Deal Numbers Fall in 3rd Quarter," *Pensions & Investments*, October 27, 2008, 37.
41. "SecondMarket Named to the Inc. 500 List of America's Fastest-Growing Private Companies," SecondMarket Holdings, September 16, 2010, https://secondmarket.com/press-releases/secondmarket-named-to-the-inc-500-list-of-americas-fastestgrowing-private-companies.html.
42. Pui-Wing Tam and Jessica E. Vascellaro, "Restless Workers in Silicon Valley Seek Ways to Cash in Early," *Wall Street Journal*, August 21, 2009, B1.
43. Bo Peabody, *Lucky or Smart?: Secrets to an Entrepreneurial Life*, New York: Random House, 2004, 7.
44. Bo Peabody, "Lucky Or Smart." *Inc.*, January 2005, www.inc.com/magazine/20050101/lucky-or-smart.html, accessed January 1, 2005.
45. Greg Walsh, "Catching Up With The Class of 1999," *Boston Business Journal*, May 15–21, 2009, boston.bizjournals.com/boston/stories/2009/05/18/story9.html, accessed May 21, 2009.
46. Galen Moore, "Consumer Goods Start-Ups Only Gainers Amid VC Slide," *Boston Business Journal*, October 23, 2009, boston.bizjournals.com/boston/stories/2009/10/26/story4.html, accessed October 23, 2009.
47. Karl H. Vesper, *New Venture Strategies*, 2nd ed., rev. ed., Alexandria, VA: Prentice Hall, 1989, 129.
48. Miriam Hill, "Drug-Industry Bosses Give Job-Seekers Advice," *Philadelphia Inquirer*, November 26, 2009, C1.
49. "Investment Program," Pennsylvania Public School Employees' Retirement System, www.psers.state.pa.us/invest/invest.htm, accessed January 1, 2008.
50. Arleen Jacobius, "Limited Partners Flexing Muscles in Negotiations," *Pensions & Investments*, August 24, 2009, 1, 23.

51. Rebecca Buckman, "Where the Smart Money Is," *Wall Street Journal*, December 18, 2006, R4.
52. Rebecca Buckman, "Venture to Nowhere," *Forbes*, January 12, 2009, 66–71.
53. Helen Kaiao Chang, "Technology companies 'cautiously optimistic' about exit strategies," *San Diego News Network*, October 16, 2009, www.sdnn.com/sandiego/2009–10–16/business-real-estate/technology-companies-cautiously-optimistic-about-exit-strategies, accessed October 16, 2009.
54. Brian Deagon, "Venture Firms Eye Private Equity, with IPO Market Still in the Dumps," *Investor's Business Daily*, December 19, 2006, A4.
55. Reinhardt Krause, "Chinese IPOs Keep Their Shine as Shin Digital TV Climbs 75%," *Investor's Business Daily*, October 8, 2007, A1.
56. Rebecca Buckman, "Green Tendrils," *Forbes*, September 21, 2009, www.forbes.com/forbes/2009/0921/opinions-cisco-systems-acquisition-heads-up.html, accessed September 21, 2009.

Chapter 10

1. Ernest Hemingway, *The Old Man and the Sea*, New York: Scribner, 1980, 61.
2. "Recoil," *Economist*, May 31, 2008, 13.
3. "The Case For Managed Futures," *Worth*, Spring–Summer 2009.
4. Russell R. Wasendorf and Thomas A. McCafferty, *All About Commodities from the Inside Out*, New York: McGraw-Hill, 1993, 208.
5. Roland Fuss, Dieter G. Kaiser, and Frank J. Fabozzi, *The Handbook of Commodity Investing*, New York: Wiley, 2008, 71.
6. Jim Rogers, *Adventure Capitalist*, New York: Random House, 2003, 337.
7. Commodity Research Bureau, *CRB Commodity Yearbook 2009*, New York: Wiley, 2009, 6T.
8. Ibid.
9. "3 Strategies to Beat Inflation," *Forbes*, December 11, 2006.
10. Daniel Fisher, "The Insidious Thief," *Forbes*, November 10, 2008, 54.
11. Robert W. Kolb and James A. Overdahl, "Futures Markets: Introduction," in *Understanding Futures Markets*, 6th ed., Malden, MA: Wiley-Blackwell, 2006, 28.
12. Roger W. Gray, "Onions Revisited," *Journal of Farm Economics*, vol. 45, no. 2, 1963, 273–276.
13. Jim Rogers, *Hot Commodities: How Anyone Can Invest Profitably in the World's Best Market*, New York: Random House Trade Paperbacks, 2004, 3.
14. Gerald Jensen, Robert R. Johnson, and Jeffrey M. Mercer, "Time Variation in the Benefits of Managed Futures," *Journal of Alternative Investments*, Spring 2003, 41–50.
15. Chicago Board of Trade, *Commodity Trading Manual*, New York: Global Professional Publishing, 1998, 377.
16. Harry M. Kat, "Managed Futures and Hedge Funds: A Match Made in Heaven," *Journal of Investment Management*, 2, no. 1, 2002, 7.
17. Ryan Abrams, Ranjan Bhaduri, and Elizabeth Flores, "Lintner Revisited: The Benefits of Managed Futures 25 Years Later," *CME Group*, 2009.
18. Bahattin Büyüksahin, Michael S. Haigh, and Michel A. Robe, "Commodities and Equities: A 'Market of One'?," *Journal of Alternative Investments*, Winter 2010, 76–95.

19. Aristotle, *Politics A Treatise on Government*, 1259, reprint, Little Books Of Wisdom: Book Jungle, 2008, 8–10.

20. Paul Katzeff, "Eli Whitney's Industrial Spark," *Investor's Business Daily*, August 19, 2009, A3.

21. BASF, "Corporate Website," www.basf.com/group/corporate/en/innovations/research-verbund/innovation-drivers/index, accessed August 1, 2009.

22. Russell R. Wasendorf and Thomas A. McCafferty, *All About Commodities from the Inside Out*, New York: McGraw-Hill, 1993.

23. Ingmar Lehmann and Alfred S. Posamentier, *The Fabulous Fibonacci Numbers*, Buffalo, NY: Prometheus Books, 2007, 182.

24. CME Group, "About Us," www.cmegroup.com, accessed July 27, 2009.

25. "Chelmsford Trading Bureau Ltd: Futures, Options, Forex, Equity," Chelmsford Trading Bureau Ltd., www.ctbfutures.com/exchanges.php.

26. *International Directory of Company Histories*, Volume 41, Kirkpatrick: St. James Press, 2001, 84.

27. ICE, "History," https://www.theice.com/history.jhtml, accessed August 1, 2009.

Chapter 11

1. Roland Fuss, Dieter G. Kaiser, and Frank J. Fabozzi, *The Handbook of Commodity Investing*, New York: Wiley, 2008.

2. Geri Smith, "The Oil Crisis Slamming Mexico," *BusinessWeek*, September 17, 2009, 36–37.

3. Peter Coy, "Commodities are down . . . hooray?" *BusinessWeek*, August 18, 2008, 26.

4. Carolyn Cui, "Commodities Zig. Stocks Do, Too," *Wall Street Journal*, October 17, 2008, C1.

5. Derek van Eck, "Commodities: Rebounding, and Then Some," *Barron's*, April 20, 2009, online.barrons.com/article/SB124000825738230461.html, accessed April 20, 2009.

6. "The Case for Managed Futures," *Worth*, Spring–Summer 2009. http://www.thehedgefundjournal.com/magazine/200909/manager-writes/the-case-for-managed-futures.php. Accessed April 20, 2009.

7. Ibid.

8. Christine Harper, "Banking on Energy," *Bloomberg Markets*, September 2008.

9. "The Case for Managed Futures," *Worth*, Spring–Summer 2009.

10. Carolyn Cui, "Commodities Lose Some of Their Luster," *Wall Street Journal*, March 20, 2008, D1.

11. Deutsche Bank Commodity Services.

12. "Bulls in a China Shop," *Economist*, August 23, 2008, www.economist.com/realarticleid.cfm?redirect_id=11986068, accessed August 23, 2008.

13. Quoted in Bernard Condon, "Can You Spell Commodity?" *Forbes*, October 30, 2006, 46.

14. Matt Hougan, "Dancing the Contango," *Financial Advisor*, February 2007, www.fa-mag.com/component/content/article/1586.html?issue=77&magazineID=1&Itemid=27, accessed February 1, 2007.

15. Ibid.

16. "The Case for Managed Futures," *Worth*, Spring–Summer 2009. http://www.thehedgefundjournal.com/magazine/200909/manager-writes/the-case-for-managed-futures.php. Accessed April 20, 2009.

17. "Mirror Mirror on the Wall, Who's the Gloomiest of Them All?" Investoralist, www.investoralist.com/experts–2009-economic-prediction/, accessed July 26, 2010.
18. Mark Gongloff, "Is the Bubble in Commodities Bursting?" *Wall Street Journal*, March 20, 2008, C1.
19. Matt Hougan, "Dancing the Contango," *Financial Advisor*, February 2007, www.fa-mag.com/component/content/article/1586.html?issue=77&magazineID=1&Itemid=27, accessed February 1, 2007.
20. Paul D. Kaplan, "Forging a New Commodity Index," Morningstar Advisor, Summer 2008, 26.
21. "About Us," Metals Economics Group, www.metalseconomics.com/aboutus.html, accessed July 26, 2010.

Chapter 12

1. Robert Huebscher, "Gold Rushes Then and Now," *Wealth Manager*, September 2008, www.wealthmanagerweb.com/Issues/2008/9/Pages/Gold-Rushes-Then-and-Now.aspx, accessed August 31, 2008.
2. Aaron Pressman, "Seeking Safety Beyond Gold," *BusinessWeek*, November 10, 2008, 68.
3. Zvi Bodie, Alex Kane, and Alan J. Marcus, *Investments*, 8th ed., New York: McGraw-Hill/Irwin, 2008, 822.
4. Jim Rogers, *Adventure Capitalist: The Ultimate Road Trip*, New York: Random House Trade Paperbacks, 2004, 313.
5. Vernon Clark, "Judge Orders Government to Return Family's Rare Coins," *Philadelphia Inquirer*, August 1, 2009.
6. Adam Aston, "How to Turn Pennies Green," *BusinessWeek*, May 5, 2008, 17.
7. Cynthia Crossen, *The Rich and How They Got That Way*, new ed., London: Nicholas Brealey Publishing Ltd, 2001, 51.
8. Miguel Bustillo, "Culture of Bling Clangs to Earth as the Recession Melts Rapper's Ice," *Wall Street Journal*, May 26, 2009, A1.
9. Roland Fuss, Dieter G. Kaiser, and Frank J. Fabozzi, *The Handbook of Commodity Investing* (Frank J. Fabozzi Series), New York: Wiley, 2008, 696.
10. Commodity Research Bureau, *The CRB Commodity Yearbook 2008*, New York: Wiley, 2008, 113.
11. Federal Reserve Bank of New York, *The Key to the Gold Vault*, New York: Federal Reserve Bank of New York, 2006, 1.
12. Cynthia Crossen, *The Rich and How They Got That Way*, London: Nicholas Brealey Publishing Ltd, 2001, 61.
13. Zahi Hawass, *Tutankhamun and the Golden Age of the Pharaohs: Official Companion Book to the Exhibition sponsored by National Geographic*, Washington, DC: National Geographic, 2005, 57.
14. Cornelius Searle Hurlbut, *Minerals and Man*, New York: Random House, 1975, 146.
15. Zahi Hawass, *Tutankhamun and the Golden Age of the Pharaohs: Official Companion Book to the Exhibition sponsored by National Geographic*, Washington, DC: National Geographic, 2005, 57.
16. Federal Reserve Bank of New York, *The Key to the Gold Vault*, 2006, 1.
17. Ibid., 1–3.
18. Cornelius Searle Hurlbut, *Minerals and Man*, New York: Random House, 1975, 146.

19. Federal Reserve Bank of New York, *The Key to the Gold Vault*, 2006, 3.
20. Ibid.
21. Ibid.
22. Cornelius Searle Hurlbut, *Minerals and Man*, 143.
23. Ian Johnson, "China Strikes Back on Trade," *Wall Street Journal*, September 14, 2009, A1.
24. Robert D. Auerbach, *Financial Markets and Institutions*, Boston: Prentice Hall College Division, 1983, 508.
25. "Executive Order 6102," About Precious Metals, www.aboutpreciousmetals.com/Money_Economics/executive_order_6102.htm, accessed July 26, 2010.
26. Benjamin Graham, *The Intelligent Investor*, 4th rev. ed., New York: Harper & Row, Publishers, 1973, 24.
27. Steve F. Forbes, "One Gold Ring He Won't Grasp," *Forbes*, December, 2008, 19–20.
28. Austin Gold Information Network, "Yearly Gold Prices since 1793," Gold Coins–Gold Information Network, www.goldinfo.net/yearly.html.
29. Federal Reserve Bank of New York, *The Key to the Gold Vault*, 2006, 1.
30. Cornelius Searle Hurlbut, *Minerals and Man*, 146.
31. Ibid.
32. Michael G. George, 2007 *Minerals Yearbook*, United States Geological Survey, 2009, 2, minerals.usgs.gov/minerals/pubs/commodity/nitrogen/myb1–2007-nitro.pdf, accessed July 26, 2010.
33. Ibid., 4.
34. Cornelius Searle Hurlbut, *Minerals and Man*, 149.
35. Ibid., 151.
36. Colin Lawrence, "Why Is Gold Different from Other Assets? An Empirical Investigation," March 2003, 2, www.goldbullion.com.au/pdf/colin_lawrence_report.pdf, accessed March 15, 2003.
37. Robert Huebscher, "Gold Rushes Then and Now," *Wealth Manager*, September 2008, www.wealthmanagerweb.com/Issues/2008/9/Pages/Gold-Rushes-Then-and-Now.aspx, accessed August 31, 2008.
38. "Gold Haven," *Bloomberg Markets*, July 2006, 24.
39. Peter A. McCay, "Slow and Steady," *Wall Street Journal*, December 18, 2006, R3.
40. Jeremy J. Siegel, *Stocks for the Long Run*, New York: McGraw-Hill, 2008, 11.
41. Morgan Stanley, Probability of Negative Return for Selected Asset Classes, chart, Morgan Stanley Global Wealth Management Asset Allocation and Investment Strategy Group, April 2009, from *Asset Allocation and Investment Strategy Slides*.
42. Daniel Fisher, "The Insidious Thief," *Forbes*, November 10, 2008, 54.
43. Jason Zweig, "Steer Clear of the New Gold Rush — March 12, 2008," CNNMoney.com, money.cnn.com/2008/03/06/pf/intelligent_apr.moneymag/index.htm?postversion=2008031218, accessed March 12, 2008.
44. Ibid.
45. Daren Fonda, "Why Gold Still Has Some Luster," *SmartMoney*, March 2009.
46. Robert D. Auerbach, *Financial Markets and Institutions*, Boston: Prentice Hall College Division, 1983, 510–511.

Chapter 13

1. Herman Melville, *Moby Dick*, New York: W.W. Norton and Company, 1967, 423.
2. Cornelius Searle Hurlbut, *Minerals and Man*, New York: Random House, 1975, 145.
3. Ramiro Salas Bravo and Meinrad Maria Grewenig, *IncaGold: 3000 Years of Advanced Civilisations—Masterpieces from Peru's Larco Museum*, Berlin: Kehrer Verlag, 2004, 7.
4. Terence N. D'Altroy, *The Incas (The Peoples of America)*, new ed., Chicago: Blackwell Publishing Limited, 2003.
5. Robert D. Auerbach, *Financial Markets and Institutions*, Boston: Prentice Hall College Division, 1983, 428.
6. Monex Precious Metals, "American Gold Buffalo Coins," www.monex.com/prods/gold_buffalo.html, accessed April 1,2010.
7. Monex Precious Metals, "Buying Gold Coins—Gold American Eagle Coins—American Eagle Gold Coins," ../AppData/Local/Temp/www.monex.com/prods/gold_eagle.html, accessed April 1, 2010.
8. Monex Precious Metals, "Gold Krugerrand Coins," ../AppData/Local/Temp/www.monex.com/prods/gold_krug.html, accessed April 1, 2010.
9. Elizabeth O'Brien, "Time to Buy Gold?" *SmartMoney*, April 2009, www.smartmoney.com/investing/economy/protect-your-money-time-to-buy-gold/, accessed April 1, 2009.
10. Chicago Board of Trade, *Commodity Trading Manual*, Chicago: Chicago Board of Trade, 1976, 145.
11. Patrick Barta, "High Costs Dig into Mine Profits," *Wall Street Journal*, August 25, 2008, A1.
12. Carolyn Cui, "Gold's Rise Is the Envy of Gold Miners," *Wall Street Journal*, May 7, 2009, C1.
13. Lauren Barack, "Looking for the Pot of Gold," *On Wall Street*, December 2008, 53.
14. Carolyn Cui, "Gold Futures Tumble Down 'Metals' Stand," *Wall Street Journal*, August 16–17, 2008, B1.
15. Tim Knepp, "Panning for Gold," *On Wall Street*, December, 2008, 71.
16. Morningstar Analysts, "Small Versus Big, 401(k) Outflows and ETFs, and More," *Morningstar Advisor*, April 1, 2009, advisor.morningstar.com/articles/article.asp?s=1&docId=16282&pgNo=3, accessed April 1, 2009.
17. Collin Lawrence, "Why Is Gold Different from Other Assets? An Empirical Investigation," March 2003, 3, www.goldbullion.com.au/pdf/colin_lawrence_report.pdf, accessed March 15, 2003.
18. Allan R. Elliott, "Gold's Rise Has Mixed Effect on Jewelers," *Investor's Business Daily*, May 26, 2009, B9.
19. "Show Them the Money," *Economist*, A Special Report on the Rich, April 4, 2009, 5–7.
20. Carolyn Cui, "Commodities Zig. Stocks Do, Too," *Wall Street Journal*, October 17, 2008, C1.
21. Carli Collins and Nicholas Larkin, "Gold Rush," *Bloomberg Markets*, May 2009, 21.

Chapter 14

1. Edward Gibbon, *The History of the Decline and Fall of the Roman Empire*, New York: Harcourt, Brace and Company, 1960, 838.
2. Andrew Blackman, "How Well Do You Know . . . Hedge Funds?" *Wall Street Journal*, July 3, 2007, R22.
3. Ibid.
4. Peter Lattman and Jenny Strasburg, "Clients Flee Cerberus, Fallen Fund Titan," *Wall Street Journal*, August 29, 2009.
5. Plato and B. Jowett, *The Dialogues of Plato, Republic: Volume 1*, 7th ed., New York: Random House, 1937, 719.
6. David Walker, "Hedge Funds Ratchet Up Their Focus on China," *Wall Street Journal*, August 20, 2009, C2.
7. Vinh Q. Tran, *Evaluating Hedge Fund Performance*, New York: Wiley, 2006, xv.
8. Andrew W. Lo, *Hedge Funds: An Analytic Perspective*, Princeton, NJ: Princeton University Press, 2008, 198.
9. Eugene F. Brigham and Joel F. Houston, *Study Guide for Brigham/Houston's Fundamentals of Financial Management, Concise Edition*, 5th ed., Mason, OH: South-Western College, 2006, 114.
10. Ibid., 122.
11. Franklin Allen, Richard A. Brealey, and Stewart C Meyers, *Principles of Corporate Finance*, 9th ed., New York: McGraw-Hill/Irwin, 2007, 193.
12. Jonathan Burton, "Revisiting the Capital Asset Pricing Model," Stanford University, www.stanford.edu/~wfsharpe/art/djam/djam.htm, accessed April 1, 2010.
13. Seeking Alpha, "In Search of Low (or Negative) Correlation Between Asset Returns," seekingalpha.com/article/28917-in-search-of-low-or-negative-correlation-between-asset-returns, accessed April 1, 2010.
14. Dion Friedland, "About Hedge Funds—Market Neutral Long/Short Equity Trading," Magnum Funds, www.magnum.com/hedgefunds/marketneutral.asp, accessed April 1, 2010.
15. Securities and Exchange Commission, "Implications of the Growth of Hedge Funds," staff report, September 2003, viii.
16. Mark Anson, "So Hedge Funds Like Volatility?" *Pensions & Investments*, October 27, 2008, 12.
17. FINRA, "Higher Costs and Risks for Higher Potential Returns," FINRA Home Page, www.finra.org/web/idcplg?IdcService=GET_PROBLEM_PAGE&siteId=www.finra.org&siteRelativeUrl=/Investors/Protectyourself/investoralerts/mutualfunds/p006028, accessed April 15, 2010.
18. U.S. Securities and Exchange Commission, "Hedging Your Bets: A Heads Up on Hedge Funds and Funds of Hedge Funds," U.S. Securities and Exchange Commission Home Page, www.sec.gov/answers/hedge.htm, accessed April 15, 2010.
19. Securities and Exchange Commission, "Implications of the Growth of Hedge Funds," staff report, September 2003, 9–10.
20. Ibid., 9.
21. Investment Company Institute, "Hedge Funds," www.ici.org/funds/abt/faqs_hedge.html.
22. Securities and Exchange Commission, "Mutual Funds," www.sec.gov/answers/mutfund.htm, accessed April 30, 2010.

23. Investment Company Institute, "Hedge Funds," www.ici.org/funds/abt/faqs_hedge.html.
24. Joseph G. Nicholas, *Investing in Hedge Funds, Revised and Updated Edition*, New York: Bloomberg Press, 2005, 70.
25. Ibid., 60.
26. Joseph G. Nicholas, "Investing in Relationships," in *Market-Neutral Investing: Long/Short Hedge Fund Strategies*, New York: Bloomberg Press, 2000, 5.
27. Hedge Fund Research, Inc., "HFRI Strategy Definitions," www.hedgefundresearch. com/index.php?fuse=indices-str, accessed February 17, 2009.
28. Ibid.
29. Ibid.
30. Vinh Q. Tran, *Evaluating Hedge Fund Performance*, 60.
31. Stuart A. McCrary, *How to Create and Manage a Hedge Fund: A Professional's Guide*, New York: Wiley, 2002, 38.
32. Hedge Fund Research, Inc., "HFRI Strategy & Regional Classifications," www.hedgefundresearch.com/index.php?fuse=indices-str, accessed April 30, 2010.
33. Hedge Fund Research, Inc., "HFRI Strategy Definitions," www.hedgefundresearch. com/index.php?fuse=indices-str, accessed February 17, 2009.
34. Ibid.
35. Ibid.
36. Ibid., accessed January 7, 2010.
37. Filippo Stefanini, *Investment Strategies of Hedge Funds*, New York: Wiley, 2006, 21.
38. Hedge Fund Research, Inc., "HFRI Strategy Definitions," www.hedgefundresearch.com/index.php?fuse=indices-str, accessed January 7, 2010.
39. Ibid.
40. Ibid.
41. Philip Coggan, *Guide to Hedge Funds: What They Are, What They Do, Their Risks, Their Advantages*, New York: Bloomberg Press, 2008, 21.
42. Ibid., 26.
43. Joseph G. Nicholas, *Investing in Hedge Funds, Revised and Updated Edition*, New York: Bloomberg Press, 2005, 26–27.
44. CalPERS On-Line, "Roadmap," CalPERS On-Line, www.calpers.ca.gov/eip-docs/ about/press/news/invest-corp/aima_roadmap.pdf, September 1, 2008.
45. Ibid.
46. Quoted in Danny Hakim, "Huge Losses Move Soros to Revamp Empire," *New York Times*, April 29, 2000, A1.
47. "The 400: 2008 Edition," *Forbes 400*, October 27, 2008, www.forbes.com/2008/09/16/ forbes–400-billionaires-lists–400list08_cx_mn_0917richamericans_land.html, accessed December 1, 2008.
48. Stephanie Baker and Tom Cahill, "The Charmed Life of Arpad Busson," *Bloomberg Markets*, February 2009, 42.
49. Landon Thomas Jr. and Jenny Anderson, "SEC Accuses Hedge Fund of Deceiving Its Investors," *New York Times*, October 14, 2005, B6.
50. "How UBS lost $38 Billion," *Economist*, April 24, 2008, www.economist.com/ research/articlesBySubject/displaystory.cfm?subjectid=549559&story_id=E1_TTDJ DNTR, accessed April 24, 2008.

Chapter 15

1. Securities and Exchange Commission, "Implications of the Growth of Hedge Funds," staff report, September 2003.
2. Stephanie Baker and Tom Cahill, "The Charmed Life of Arpad Busson," *Bloomberg Markets*, February 2009.
3. "Investors Yanked $152 Billion out of Hedge Funds in Q4," Reuters, January 21, 2009.
4. Paul Katzeff, "Record $70 Bill Flees from Stock Funds," *Investor's Business Daily*, November 28, 2008. A7.
5. "Difference a Year Makes," *Investor's Business Daily*, December 2, 2008. A7.
6. Sharon Reier, "From Jones to LTCM: A Short (-Selling) History," *International Herald Tribune*, December 2, 2000, www.nytimes.com/2000/12/02/your-money/02iht-mhist.t.html, accessed November 15, 2009.
7. Hedge Funds Jump into Private Equity," *BusinessWeek*, February 26, 2007, www.businessweek.com/magazine/content/07_09/b4023048.htm, accessed February 26, 2007.
8. "iPorn.com Acquired by AdultVest!" Reuters, April 11, 2008.
9. Chelsea Emery, "Bay Harbour Affiliate Set to Acquire Retailer Steve & Barry's Following Auction of Company's," Reuters, August 21, 2008.
10. Lori Becker, "Aon Approves Hedge Fund's Takeover Bid," *Palm Beach Post*, May 5, 2007.
11. Mark Fitzgerald, "Hedge Fund Wins Control of 'Chicago Sun-Times' Parent," *Editor and Publisher*, January 17, 2009, www.editorandpublisher.com/RedirectNew.aspx?Page=http://www.editorandpublisher.com/home.aspx, accessed January 17, 2009.
12. "James River to Be Acquired by DE Shaw for $575mln," Reuters, August 21, 2008, www.reuters.com/article/idUSN1146711720070611, accessed August 21, 2008.
13. Bill Birnbaum, "Kmart to Acquire Sears. Goodbye, Kmart," *Business Strategies Newsletter*, January–March 2005.
14. John Spence, "Simon, Farallon Team Up to Buy Mall REIT," *MarketWatch*, February 16, 2007, www.marketwatch.com/story/mills-agrees-to-be-acquired-by-simon-property-hedge-fund, accessed February 16, 2007.
15. Digital River, "News & Events," phx.corporate-ir.net/phoenix.zhtml?c=64379&p=irol-newsArticle&ID=997164&highlight=, accessed April 1, 2010.
16. Vidya Ram, "Man Group Standing Tall," *Forbes*, May 29, 2008, www.forbes.com/2008/05/29/man-ahl-fund-markets-equities-cx_vr_markets16.html, accessed May 29, 2008.
17. "RAB Capital Acquire 20% Stake in Japan's Prestige AM," *Hedge Funds Review*, November 14, 2007.
18. "Soros Directs British-Steered Hedge Funds Take-Over of IndyMac Bank," Larouche Pack, January 5, 2009, www.larouchepac.com/news/2009/01/05/soros-directs-british-steered-hedge-funds-take-over-indymac-.html, accessed January 5, 2009.
19. Mathew Goldstein, "Hedge Funds Jump into Private Equity," *BusinessWeek*, February 26, 2007, 46.
20. "Lifting the Lid," *Economist*, January 27, 2007, 75.
21. Ibid.
22. Anthony Effinger, "High-Wire Act at Fortress," *Bloomberg Markets*, March 2009.

23. Katherine Burton and Adam Levy, "The Secrets of Ken Griffin," *Bloomberg Markets,* June 2005, 39–48.
24. Hedge Fund Research, Inc., "HFRI Strategy Definitions," www.hedgefundresearch. com/index.php?fuse=indices-str, accessed February 17, 2009.
25. Allistar Barr, "Amid Industry Losses, Some Managers Perform," *MarketWatch,* January 9, 2009, www.marketwatch.com/story/correct-amid-big-industry-losses-in–2008-some-managers-perform, accessed January 9, 2009.
26. Saijel Kishan, "Clive Capital Hedge Funds Gains 17.6% in Quarter," *Bloomberg, Markets* www.bloomberg.com/apps/news?pid=20601085&sid=acxpk_bkGikw&refer =europe, accessed April 18, 2008.
27. Gregory Zuckerman and Henny Sender, "Ex-Trader Creates Hot Hedge Fund, and a Traffic Jam," *Wall Street Journal,* January 12, 2005, A1.
28. Richard Teitelbaum, "The Richest Hedge Funds: John Paulson Strikes Again," *Bloomberg Markets,* January 2009, 40.
29. "Craig Effron: Getting a Grip on Risk," *Bloomberg Markets,* November 2007.
30. "Renaissance Hedge Fund: Only Scientists Need Apply," Reuters, May 22, 2007.
31. Richard Teitelbaum, "The Richest Hedge Funds: John Paulson Strikes Again," *Bloomberg Markets,* January 2009, 33–48.
32. Joseph Pereira, "Jeffrey Vinik Becomes Latest in Hedge Funds to Step Back," *Wall Street Journal,* October 27, 2000, C1.
33. Paul Katzeff and Peter McKennan, "$4.2 Billion Vinik Hedge Fund to Liquidate," *Investor's Business Daily,* October 23, 2000, 9.
34. Richard Teitelbaum, "Empire," *Bloomberg Markets,* October 2006.
35. Ibid.
36. "LTCM," Money Science, www.moneyscience.com/Information_Base/Long_ Term_Capital_Management_(LTCM).html, accessed April 15, 2010.
37. Jenny Strasburg, "As Markets Swing, Meriwether Hears Echoes of His Own Collapse—LTCM Lost Billions a Decade Ago; Now, a Second Fall?" *Wall Street Journal,* September 20, 2008, B1.
38. Ellen Joan Pollock, Steve Stecklow, Michael Allen, Mitchell Pacelle, and Deborah Lohse, "Marty's World: What Life Was Like In Frankel's Mansion as It All Unraveled," *Wall Street Journal,* July 16, 1999, A1.
39. Bernard Condon, "Bayou Bog," *Forbes,* February 26, 2007, www.forbes.com/ forbes/2007/0226/044b.html, accessed February 26, 2007.
40. Katherine Burton and Rob Burton, "Bayou Fraud Exposes Tale of Lies, Drugs, Violence," *Bloomberg Markets,* accessed October 27, 2005.
41. Monee Fields-White, "Kirk Wright's Razzle-Dazzle Play," *Bloomberg Markets,* October 2006.
42. Katherine Burton and Jenny Strasburg, "Amaranth's $6.6 Billion Slide Began with Trader's Bid to Quit," Bloomberg, www.bloomberg.com/apps/news?pid=20601082 &sid=aRJS57CQQbeE&refer=canada, accessed December 6, 2006.
43. Neil Weinberg, "Trading Up," *Forbes,* October 15, 2007, 44.
44. Jenny Strasburg and Katherine Burton, "Sowood Funds Lose More Than 50% as Debt Markets Fall," *Bloomberg Markets,* www.bloomberg.com/apps/news? pid=20601103&sid=a5He2yClHjJE, accessed July 31, 2007.
45. Jenny Strasburg and David Enrich, "Citigroup to Close Hedge Fund; Blow to CEO," *Wall Street Journal,* June 12, 2008, A1.

46. David Enrich, "Citigroup's Pandit Faces Test as Pressure on Bank Grows," *Wall Street Journal*, May 6, 2008, A1.

47. Jonathan Stempel, "Citigroup Stock Falls Below $1 for the First Time," Reuters, March 5, 2009, www.reuters.com/article/idUSN0532847720090305, accessed March 5, 2009.

48. David Enrich and Monica Langley, "Citigroup Chafes under U.S. Oversees," *Wall Street Journal*, February 25, 2009, A1.

49. Amir Efrati, Tom Lauricella, and Dionne Searcey, "Top Broker Accused of $50 Billion Fraud," *Wall Street Journal*, December 12, 2008, A1.

50. "Madoff Affair: Going Down Quietly," *Economist*, March 14, 2009, 79.

Chapter 16

1. Matthew Miller and Duncan Greenberg, eds. "The 400 Richest People In America," *Forbes*, October 6, 2008, 44.

2. Joseph A. Dear, *Written Statement Prepared For: U.S. Senate Banking Subcommittee on Securities, Insurance and Investment Re: Regulating Hedge Funds and Other Private Investment Pools*, July 15, 2009, www.calpers.ca.gov/eip-docs/about/press/news/invest-corp/dear-senate-testimony-regulating-hedge-funds.pdf, accessed August 1, 2009.

3. Andrew W. Lo, *Hedge Funds: An Analytic Perspective*, Princeton, NJ: Princeton University Press, 2008, 13.

4. Richard Teitelbaum, "The Richest Hedge Funds," *Bloomberg Markets*, January 2009, 46.

5. Cicero, *The Republic and The Laws*, New York: Oxford University Press, 1998, 3.

6. Vinh Q. Tran, *Evaluating Hedge Fund Performance*, New York: Wiley, 2006, 31.

7. *In Brief: Hewitt Investment Group Hedge Fund of Funds*, October 2005.

8. Scott Schweighauser, "Wrong Turn to Separate Account Hedge Funds," *Pensions & Investments*, October 5, 2009, 12, 28.

9. Christine Williamson "Segregated Funds Pique Interest of Large Investors," *Pensions & Investments*, October 5, 2009, 3, 43.

10. Robert F. Whitelaw and Sujeet Banerjee, "Hedge Funds for the Rest of Us," *Journal of Indexes*, July/August 2007, 12.

11. Matthew Goldstein, "The Humbling of Hedge Funds," *BusinessWeek*, December 29, 2008, 26.

12. Robert F. Whitelaw and Sujeet Banerjee, "Hedge Funds for the Rest of Us," *Journal of Indexes*, July/August 2007, 12.

13. "The SEC Isn't Finished with Hedge Funds,"*BusinessWeek*, July 17, 2006, 34.

14. Ibid.

15. Andrew W. Lo, *Hedge Funds: An Analytic Perspective*, Princeton, NJ: Princeton University Press, 2008, 129.

Chapter 17

1. Henry David Thoreau, *Walden and "Civil Disobedience,"* New York: Signet Classic, 1960, 141.

2. "Largest Hedge Funds" chart, *Pensions & Investments*, December 27, 2004.
3. Richard Teitelbaum, "World's Most Profitable Hedge Funds," *Bloomberg Markets*, January 2009, 33–48.
4. 2008 Data Book, *Pensions & Investments*, December 22, 2008, 15–43.

Chapter 18

1. To The President's Working Group On Financial Markets, Principles and Best Practices for Hedge Fund Investors, Report Of The Investors' Committee, April 15, 2008, www.treasury.gov/press/releases/reports/investors'committeereportapril152008.pdf, accessed August 1, 2008.
2. "Hedging Your Bets: A Heads Up on Hedge Funds and Funds of Hedge Funds," U.S. Securities and Exchange Commission (Home Page), www.sec.gov/answers/hedge.htm, accessed August 1, 2009.
3. Robert F. Whitelaw and Sujeet Banerjee, "Hedge Funds for the Rest of Us," *Journal of Indexes*, July/August 2007, 14.
4. "Hedge Index," Credit Suisse, www.hedgeindex.com/hedgeindex/en/indexmethodology.aspx?cy=USD&indexname=HEDG, accessed August 1, 2008.
5. Ibid.
6. Greenwich Alternative Investments, "About Us," www.greenwichai.com/index.php?option=com_content&view=article&id=31&Itemid=9, accessed August 1, 2008.
7. "Hedge Fund Indicies," MSCI, www.mscibarra.com/resources/pdfs/HFI_faq.pdf, accessed August 1, 2008.
8. Janet Paskin, "Funds Try 'Hedge' Approach in Effort to Trim Stock Losses," *Wall Street Journal*, August 3, 2009, R1.
9. "Finance and Economics: The Feeling is Mutual," *Economist*, January 9, 2010, 75.
10. Eleanor Laise, "Hedge Fund AQR Goes 'Mom and Pop'" *Wall Street Journal*, January 6, 2010, C1.
11. Aberdeen Equity Long-Short Fund, www.aberdeen-asset.us, accessed May 25, 2010.
12. DWS Investing, "DWS Disciplined Market Neutral Fund," Deutsche Bank Group, 2009, 3.
13. Shefali Anand, "Leverage Shakes Up Mutual Funds, Which Discover a Strategy's Downside," *Wall Street Journal*, January 24–25, 2009, B2.
14. Ibid.
15. Joseph Nicolas, *Investing in Hedge Funds, Revised and Updated Edition*, New York: Bloomberg Press, 2005, 35.
16. Morgan Stanley, "Graystone Research, Hedge Fund Review and Outlook," Q1, 2009.
17. Lisa Kassenaar and Christine Harper,"Mack Fights Back," *Bloomberg Markets*, March 2009.
18. Ben Warwick,"Steady the Course: Although Hedge Funds Suffered Losses, the Asset Class Remains Viable," *Wealth Manager*, December 2008.
19. JPMorgan, "Insights: The Buyer's Guide to 130/30 Equity Strategies," JPMorgan Asset Management, 8.
20. Peter Lattman, Jenny Strasburg, Naftali Bendavid, "Congress Has Hedge Funds, Buyout Firms in Tax Sights," *Wall Street Journal*, January 7, 2010, C1.

21. Richard Teitelbaum, "Bullish at the Brink," *Bloomberg Markets*, February 2010.

22. Tomako Yamazaki, *Bloomberg Business Week*, February 3, 2010.

23. Jenny Strasburg and Craig Karmin, "CalPERS Tells Hedge Funds to Fix Terms—Or Else," *Wall Street Journal*, March 28–29, 2009, B1.

24. Ibid.

25. Ibid.

26. Scott Patterson, "Black Swan Trader Bets Reputation on Inflation," *Wall Street Journal*, June 17, 2009, C1.

27. Ben Warwick, "Steady the Course: Although Hedge Funds Suffered Losses, the Asset Class Remains Viable," *Wealth Manager*, December 2009.

28. Goldman Sachs, "Hedge Fund Replication and the Goldman Sachs Absolute Return Tracker Index," *White Paper*, 2008, 5.

29. Christine Williamson, "North America Set to Power a Resurgence," *Pensions & Investments*, 3, 28.

30. Ibid.

31. Mark Cobley, "Shell Fund to Expand Alternative Investments," *Wall Street Journal*, October 12, 2009, C8.

32. Barry B. Burr, "Boeing Sets Alternatives Course," *Pensions & Investments*, 1, 38.

33. Halah Touryalai, "A Hedge Fund Resurgence," *Registered Rep*, January 2010, registeredrep.com/investing/altinvestments/finance_hedge_fund_resurgence/, accessed January 8, 2010.

Index

About the Author

Stephen Todd Walker is presently a Managing Director Oppenheimer & Co., Inc. Mr. Walker works with many CEO's of large publicly traded companies as well as entrepreneurs from privately held growth companies. He also advises family offices. His clients include Forbes 400 members as well as some of the most affluent families around the world. Most recently he served as a Senior Vice President, Corporate Client Group Director for Global Wealth Management at Morgan Stanley. While at Morgan Stanley, he was named a member of the prestigious Chairman's Group in recognition of his outstanding achievement. Prior to joining Morgan Stanley, he served as a Director of Deutsche Bank Alex. Brown, Deutsche Bank's North American investment banking and brokerage business. He was one of the youngest Directors in Alex. Brown history and one of the top wealth managers in the country. Mr. Walker helped grow Alex. Brown's Corporate & Executive Services Group from its infancy into one of the most successful operations of the firm. He was also part of Alex. Brown's elite Flagship group. While at Deutsche Bank, he managed large corporate cash accounts and retirement plans of both private and publicly traded companies for the bank's Global Investment Banking division. In addition, he handled large restricted stock transactions for global corporations and ultra high net worth clients.

Mr. Walker has over 20 years finance experience. He holds an MBA degree in finance from Temple University's Fox School of Business and Management and a BA degree in English from Kenyon College. He completed the Philadelphia Municipal Bond School and a three-year finance course conducted by the Wharton School at the Securities Industry Institute, sponsored by the Securities Industry Association. He was named to *The Philadelphia Business Journal's* "Forty Under 40," which honors the top young entrepreneurs in the Philadelphia area. In 2003, *RealPhilly* wrote an article about Mr. Walker titled "Managing risk has its reward." He was also featured in *The Philadelphia Business Journal's* October 3, 2008 issue titled "Winner's Circle: Top Wealth Advisors" which presented the top 25 wealth managers in the greater Philadelphia area culled from the 7,000 advisors in Pennsylvania and New Jersey who are employed by national and international securities firms. On February 9, 2009, Mr. Walker was named by *Barron's* as one of "The Top 1,000 Advisers" in the United States and was also named as one of the top 25 "Wealth Advisers" in *The Philadelphia Business Journal* 2009 Book of Lists.

Mr. Walker served as a Director of the Board of Big Brothers/Big Sisters of Montgomery County and is involved with many other charitable organizations including the Boy Scouts of America, Red Cross, Philadelphia Art Museum, Philadelphia Zoo, Philadelphia Orchestra, Franklin Institute, and United Way. He serves on the Board of Directors for The Space Shuttle Children's Fund, a non-profit organization and the Please Touch Museum for Children. He is also a member of various clubs including The Merion Cricket Club, Pyramid Club, Union League of Philadelphia, Ocean Reef Club, and Yale Club.